Rin Mikimoto

2

Kiss Me at the Stroke of Midnight

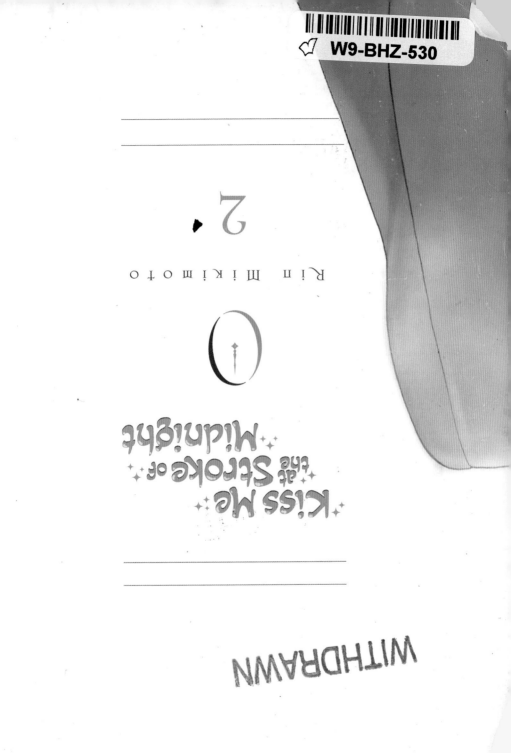

Contents

STORY. 4

Is That Really What Ayase-san is Like?

004

STORY. 5

Obviously

049

STORY. 6

Making It Work

089

STORY. 7

Pay Attention to Me, Too

131

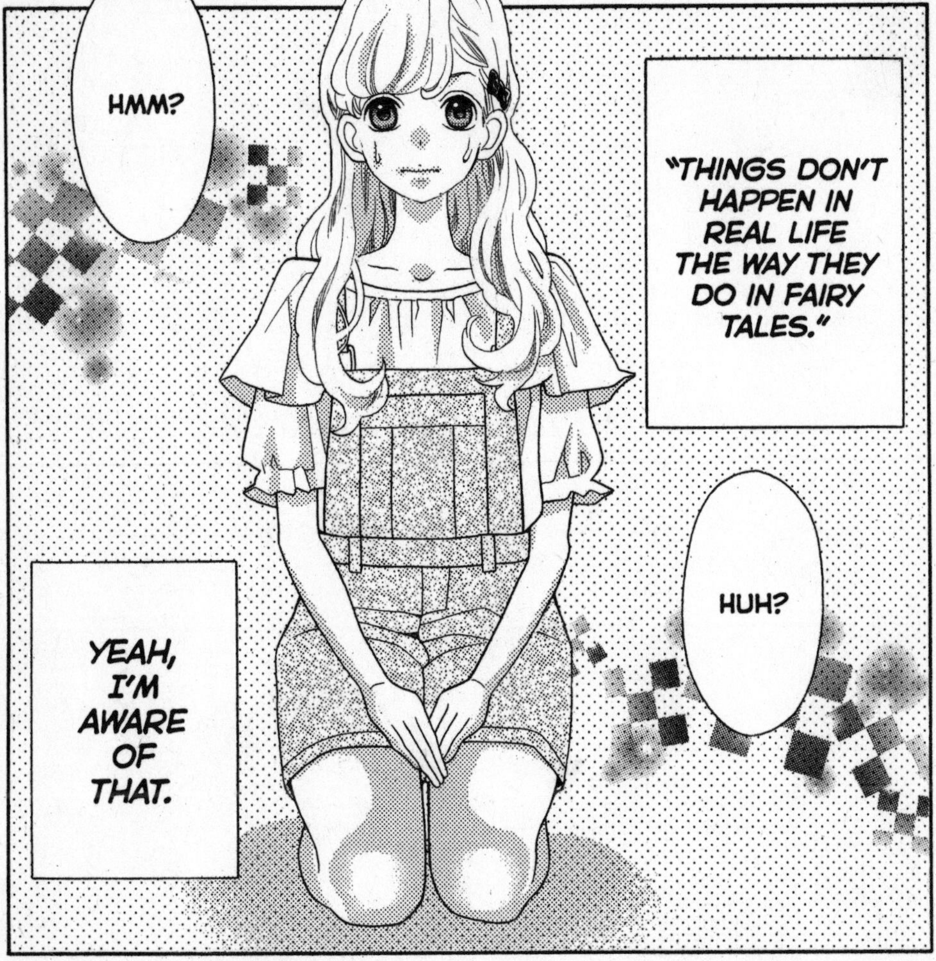
"THINGS DON'T HAPPEN IN REAL LIFE THE WAY THEY DO IN FAIRY TALES."
HMM?
HUH?
YEAH, I'M AWARE OF THAT.

STORY&CAST

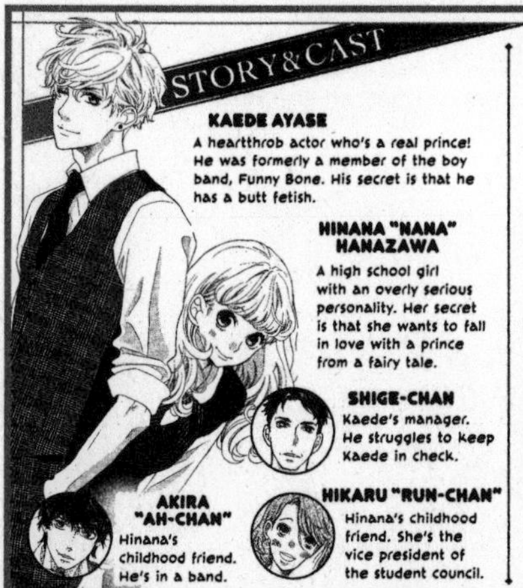

KAEDE AYASE
A heartthrob actor who's a real prince! He was formerly a member of the boy band, Funny Bone. His secret is that he has a butt fetish.

HINANA "NANA" HANAZAWA
A high school girl with an overly serious personality. Her secret is that she wants to fall in love with a prince from a fairy tale.

SHIGE-CHAN
Kaede's manager. He struggles to keep Kaede in check.

HIKARU "RUN-CHAN"
Hinana's childhood friend. She's the vice president of the student council.

AKIRA "AH-CHAN"
Hinana's childhood friend. He's in a band.

Kiss Me at the Stroke of Midnight

Hinana, a high school girl, dreams of a fairy-tale romance with a prince. And when she meets the famous heartthrob, Kaede, her dream becomes a reality...! Last Saturday, they met up for the first time.♥ After eating lunch, they went to Kaede's place, where Hinana's heart was fluttering. Before long, she finds herself under the shadow of a mystery girl named Scarlet—but it turns out that Scarlet is just Kaede's pet dog! Just as the misunderstanding was cleared, Kaede's manager, Shige-chan, appears!

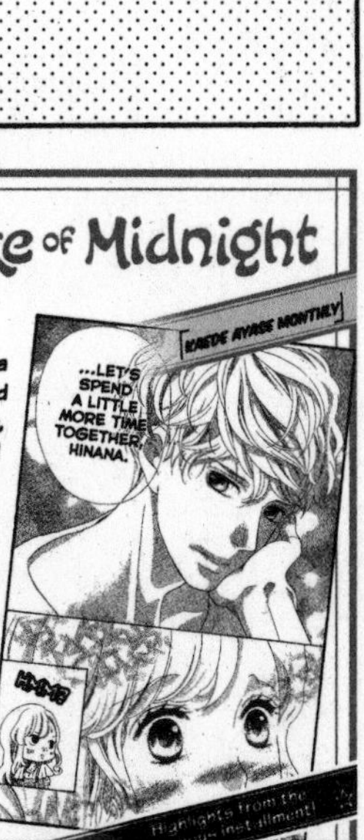
KAEDE AYASE MONTHLY
...LET'S SPEND A LITTLE MORE TIME TOGETHER, HINANA.
Highlights from the previous installment!

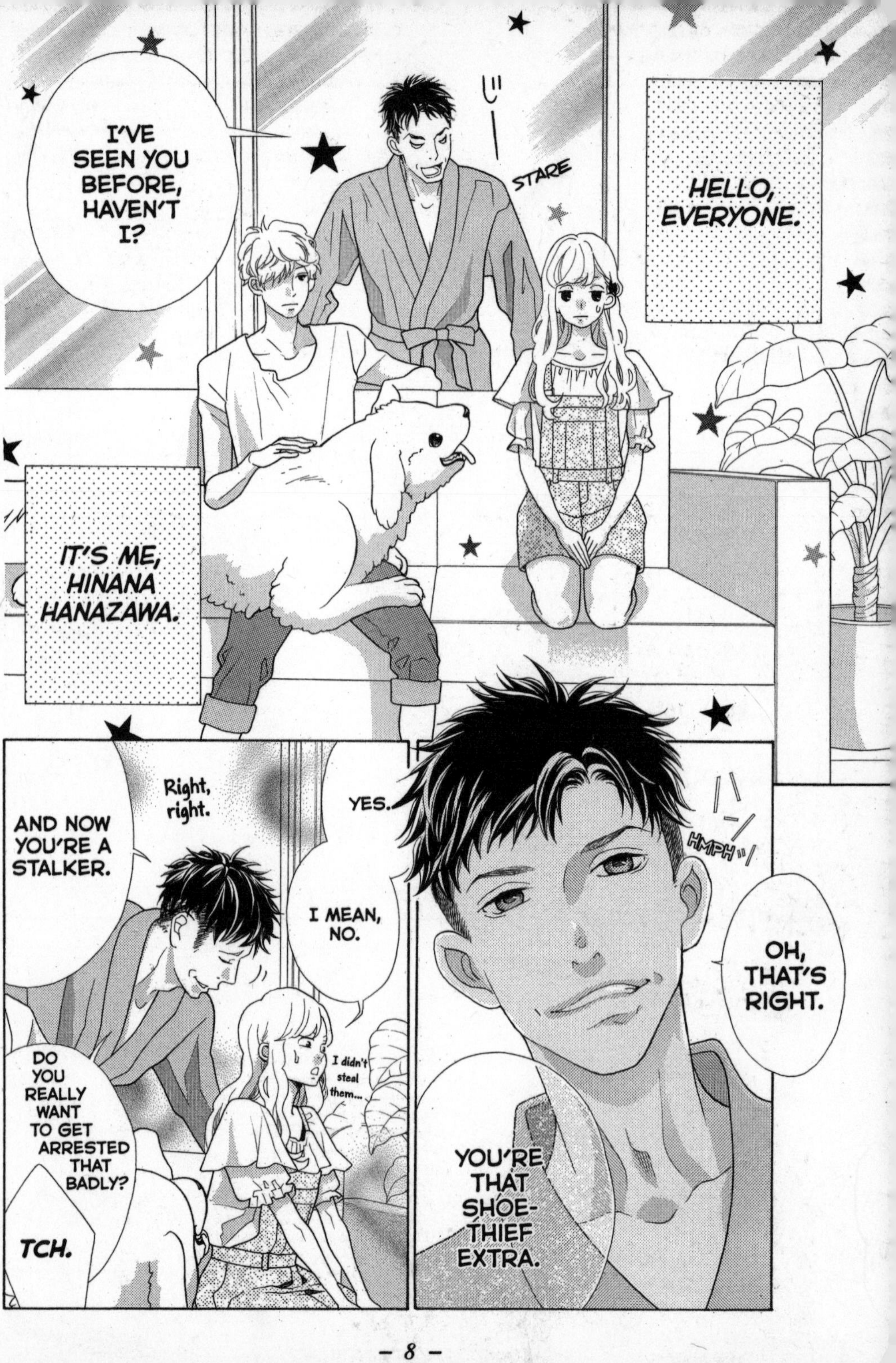
HELLO, EVERYONE.
IT'S ME, HINANA HANAZAWA.
じー
STARE
I'VE SEEN YOU BEFORE, HAVEN'T I?
HMPH
OH, THAT'S RIGHT.
YOU'RE THAT SHOE-THIEF EXTRA.
YES.
I MEAN, NO.
Right, right.
AND NOW YOU'RE A STALKER.
I didn't steal them...
DO YOU REALLY WANT TO GET ARRESTED THAT BADLY?
TCH.

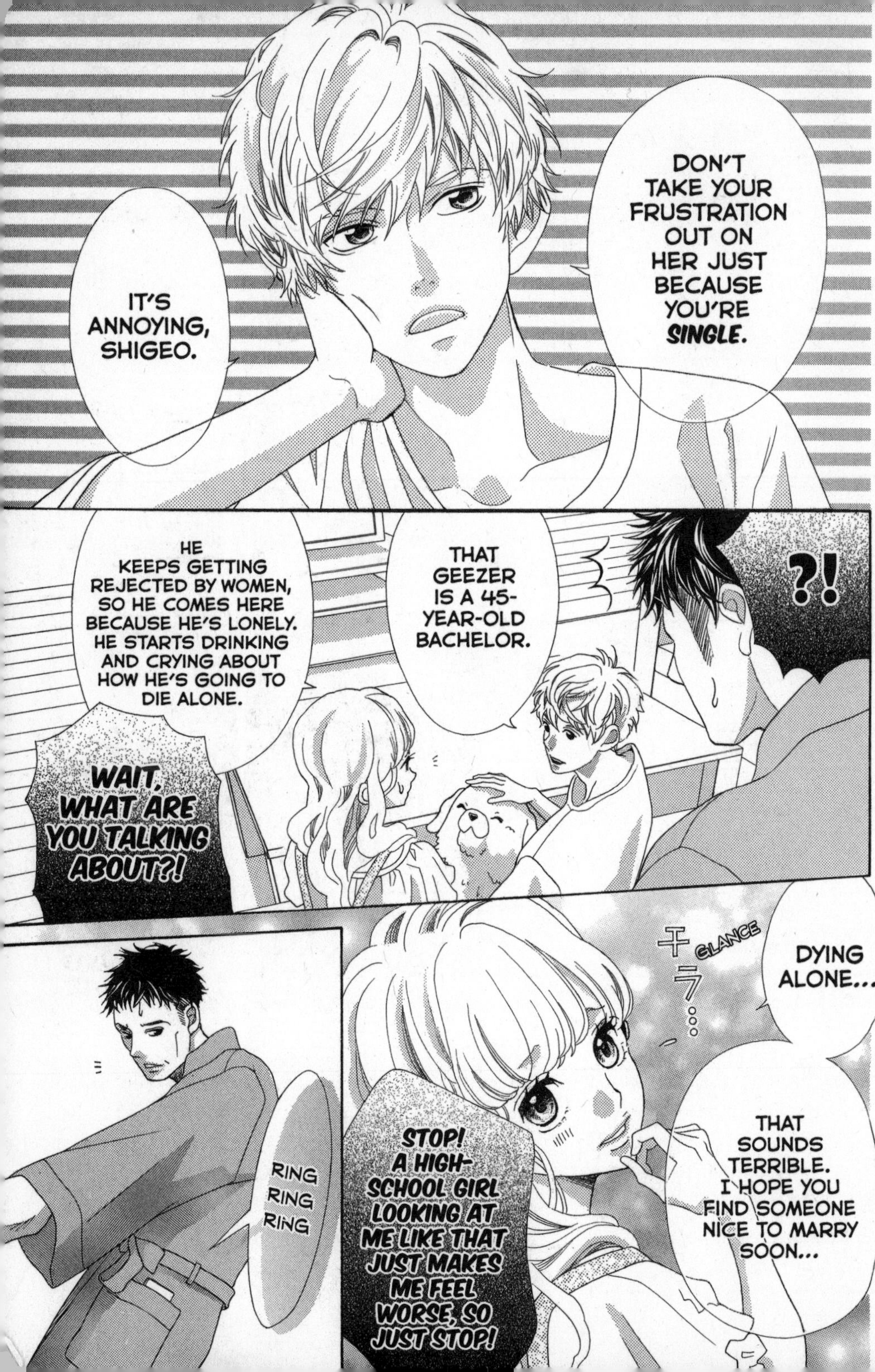
DON'T TAKE YOUR FRUSTRATION OUT ON HER JUST BECAUSE YOU'RE SINGLE.
IT'S ANNOYING, SHIGEO.
?!
THAT GEEZER IS A 45-YEAR-OLD BACHELOR.
HE KEEPS GETTING REJECTED BY WOMEN, SO HE COMES HERE BECAUSE HE'S LONELY. HE STARTS DRINKING AND CRYING ABOUT HOW HE'S GOING TO DIE ALONE.
WAIT, WHAT ARE YOU TALKING ABOUT?!
チラ…
GLANCE
DYING ALONE...
THAT SOUNDS TERRIBLE. I HOPE YOU FIND SOMEONE NICE TO MARRY SOON...
STOP! A HIGH-SCHOOL GIRL LOOKING AT ME LIKE THAT JUST MAKES ME FEEL WORSE, SO JUST STOP!
RING RING RING

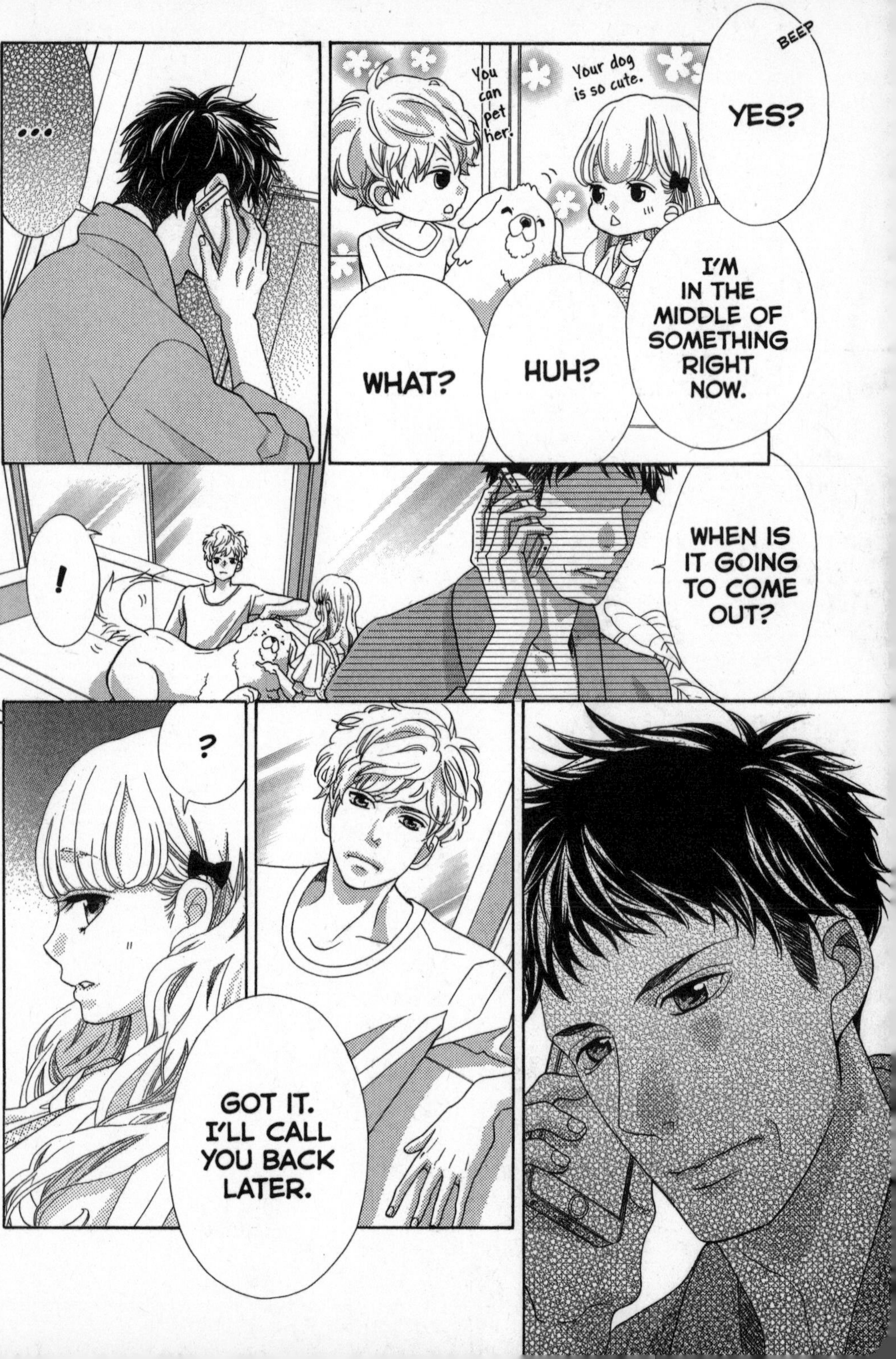
BEEP
YES?
Your dog is so cute.
You can pet her.
I'M IN THE MIDDLE OF SOMETHING RIGHT NOW.
HUH?
WHAT?
...
WHEN IS IT GOING TO COME OUT?
!
GOT IT. I'LL CALL YOU BACK LATER.
?

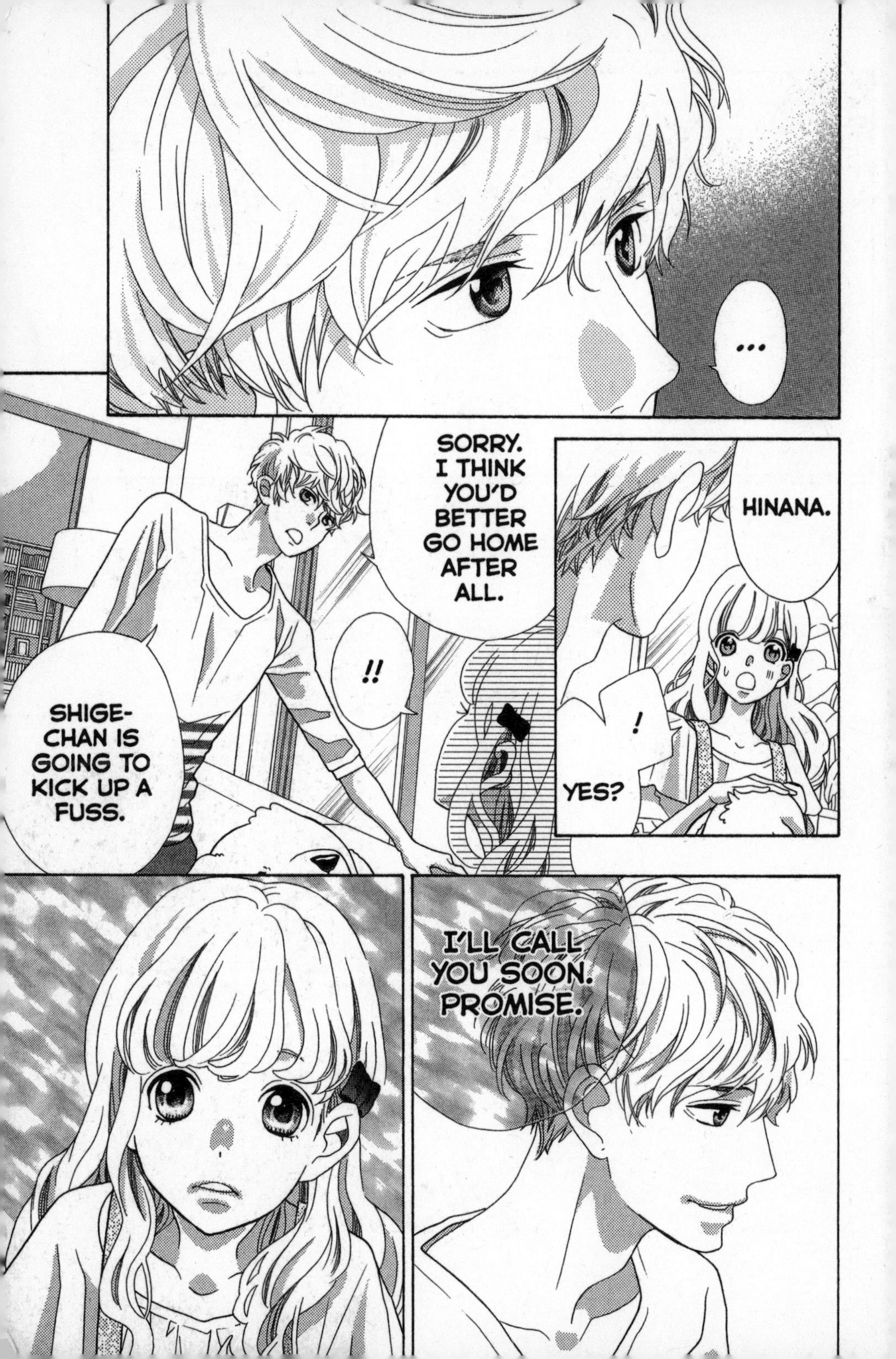
...
HINANA.
!
YES?
SORRY. I THINK YOU'D BETTER GO HOME AFTER ALL.
!!
SHIGE-CHAN IS GOING TO KICK UP A FUSS.
I'LL CALL YOU SOON. PROMISE.

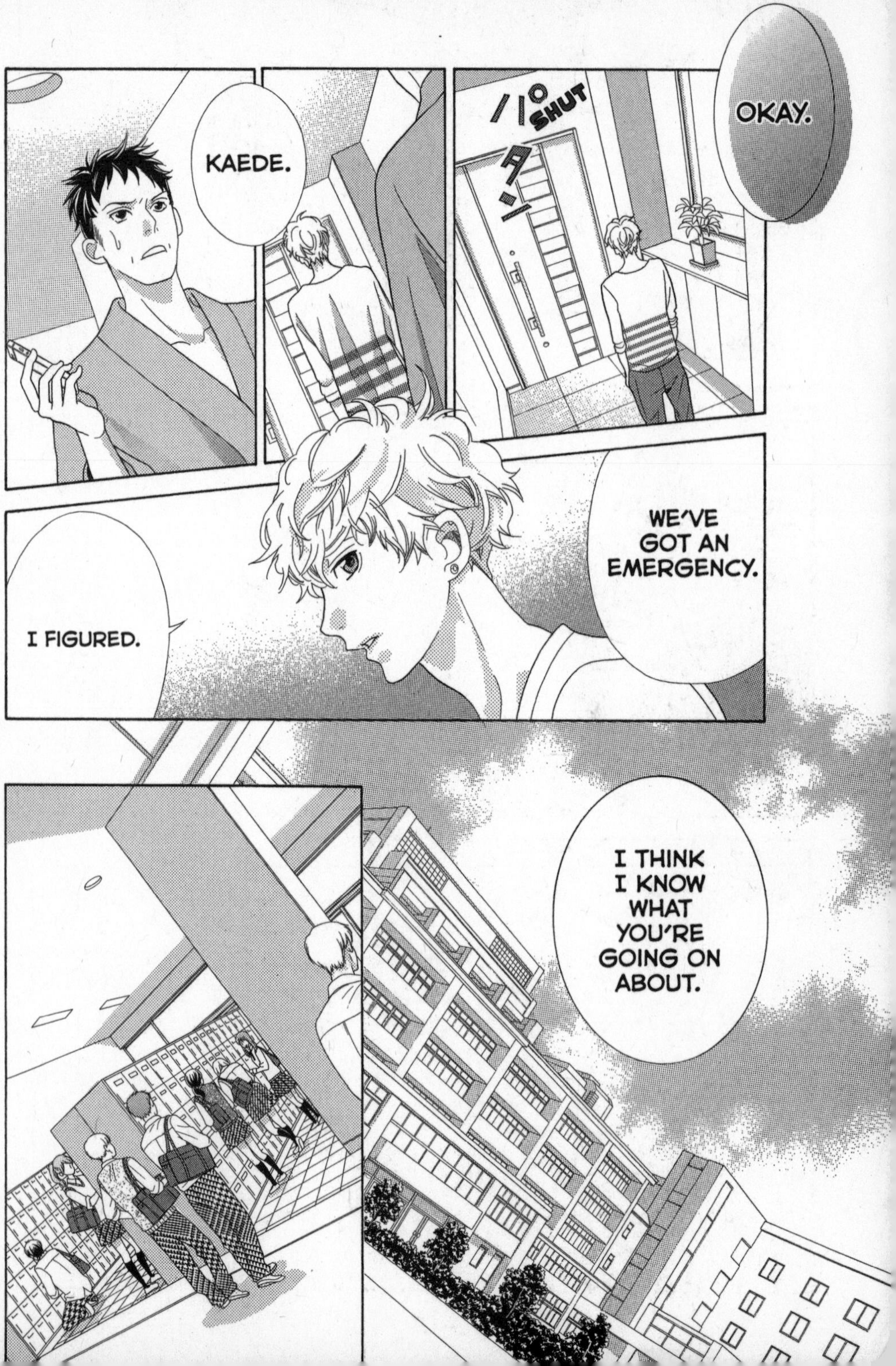
OKAY.
SHUT
KAEDE.
WE'VE GOT AN EMERGENCY.
I FIGURED.
I THINK I KNOW WHAT YOU'RE GOING ON ABOUT.

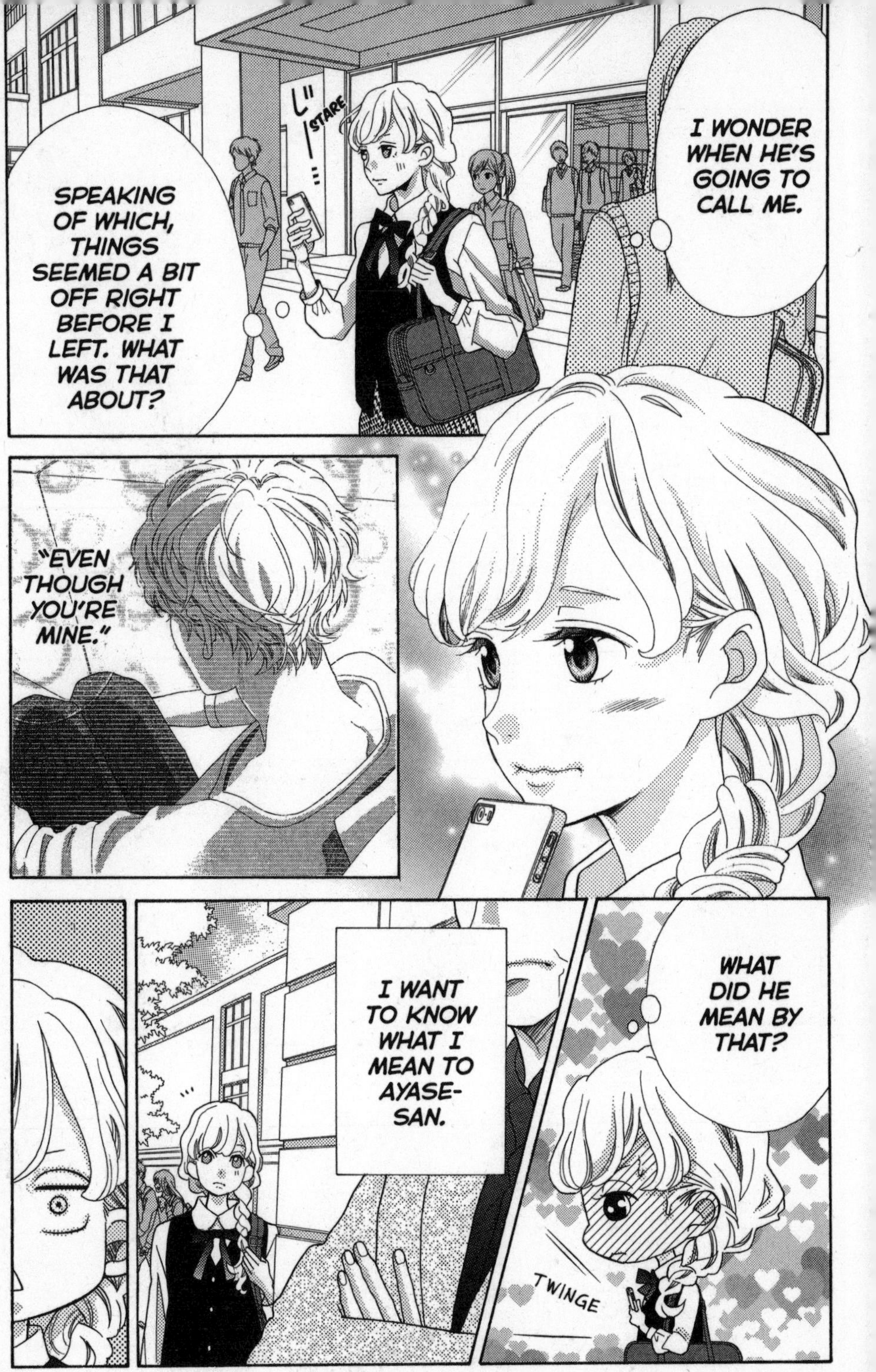
I WONDER WHEN HE'S GOING TO CALL ME.
STARE
SPEAKING OF WHICH, THINGS SEEMED A BIT OFF RIGHT BEFORE I LEFT. WHAT WAS THAT ABOUT?
"EVEN THOUGH YOU'RE MINE."
WHAT DID HE MEAN BY THAT?
TWINGE
I WANT TO KNOW WHAT I MEAN TO AYASE-SAN.
...

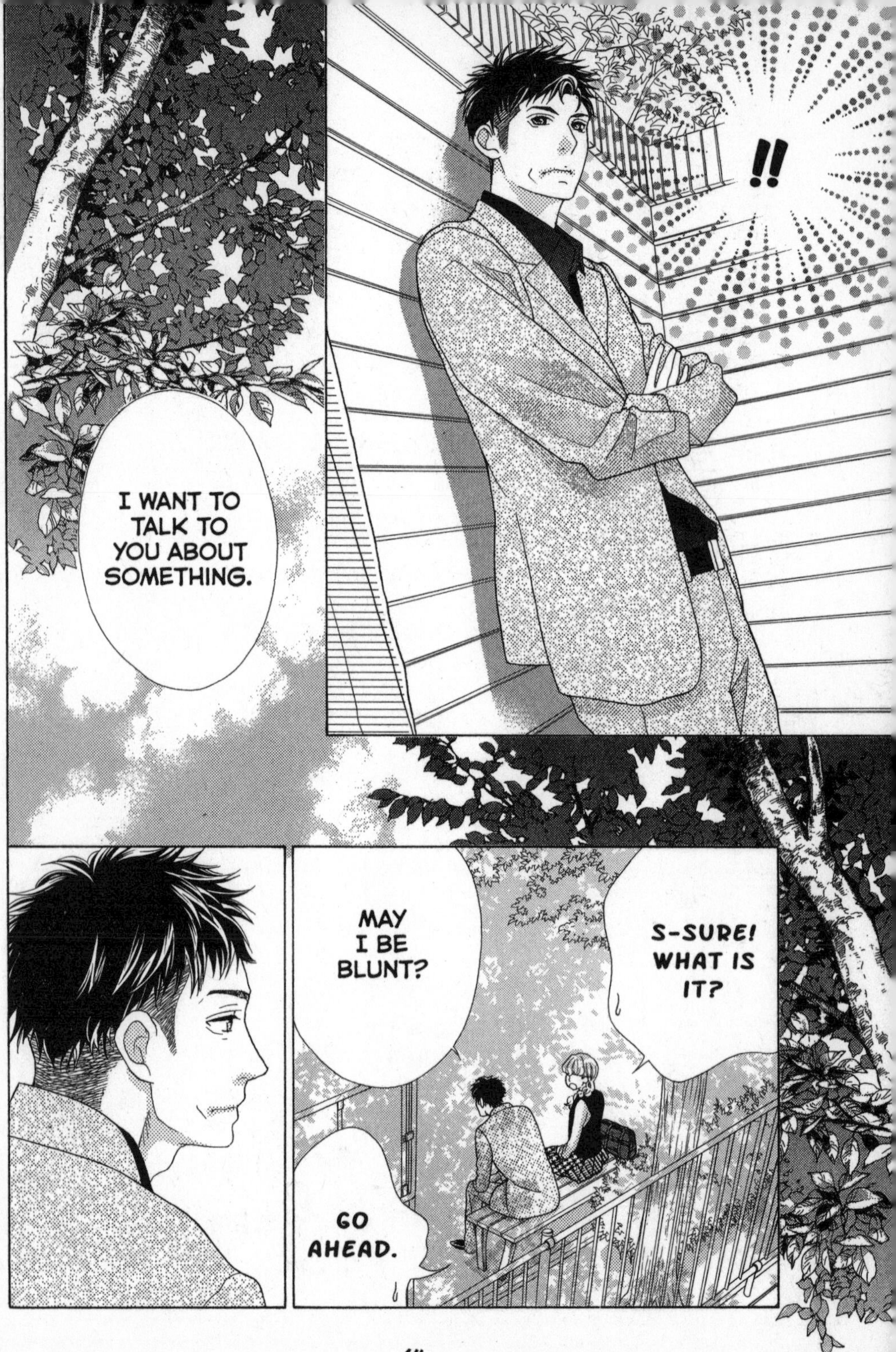
!!
I WANT TO TALK TO YOU ABOUT SOMETHING.
S-SURE! WHAT IS IT?
MAY I BE BLUNT?
GO AHEAD.

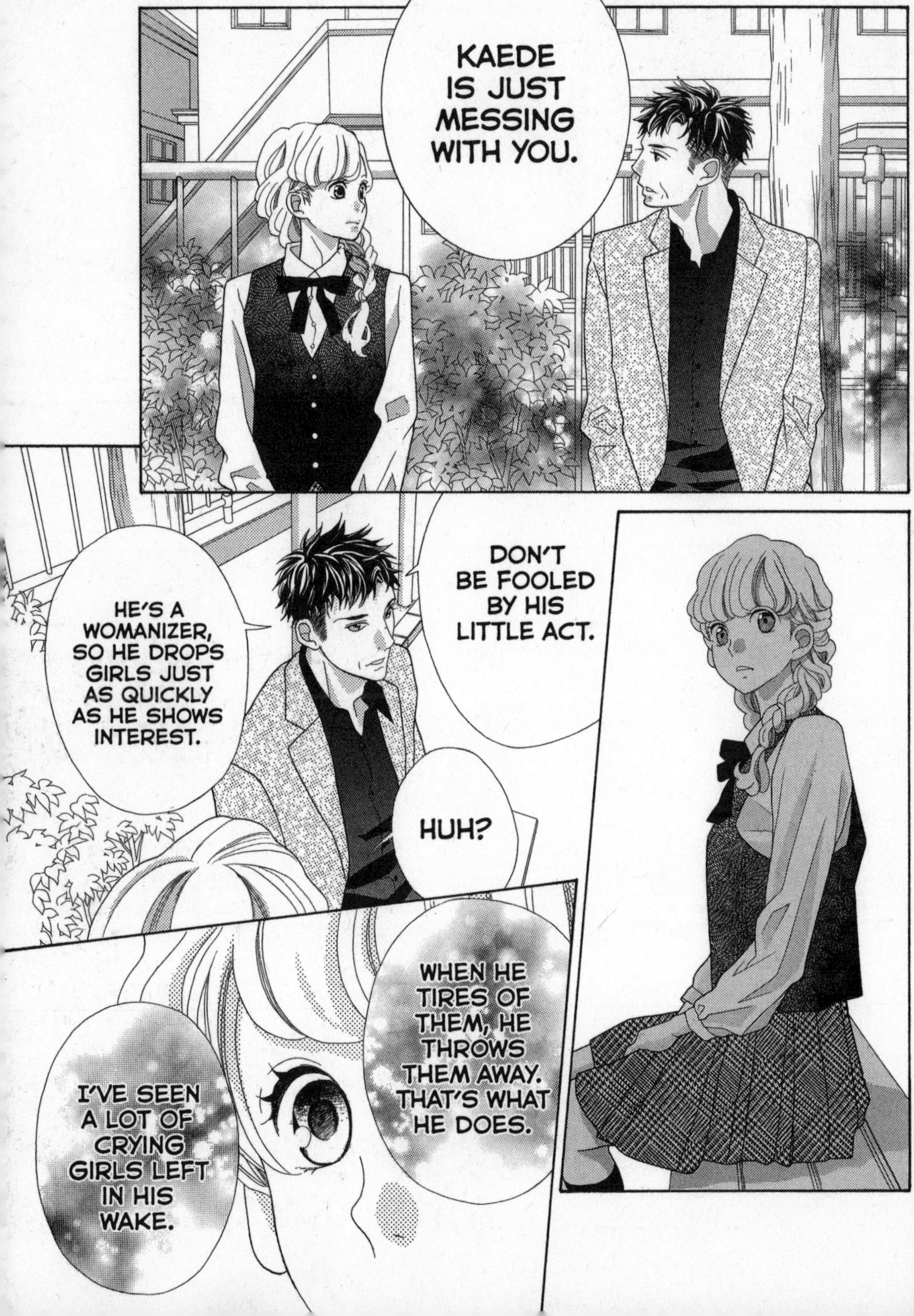
KAEDE IS JUST MESSING WITH YOU.
DON'T BE FOOLED BY HIS LITTLE ACT.
HE'S A WOMANIZER, SO HE DROPS GIRLS JUST AS QUICKLY AS HE SHOWS INTEREST.
HUH?
WHEN HE TIRES OF THEM, HE THROWS THEM AWAY. THAT'S WHAT HE DOES.
I'VE SEEN A LOT OF CRYING GIRLS LEFT IN HIS WAKE.

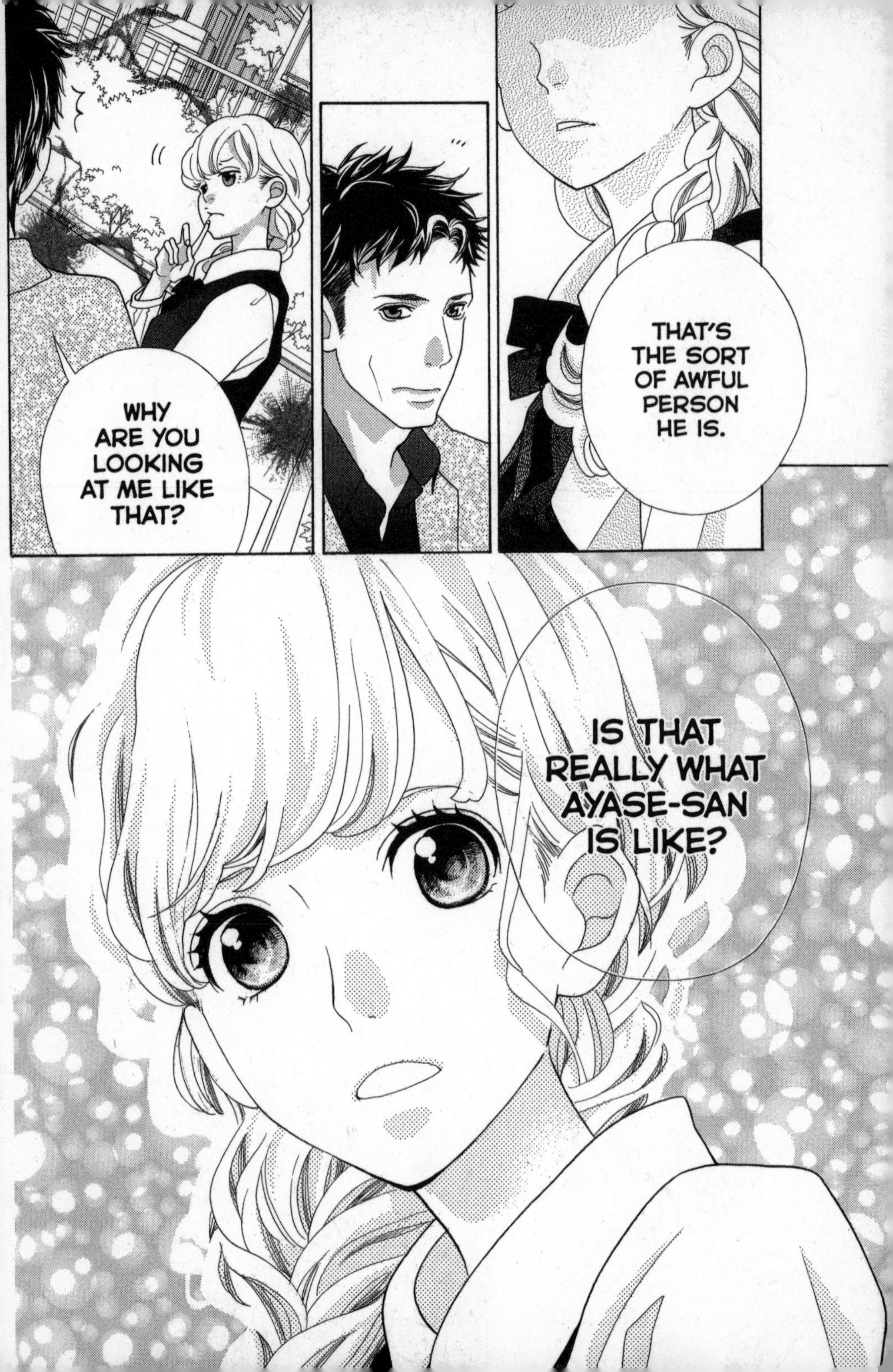
THAT'S THE SORT OF AWFUL PERSON HE IS.
WHY ARE YOU LOOKING AT ME LIKE THAT?
IS THAT REALLY WHAT AYASE-SAN IS LIKE?

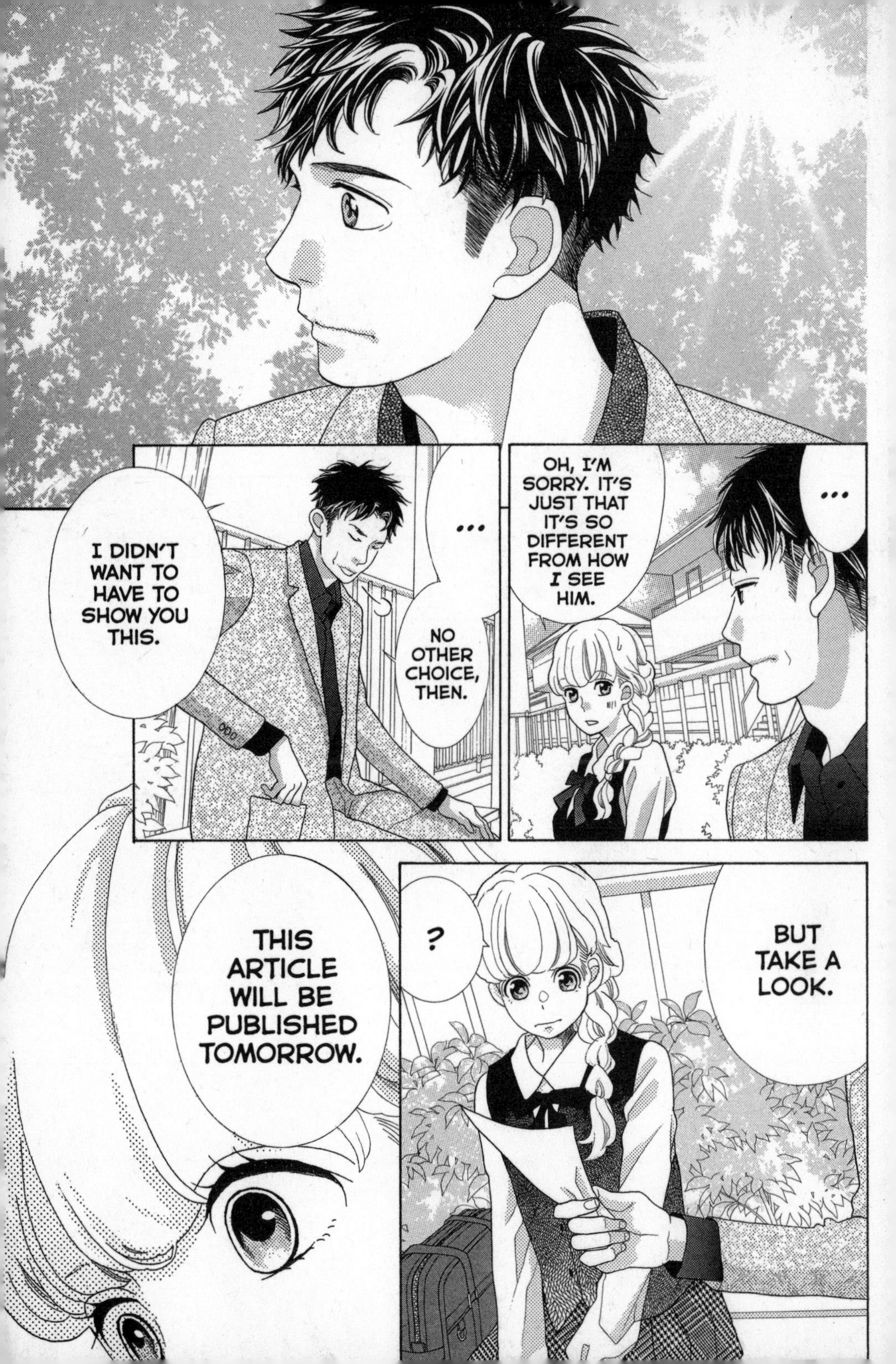
...
OH, I'M SORRY. IT'S JUST THAT IT'S SO DIFFERENT FROM HOW *I* SEE HIM.
...
NO OTHER CHOICE, THEN.
I DIDN'T WANT TO HAVE TO SHOW YOU THIS.
BUT TAKE A LOOK.
?
THIS ARTICLE WILL BE PUBLISHED TOMORROW.

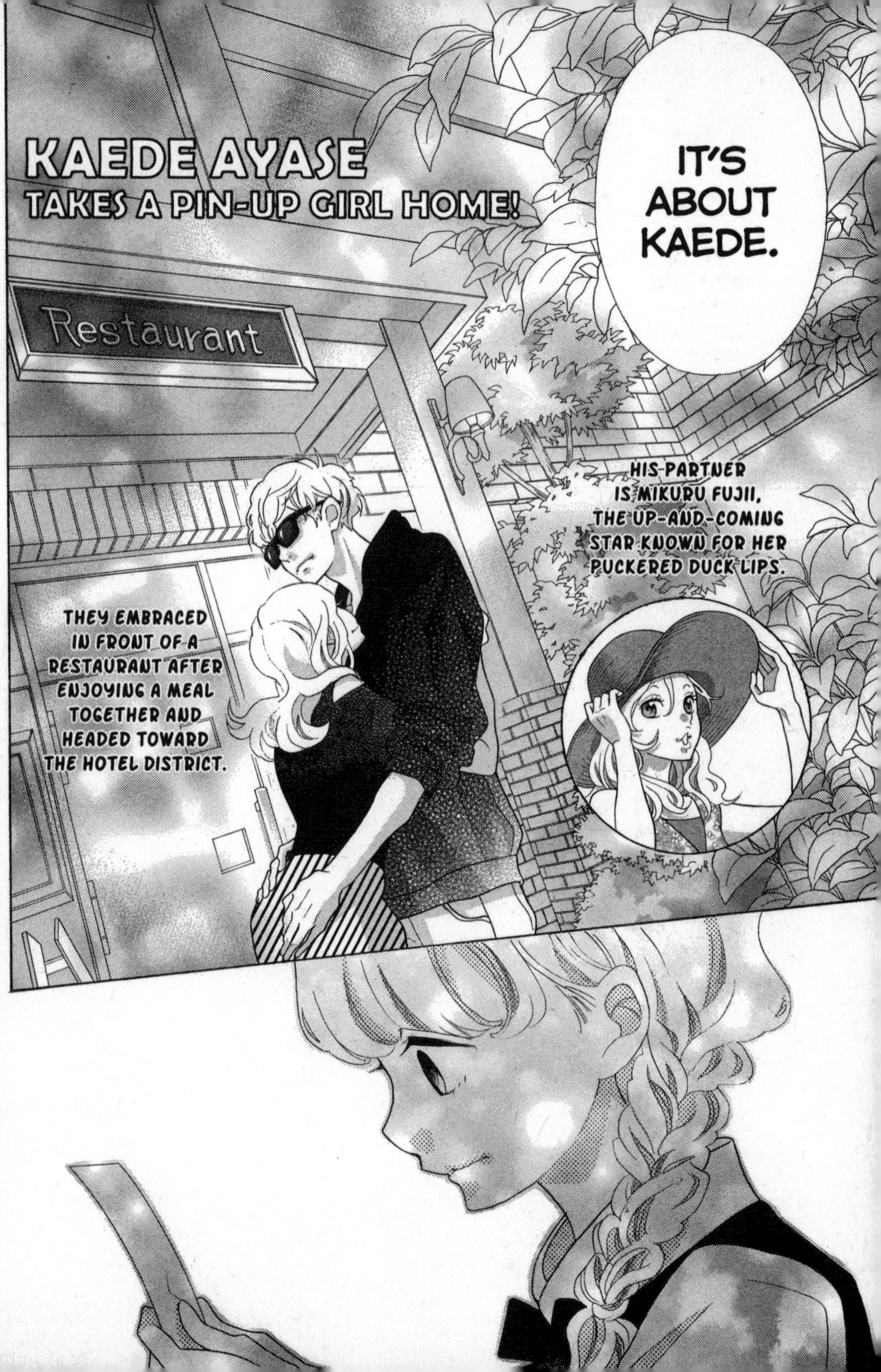

IT'S ABOUT KAEDE.
KAEDE AYASE TAKES A PIN-UP GIRL HOME!
Restaurant
HIS PARTNER IS MIKURU FUJII, THE UP-AND-COMING STAR KNOWN FOR HER PUCKERED DUCK LIPS.
THEY EMBRACED IN FRONT OF A RESTAURANT AFTER ENJOYING A MEAL TOGETHER AND HEADED TOWARD THE HOTEL DISTRICT.

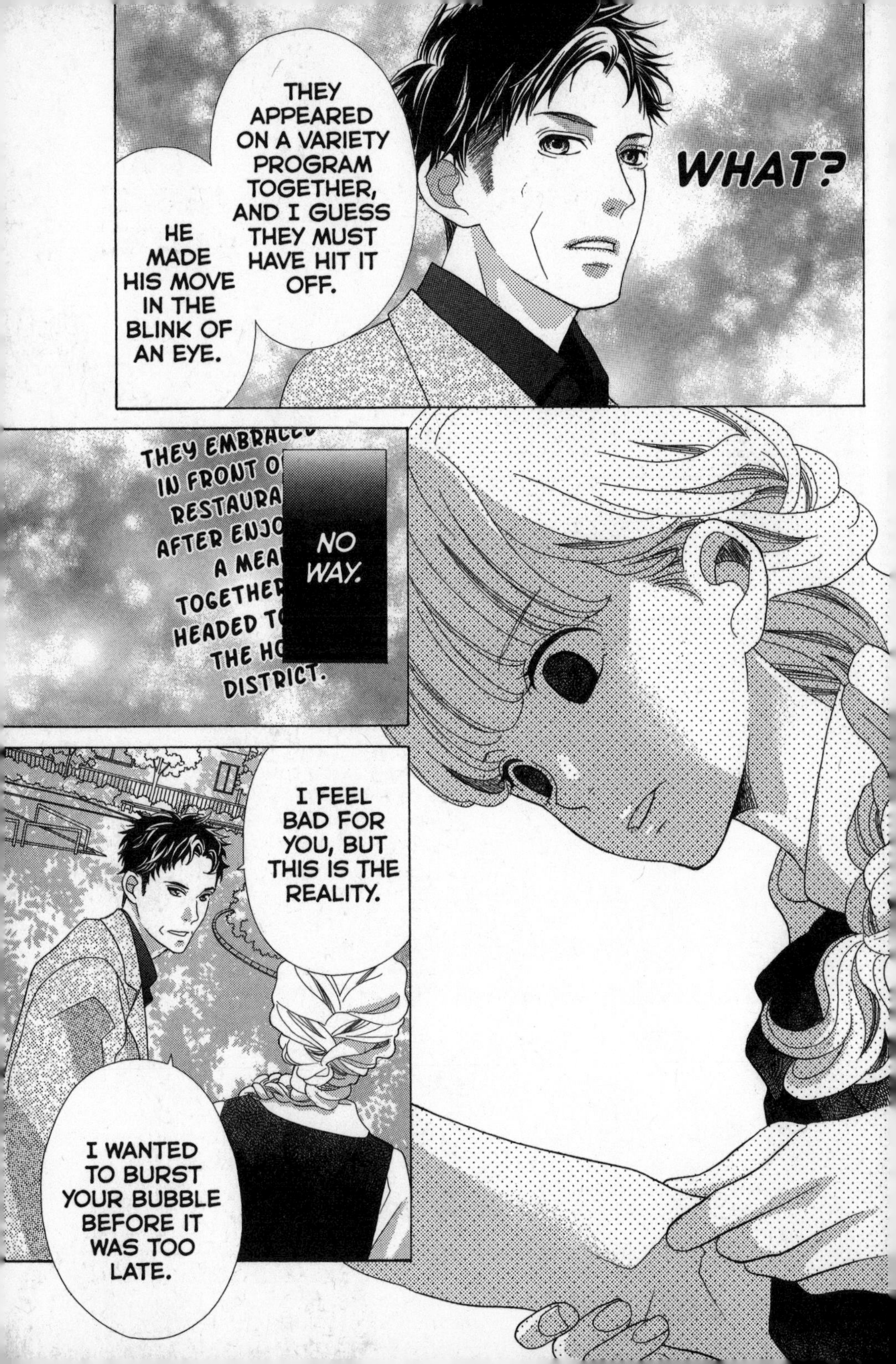

WHAT?
THEY APPEARED ON A VARIETY PROGRAM TOGETHER, AND I GUESS THEY MUST HAVE HIT IT OFF.
HE MADE HIS MOVE IN THE BLINK OF AN EYE.
NO WAY.
THEY EMBRAC IN FRONT O RESTAURA AFTER ENJO A MEA TOGETHER HEADED TO THE HO DISTRICT.
I FEEL BAD FOR YOU, BUT THIS IS THE REALITY.
I WANTED TO BURST YOUR BUBBLE BEFORE IT WAS TOO LATE.

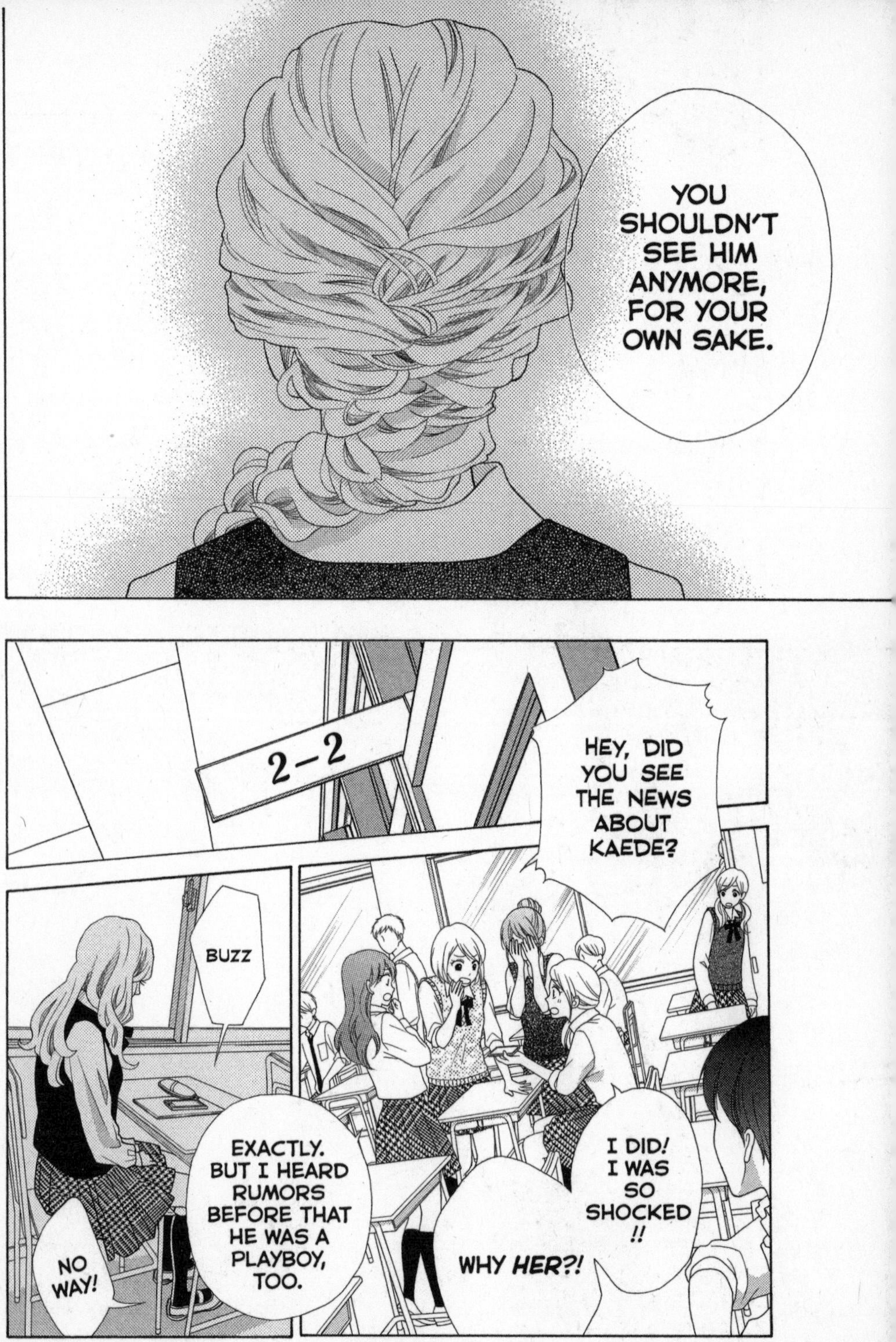
YOU SHOULDN'T SEE HIM ANYMORE, FOR YOUR OWN SAKE.
2-2
HEY, DID YOU SEE THE NEWS ABOUT KAEDE?
I DID! I WAS SO SHOCKED!!
WHY *HER*?!
EXACTLY. BUT I HEARD RUMORS BEFORE THAT HE WAS A PLAYBOY, TOO.
BUZZ
NO WAY!

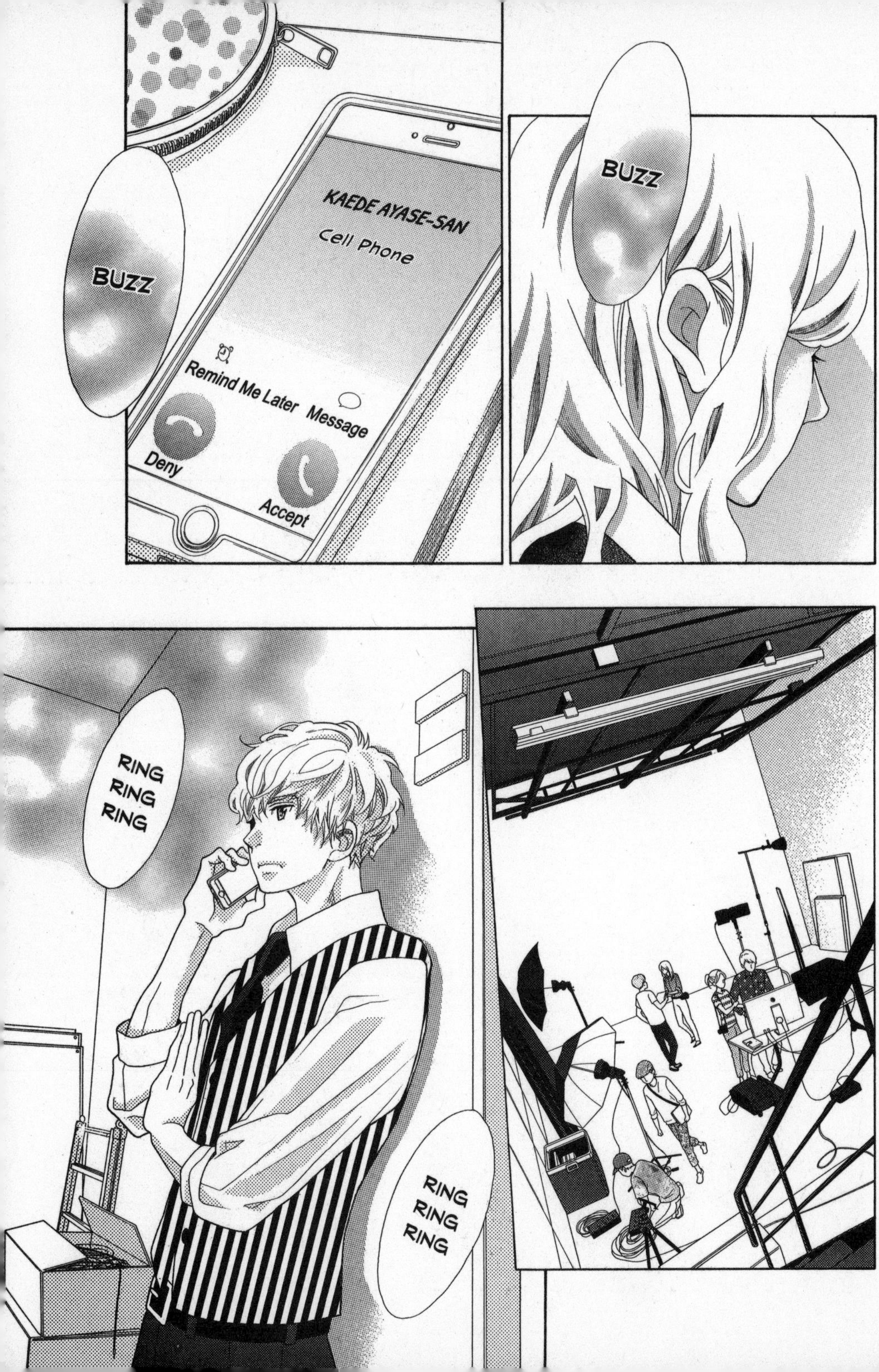
BUZZ
KAEDE AYASE-SAN
Cell Phone
BUZZ
Remind Me Later
Message
Deny
Accept
RING
RING
RING
RING
RING
RING

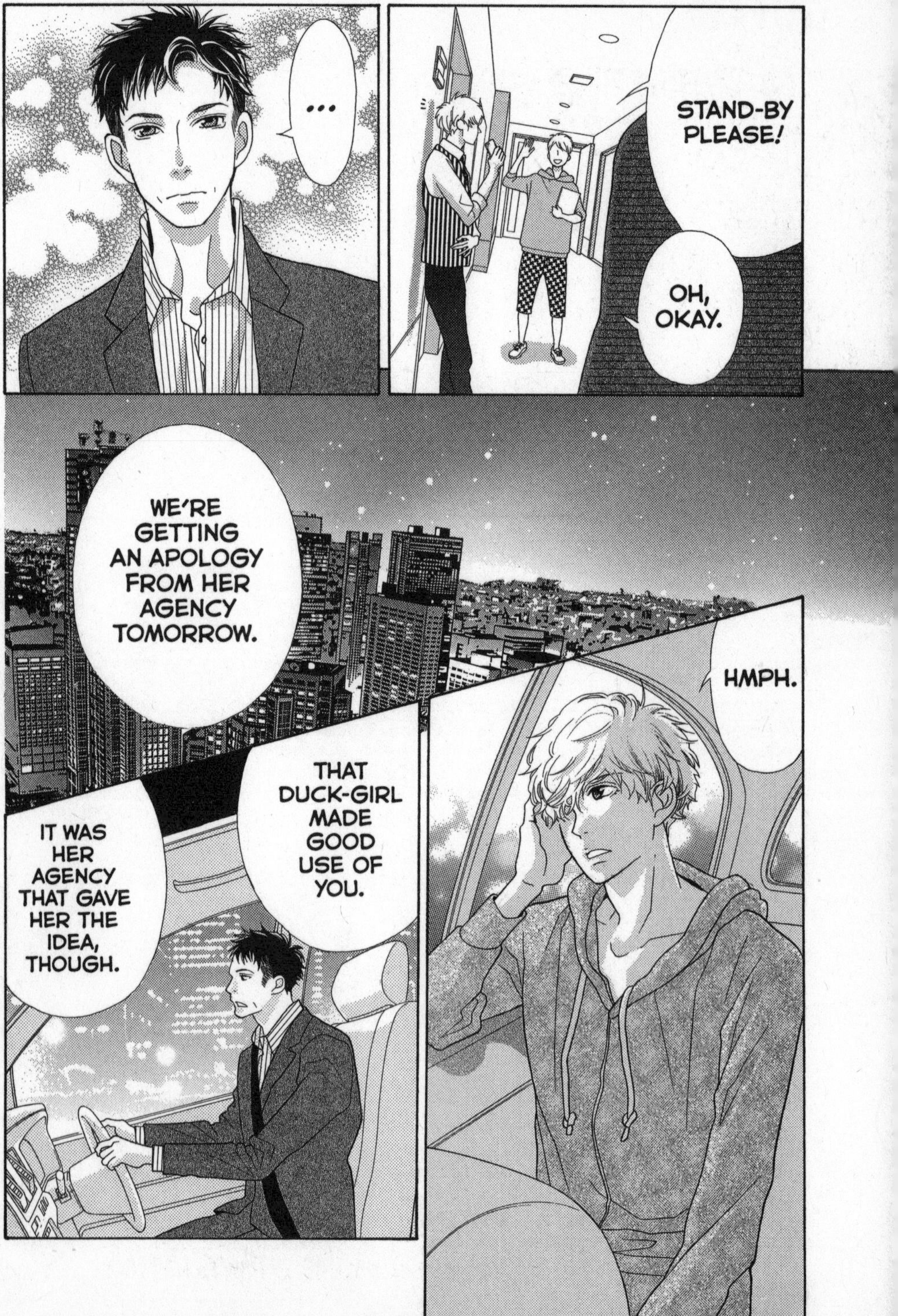
STAND-BY PLEASE!
OH, OKAY.
...
WE'RE GETTING AN APOLOGY FROM HER AGENCY TOMORROW.
HMPH.
THAT DUCK-GIRL MADE GOOD USE OF YOU.
IT WAS HER AGENCY THAT GAVE HER THE IDEA, THOUGH.

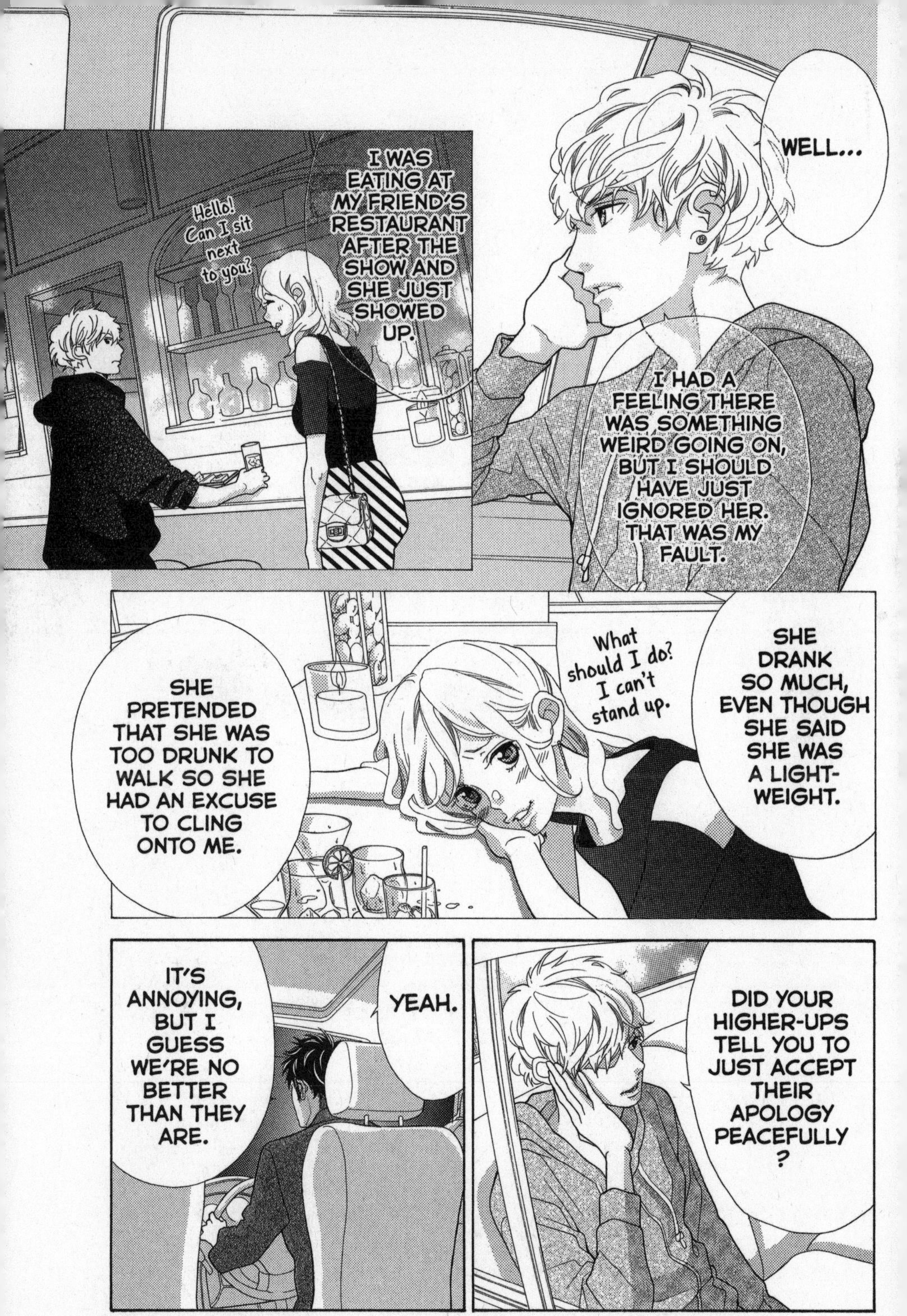
WELL...
I WAS EATING AT MY FRIEND'S RESTAURANT AFTER THE SHOW AND SHE JUST SHOWED UP.
Hello! Can I sit next to you?
I HAD A FEELING THERE WAS SOMETHING WEIRD GOING ON, BUT I SHOULD HAVE JUST IGNORED HER. THAT WAS MY FAULT.
SHE DRANK SO MUCH, EVEN THOUGH SHE SAID SHE WAS A LIGHT-WEIGHT.
What should I do? I can't stand up.
SHE PRETENDED THAT SHE WAS TOO DRUNK TO WALK SO SHE HAD AN EXCUSE TO CLING ONTO ME.
DID YOUR HIGHER-UPS TELL YOU TO JUST ACCEPT THEIR APOLOGY PEACEFULLY?
YEAH.
IT'S ANNOYING, BUT I GUESS WE'RE NO BETTER THAN THEY ARE.

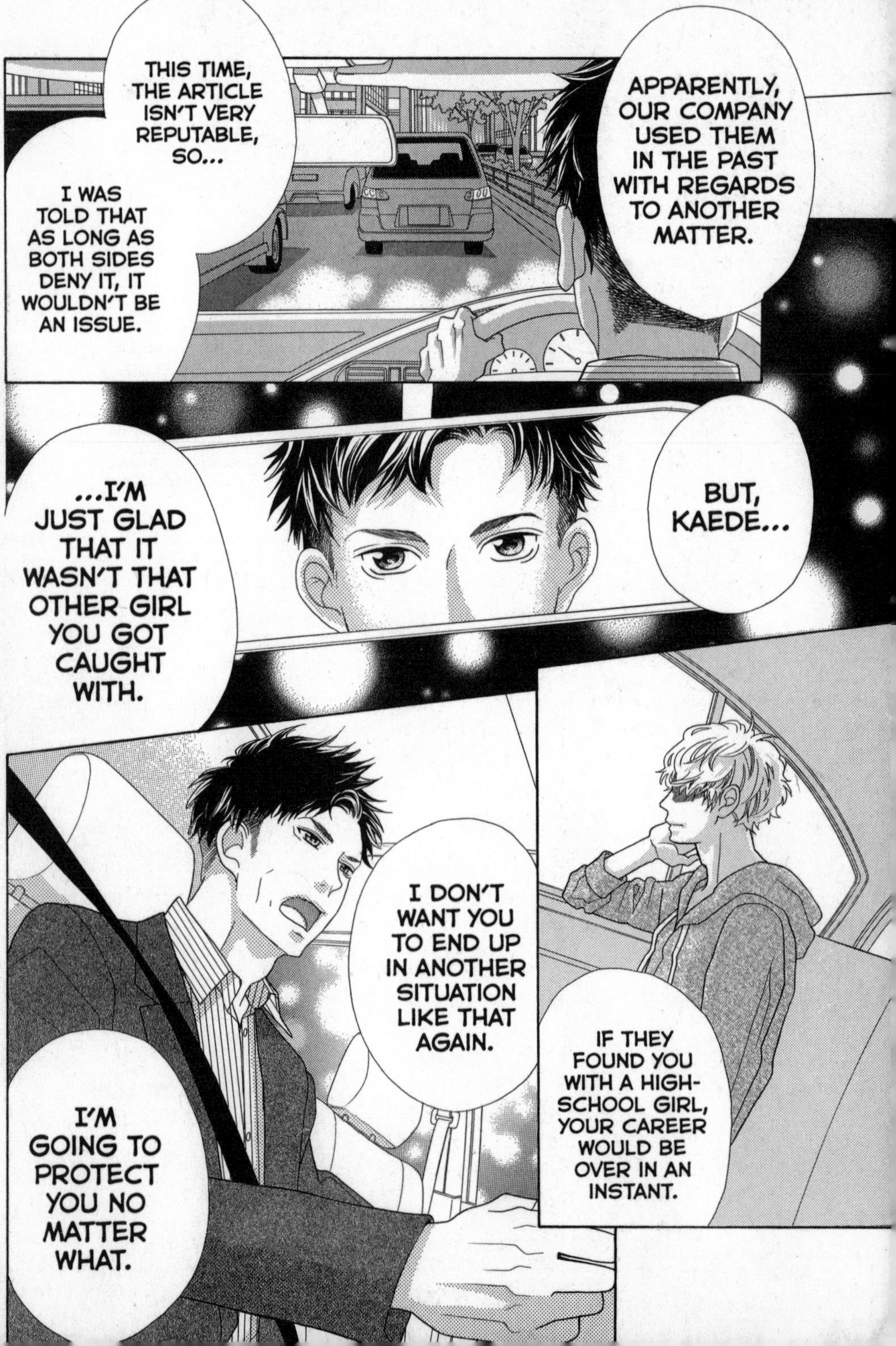
APPARENTLY, OUR COMPANY USED THEM IN THE PAST WITH REGARDS TO ANOTHER MATTER.
THIS TIME, THE ARTICLE ISN'T VERY REPUTABLE, SO...
I WAS TOLD THAT AS LONG AS BOTH SIDES DENY IT, IT WOULDN'T BE AN ISSUE.
BUT, KAEDE...
...I'M JUST GLAD THAT IT WASN'T THAT OTHER GIRL YOU GOT CAUGHT WITH.
IF THEY FOUND YOU WITH A HIGH-SCHOOL GIRL, YOUR CAREER WOULD BE OVER IN AN INSTANT.
I DON'T WANT YOU TO END UP IN ANOTHER SITUATION LIKE THAT AGAIN.
I'M GOING TO PROTECT YOU NO MATTER WHAT.

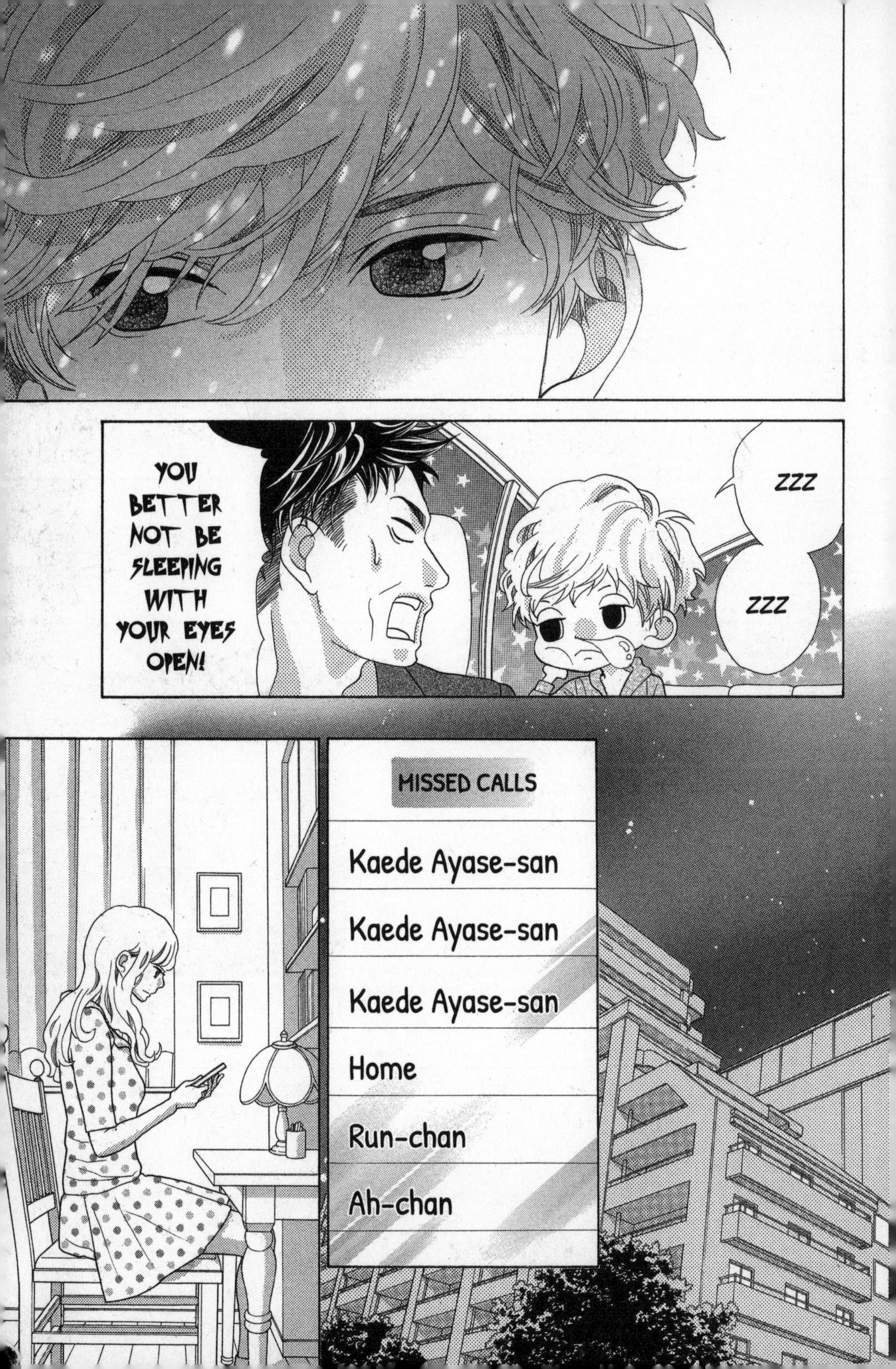
ZZZ
ZZZ
YOU BETTER NOT BE SLEEPING WITH YOUR EYES OPEN!
MISSED CALLS
Kaede Ayase-san
Kaede Ayase-san
Kaede Ayase-san
Home
Run-chan
Ah-chan

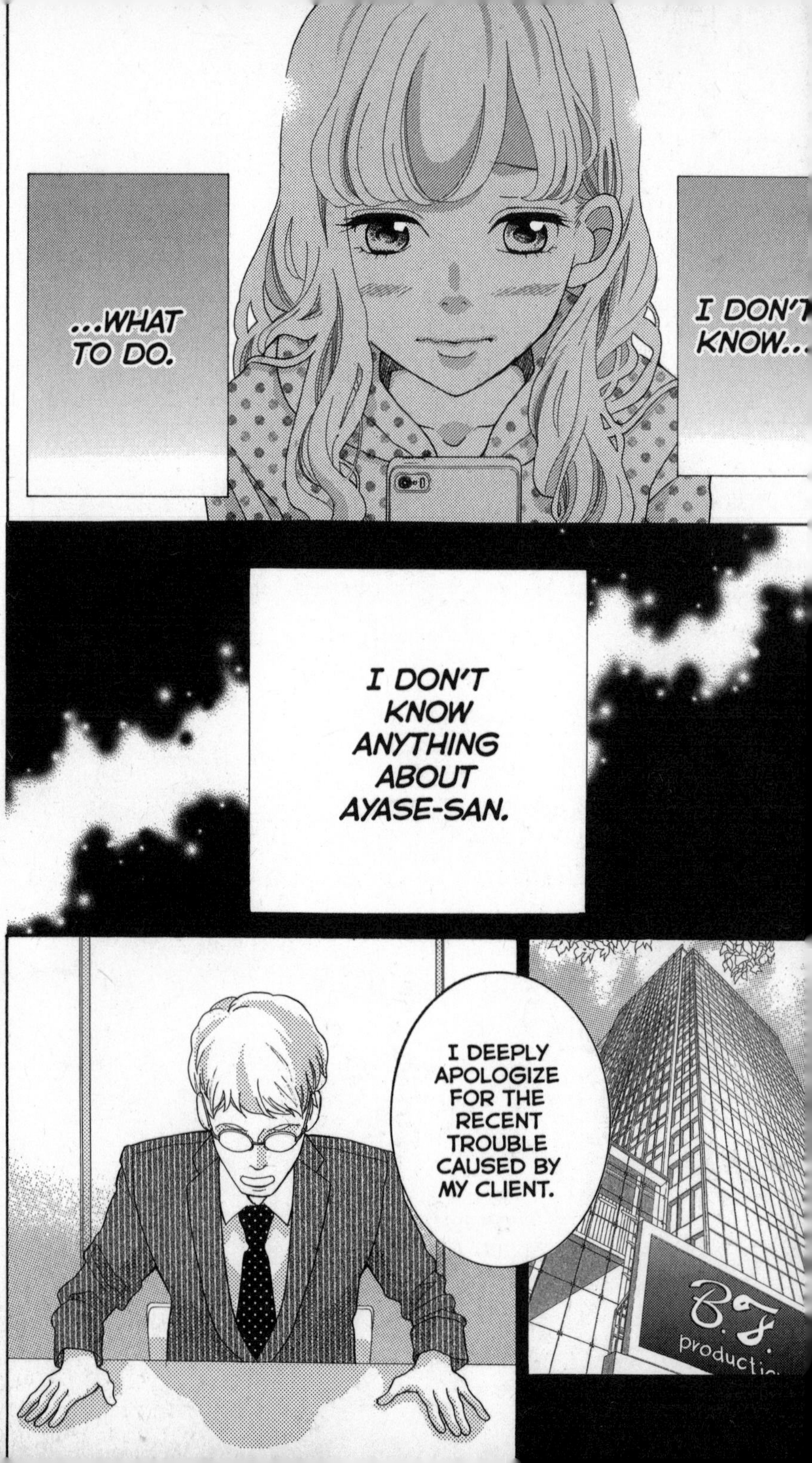
I DON'T KNOW...
...WHAT TO DO.
I DON'T KNOW ANYTHING ABOUT AYASE-SAN.
I DEEPLY APOLOGIZE FOR THE RECENT TROUBLE CAUSED BY MY CLIENT.

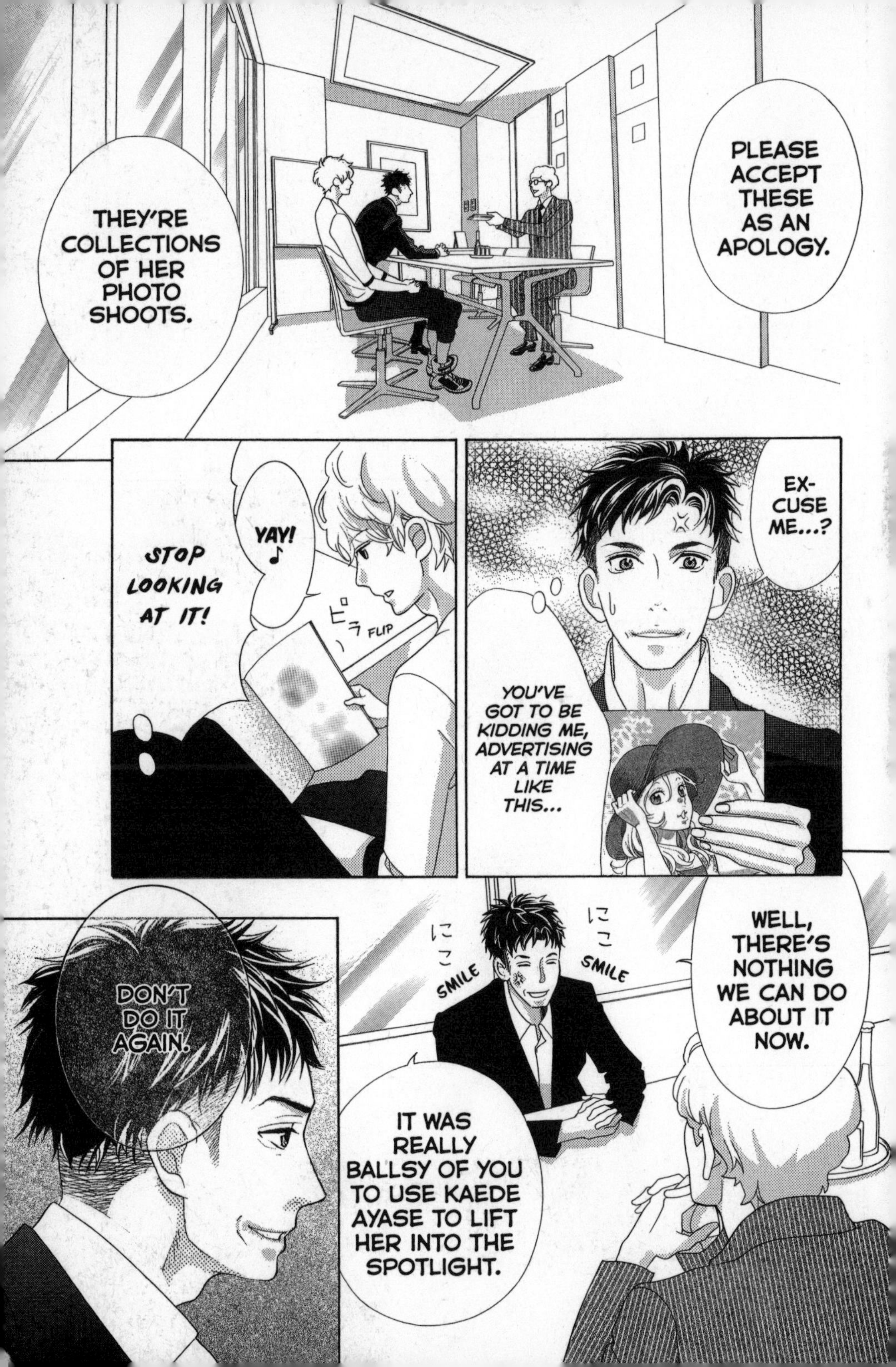
PLEASE ACCEPT THESE AS AN APOLOGY.
THEY'RE COLLECTIONS OF HER PHOTO SHOOTS.
EX-CUSE ME...?
YOU'VE GOT TO BE KIDDING ME, ADVERTISING AT A TIME LIKE THIS...
YAY! ♪
ピラ FLIP
STOP LOOKING AT IT!
WELL, THERE'S NOTHING WE CAN DO ABOUT IT NOW.
にこ SMILE
にこ SMILE
IT WAS REALLY BALLSY OF YOU TO USE KAEDE AYASE TO LIFT HER INTO THE SPOTLIGHT.
DON'T DO IT AGAIN.

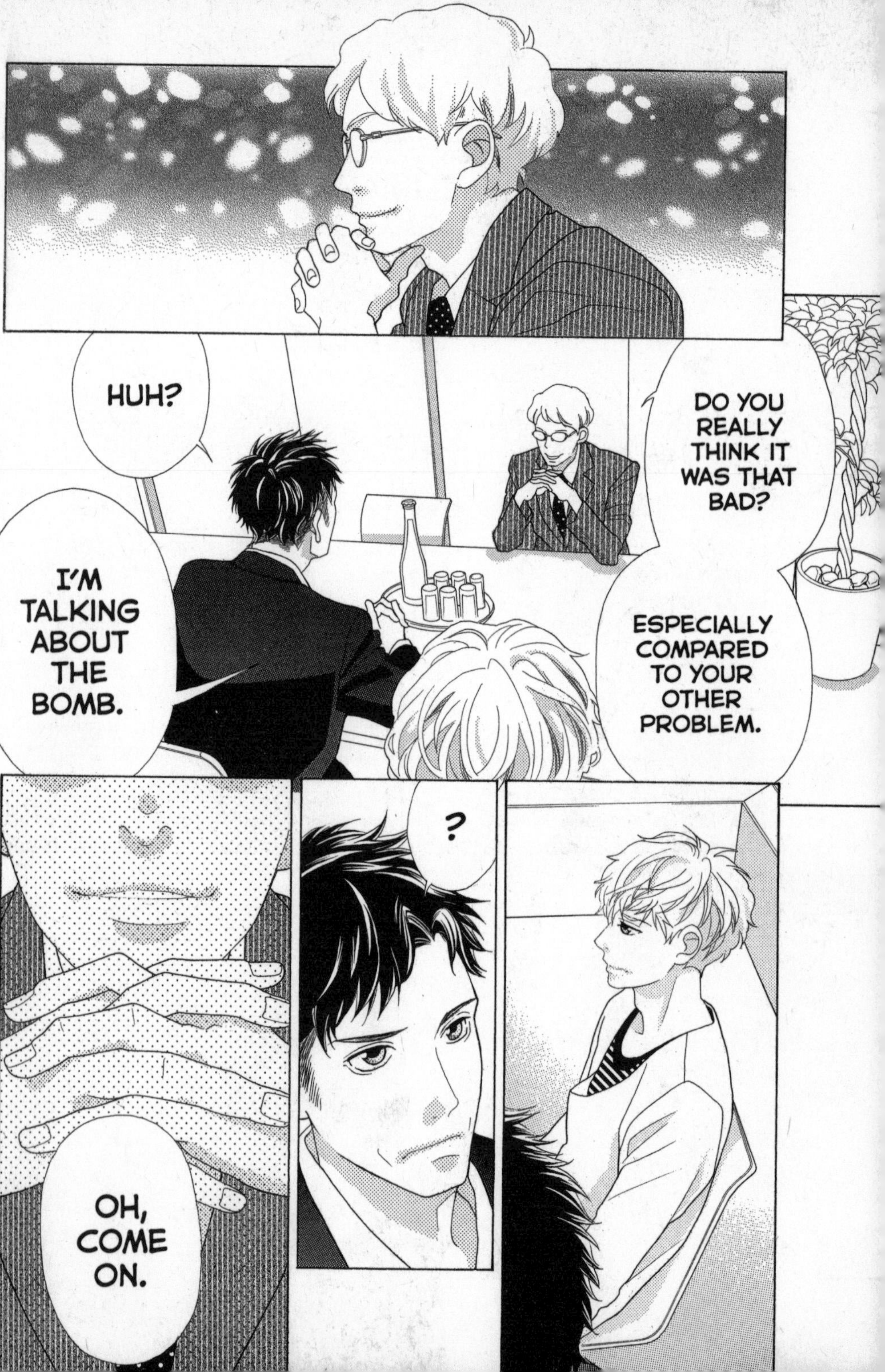
DO YOU REALLY THINK IT WAS THAT BAD?
HUH?
ESPECIALLY COMPARED TO YOUR OTHER PROBLEM.
I'M TALKING ABOUT THE BOMB.
?
OH, COME ON.

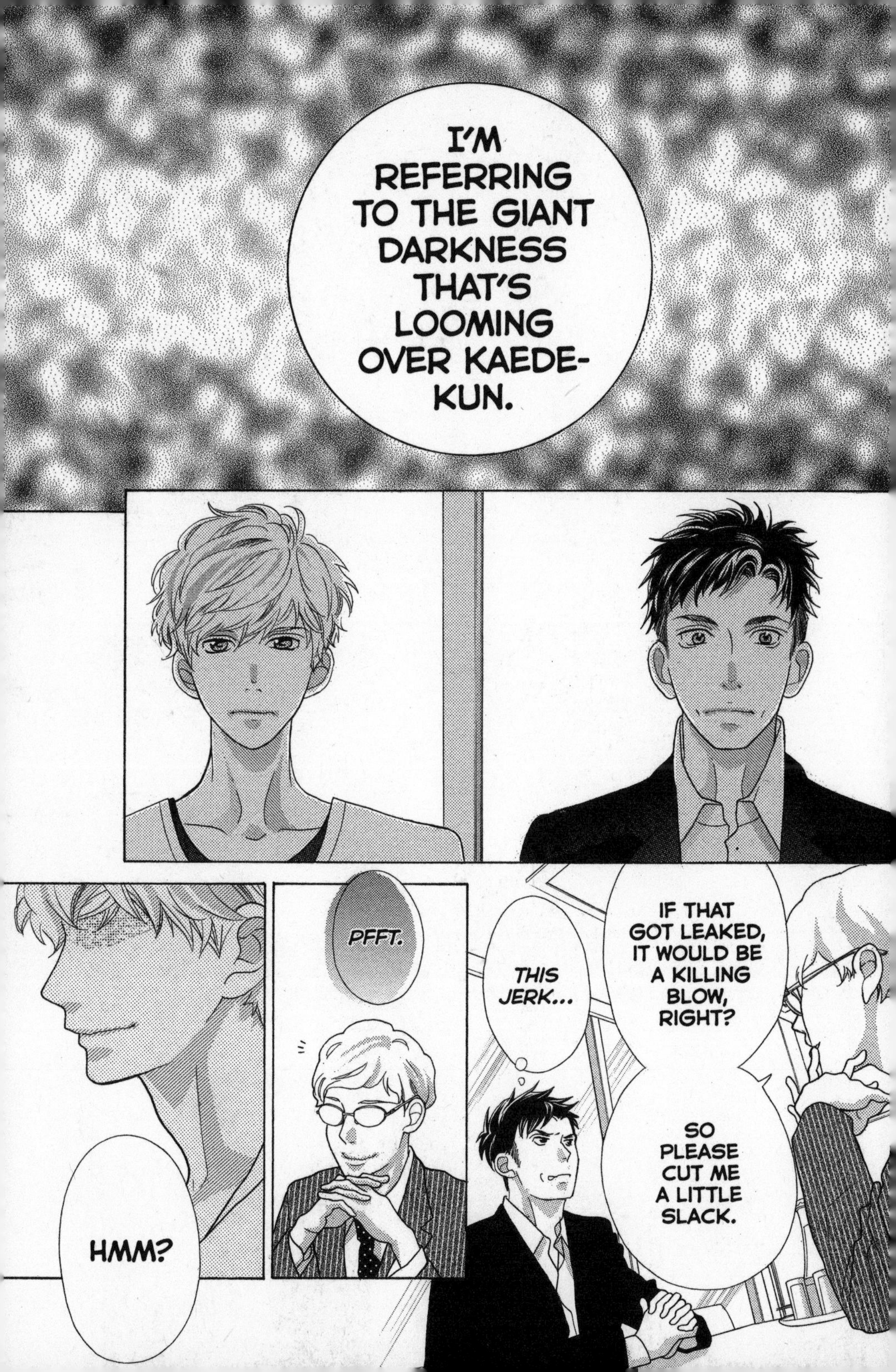
I'M REFERRING TO THE GIANT DARKNESS THAT'S LOOMING OVER KAEDE-KUN.
IF THAT GOT LEAKED, IT WOULD BE A KILLING BLOW, RIGHT?
THIS JERK...
SO PLEASE CUT ME A LITTLE SLACK.
PFFT.
HMM?

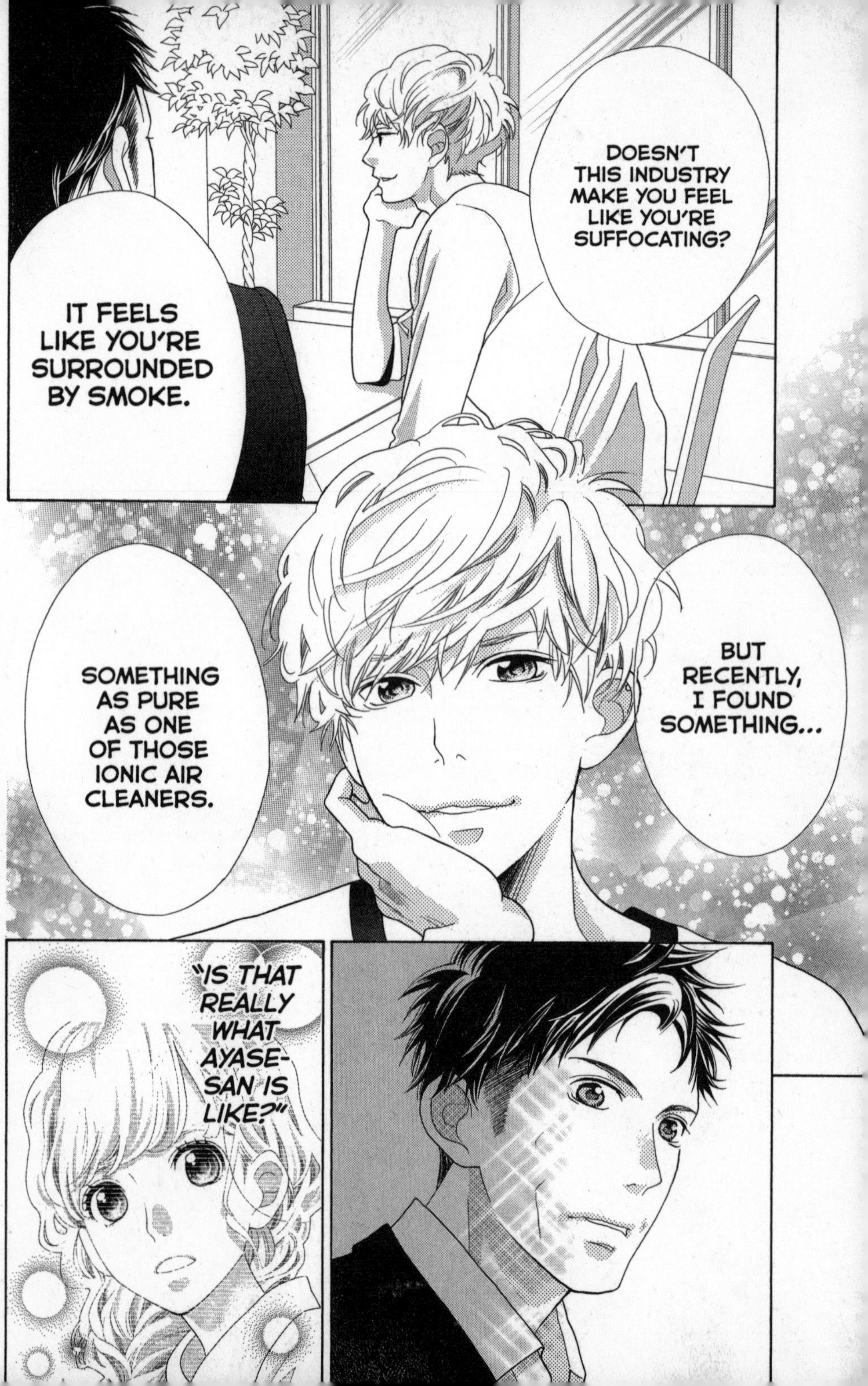
DOESN'T THIS INDUSTRY MAKE YOU FEEL LIKE YOU'RE SUFFOCATING?
IT FEELS LIKE YOU'RE SURROUNDED BY SMOKE.
BUT RECENTLY, I FOUND SOMETHING...
SOMETHING AS PURE AS ONE OF THOSE IONIC AIR CLEANERS.
"IS THAT REALLY WHAT AYASE-SAN IS LIKE?"

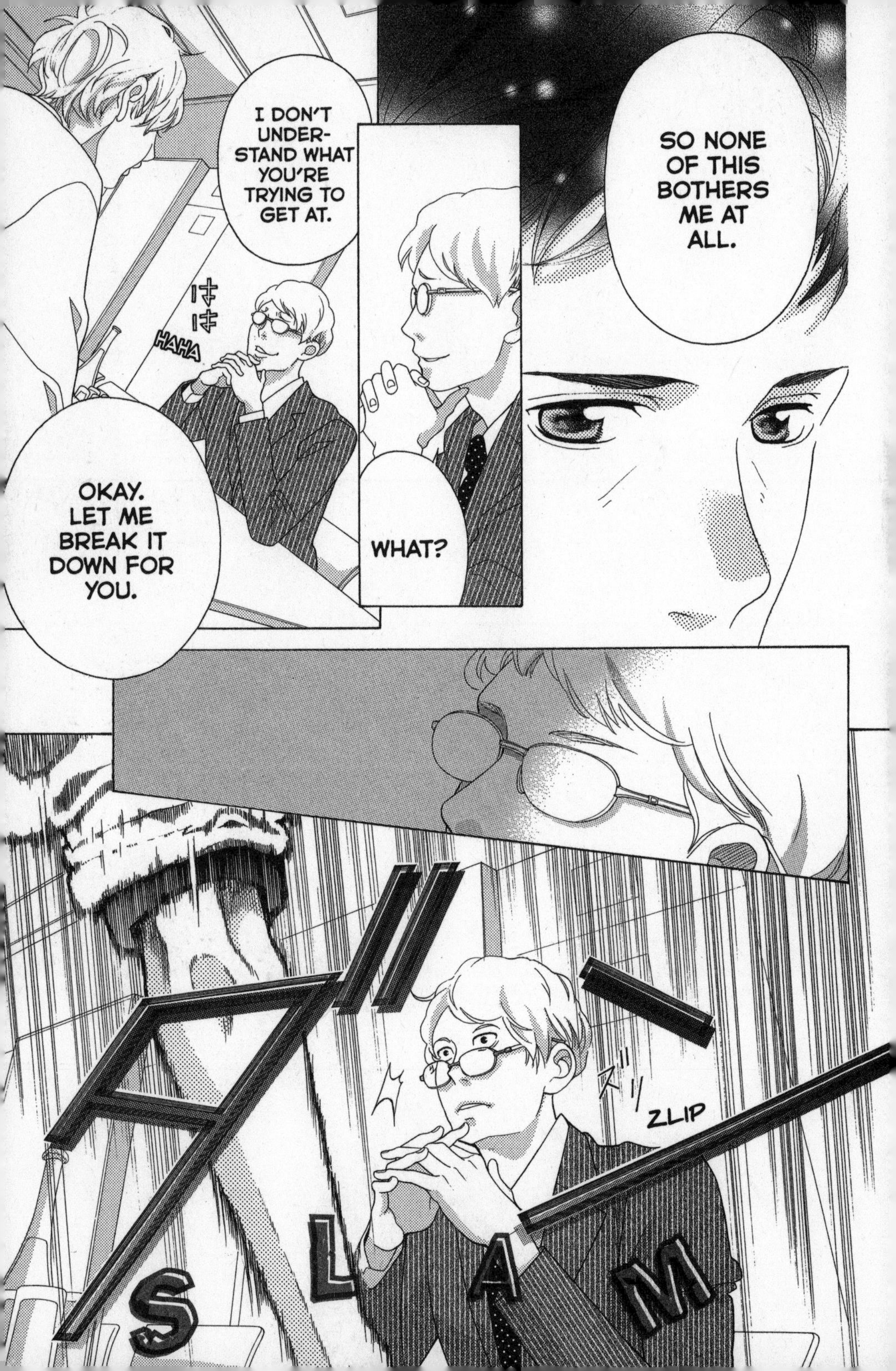
SO NONE OF THIS BOTHERS ME AT ALL.
WHAT?
I DON'T UNDER-STAND WHAT YOU'RE TRYING TO GET AT.
はは
HAHA
OKAY. LET ME BREAK IT DOWN FOR YOU.
ズリ
ZLIP
SLAM

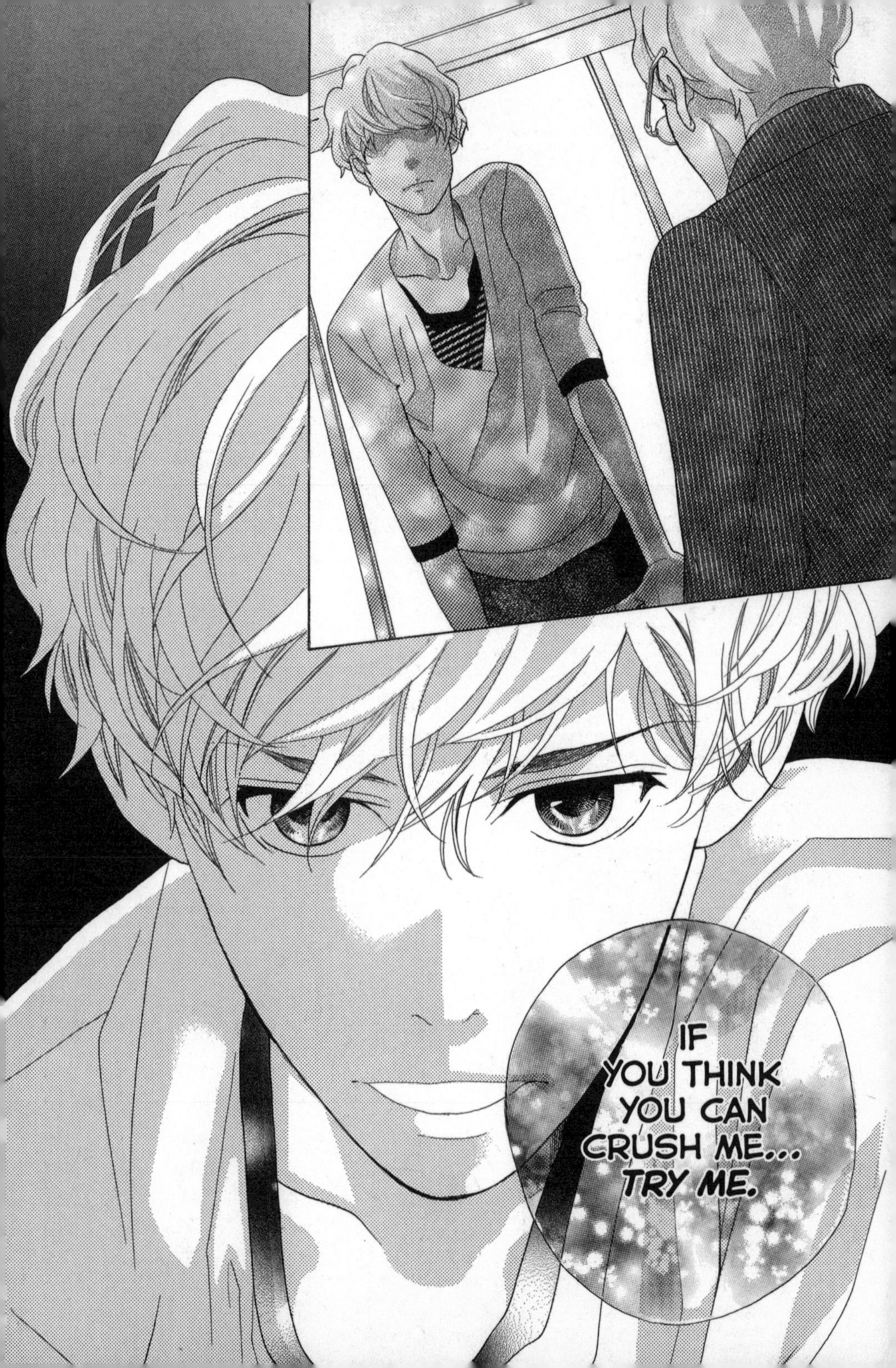
IF YOU THINK YOU CAN CRUSH ME... TRY ME.

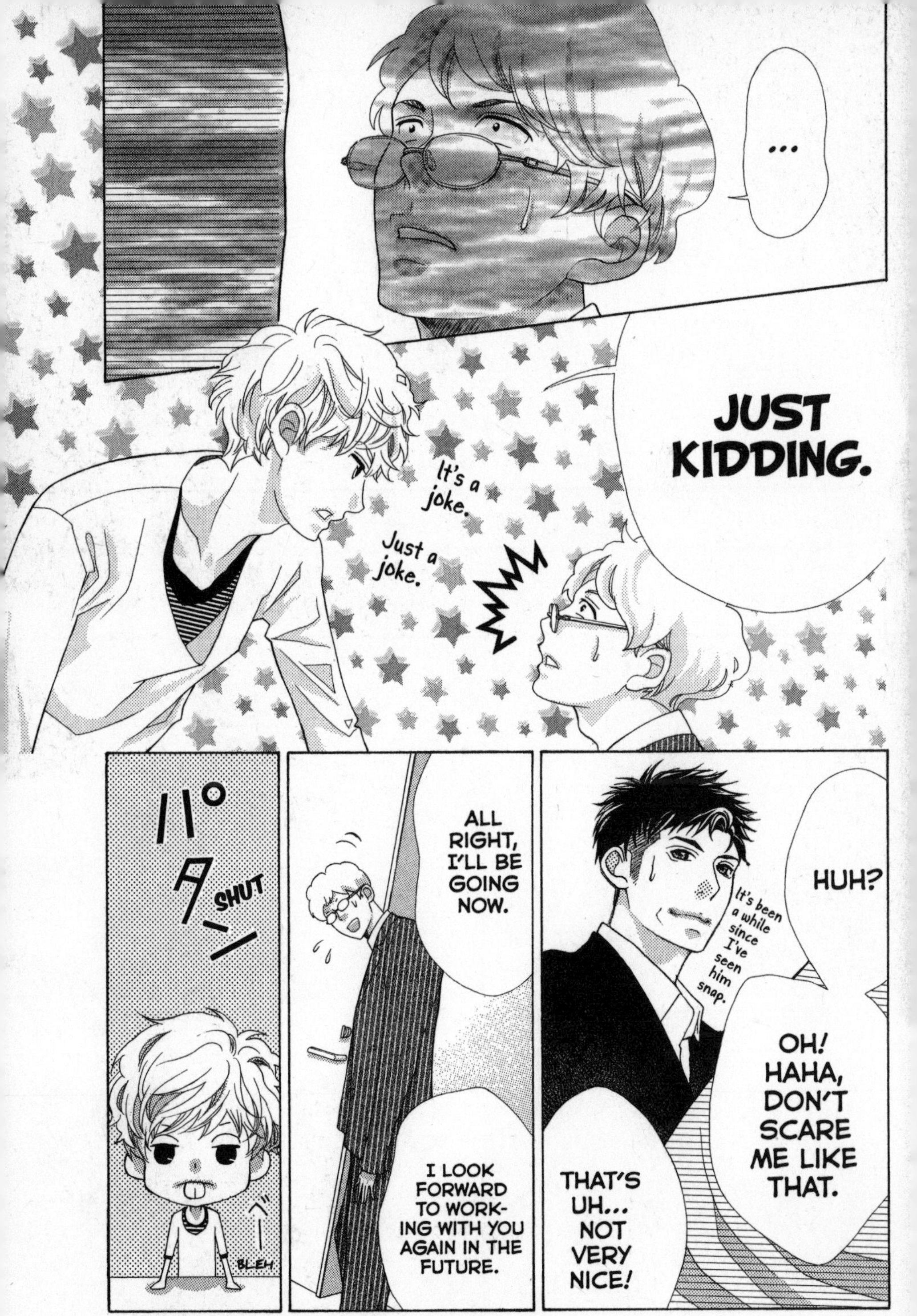
...
JUST KIDDING.
It's a joke.
Just a joke.
HUH?
It's been a while since I've seen him snap.
OH! HAHA, DON'T SCARE ME LIKE THAT.
THAT'S UH... NOT VERY NICE!
ALL RIGHT, I'LL BE GOING NOW.
I LOOK FORWARD TO WORKING WITH YOU AGAIN IN THE FUTURE.
パタン
SHUT
BLEH

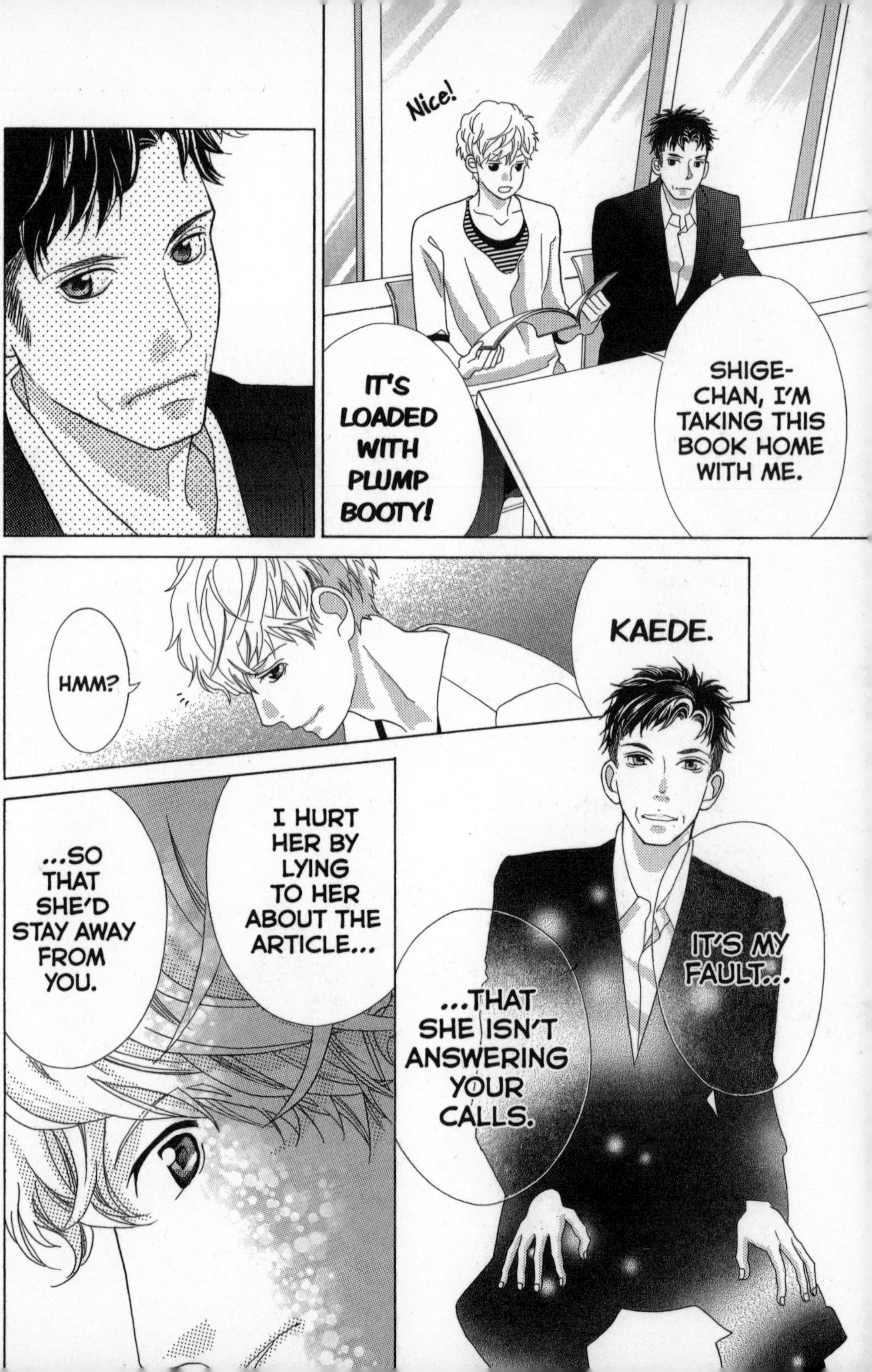
Nice!
SHIGE-CHAN, I'M TAKING THIS BOOK HOME WITH ME.
IT'S LOADED WITH PLUMP BOOTY!
KAEDE.
HMM?
IT'S MY FAULT...
...THAT SHE ISN'T ANSWERING YOUR CALLS.
I HURT HER BY LYING TO HER ABOUT THE ARTICLE...
...SO THAT SHE'D STAY AWAY FROM YOU.

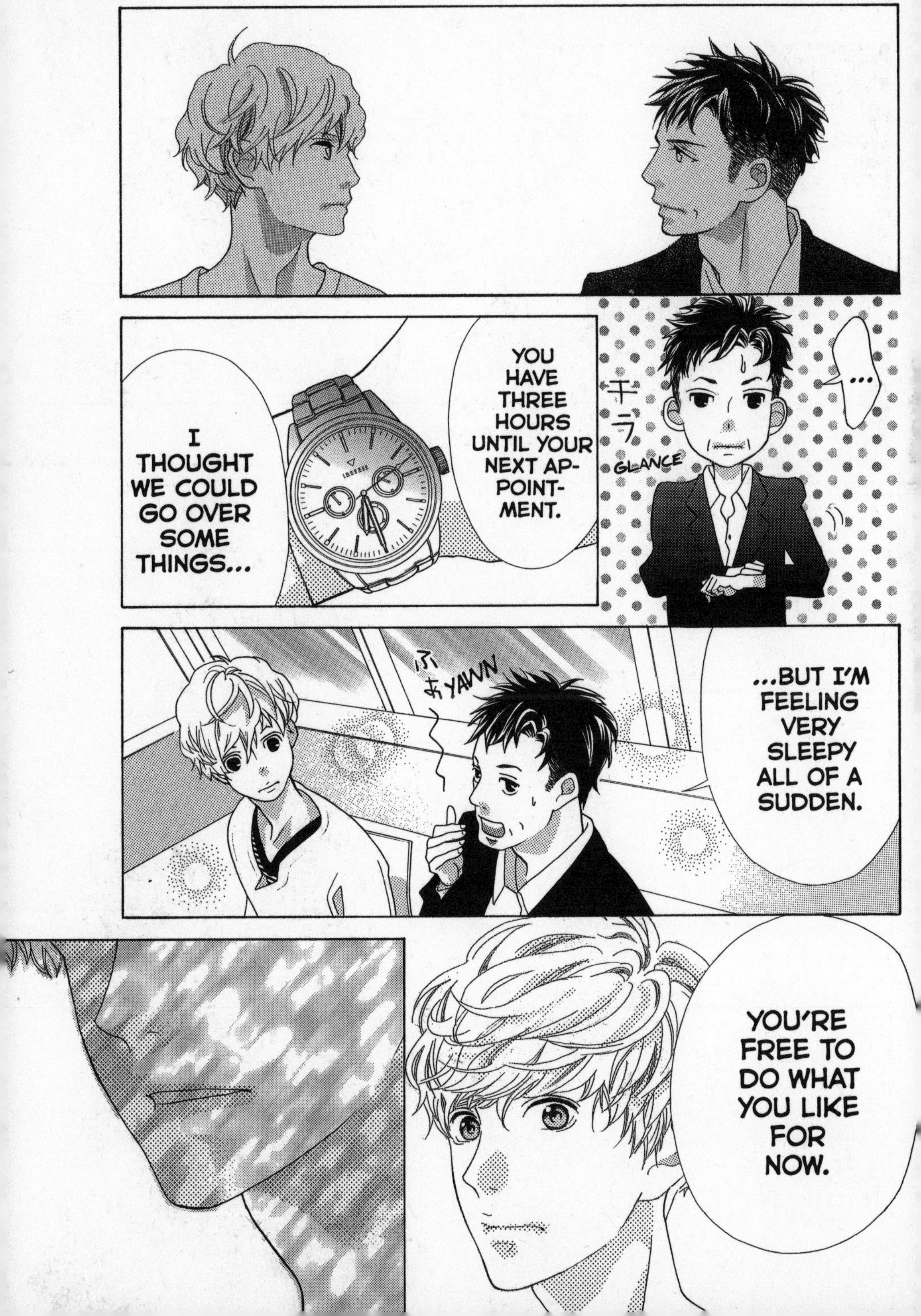
...
GLANCE
YOU HAVE THREE HOURS UNTIL YOUR NEXT AP-POINT-MENT.
I THOUGHT WE COULD GO OVER SOME THINGS...
...BUT I'M FEELING VERY SLEEPY ALL OF A SUDDEN.
ふあ YAWN
YOU'RE FREE TO DO WHAT YOU LIKE FOR NOW.

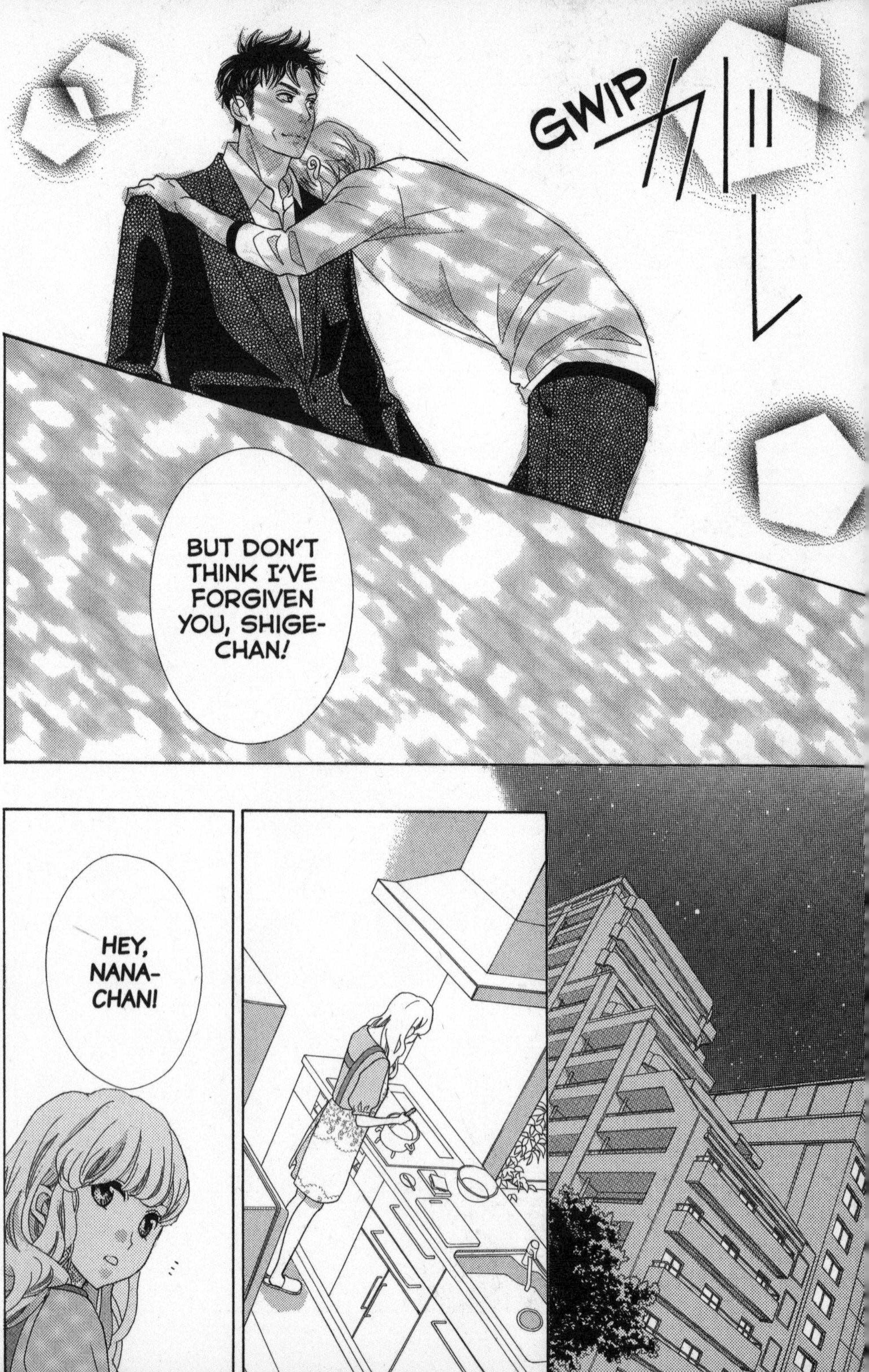
GWIP
BUT DON'T THINK I'VE FORGIVEN YOU, SHIGE-CHAN!
HEY, NANA-CHAN!

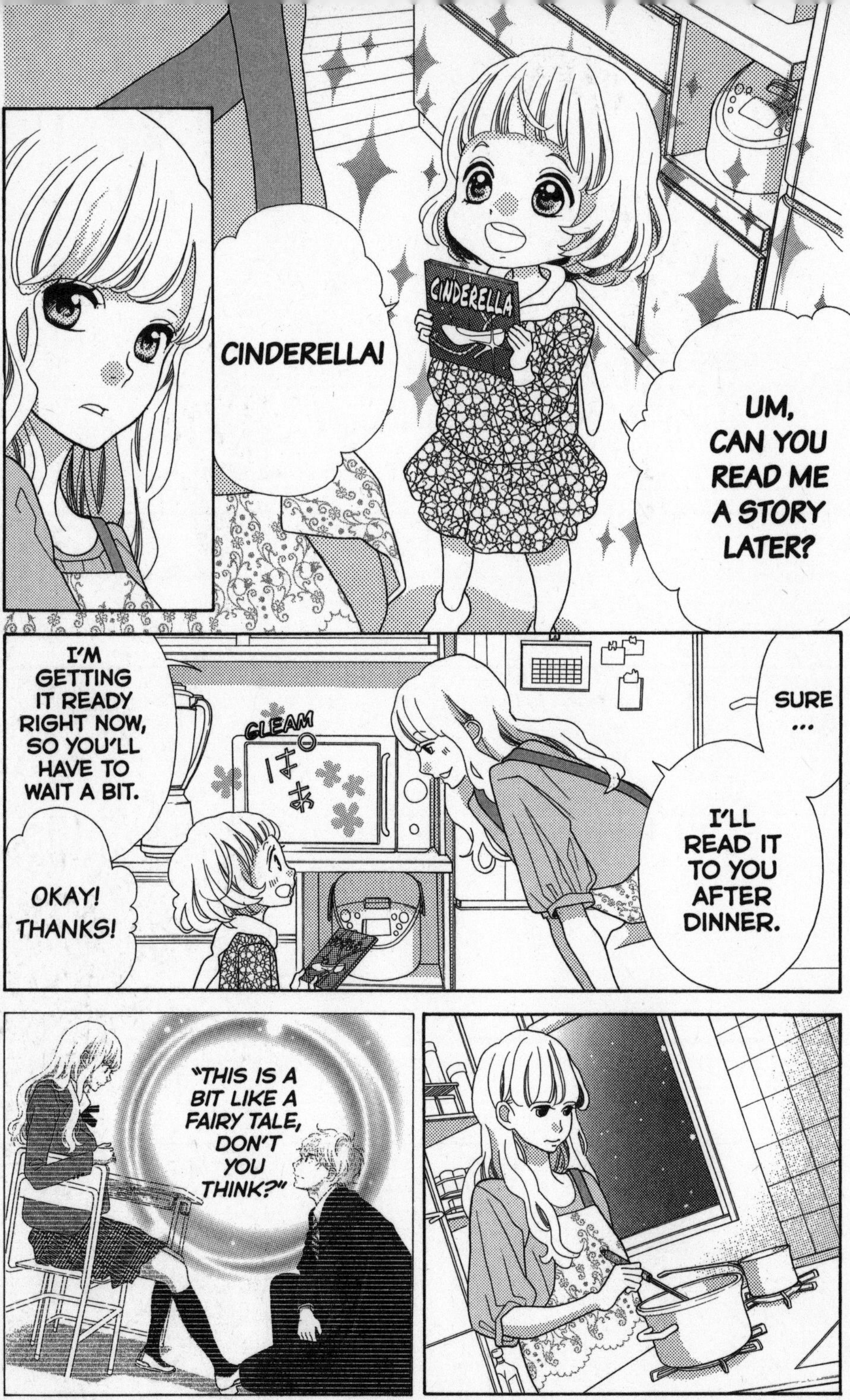
CINDERELLA
UM, CAN YOU READ ME A STORY LATER?
CINDERELLA!
SURE ...
I'LL READ IT TO YOU AFTER DINNER.
I'M GETTING IT READY RIGHT NOW, SO YOU'LL HAVE TO WAIT A BIT.
GLEAM
OKAY! THANKS!
"THIS IS A BIT LIKE A FAIRY TALE, DON'T YOU THINK?"

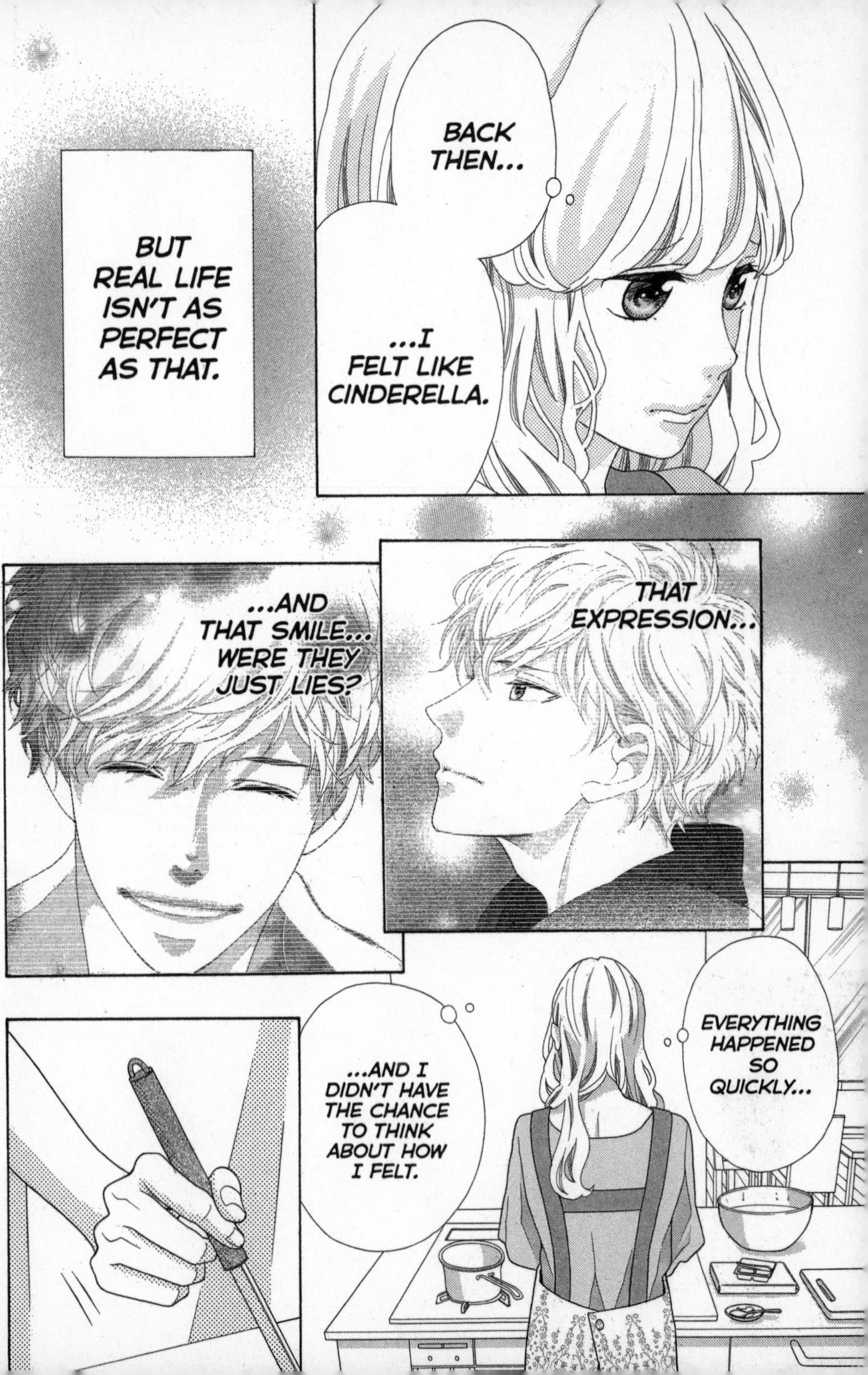
BACK THEN...
...I FELT LIKE CINDERELLA.
BUT REAL LIFE ISN'T AS PERFECT AS THAT.
THAT EXPRESSION...
...AND THAT SMILE... WERE THEY JUST LIES?
EVERYTHING HAPPENED SO QUICKLY...
...AND I DIDN'T HAVE THE CHANCE TO THINK ABOUT HOW I FELT.

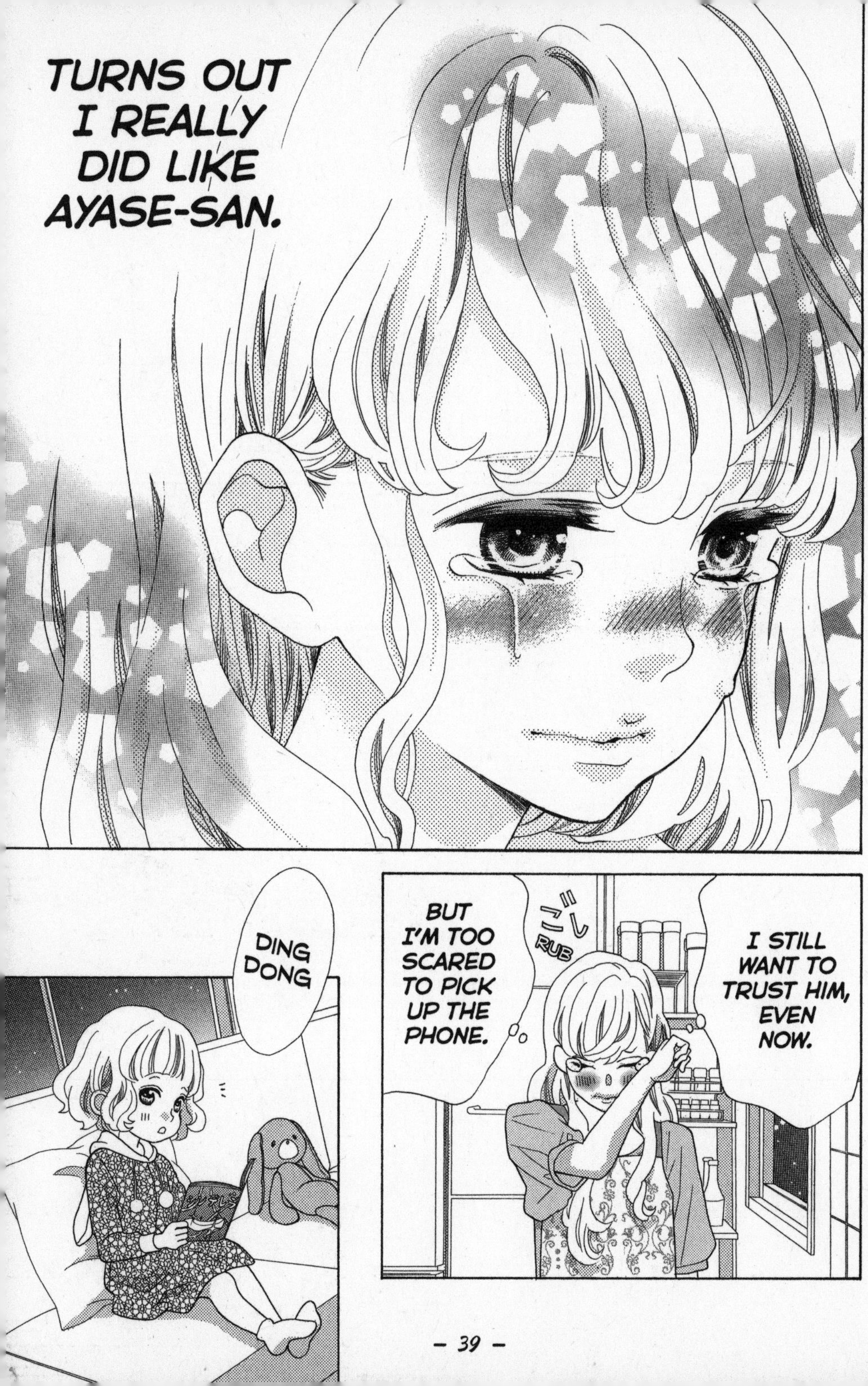
TURNS OUT I REALLY DID LIKE AYASE-SAN.
I STILL WANT TO TRUST HIM, EVEN NOW.
RUB
BUT I'M TOO SCARED TO PICK UP THE PHONE.
DING DONG

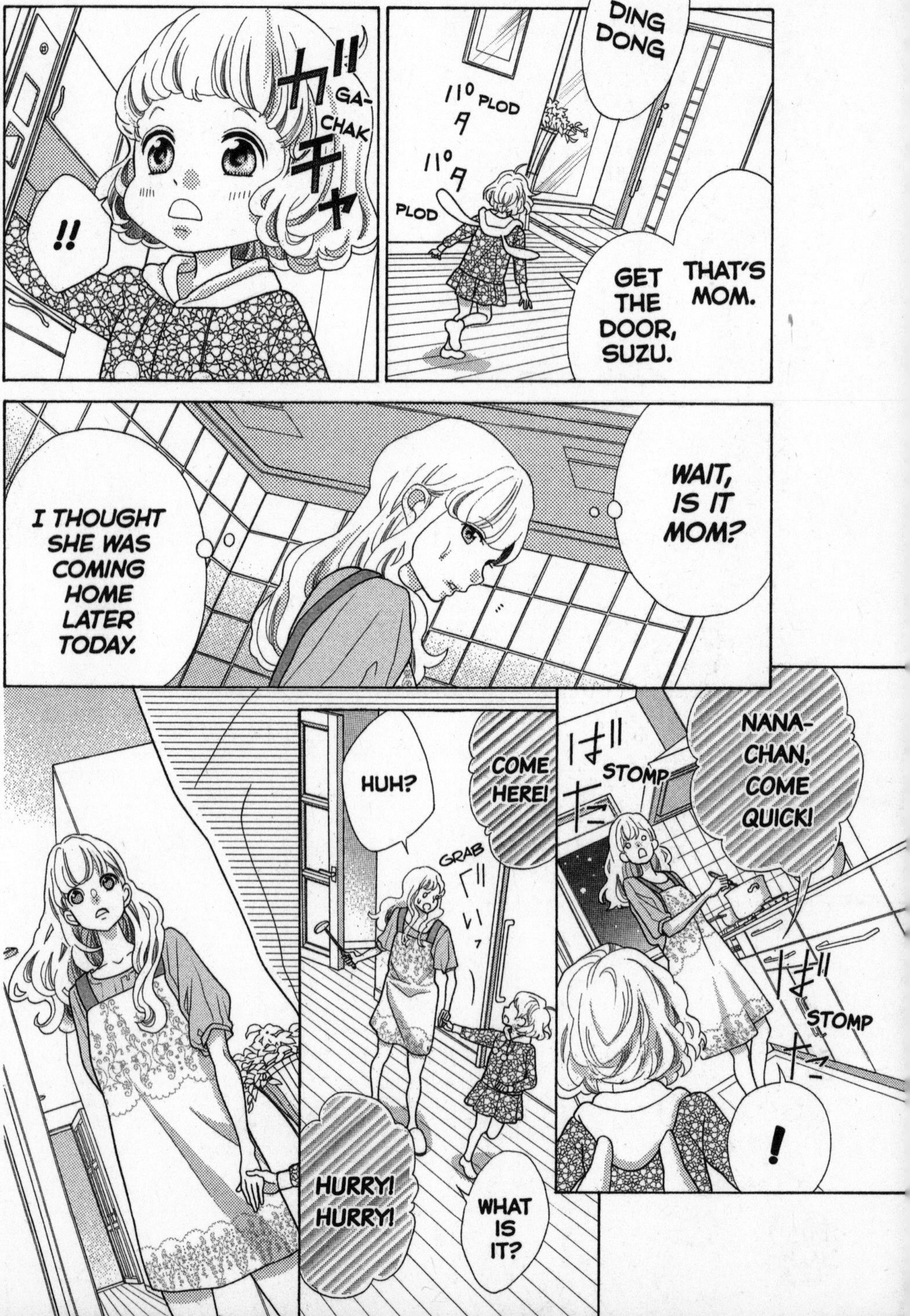

DING DONG
PLOD
PLOD
THAT'S MOM.
GET THE DOOR, SUZU.
GA-CHAK
!!
WAIT, IS IT MOM?
I THOUGHT SHE WAS COMING HOME LATER TODAY.
NANA-CHAN, COME QUICK!
STOMP
STOMP
!
COME HERE!
HUH?
GRAB
HURRY! HURRY!
WHAT IS IT?

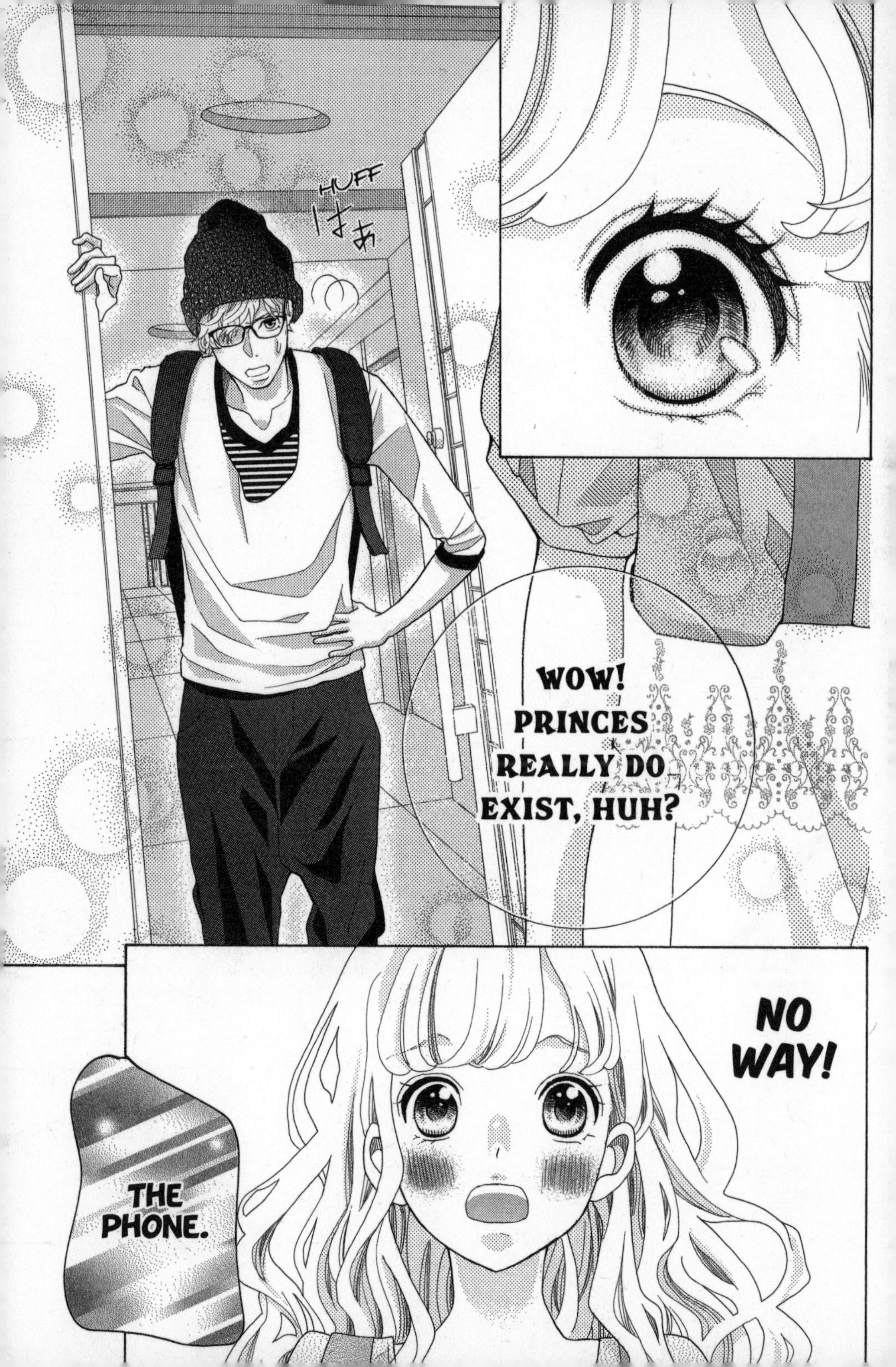
WOW! PRINCES REALLY DO EXIST, HUH?
HUFF
はぁ
NO WAY!
THE PHONE.

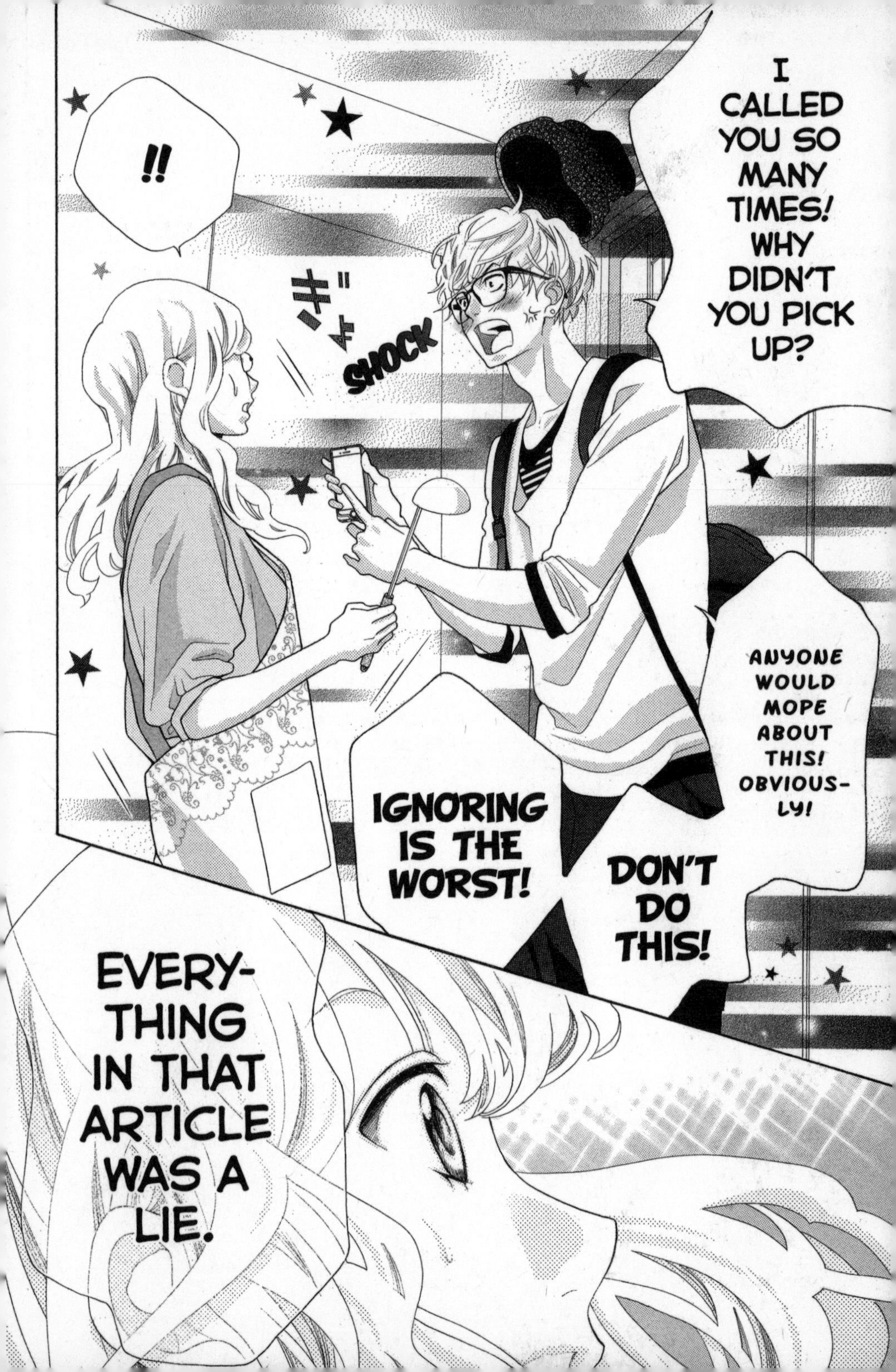
I CALLED YOU SO MANY TIMES! WHY DIDN'T YOU PICK UP?
!!
ぎょ
SHOCK
ANYONE WOULD MOPE ABOUT THIS! OBVIOUS-LY!
DON'T DO THIS!
IGNORING IS THE WORST!
EVERY-THING IN THAT ARTICLE WAS A LIE.

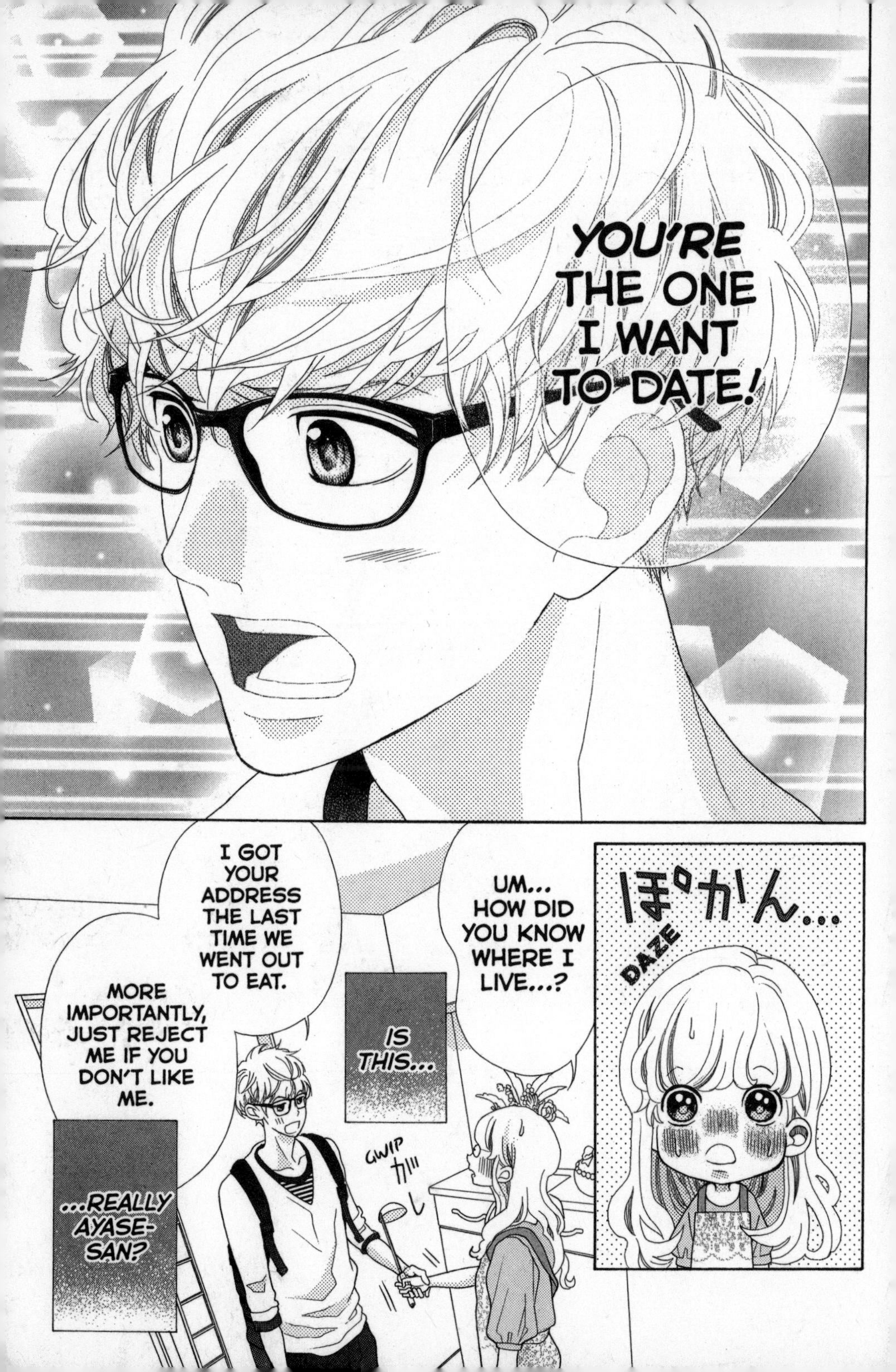
YOU'RE THE ONE I WANT TO DATE!
ぽかん...
DAZE
UM... HOW DID YOU KNOW WHERE I LIVE...?
I GOT YOUR ADDRESS THE LAST TIME WE WENT OUT TO EAT.
MORE IMPORTANTLY, JUST REJECT ME IF YOU DON'T LIKE ME.
IS THIS...
GWIP
...REALLY AYASE-SAN?

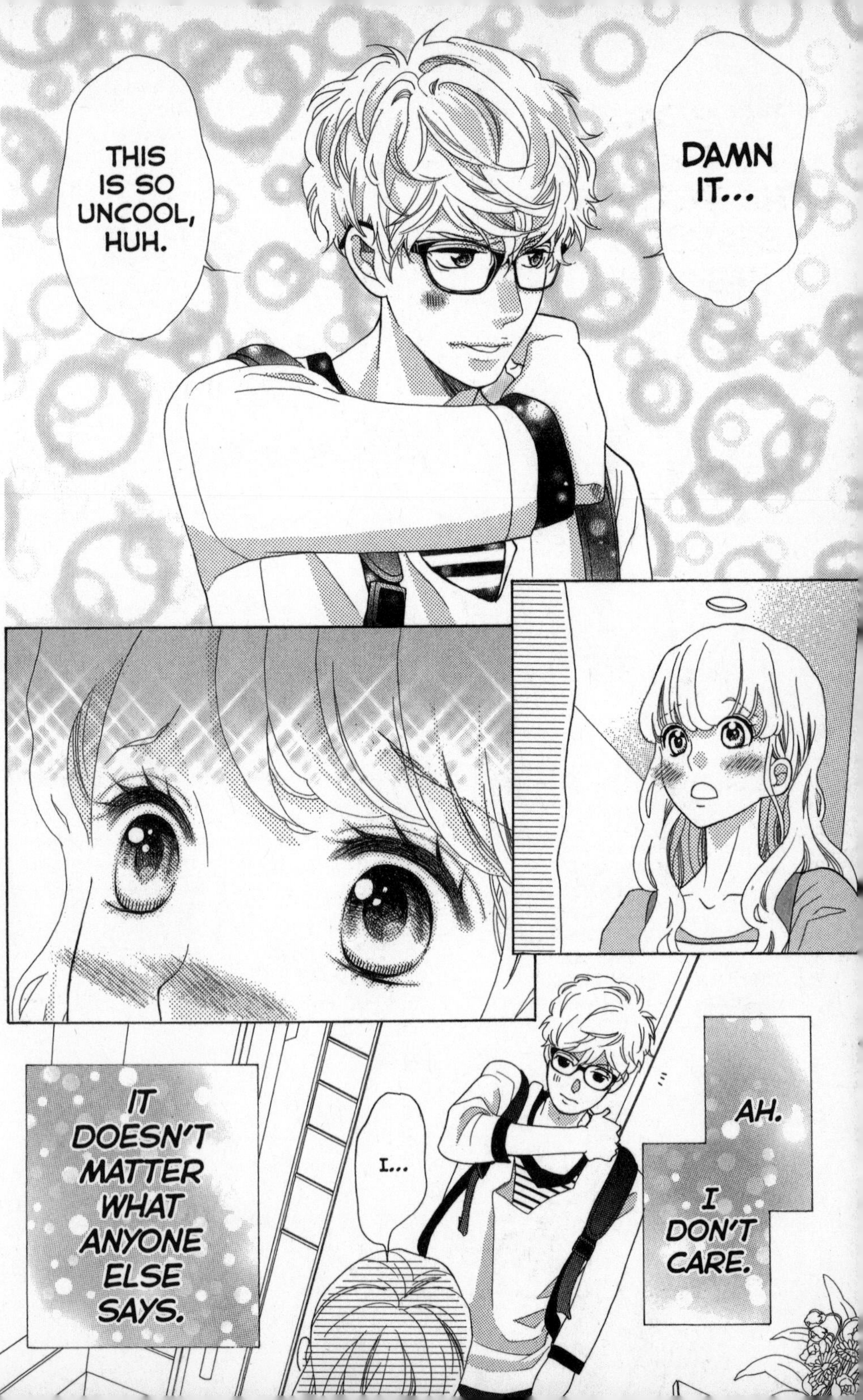
DAMN IT...
THIS IS SO UNCOOL, HUH.
AH.
I DON'T CARE.
I...
IT DOESN'T MATTER WHAT ANYONE ELSE SAYS.

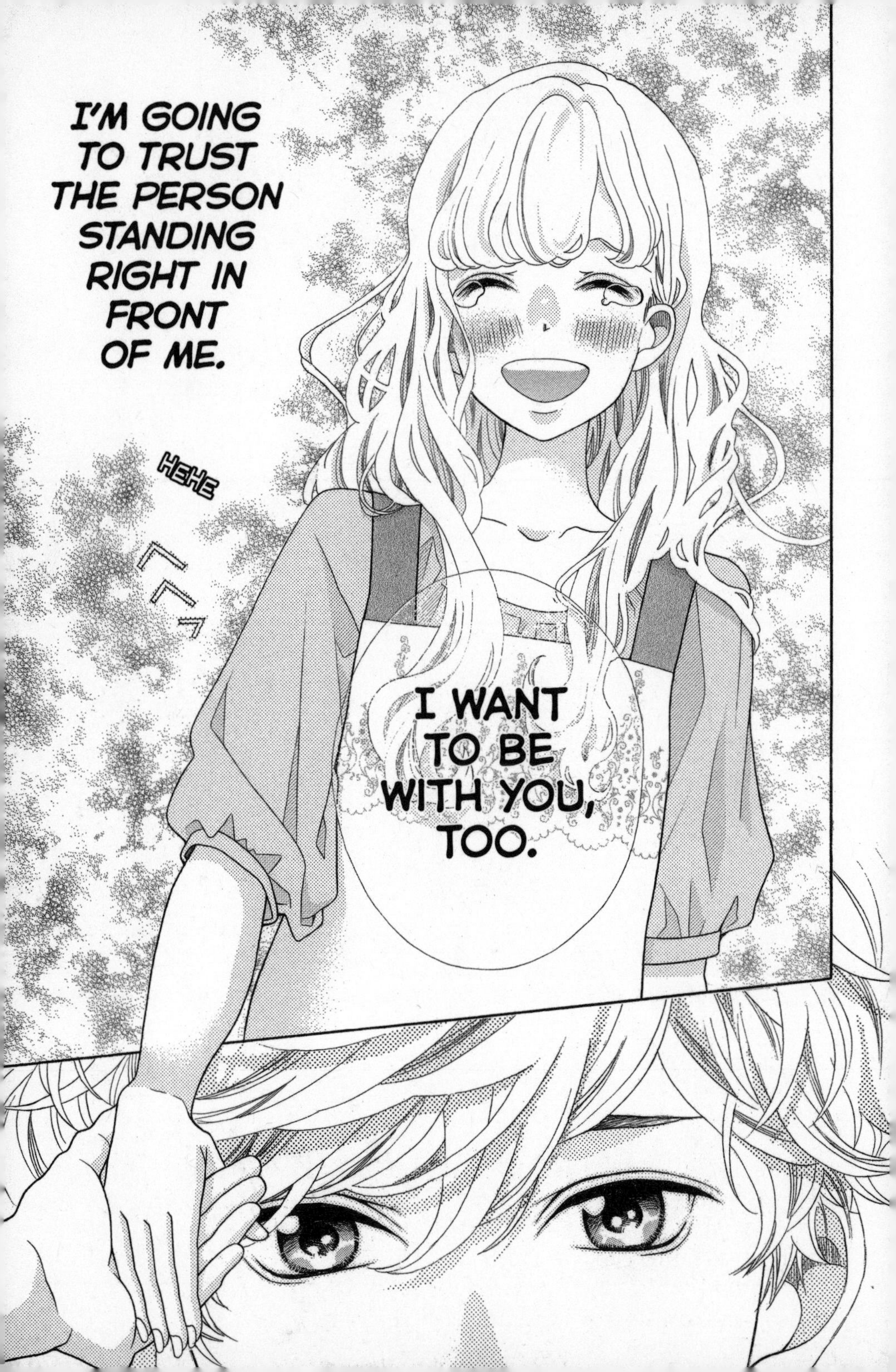

I'M GOING TO TRUST THE PERSON STANDING RIGHT IN FRONT OF ME.
HEHE
I WANT TO BE WITH YOU, TOO.

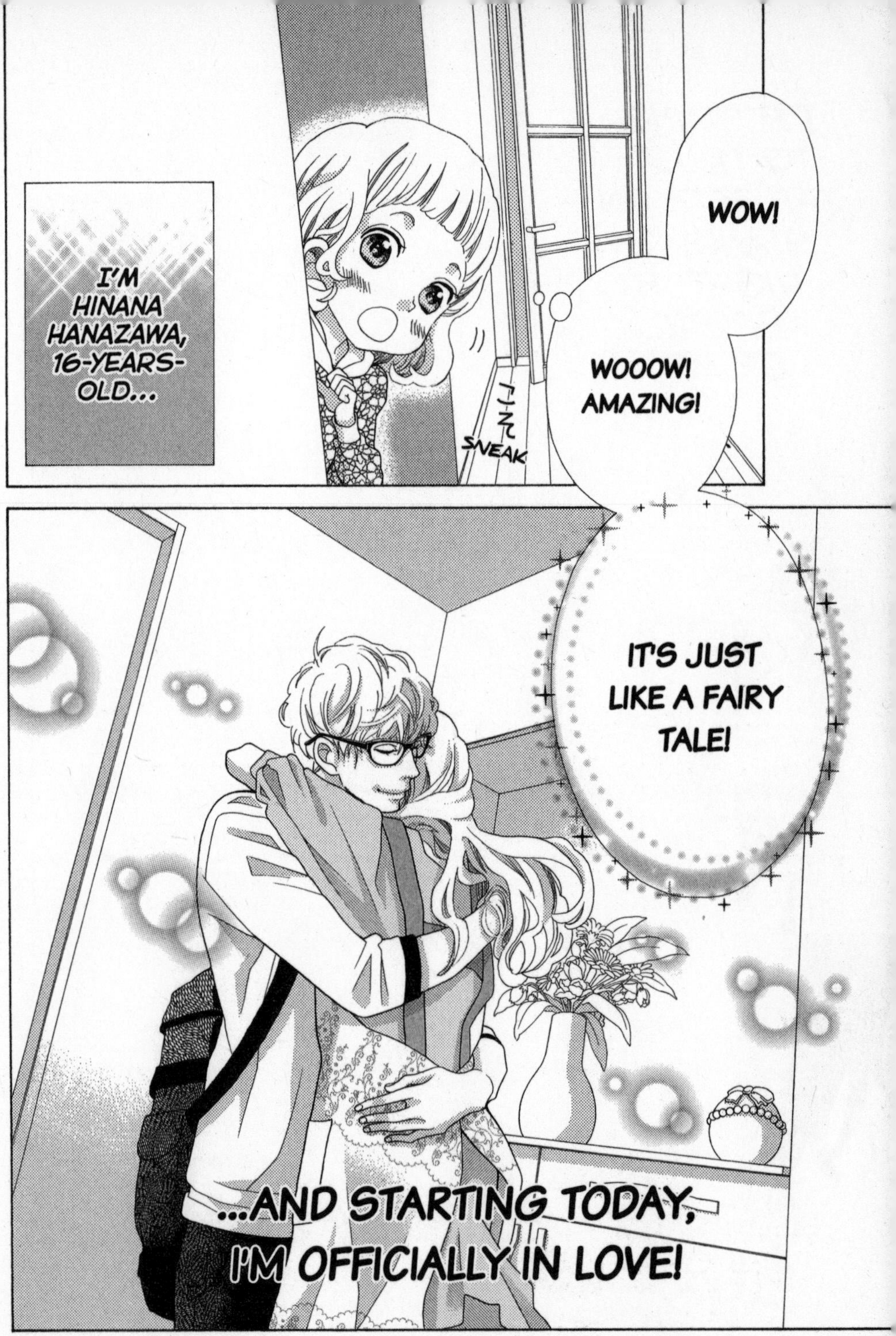
WOW!
WOOOW! AMAZING!
SNEAK
I'M HINANA HANAZAWA, 16-YEARS-OLD...
IT'S JUST LIKE A FAIRY TALE!
...AND STARTING TODAY, I'M OFFICIALLY IN LOVE!

Kiss Me
at the Stroke of
Midnight

Kiss Me at the Stroke of Midnight

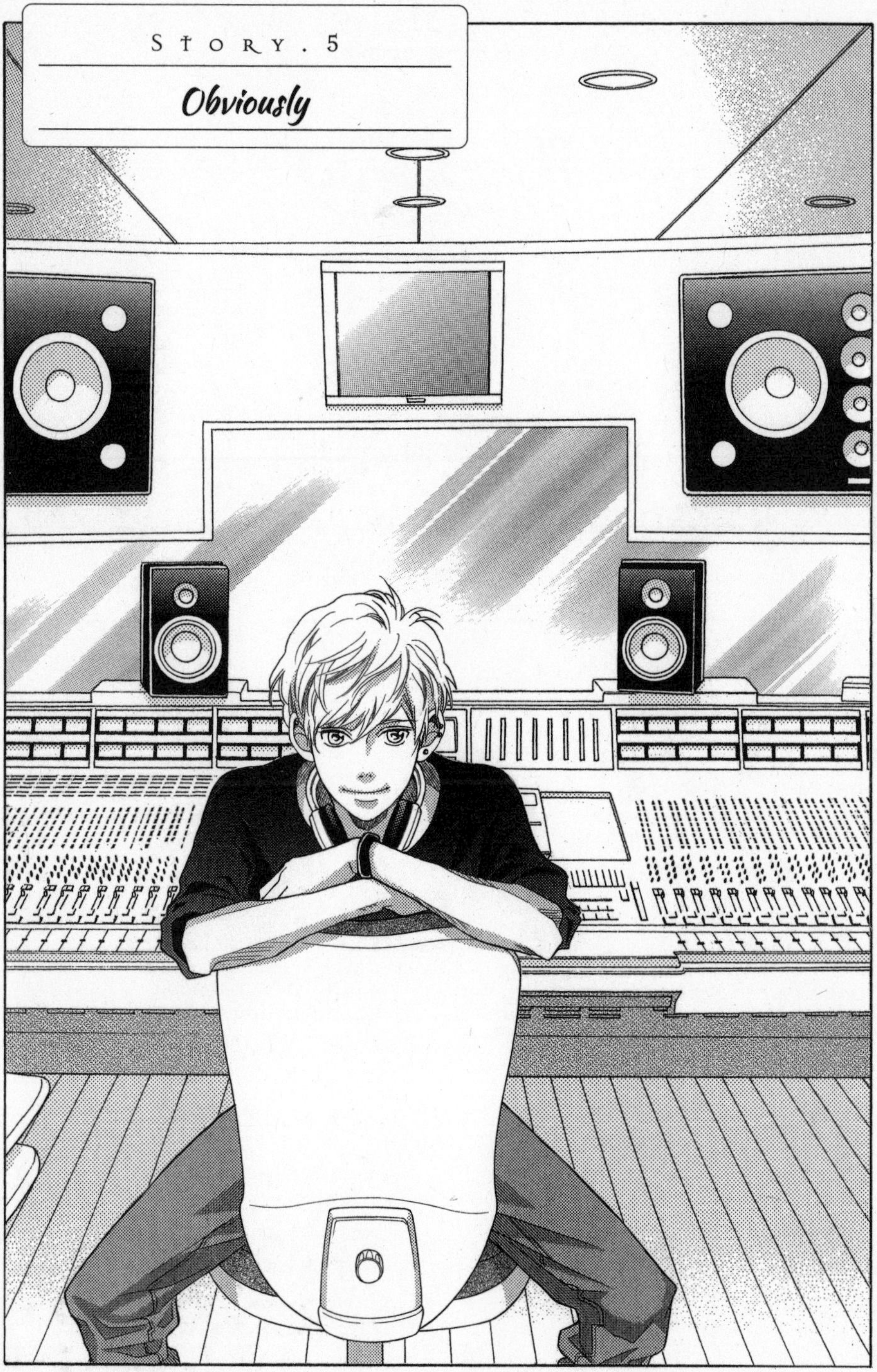
Story. 5
Obviously

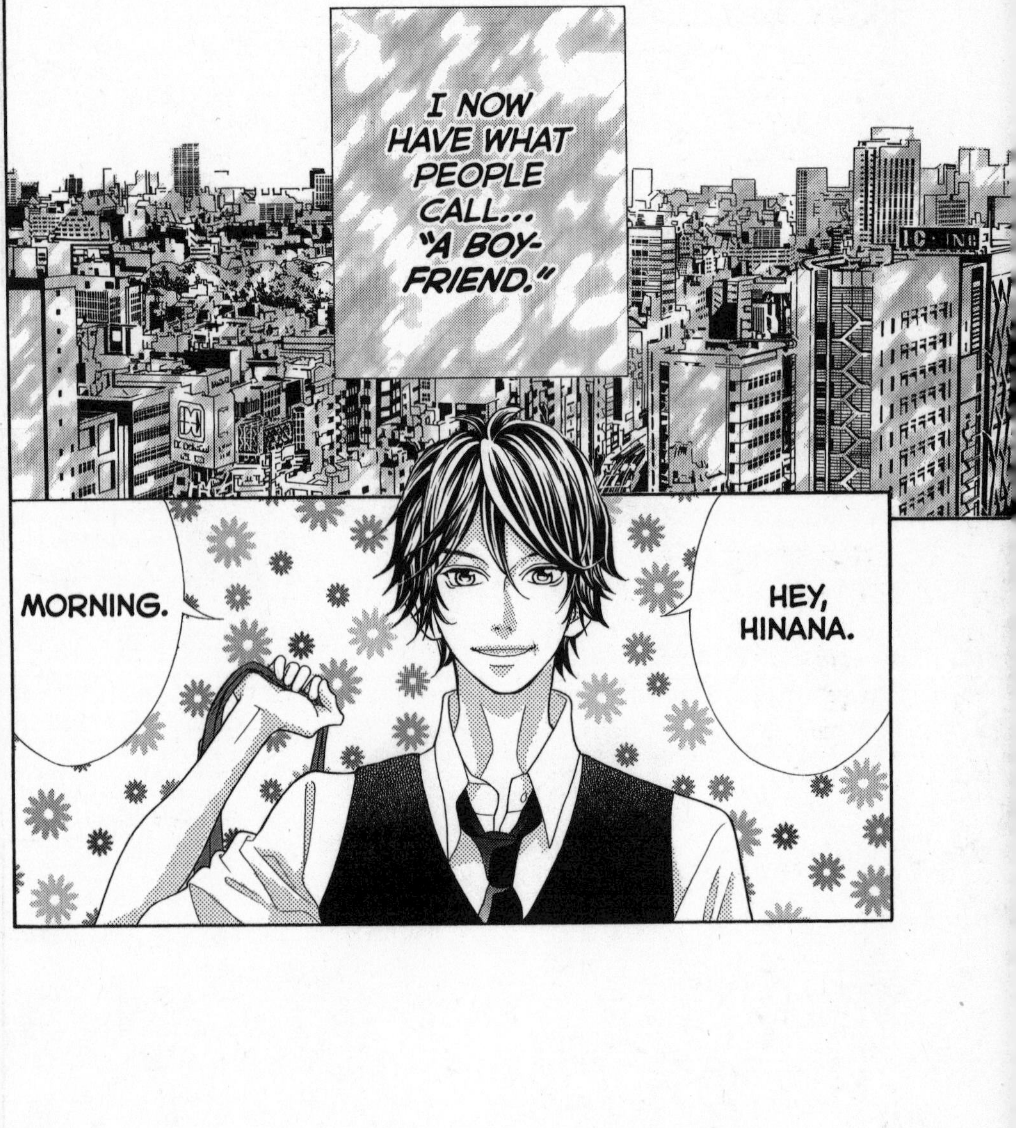
I NOW HAVE WHAT PEOPLE CALL... "A BOY-FRIEND."
HEY, HINANA.
MORNING.

Kiss Me at the Stroke of Midnight

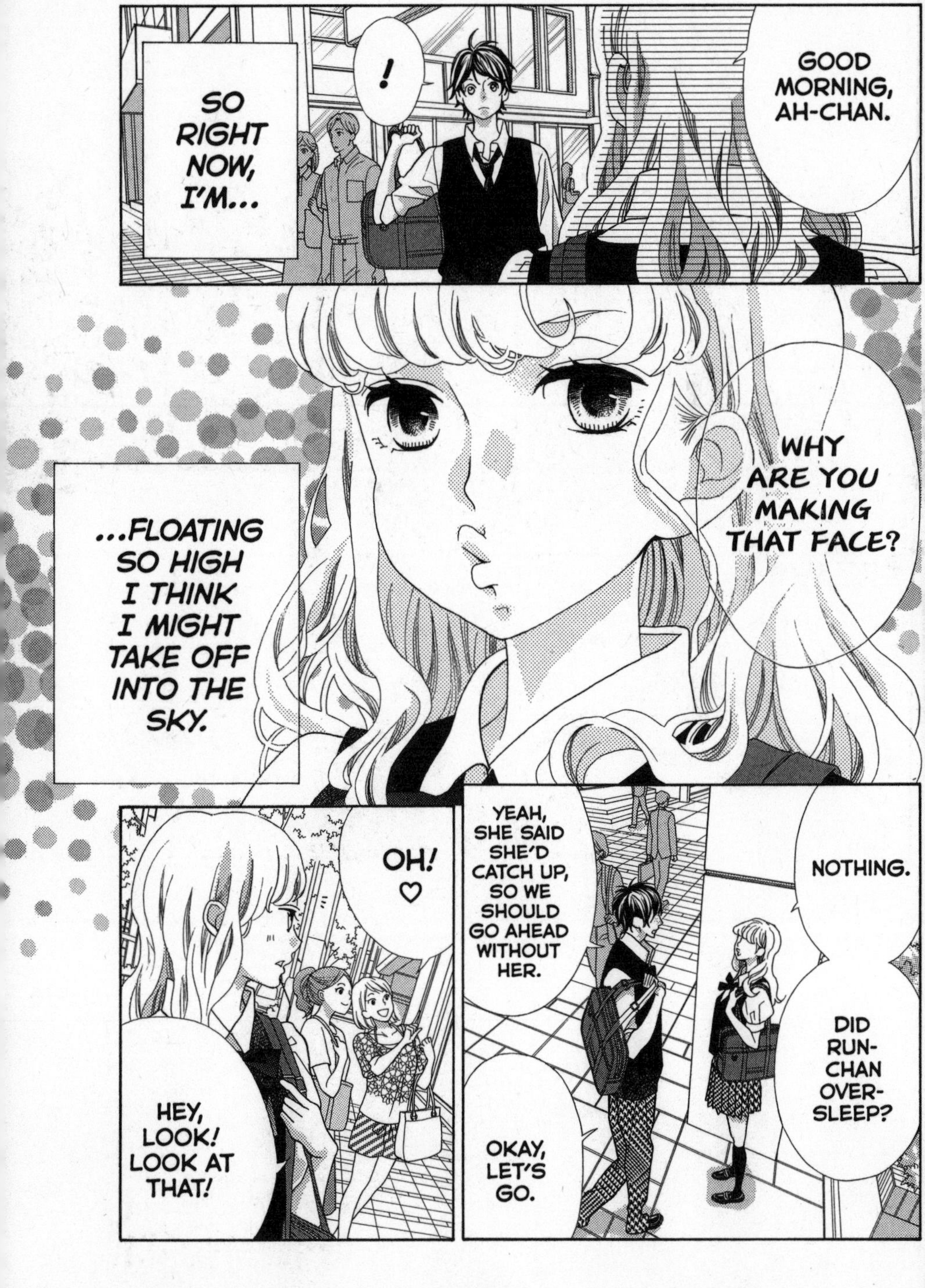
GOOD MORNING, AH-CHAN.
!
SO RIGHT NOW, I'M...
WHY ARE YOU MAKING THAT FACE?
...FLOATING SO HIGH I THINK I MIGHT TAKE OFF INTO THE SKY.
NOTHING.
DID RUN-CHAN OVER-SLEEP?
YEAH, SHE SAID SHE'D CATCH UP, SO WE SHOULD GO AHEAD WITHOUT HER.
OKAY, LET'S GO.
OH! ♡
HEY, LOOK! LOOK AT THAT!

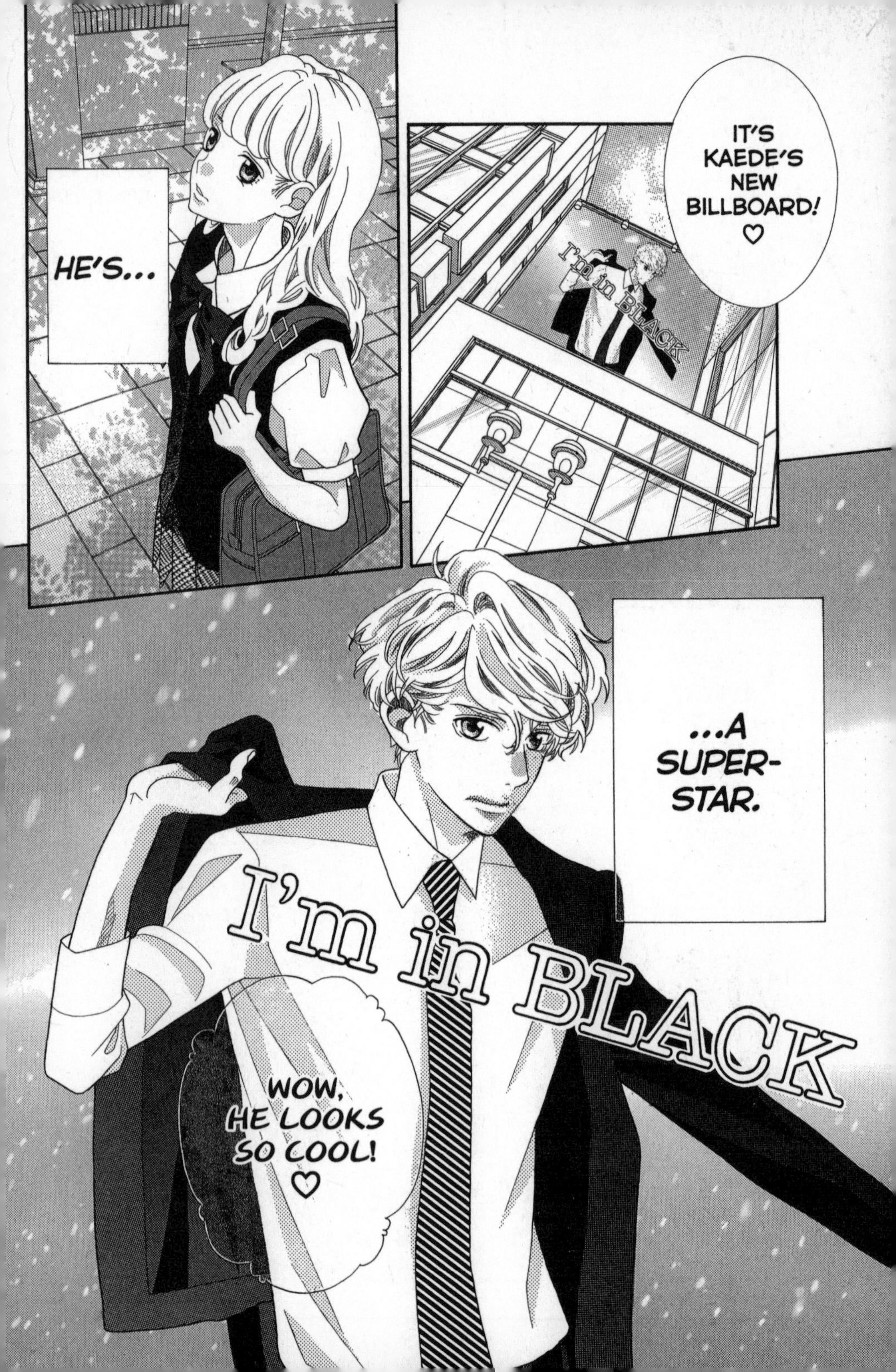
IT'S KAEDE'S NEW BILLBOARD! ♡
I'm in BLACK
HE'S...
...A SUPER-STAR.
I'm in BLACK
WOW, HE LOOKS SO COOL! ♡

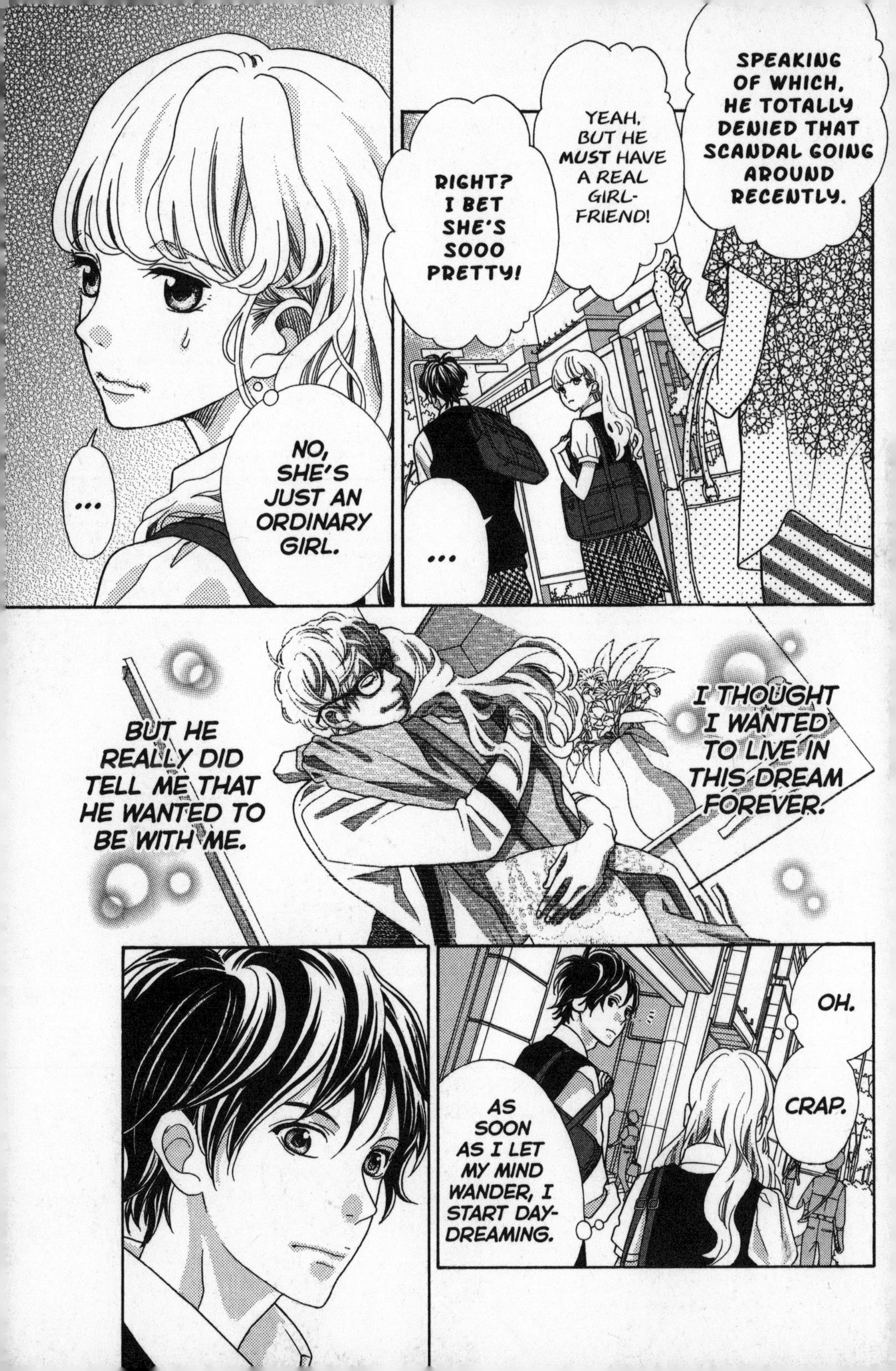
SPEAKING OF WHICH, HE TOTALLY DENIED THAT SCANDAL GOING AROUND RECENTLY.
YEAH, BUT HE MUST HAVE A REAL GIRLFRIEND!
RIGHT? I BET SHE'S SOOO PRETTY!
...
NO, SHE'S JUST AN ORDINARY GIRL.
...
I THOUGHT I WANTED TO LIVE IN THIS DREAM FOREVER.
BUT HE REALLY DID TELL ME THAT HE WANTED TO BE WITH ME.
OH.
CRAP.
AS SOON AS I LET MY MIND WANDER, I START DAYDREAMING.

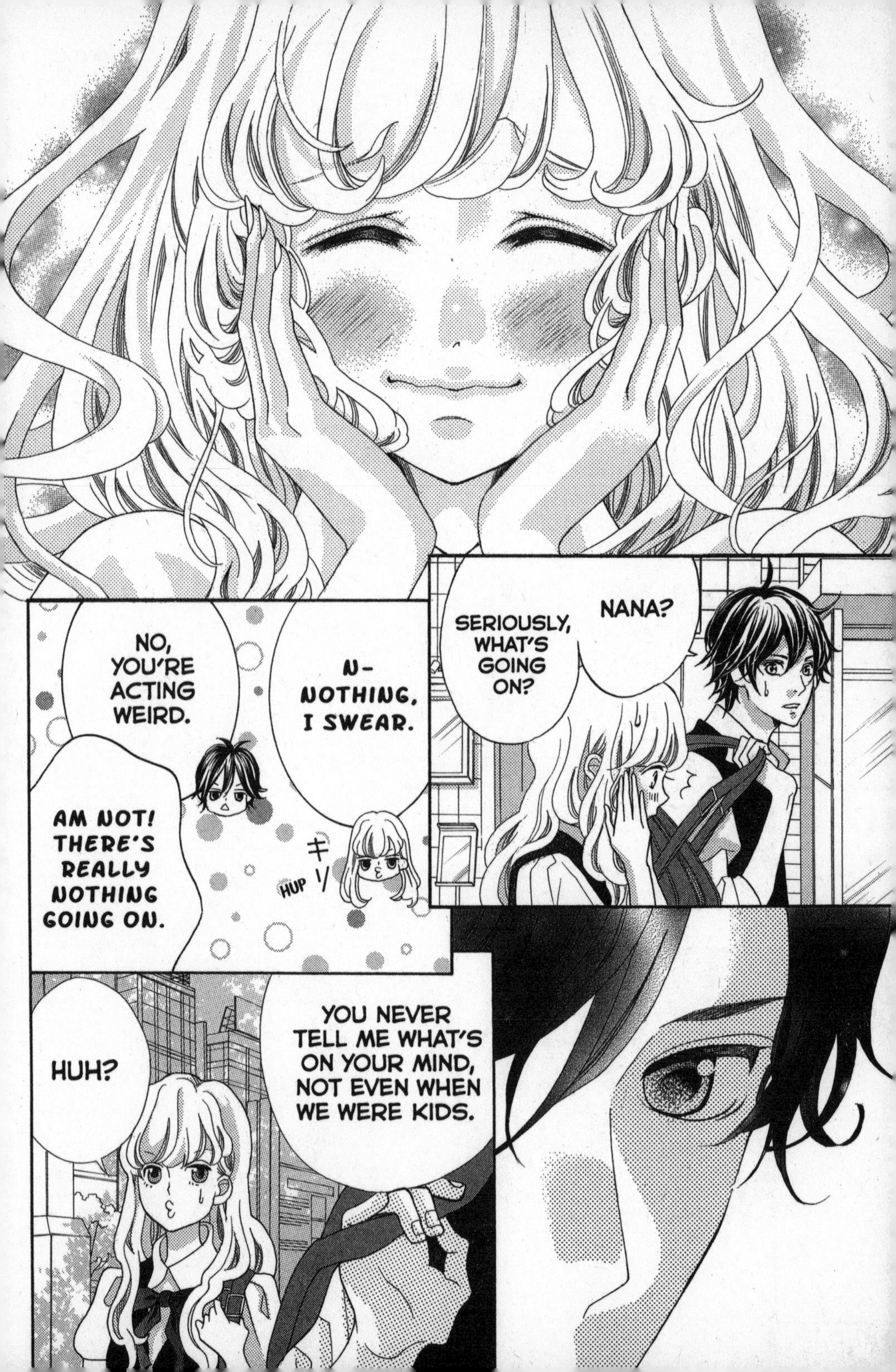
NANA?
SERIOUSLY, WHAT'S GOING ON?
N-NOTHING, I SWEAR.
NO, YOU'RE ACTING WEIRD.
キリ
HUP
AM NOT! THERE'S REALLY NOTHING GOING ON.
YOU NEVER TELL ME WHAT'S ON YOUR MIND, NOT EVEN WHEN WE WERE KIDS.
HUH?

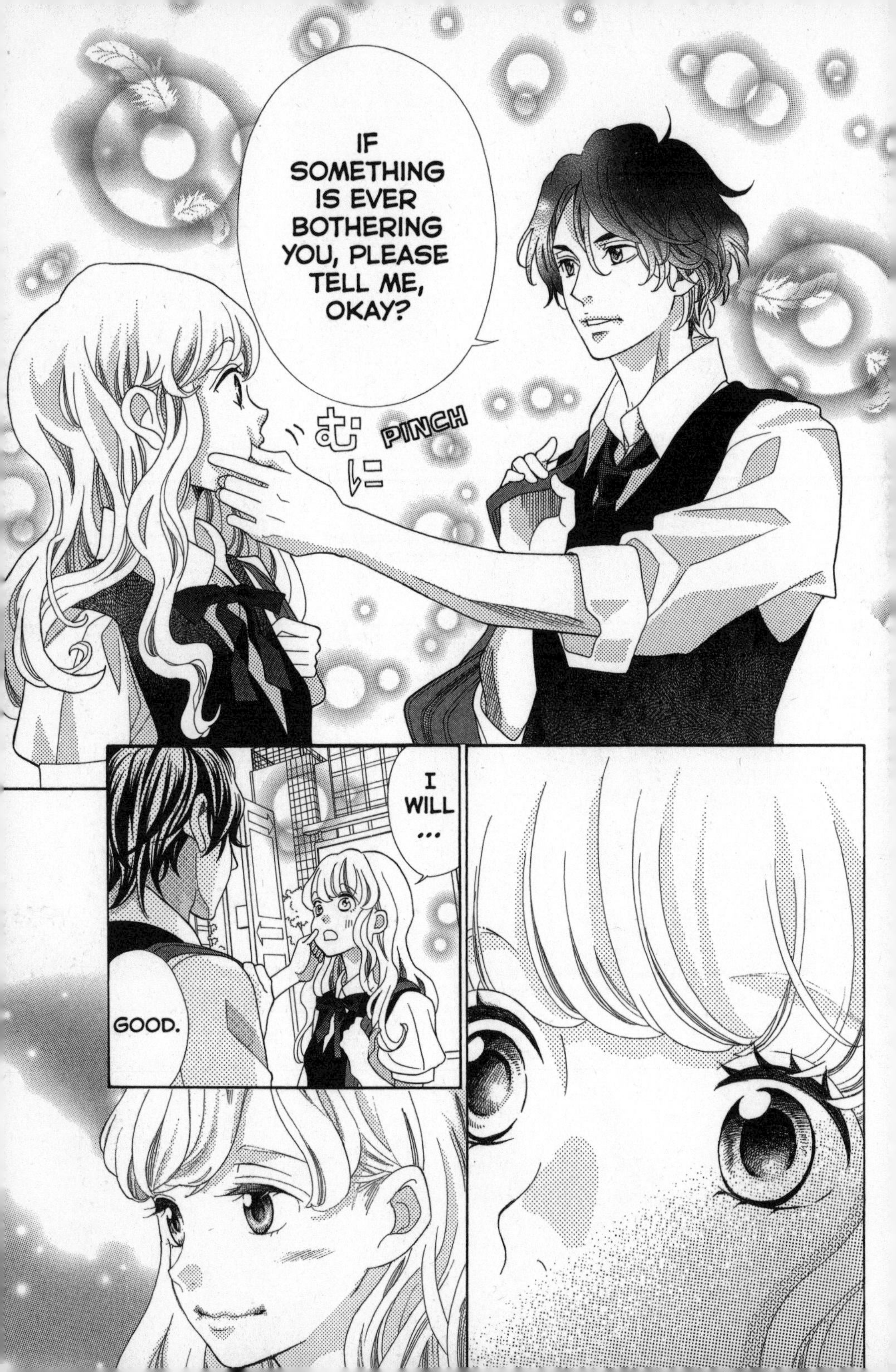
IF SOMETHING IS EVER BOTHERING YOU, PLEASE TELL ME, OKAY?
むに
PINCH
I WILL...
GOOD.

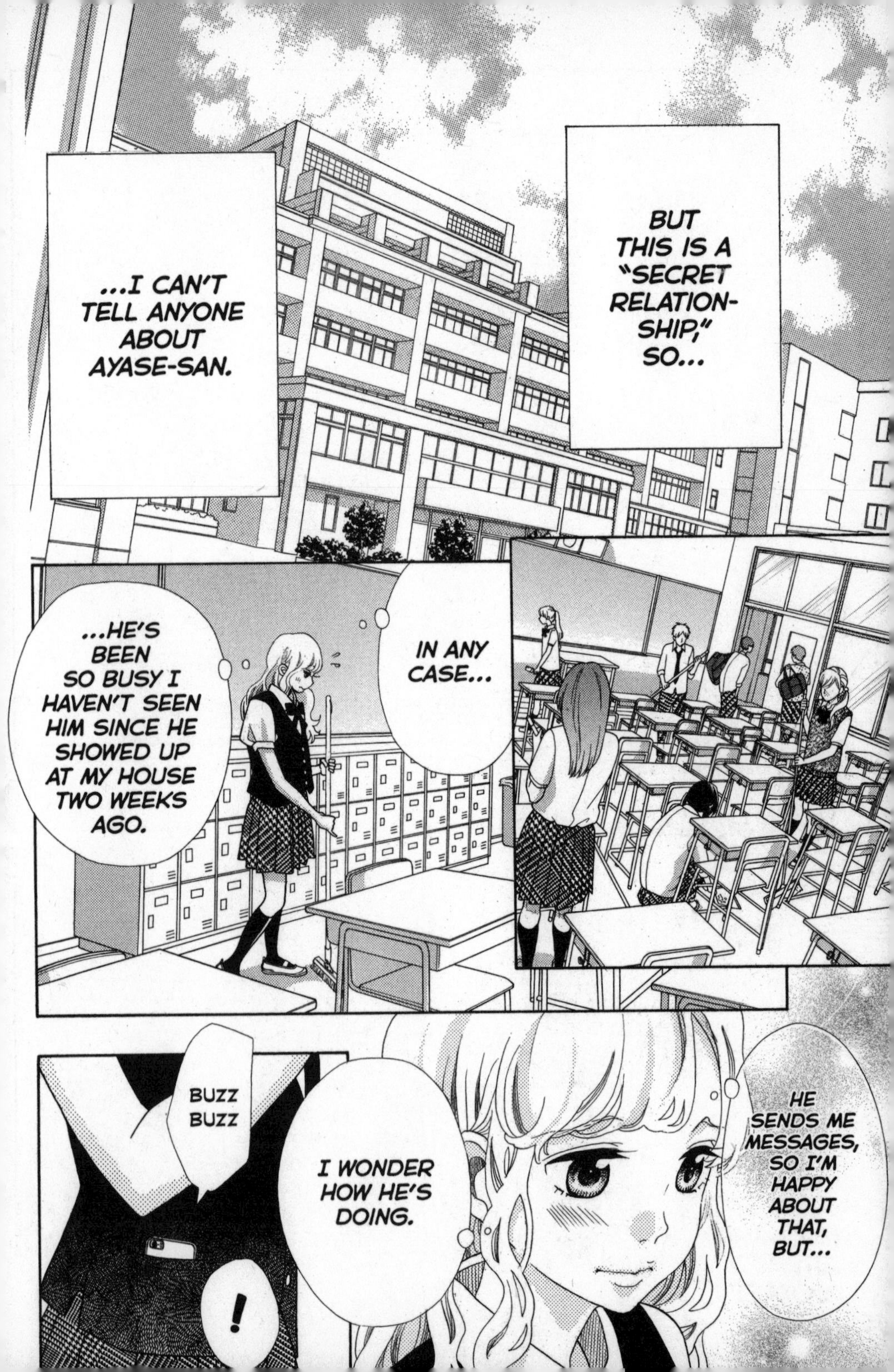
BUT THIS IS A "SECRET RELATIONSHIP," SO...
...I CAN'T TELL ANYONE ABOUT AYASE-SAN.
IN ANY CASE...
...HE'S BEEN SO BUSY I HAVEN'T SEEN HIM SINCE HE SHOWED UP AT MY HOUSE TWO WEEKS AGO.
HE SENDS ME MESSAGES, SO I'M HAPPY ABOUT THAT, BUT...
I WONDER HOW HE'S DOING.
BUZZ BUZZ
!

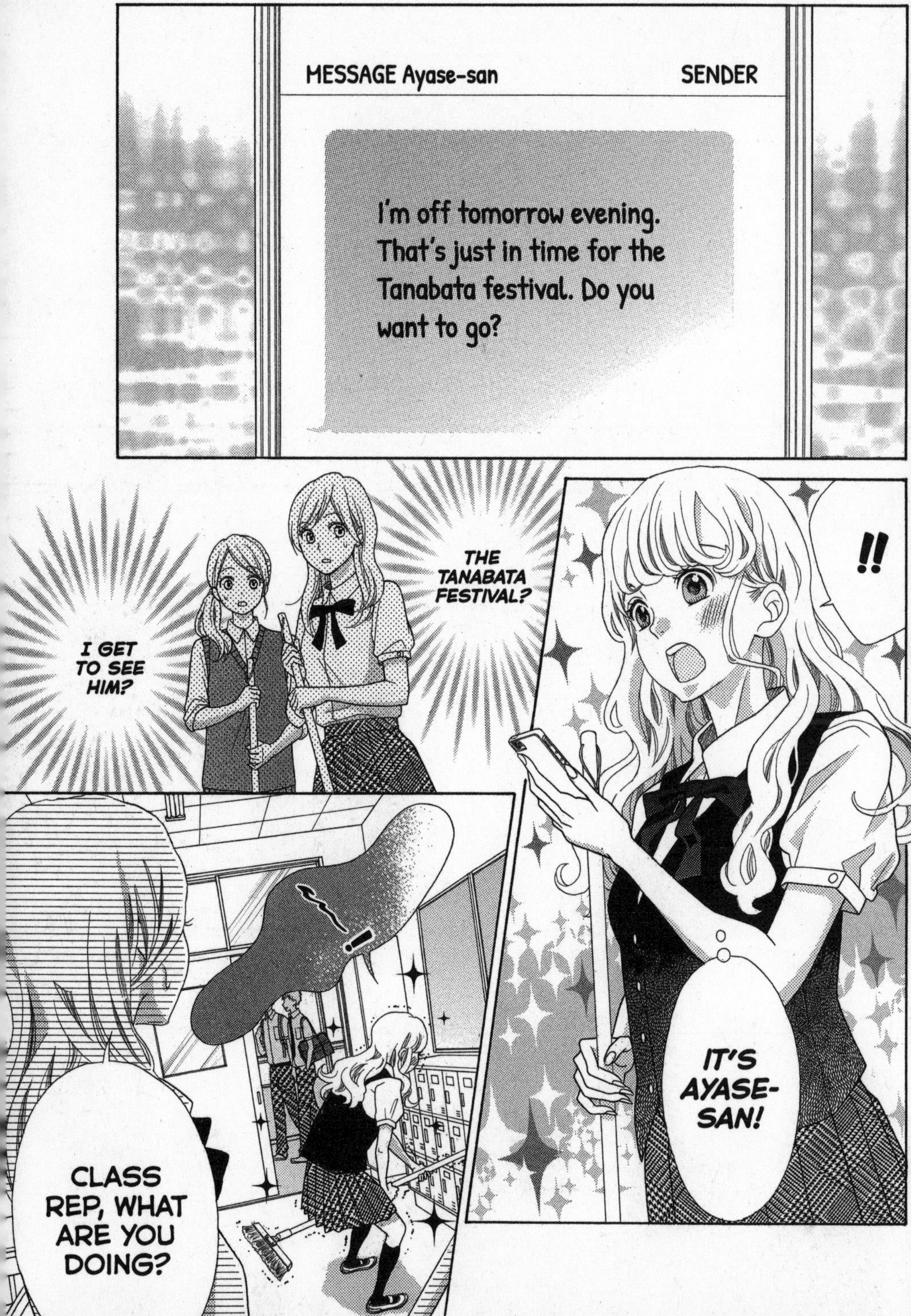
MESSAGE Ayase-san
SENDER
I'm off tomorrow evening. That's just in time for the Tanabata festival. Do you want to go?
!!
IT'S AYASE-SAN!
THE TANABATA FESTIVAL?
I GET TO SEE HIM?
CLASS REP, WHAT ARE YOU DOING?

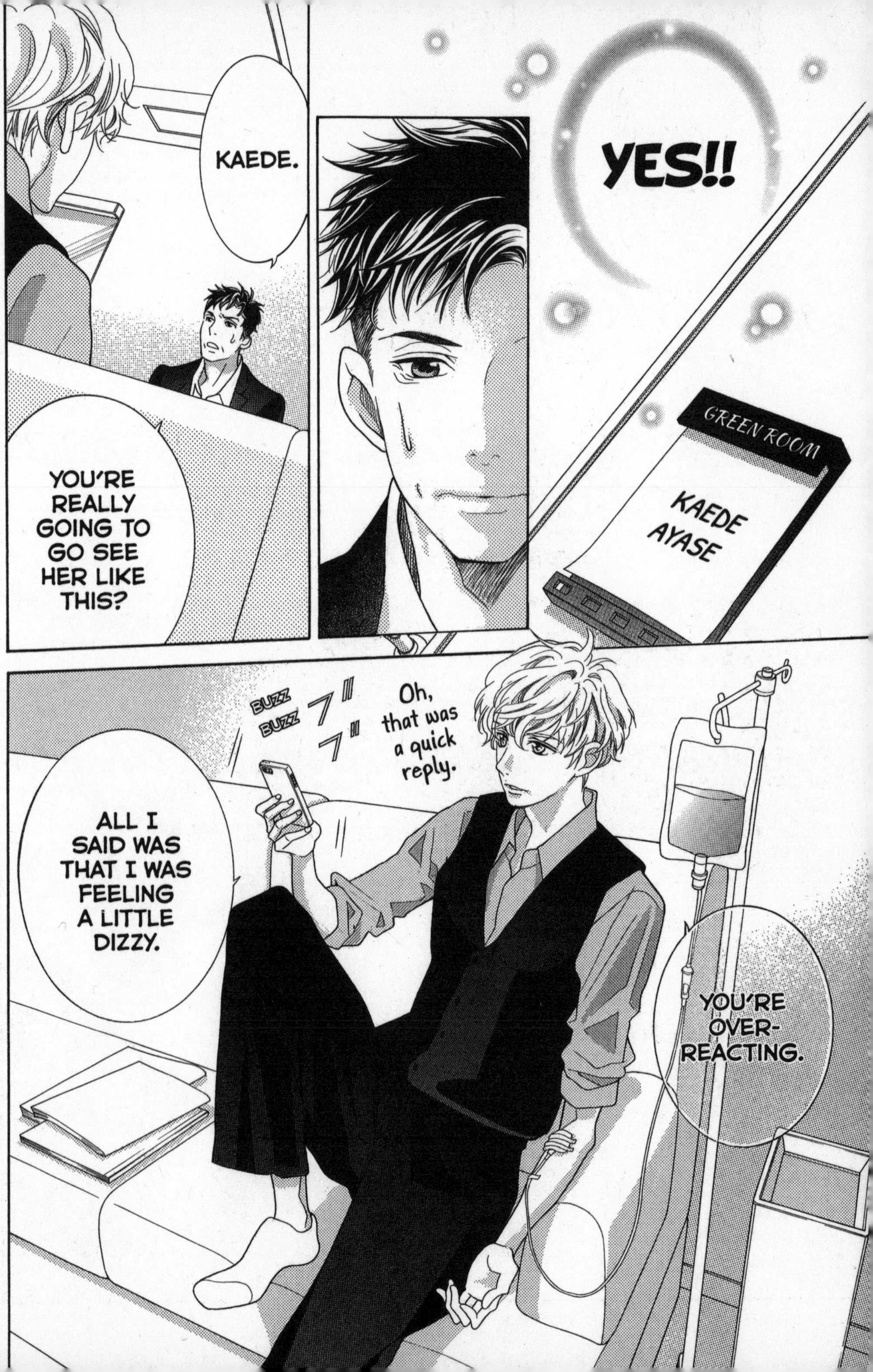
YES!!
GREEN ROOM
KAEDE AYASE
KAEDE.
YOU'RE REALLY GOING TO GO SEE HER LIKE THIS?
Oh, that was a quick reply.
BUZZ BUZZ
ALL I SAID WAS THAT I WAS FEELING A LITTLE DIZZY.
YOU'RE OVER-REACTING.

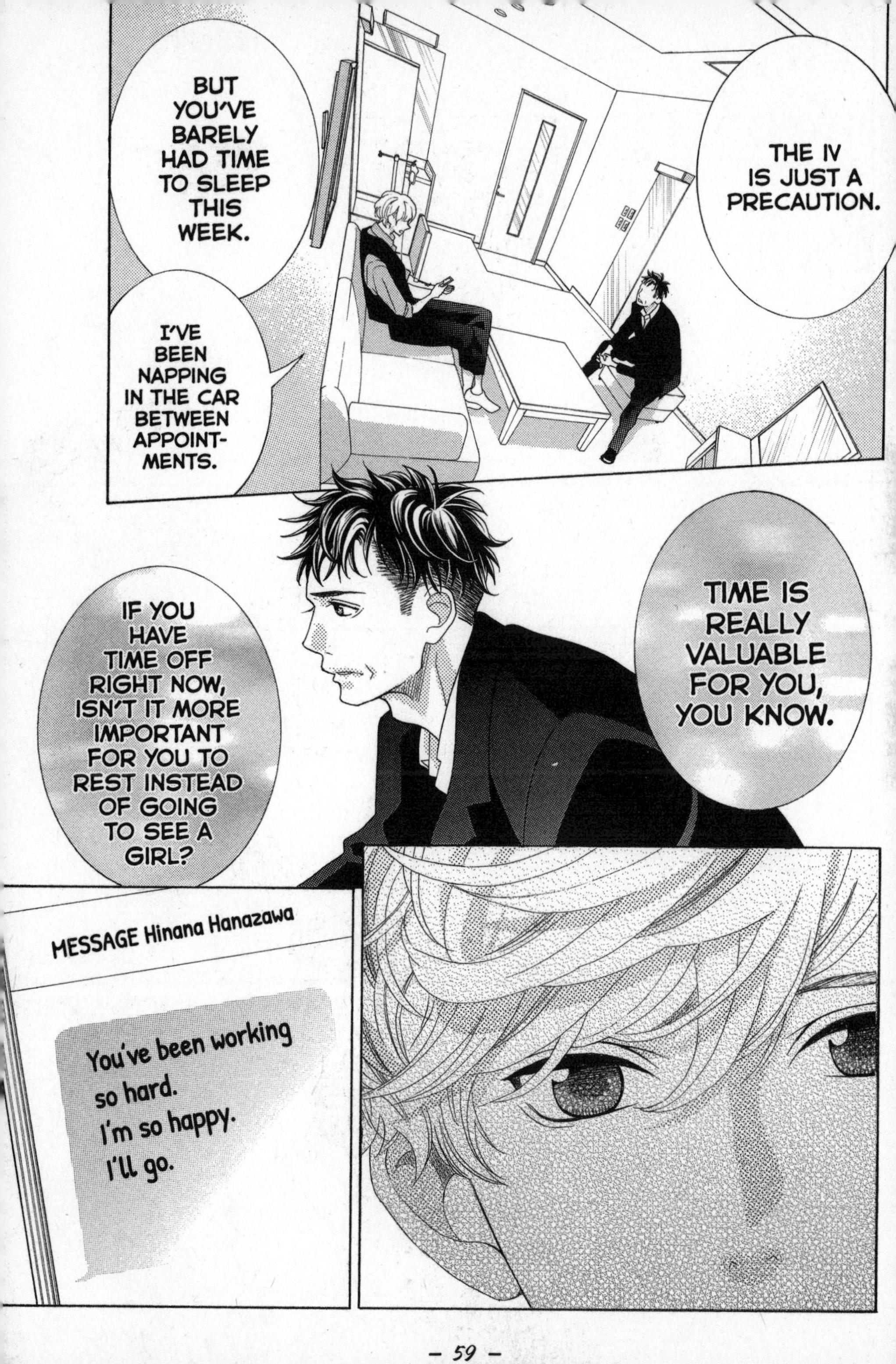
THE IV IS JUST A PRECAUTION.
BUT YOU'VE BARELY HAD TIME TO SLEEP THIS WEEK.
I'VE BEEN NAPPING IN THE CAR BETWEEN APPOINT-MENTS.
TIME IS REALLY VALUABLE FOR YOU, YOU KNOW.
IF YOU HAVE TIME OFF RIGHT NOW, ISN'T IT MORE IMPORTANT FOR YOU TO REST INSTEAD OF GOING TO SEE A GIRL?
MESSAGE Hinana Hanazawa
You've been working so hard. I'm so happy. I'll go.

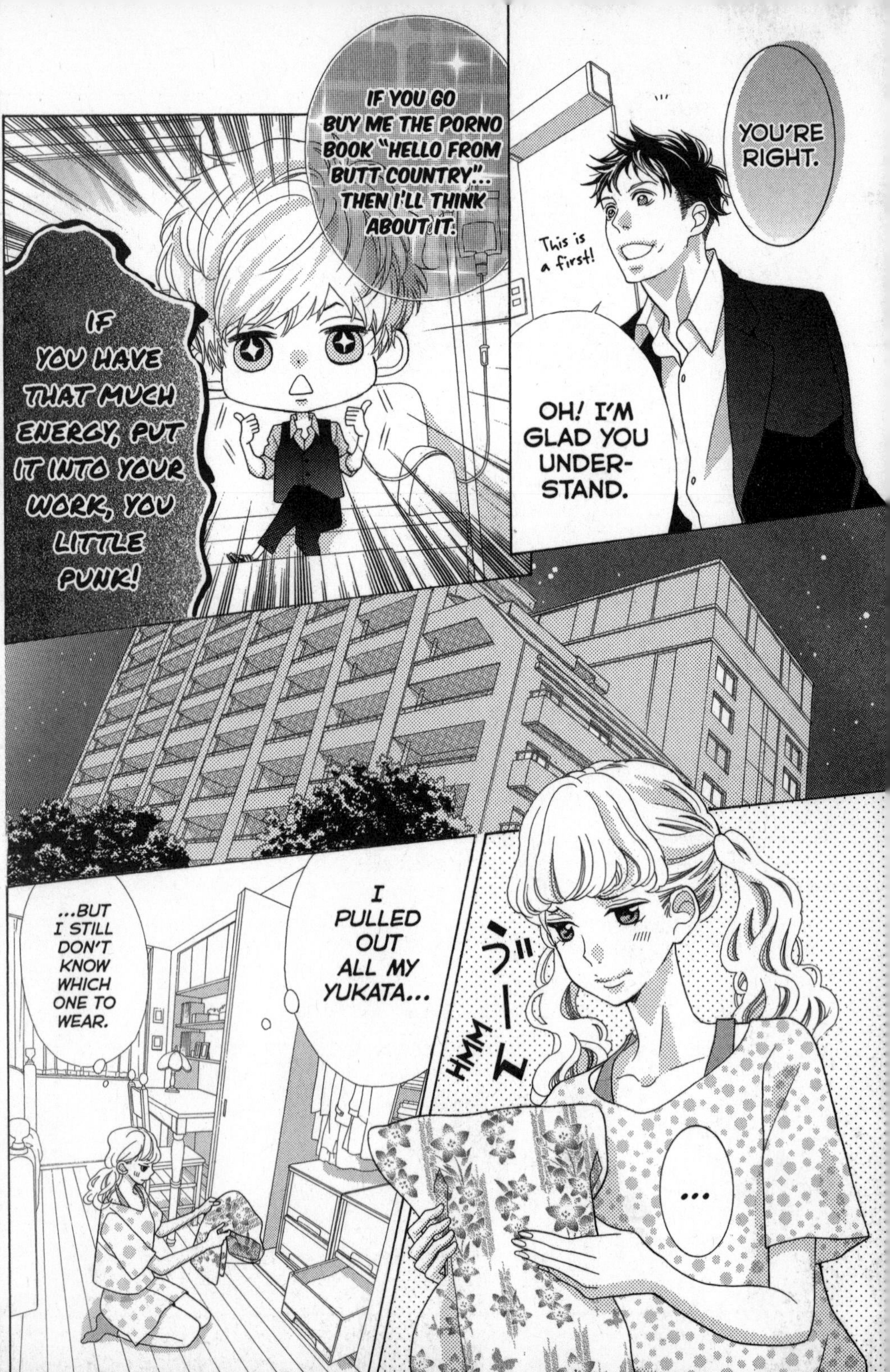
YOU'RE RIGHT.
This is a first!
OH! I'M GLAD YOU UNDERSTAND.
IF YOU GO BUY ME THE PORNO BOOK "HELLO FROM BUTT COUNTRY"... THEN I'LL THINK ABOUT IT.
IF YOU HAVE THAT MUCH ENERGY, PUT IT INTO YOUR WORK, YOU LITTLE PUNK!
HMM
...
I PULLED OUT ALL MY YUKATA...
...BUT I STILL DON'T KNOW WHICH ONE TO WEAR.

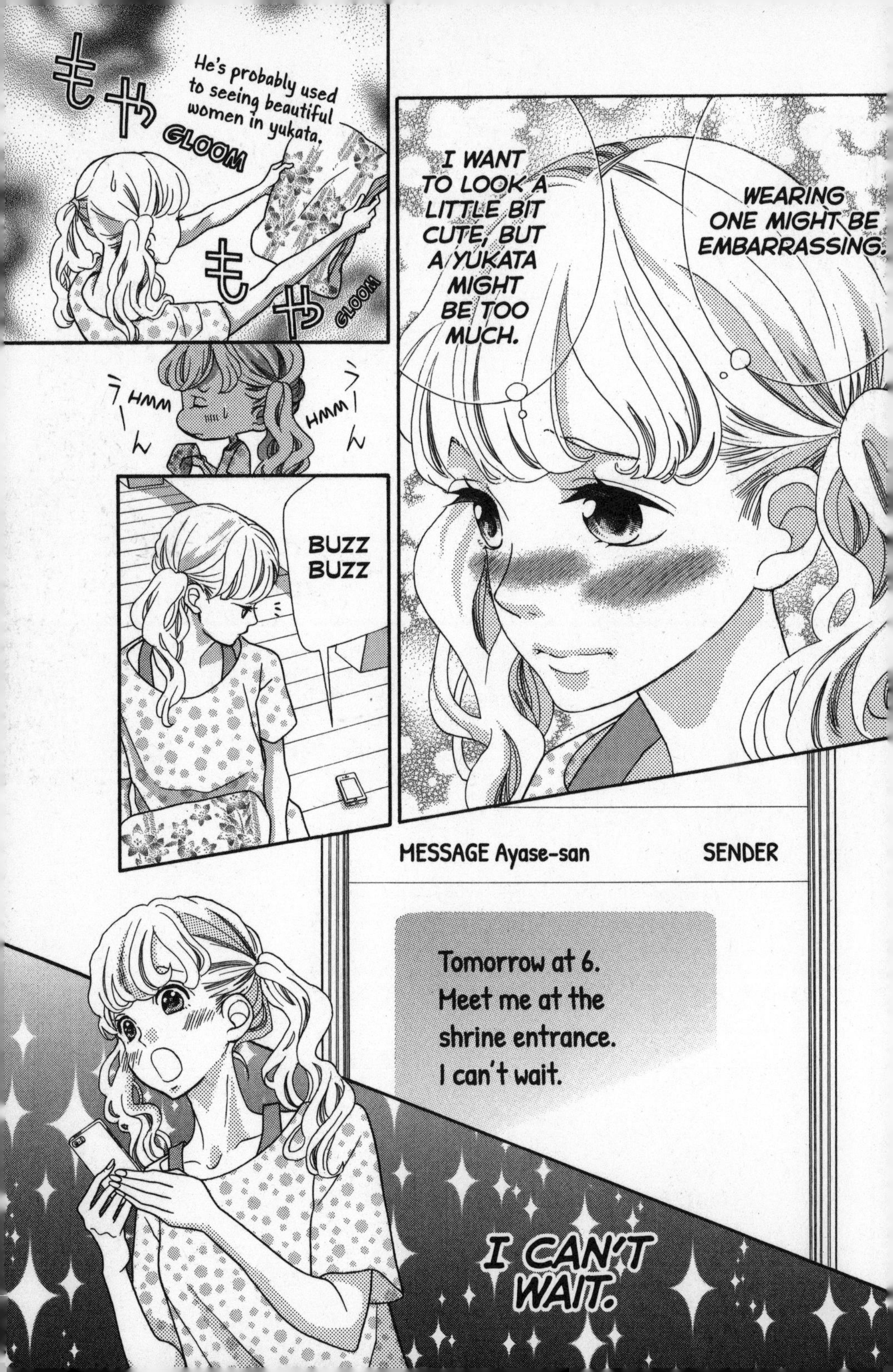

WEARING ONE MIGHT BE EMBARRASSING.
I WANT TO LOOK A LITTLE BIT CUTE, BUT A YUKATA MIGHT BE TOO MUCH.
He's probably used to seeing beautiful women in yukata.
もや GLOOM
もや GLOOM
HMM
HMM
BUZZ BUZZ
MESSAGE Ayase-san
SENDER
Tomorrow at 6.
Meet me at the shrine entrance.
I can't wait.
I CAN'T WAIT.

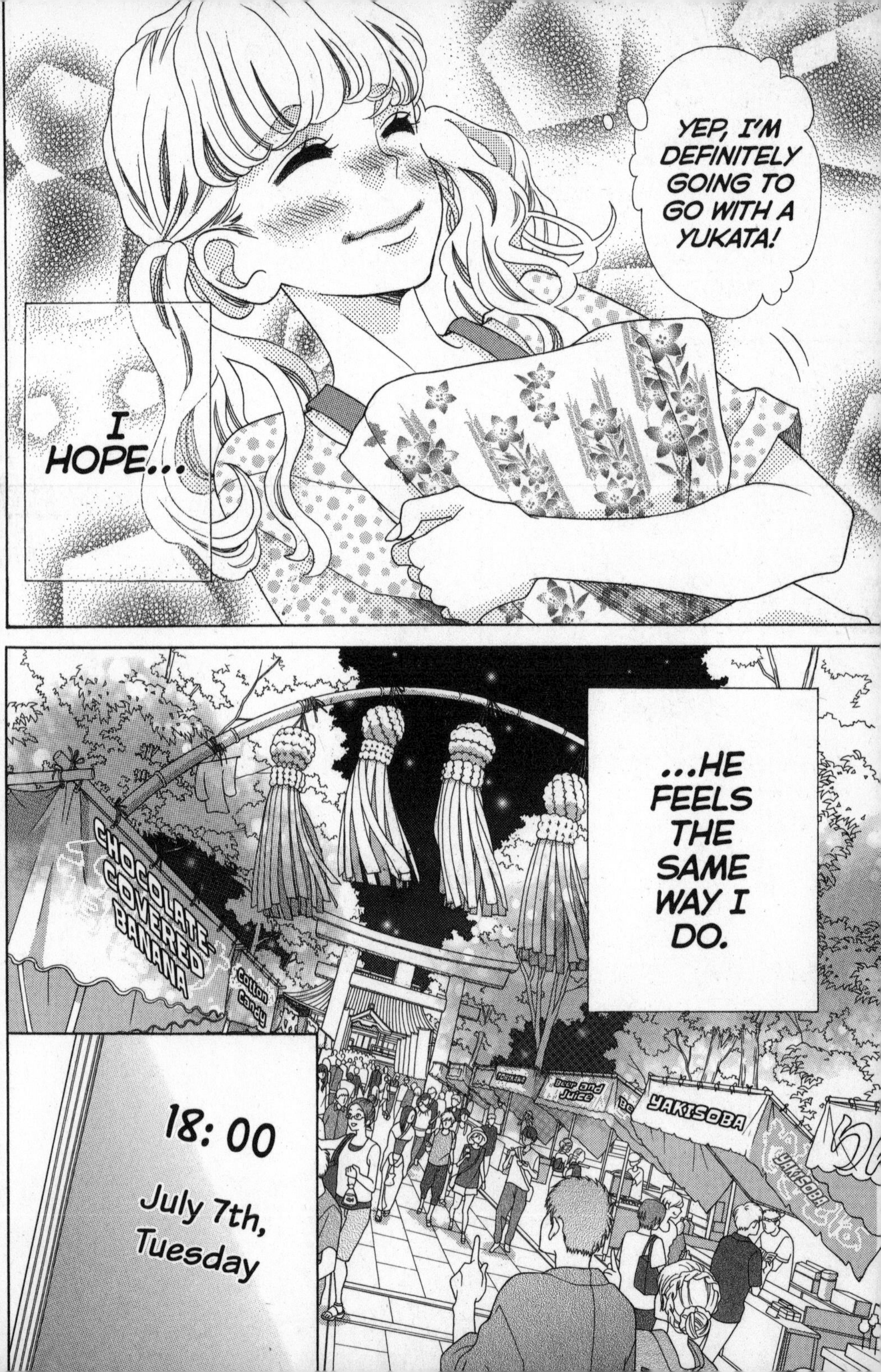
YEP, I'M DEFINITELY GOING TO GO WITH A YUKATA!
I HOPE...
...HE FEELS THE SAME WAY I DO.
CHOCOLATE-COVERED BANANA
Cotton Candy
Beer and Juice
YAKISOBA
YAKISOBA
18: 00
July 7th, Tuesday

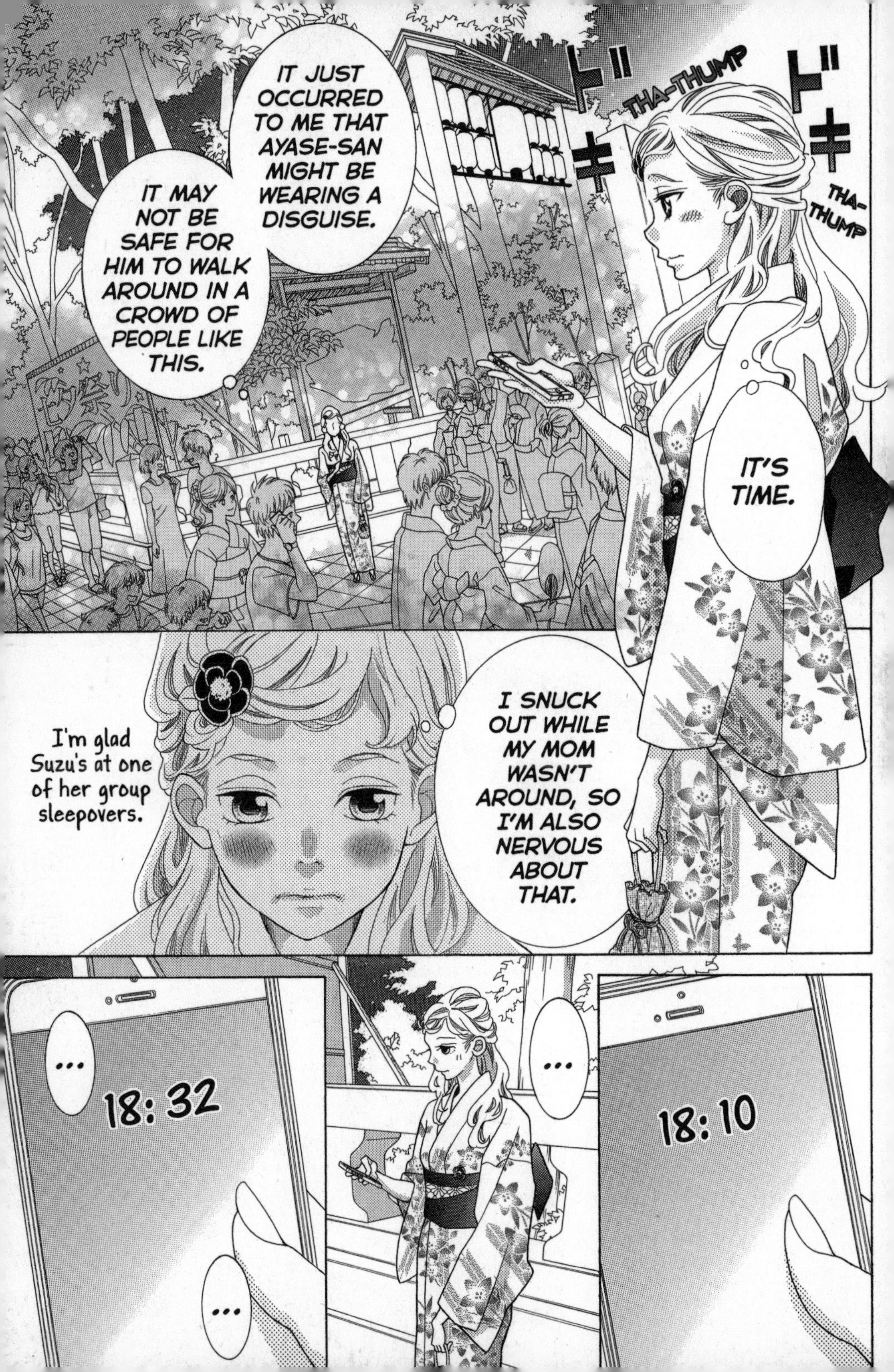
THA-THUMP
THA-THUMP
IT'S TIME.
IT JUST OCCURRED TO ME THAT AYASE-SAN MIGHT BE WEARING A DISGUISE.
IT MAY NOT BE SAFE FOR HIM TO WALK AROUND IN A CROWD OF PEOPLE LIKE THIS.
I SNUCK OUT WHILE MY MOM WASN'T AROUND, SO I'M ALSO NERVOUS ABOUT THAT.
I'm glad Suzu's at one of her group sleepovers.
...
18: 10
...
18: 32
...

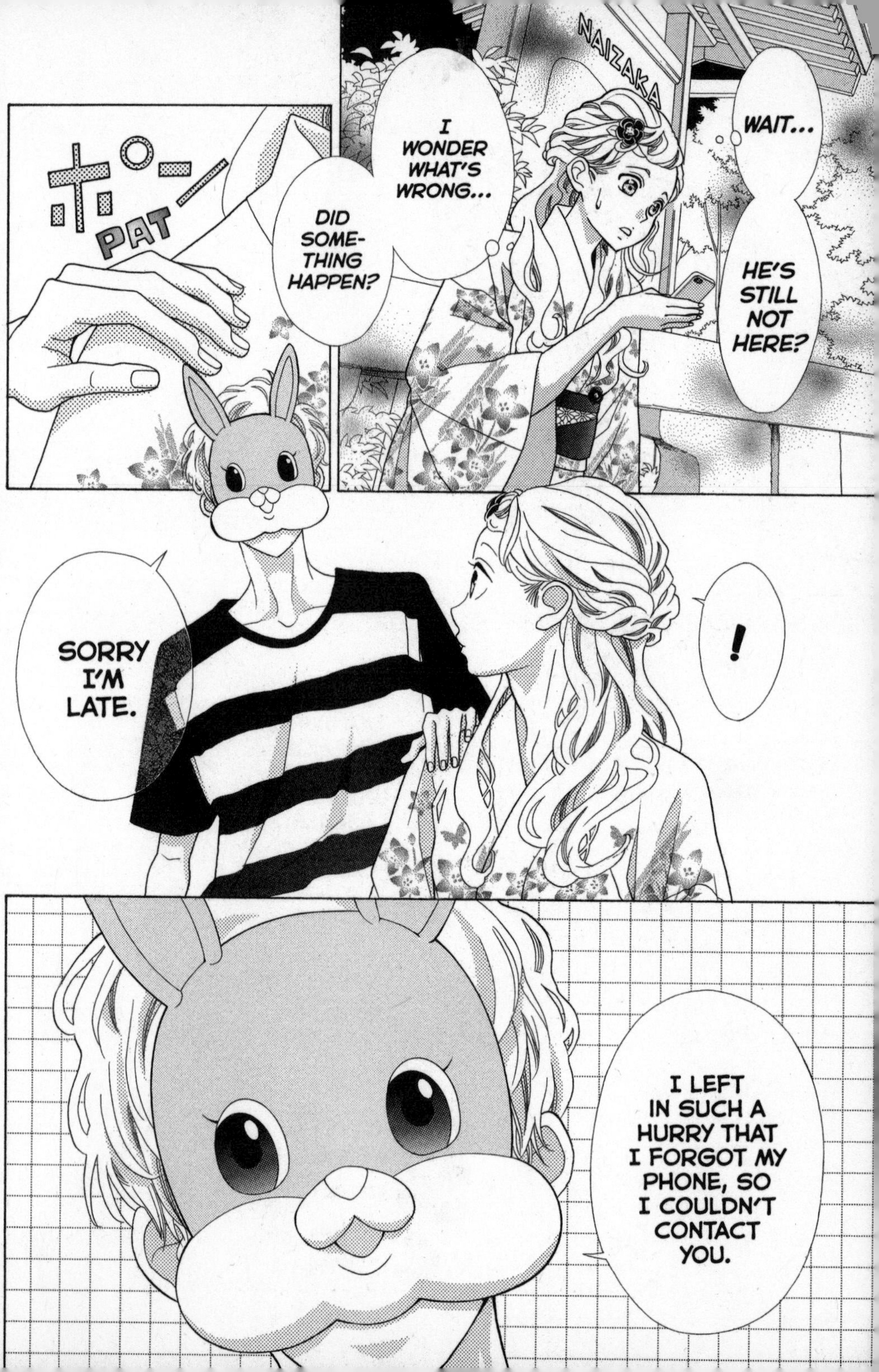
NAIZAKA
WAIT...
HE'S STILL NOT HERE?
I WONDER WHAT'S WRONG...
DID SOME-THING HAPPEN?
PAT
!
SORRY I'M LATE.
I LEFT IN SUCH A HURRY THAT I FORGOT MY PHONE, SO I COULDN'T CONTACT YOU.

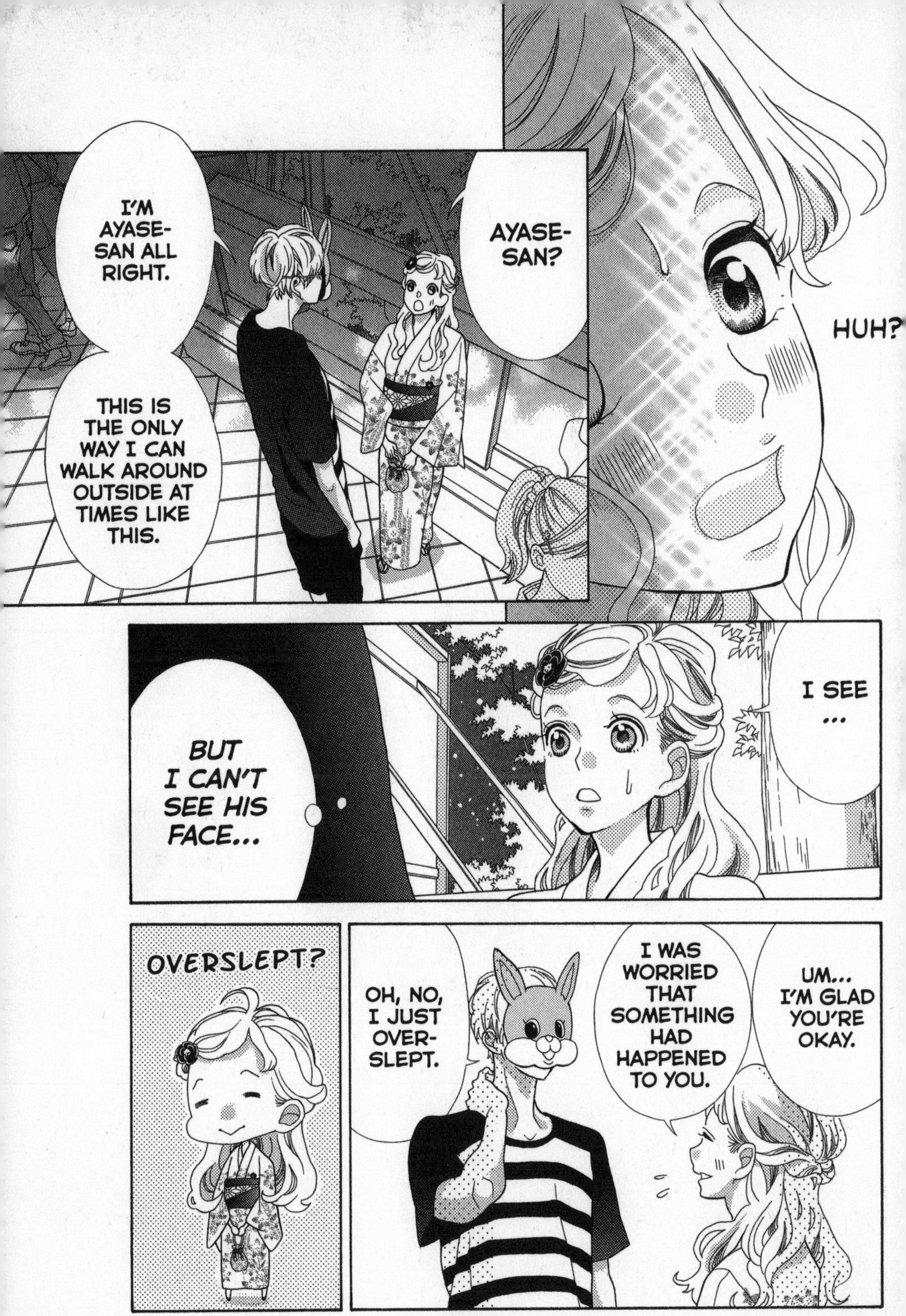
HUH?
AYASE-SAN?
I'M AYASE-SAN ALL RIGHT.
THIS IS THE ONLY WAY I CAN WALK AROUND OUTSIDE AT TIMES LIKE THIS.
I SEE...
BUT I CAN'T SEE HIS FACE...
UM... I'M GLAD YOU'RE OKAY.
I WAS WORRIED THAT SOMETHING HAD HAPPENED TO YOU.
OH, NO, I JUST OVER-SLEPT.
OVERSLEPT?

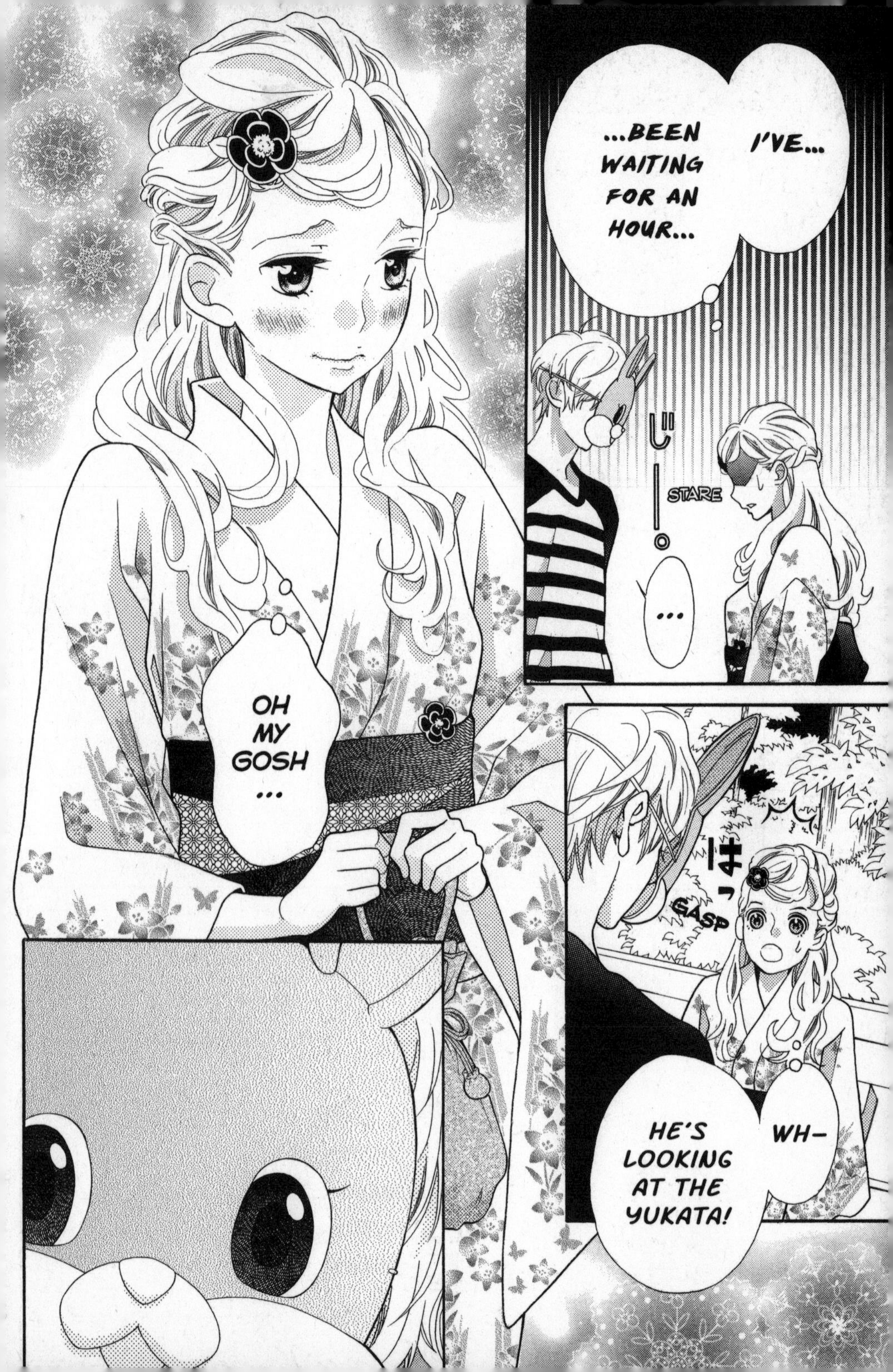
I'VE...
...BEEN WAITING FOR AN HOUR...
じー。
STARE
...
はっ
GASP
WH-
HE'S LOOKING AT THE YUKATA!
OH MY GOSH ...

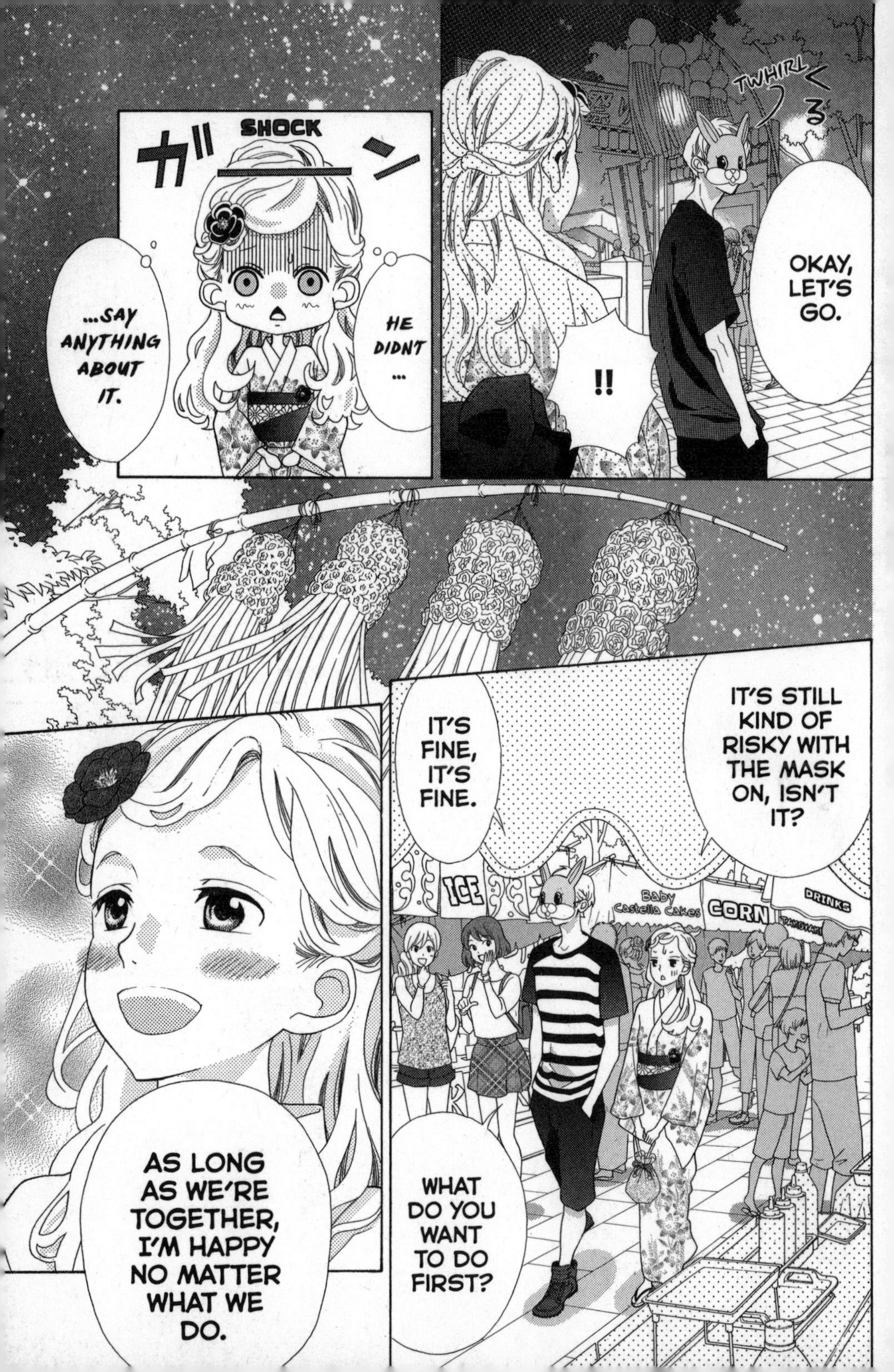
TWHIRL
くるっ
OKAY, LET'S GO.
!!
SHOCK
ガーン
HE DIDN'T ...
...SAY ANYTHING ABOUT IT.
IT'S STILL KIND OF RISKY WITH THE MASK ON, ISN'T IT?
IT'S FINE, IT'S FINE.
DRINKS
TAKOYAKI
CORN
Baby Castella Cakes
ICE
WHAT DO YOU WANT TO DO FIRST?
AS LONG AS WE'RE TOGETHER, I'M HAPPY NO MATTER WHAT WE DO.

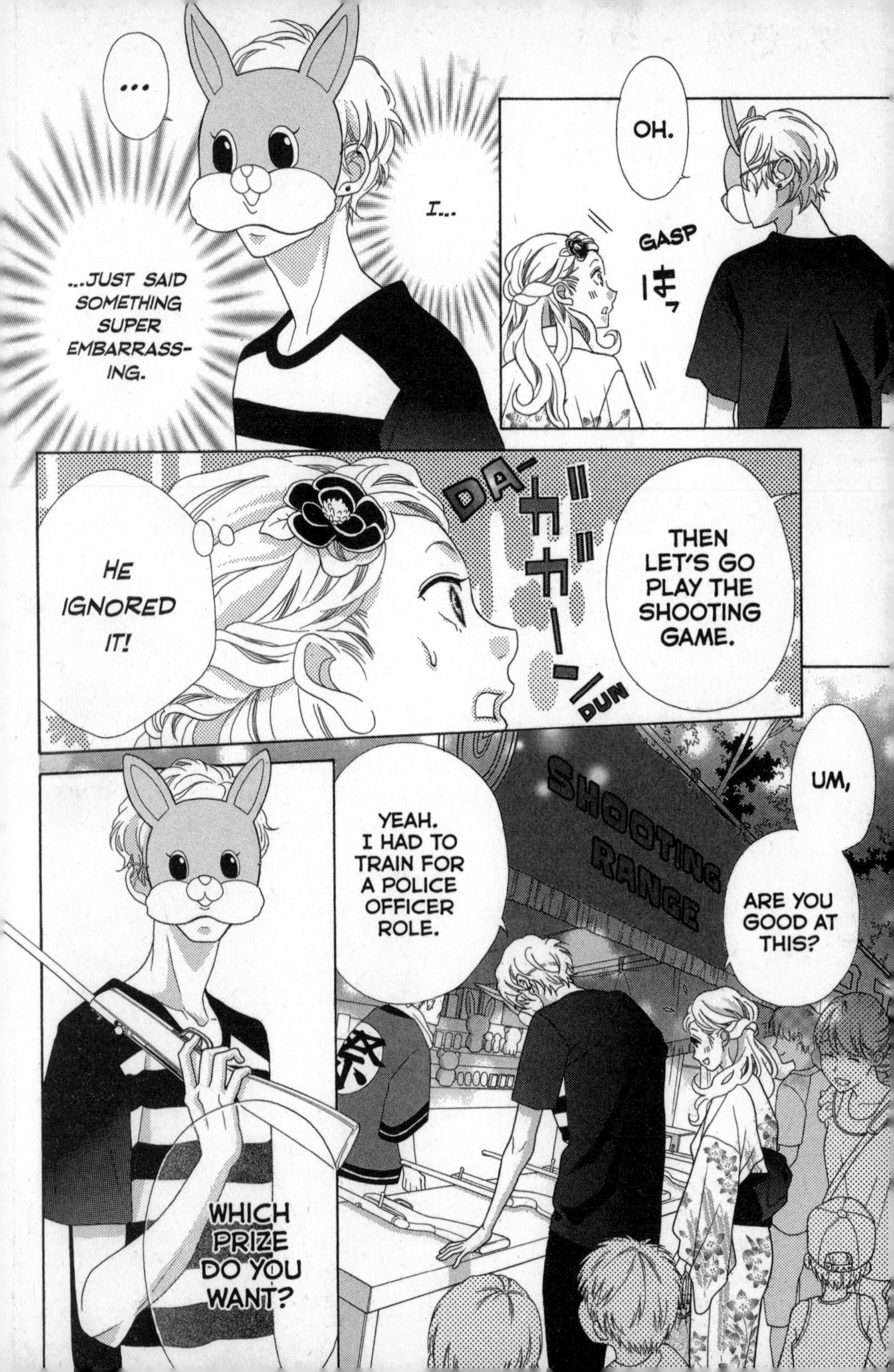
OH.
GASP
はっ
...
I...
...JUST SAID SOMETHING SUPER EMBARRASSING.
THEN LET'S GO PLAY THE SHOOTING GAME.
DA
ガーン
DUN
HE IGNORED IT!
UM,
ARE YOU GOOD AT THIS?
SHOOTING RANGE
YEAH. I HAD TO TRAIN FOR A POLICE OFFICER ROLE.
祭
WHICH PRIZE DO YOU WANT?

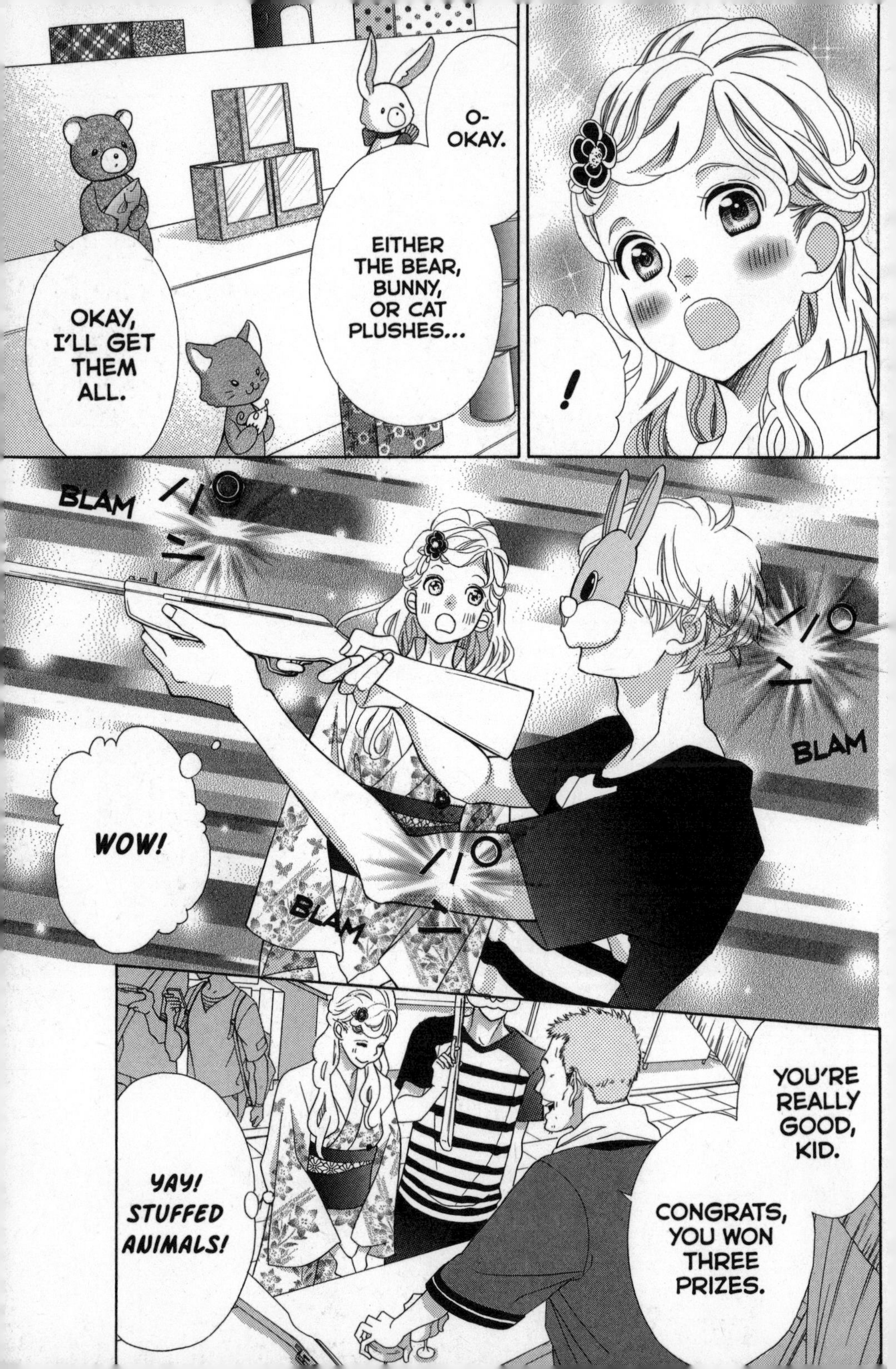
!
O-OKAY.
EITHER THE BEAR, BUNNY, OR CAT PLUSHES...
OKAY, I'LL GET THEM ALL.
BLAM
BLAM
WOW!
BLAM
YOU'RE REALLY GOOD, KID.
CONGRATS, YOU WON THREE PRIZES.
YAY! STUFFED ANIMALS!

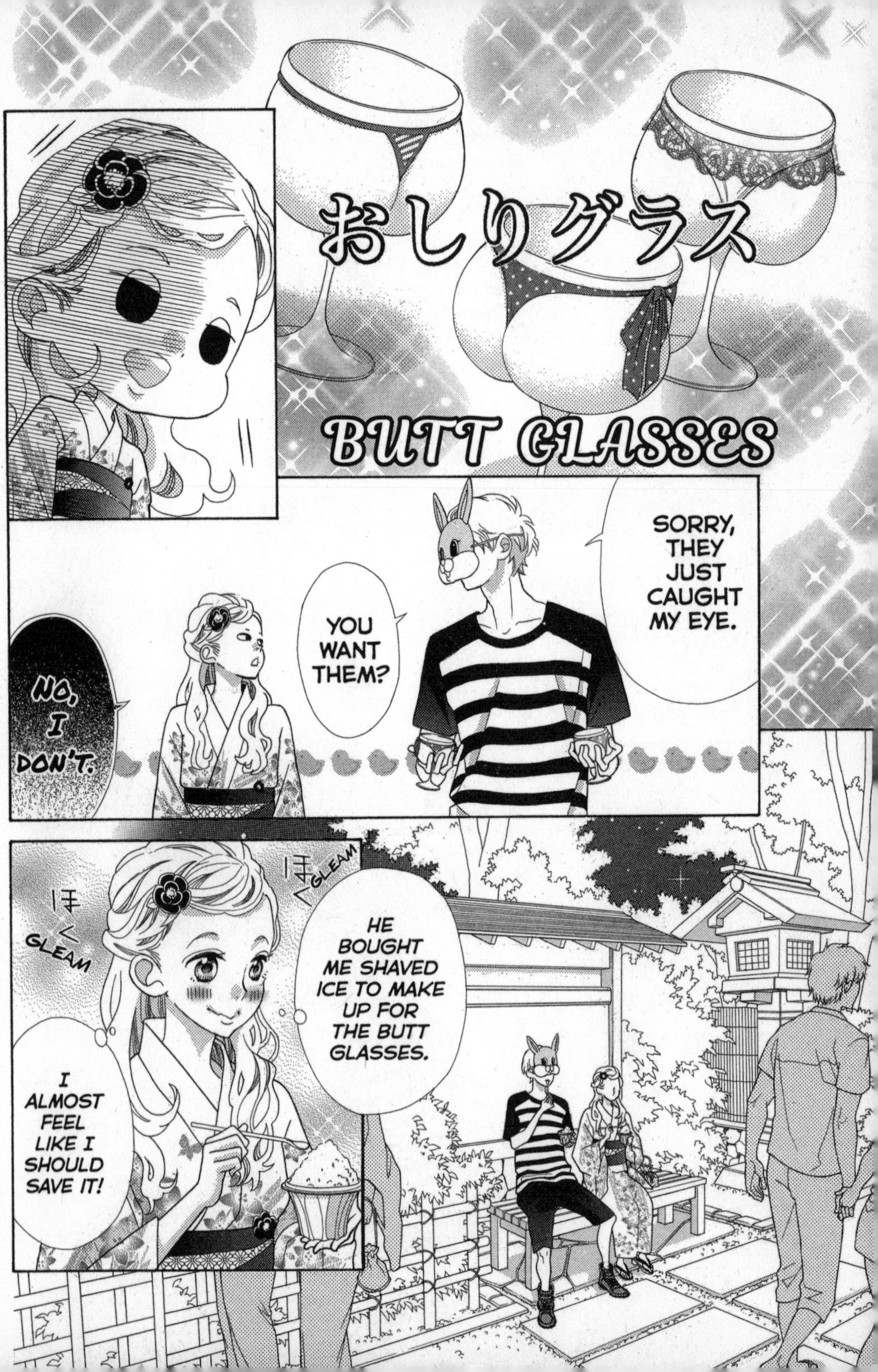
おしりグラス
BUTT GLASSES
SORRY, THEY JUST CAUGHT MY EYE.
YOU WANT THEM?
NO, I DON'T.
HE BOUGHT ME SHAVED ICE TO MAKE UP FOR THE BUTT GLASSES.
ほ GLEAM
ほ GLEAM
I ALMOST FEEL LIKE I SHOULD SAVE IT!

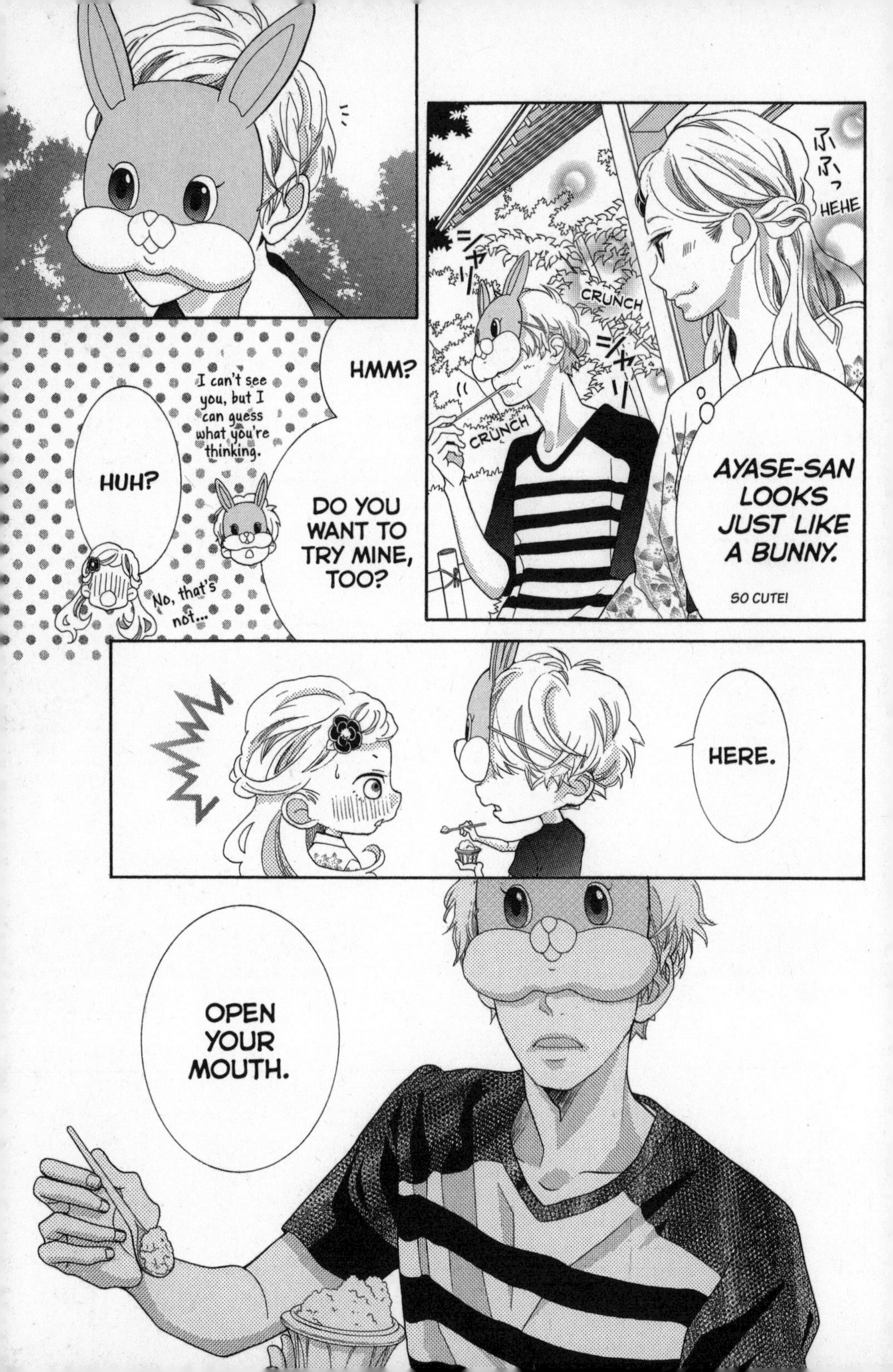
ふふっ
HEHE
シャリ
CRUNCH
シャリ
CRUNCH
AYASE-SAN LOOKS JUST LIKE A BUNNY.
SO CUTE!
HMM?
DO YOU WANT TO TRY MINE, TOO?
I can't see you, but I can guess what you're thinking.
HUH?
No, that's not...
HERE.
OPEN YOUR MOUTH.

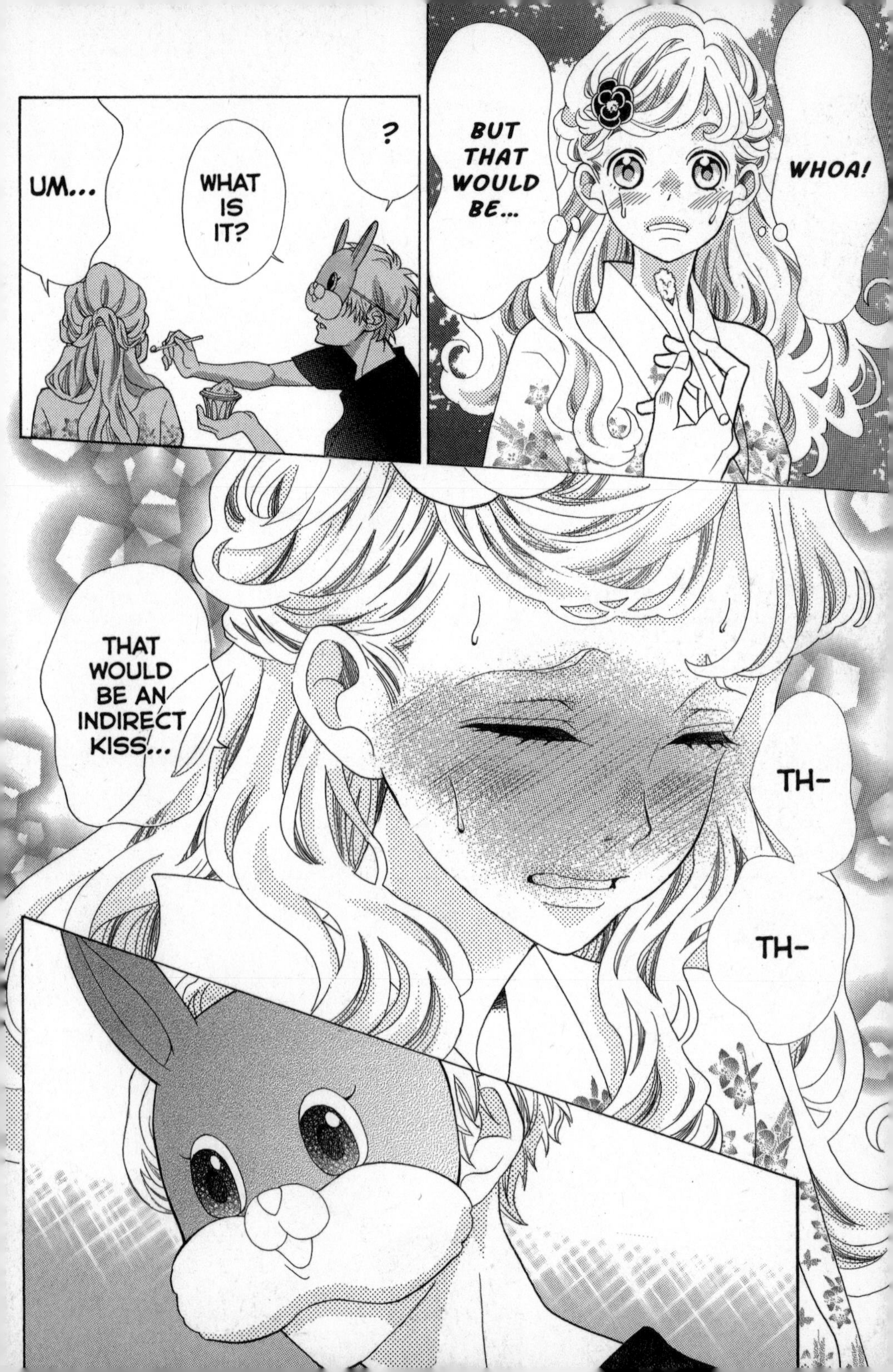
WHOA!
BUT THAT WOULD BE...
?
WHAT IS IT?
UM...
TH-
TH-
THAT WOULD BE AN INDIRECT KISS...

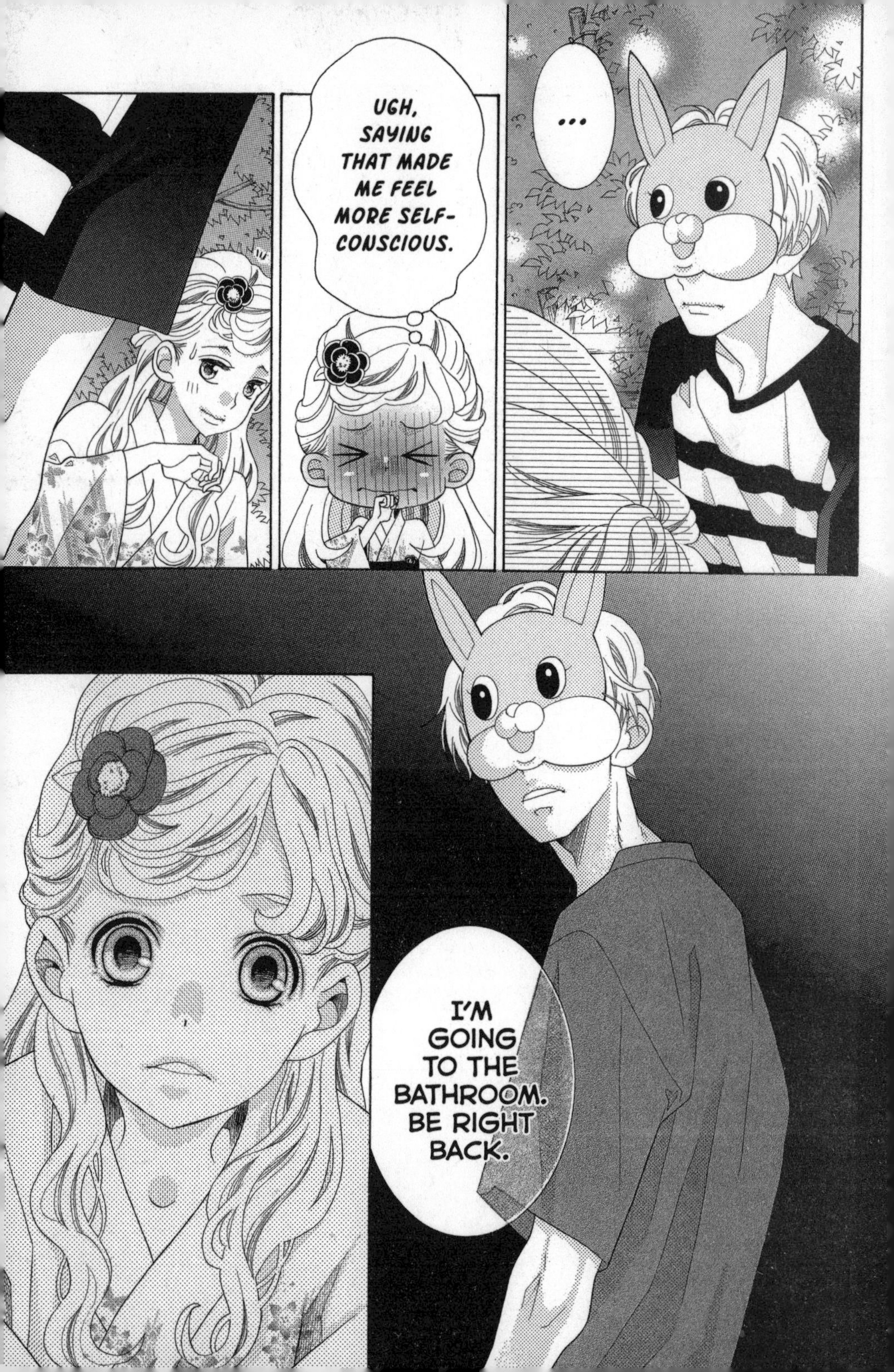
...
UGH, SAYING THAT MADE ME FEEL MORE SELF-CONSCIOUS.
I'M GOING TO THE BATHROOM. BE RIGHT BACK.

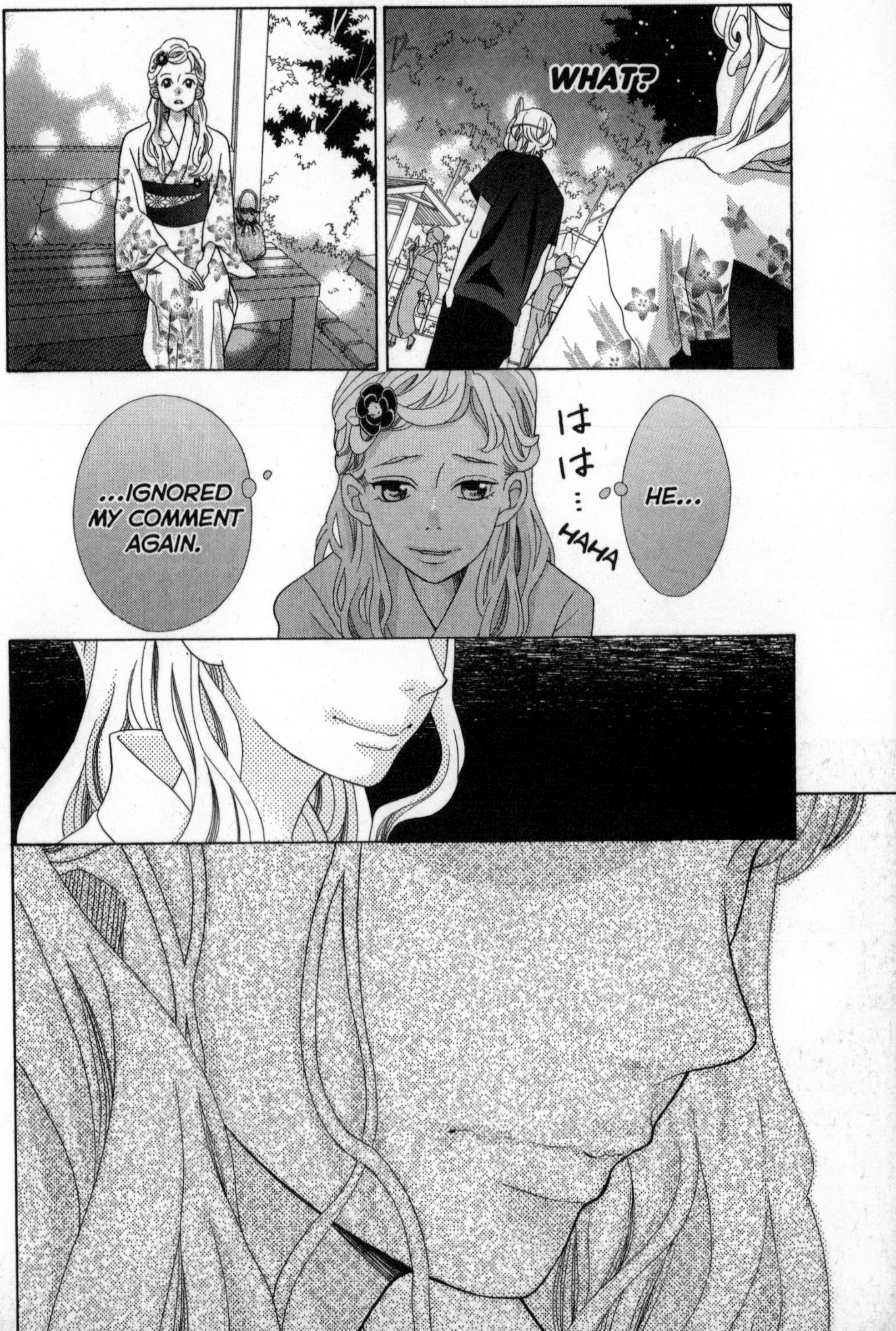
WHAT?
HE...
はは…
HAHA
...IGNORED MY COMMENT AGAIN.

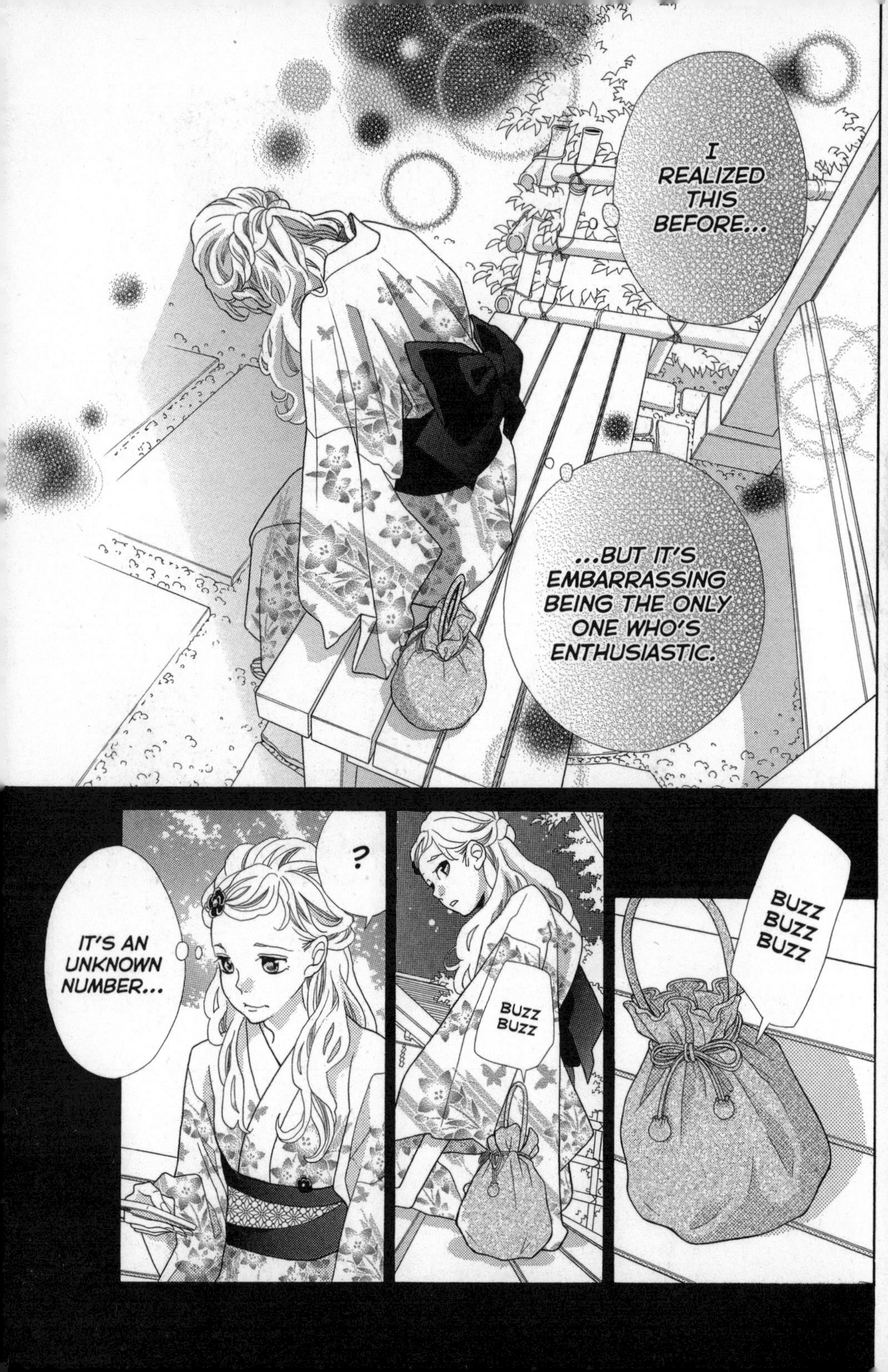
I REALIZED THIS BEFORE...
...BUT IT'S EMBARRASSING BEING THE ONLY ONE WHO'S ENTHUSIASTIC.
BUZZ BUZZ BUZZ
BUZZ BUZZ
?
IT'S AN UNKNOWN NUMBER...

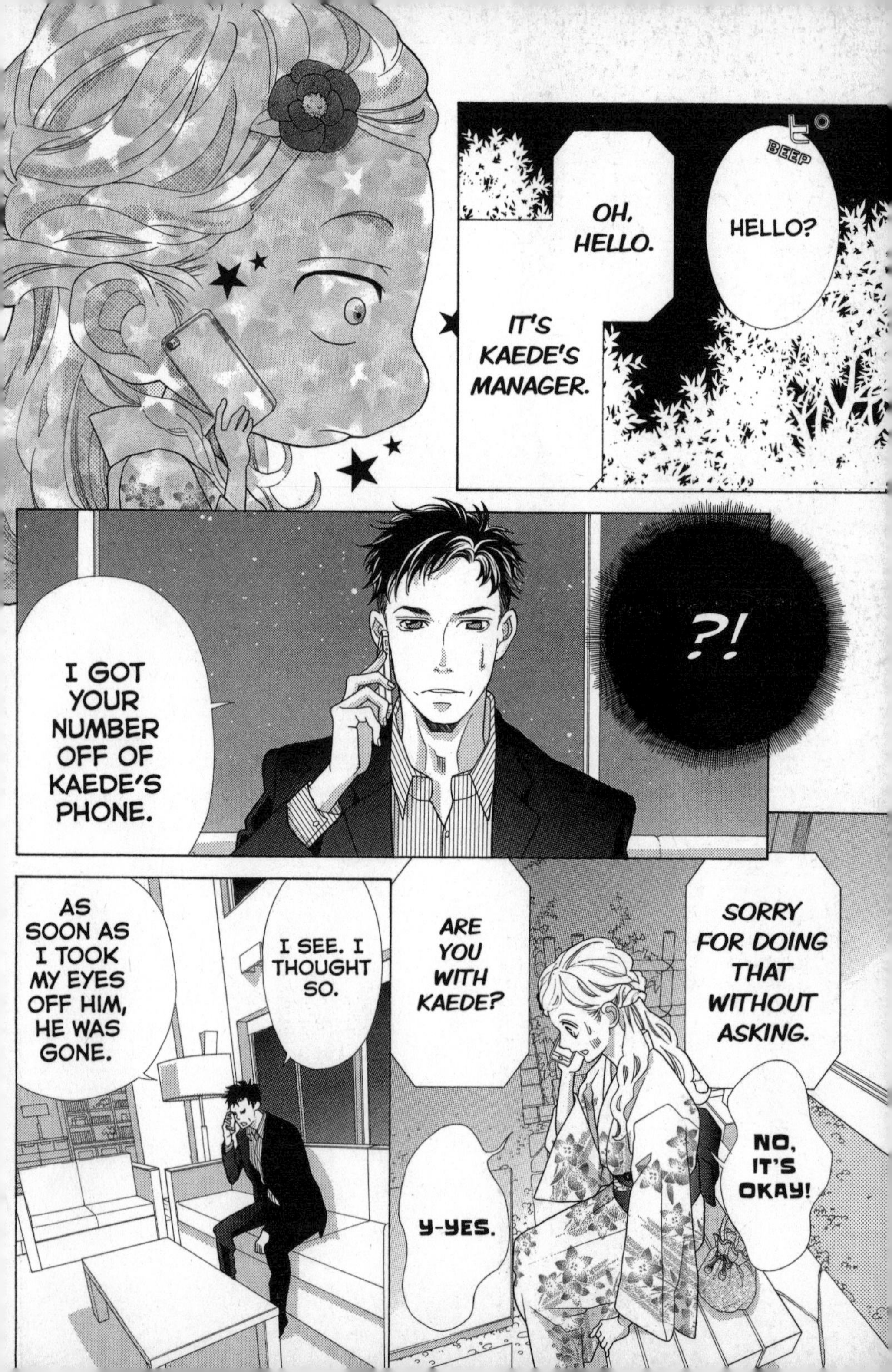
BEEP
HELLO?
OH, HELLO.
IT'S KAEDE'S MANAGER.
?!
I GOT YOUR NUMBER OFF OF KAEDE'S PHONE.
SORRY FOR DOING THAT WITHOUT ASKING.
NO, IT'S OKAY!
ARE YOU WITH KAEDE?
Y-YES.
I SEE. I THOUGHT SO.
AS SOON AS I TOOK MY EYES OFF HIM, HE WAS GONE.

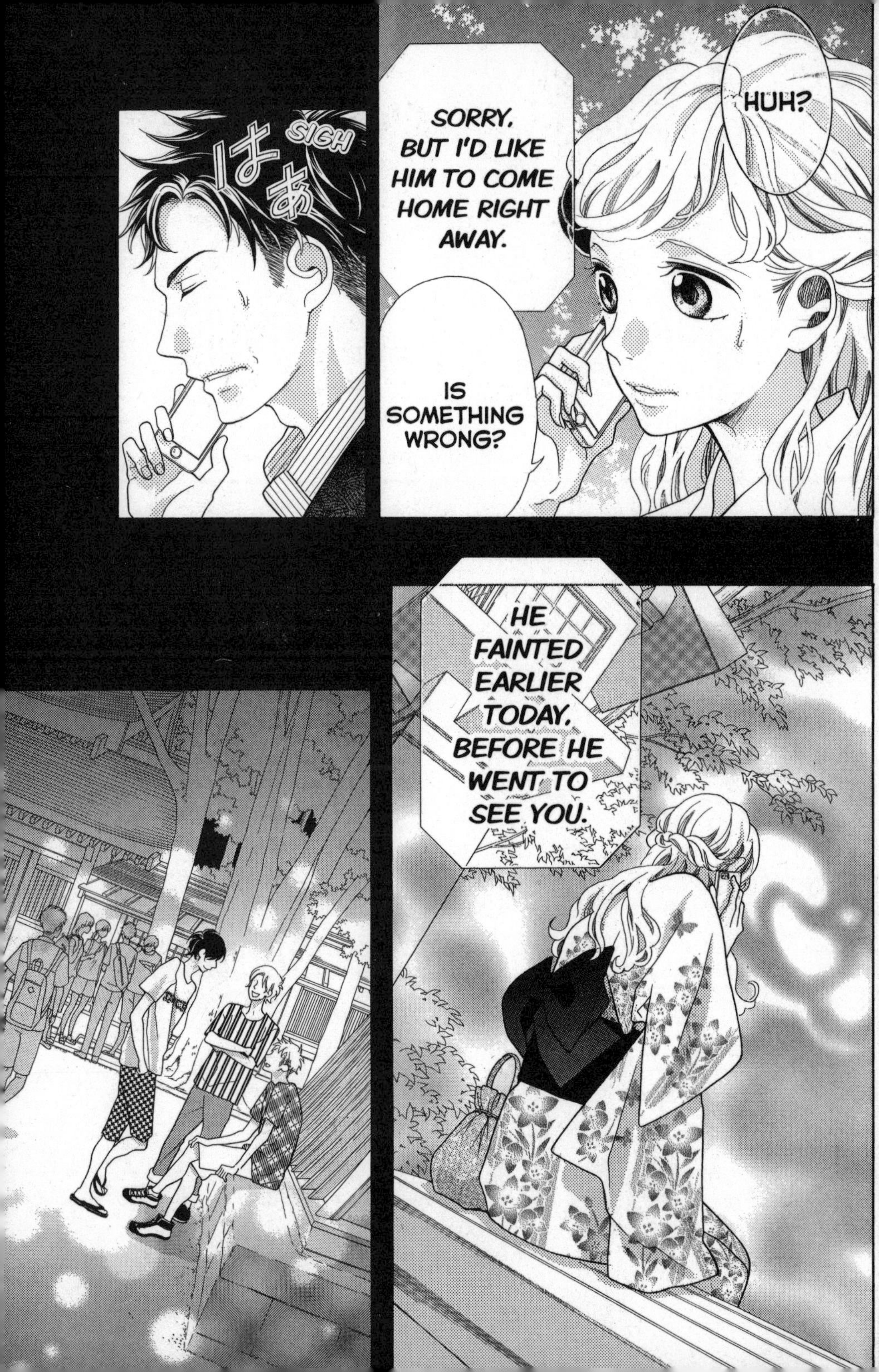
HUH?
SORRY, BUT I'D LIKE HIM TO COME HOME RIGHT AWAY.
IS SOMETHING WRONG?
はあ
SIGH
HE FAINTED EARLIER TODAY, BEFORE HE WENT TO SEE YOU.

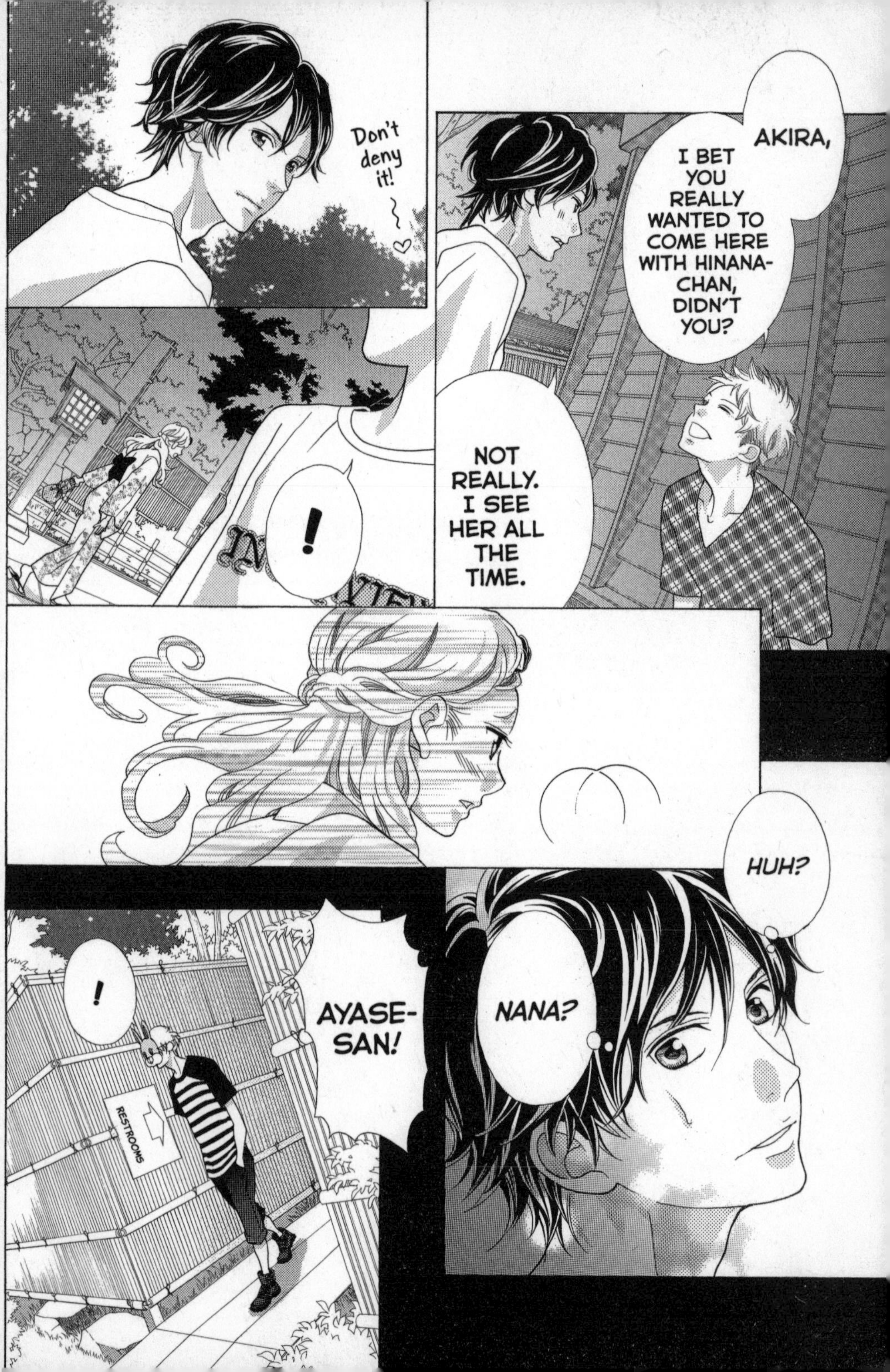
AKIRA, I BET YOU REALLY WANTED TO COME HERE WITH HINANA-CHAN, DIDN'T YOU?
NOT REALLY. I SEE HER ALL THE TIME.
Don't deny it!
!
HUH?
NANA?
AYASE-SAN!
!
RESTROOMS

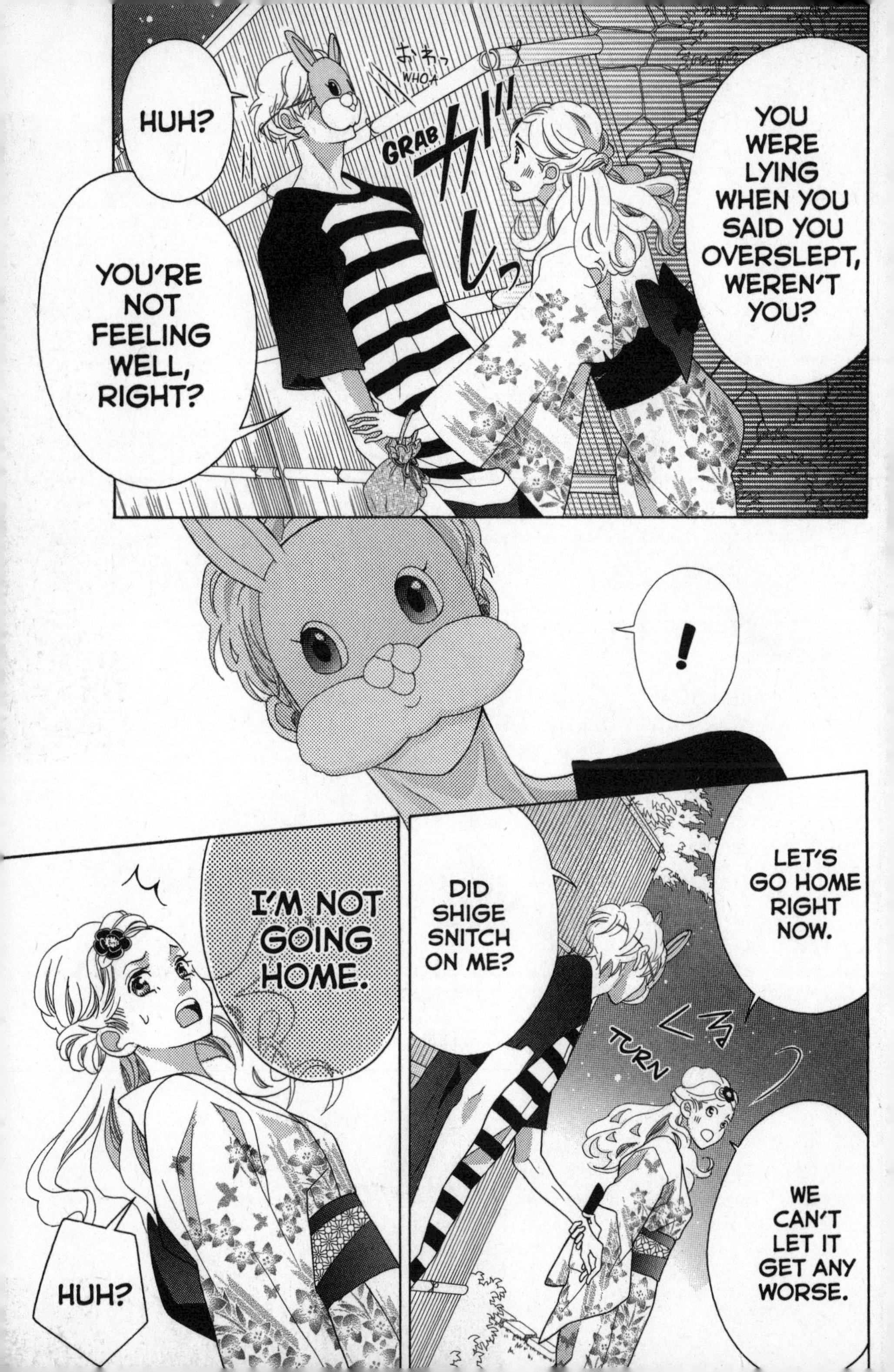

YOU WERE LYING WHEN YOU SAID YOU OVERSLEPT, WEREN'T YOU?
GRAB
WHOA
HUH?
YOU'RE NOT FEELING WELL, RIGHT?
!
LET'S GO HOME RIGHT NOW.
DID SHIGE SNITCH ON ME?
TURN
WE CAN'T LET IT GET ANY WORSE.
I'M NOT GOING HOME.
HUH?

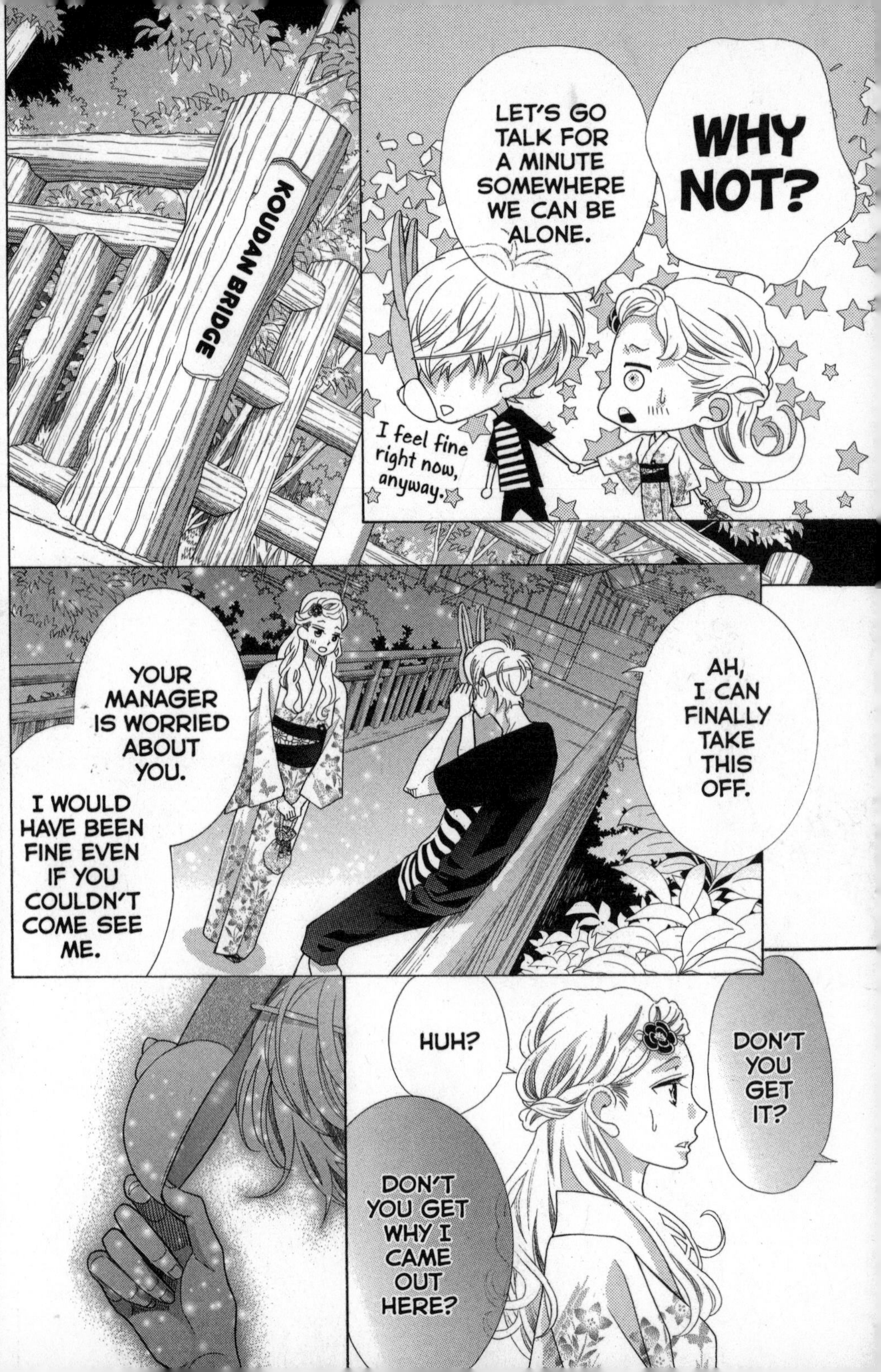
WHY NOT?
LET'S GO TALK FOR A MINUTE SOMEWHERE WE CAN BE ALONE.
I feel fine right now, anyway.
KOUDAN BRIDGE
AH, I CAN FINALLY TAKE THIS OFF.
YOUR MANAGER IS WORRIED ABOUT YOU.
I WOULD HAVE BEEN FINE EVEN IF YOU COULDN'T COME SEE ME.
DON'T YOU GET IT?
HUH?
DON'T YOU GET WHY I CAME OUT HERE?

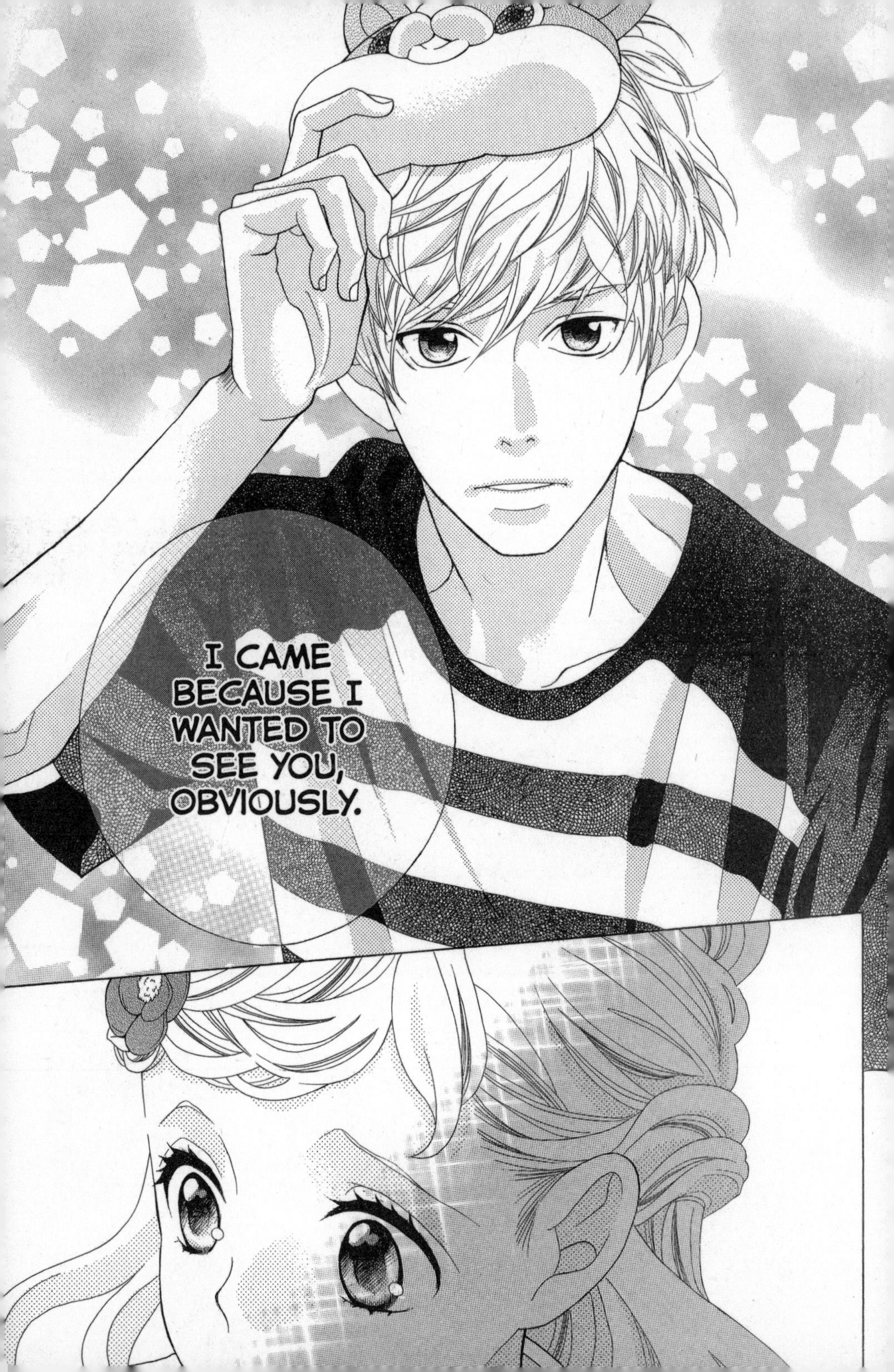
I CAME BECAUSE I WANTED TO SEE YOU, OBVIOUSLY.

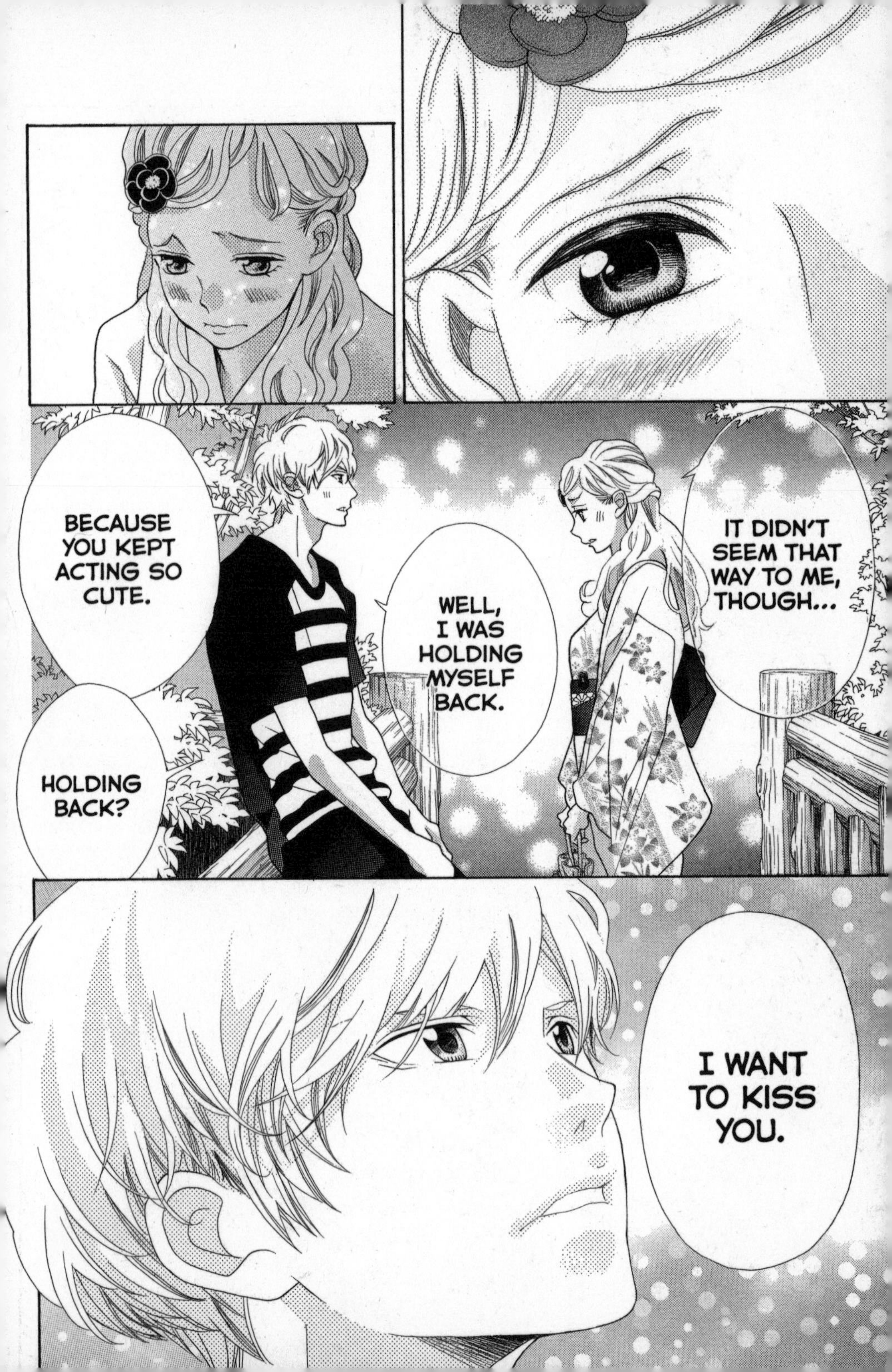
IT DIDN'T SEEM THAT WAY TO ME, THOUGH...
WELL, I WAS HOLDING MYSELF BACK.
BECAUSE YOU KEPT ACTING SO CUTE.
HOLDING BACK?
I WANT TO KISS YOU.

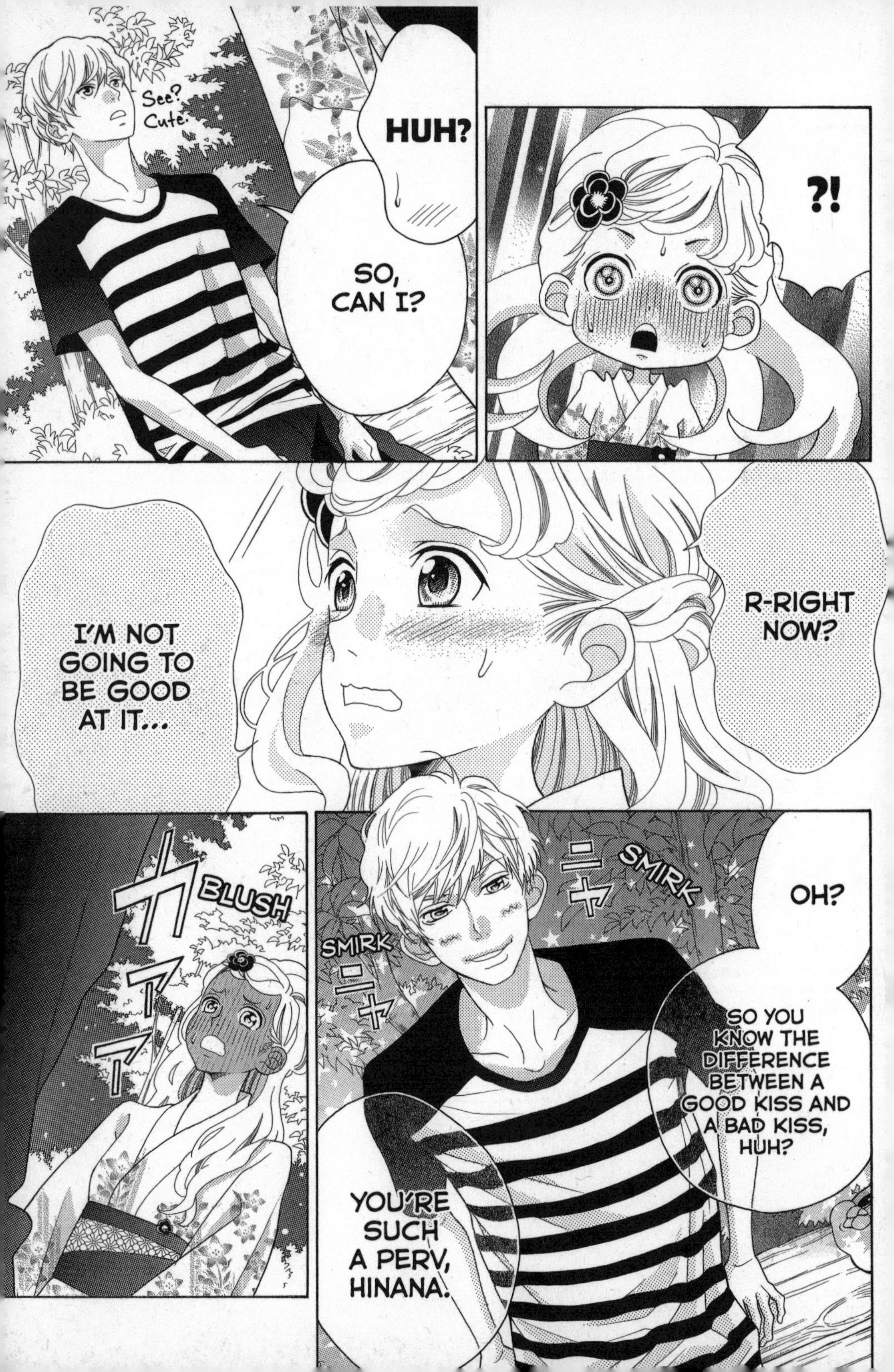
?!
HUH?
SO, CAN I?
See? Cute.
R-RIGHT NOW?
I'M NOT GOING TO BE GOOD AT IT...
OH?
SMIRK
SO YOU KNOW THE DIFFERENCE BETWEEN A GOOD KISS AND A BAD KISS, HUH?
SMIRK
YOU'RE SUCH A PERV, HINANA.
BLUSH

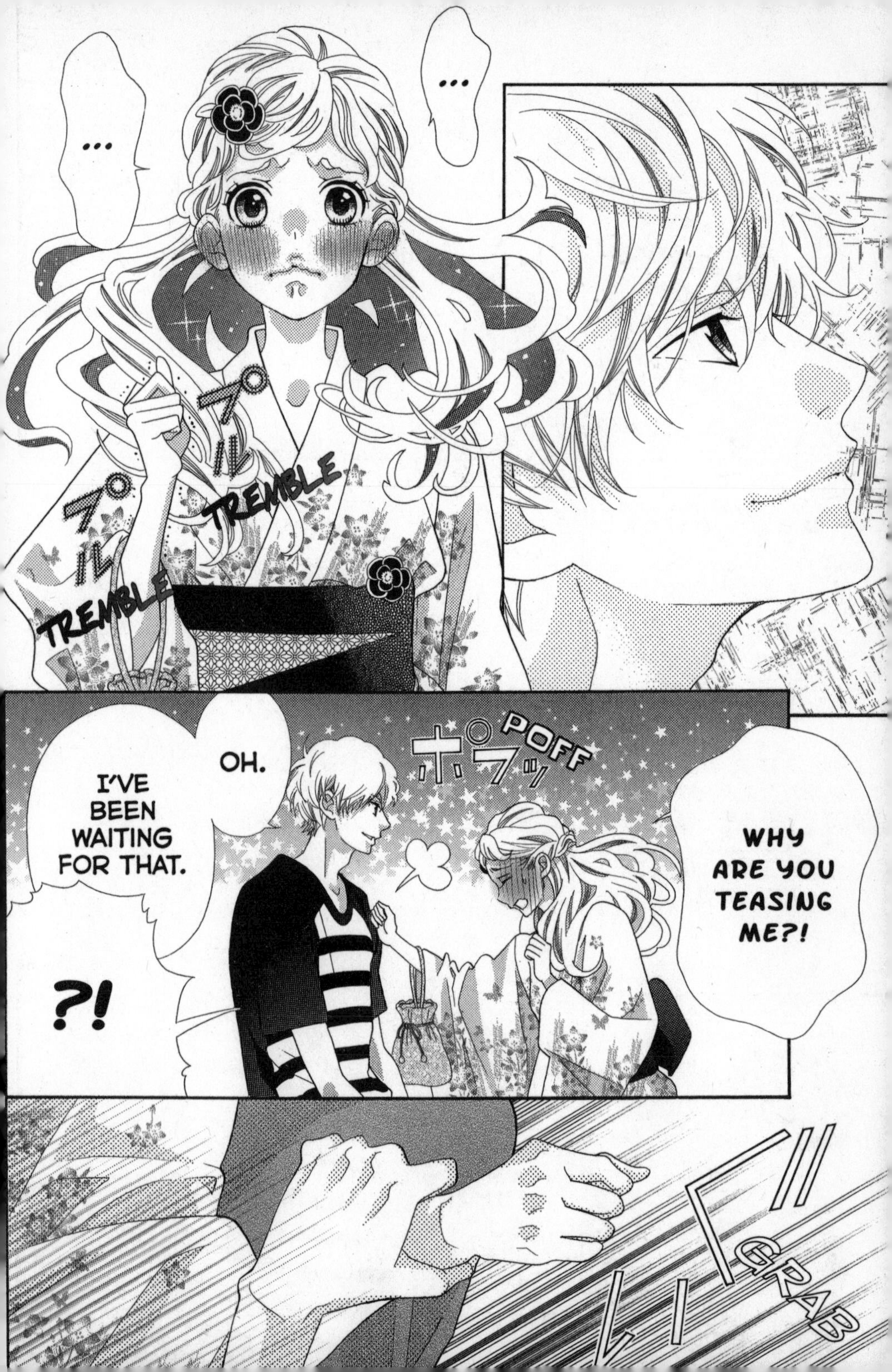

...
...
プル TREMBLE
プル TREMBLE
WHY ARE YOU TEASING ME?!
ポフッ POFF
OH.
I'VE BEEN WAITING FOR THAT.
?!
GRAB

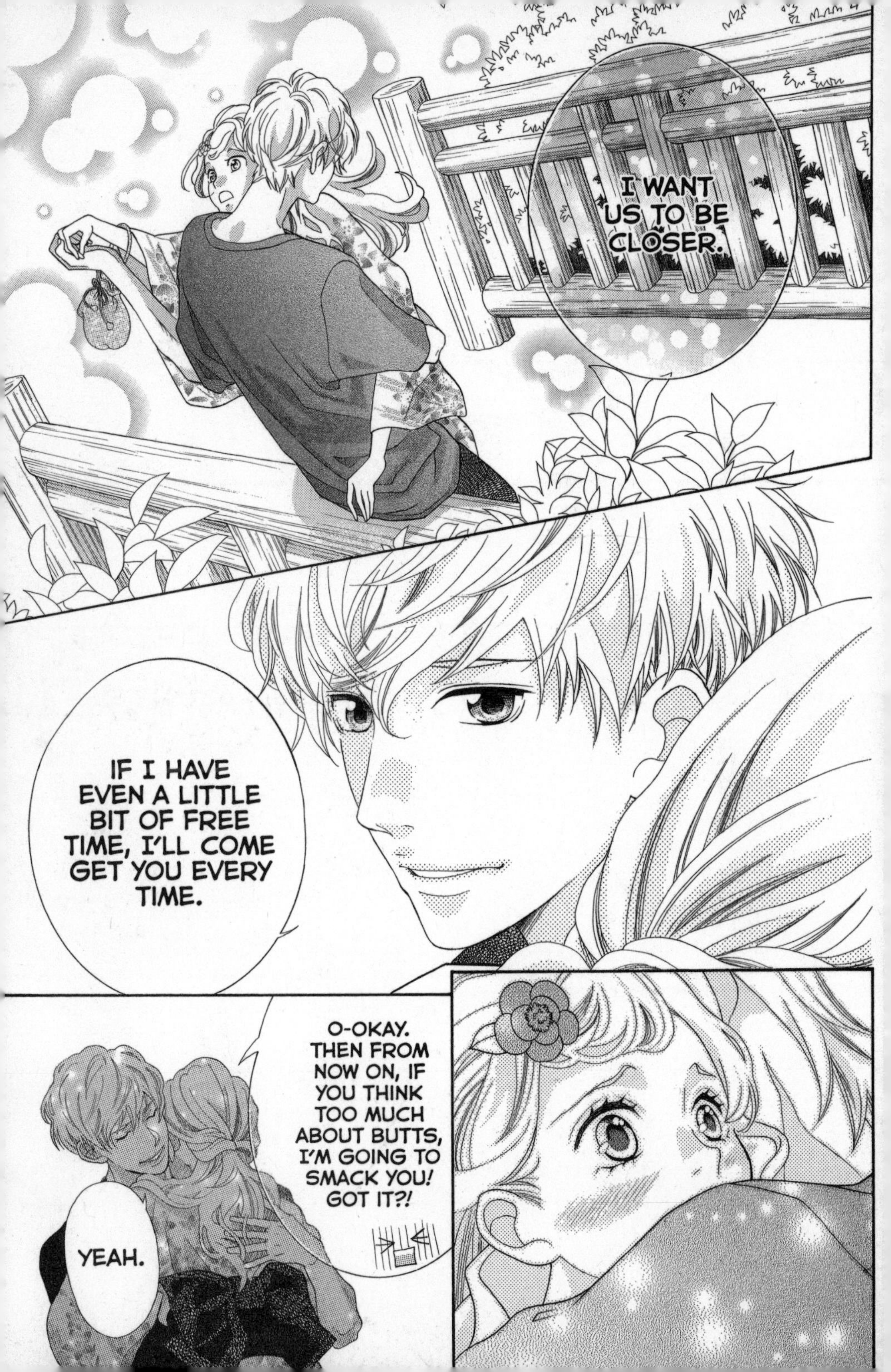
I WANT US TO BE CLOSER.
IF I HAVE EVEN A LITTLE BIT OF FREE TIME, I'LL COME GET YOU EVERY TIME.
O-OKAY. THEN FROM NOW ON, IF YOU THINK TOO MUCH ABOUT BUTTS, I'M GOING TO SMACK YOU! GOT IT?!
YEAH.

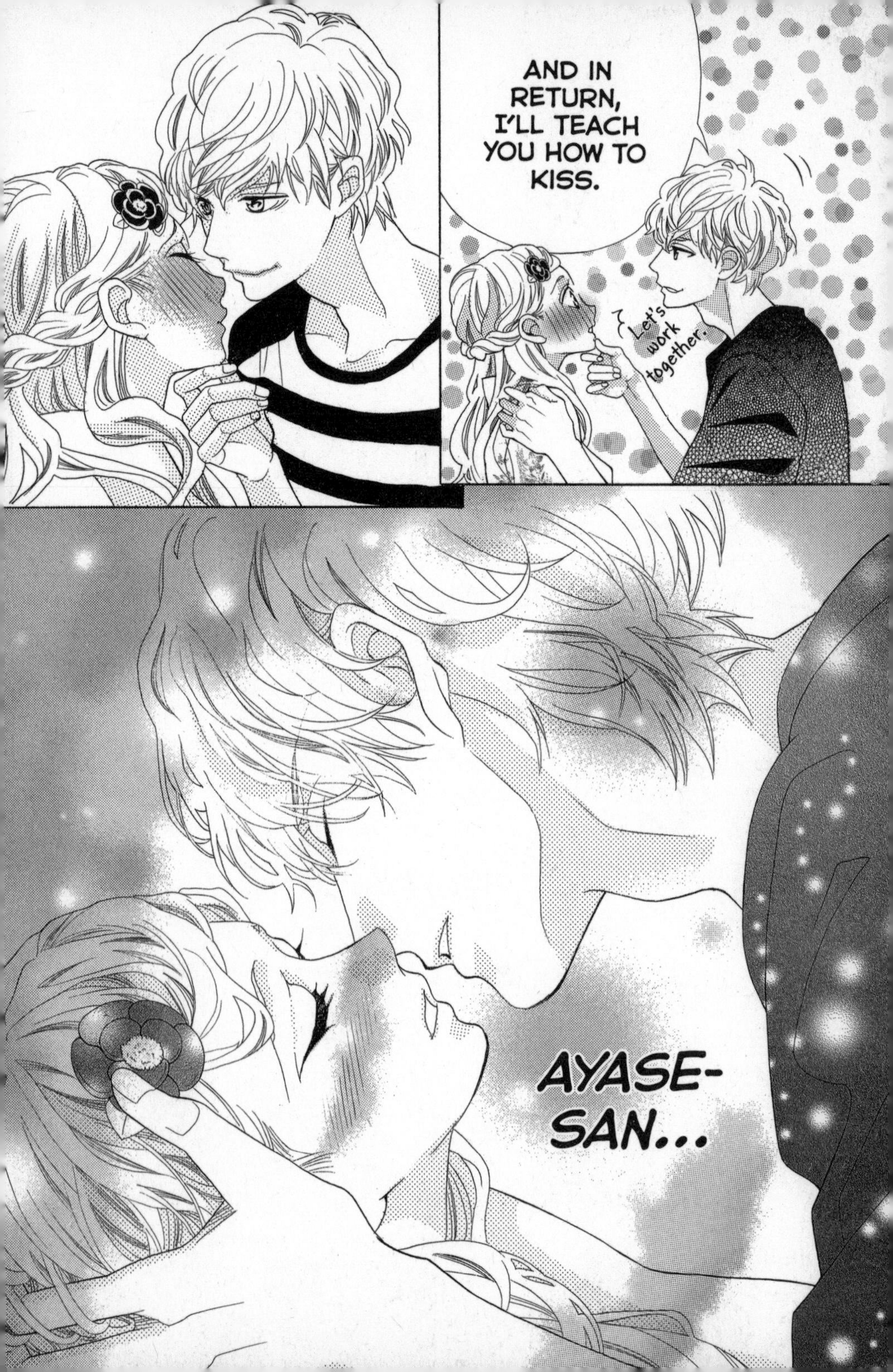
AND IN RETURN, I'LL TEACH YOU HOW TO KISS.
Let's work together.
AYASE-SAN...

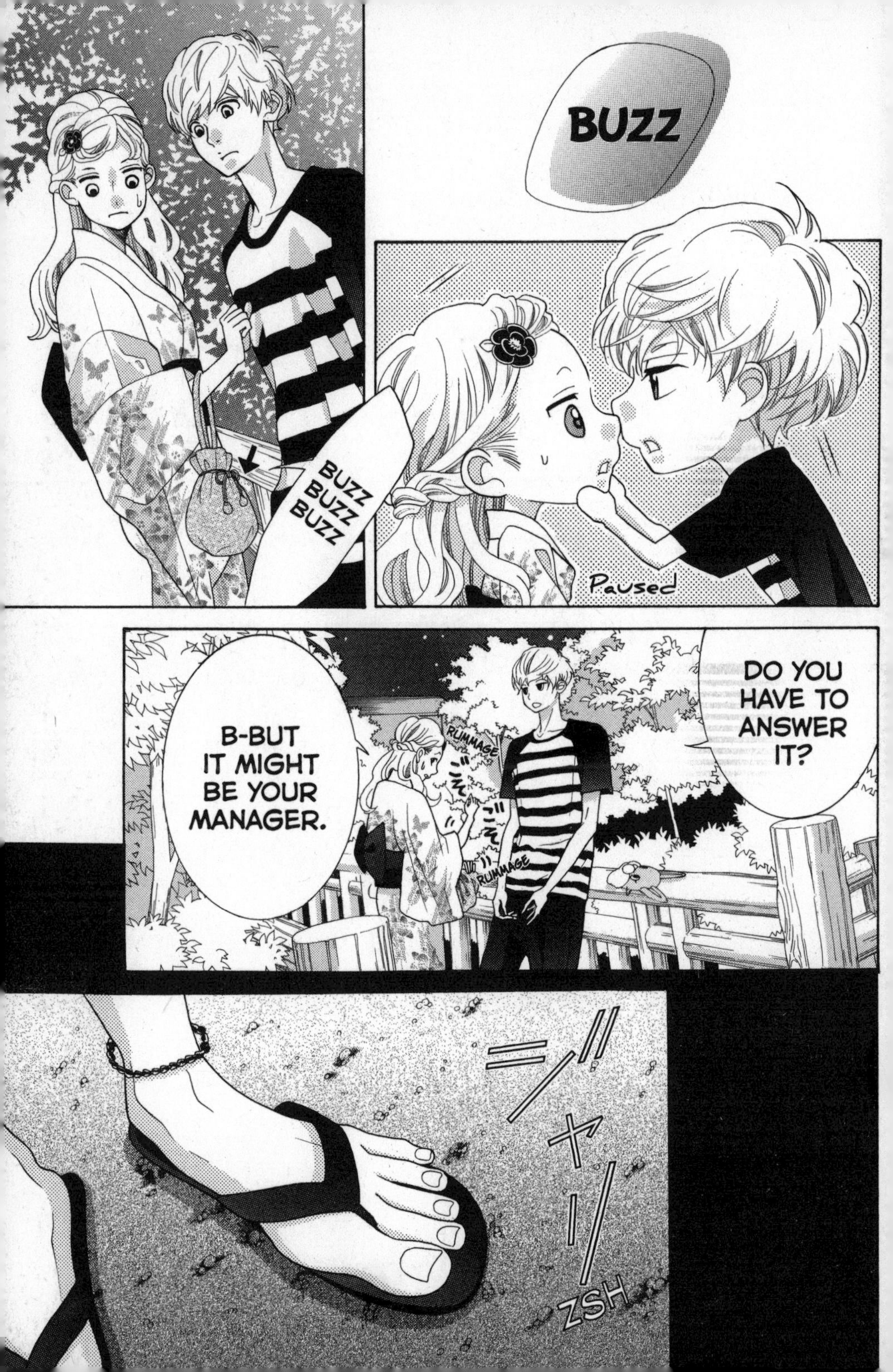
BUZZ
Paused
BUZZ BUZZ BUZZ
DO YOU HAVE TO ANSWER IT?
RUMMAGE
B-BUT IT MIGHT BE YOUR MANAGER.
RUMMAGE
ZSH

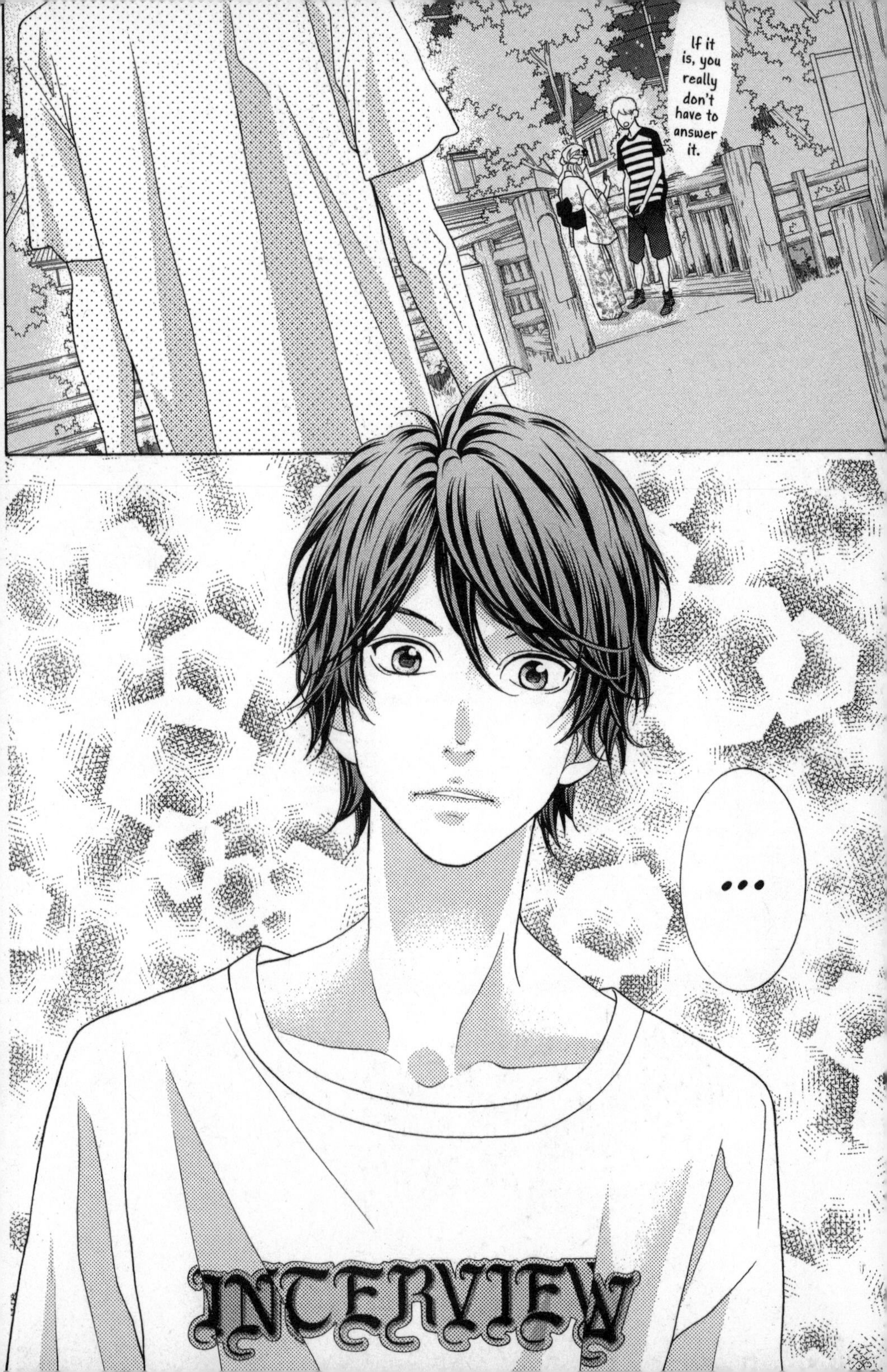
If it is, you really don't have to answer it.
...
INTERVIEW

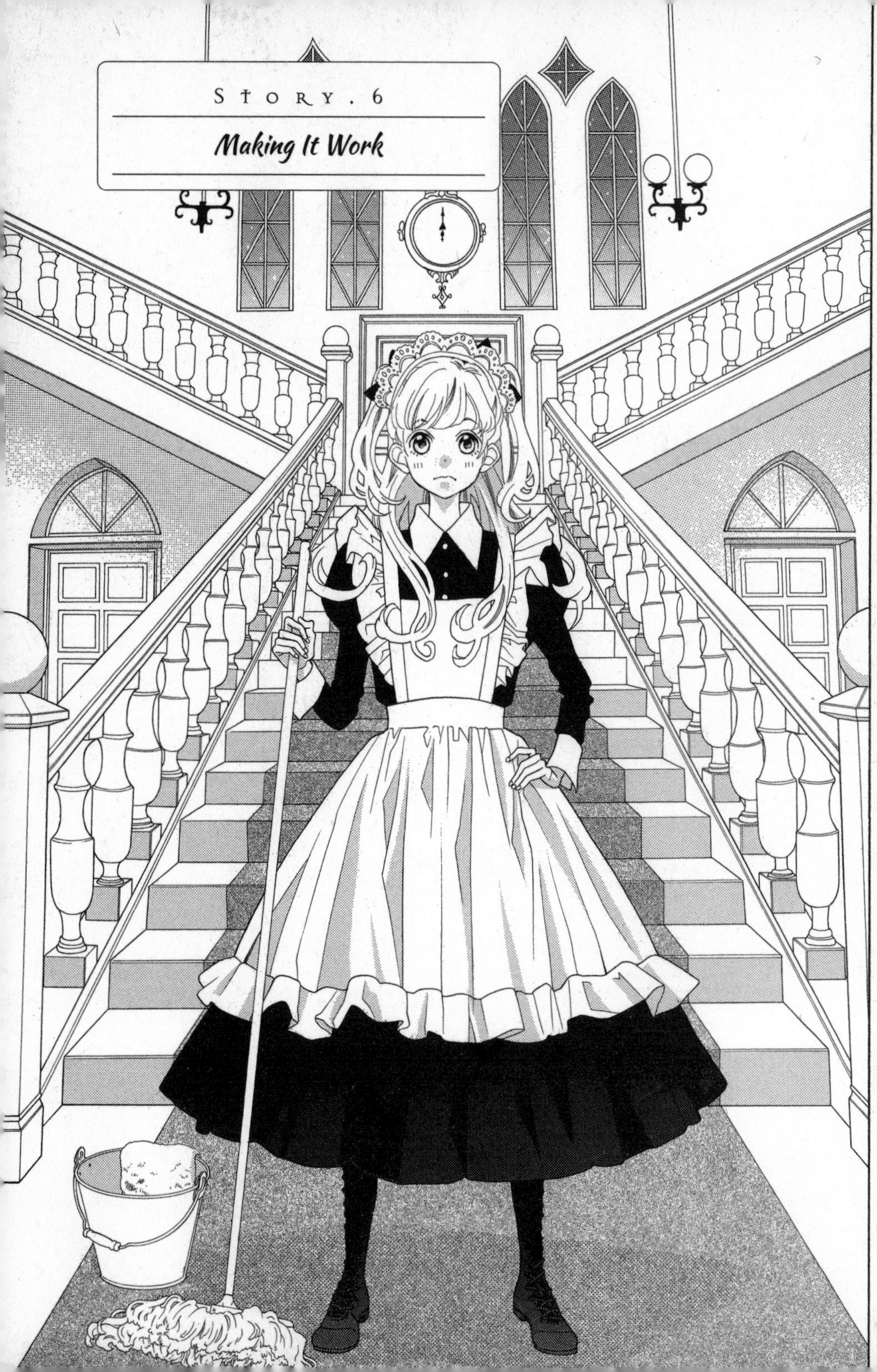
STORY. 6
Making It Work

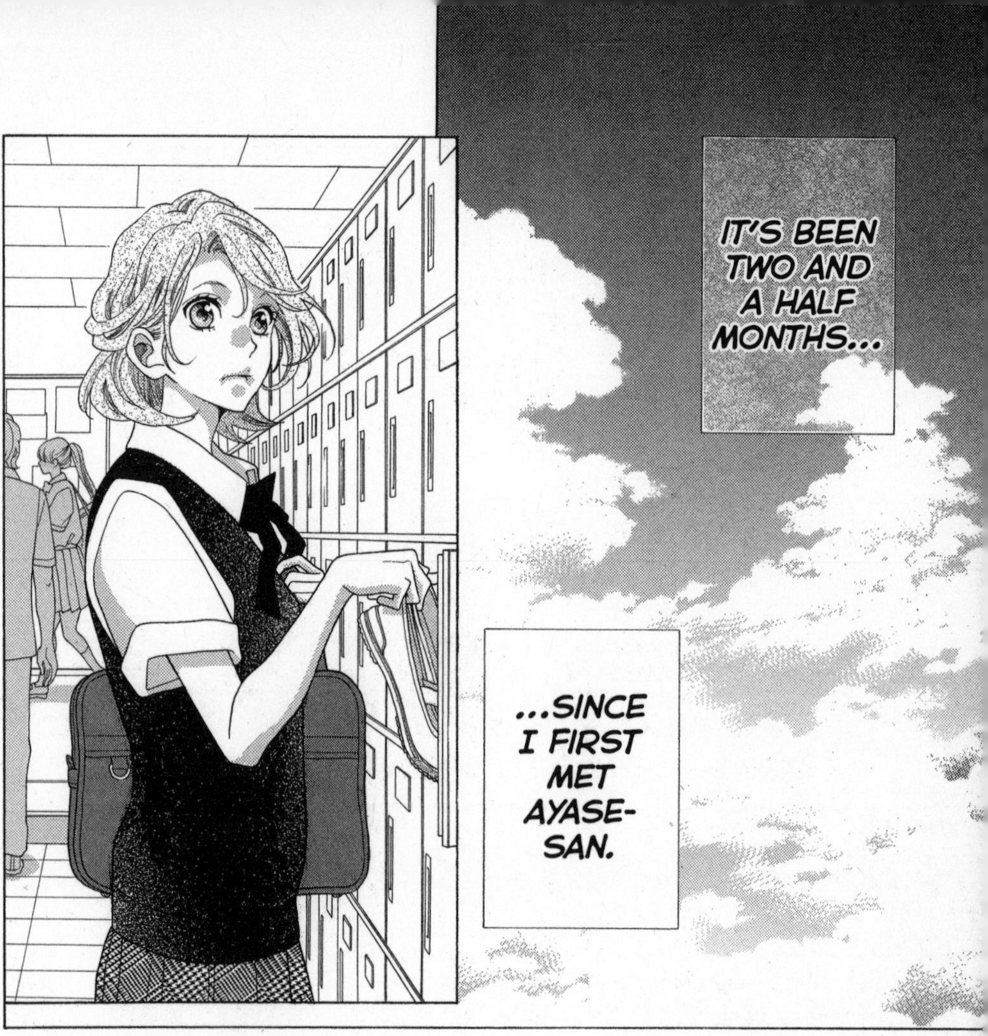
IT'S BEEN TWO AND A HALF MONTHS...
...SINCE I FIRST MET AYASE-SAN.

Kiss Me at the Stroke of Midnight

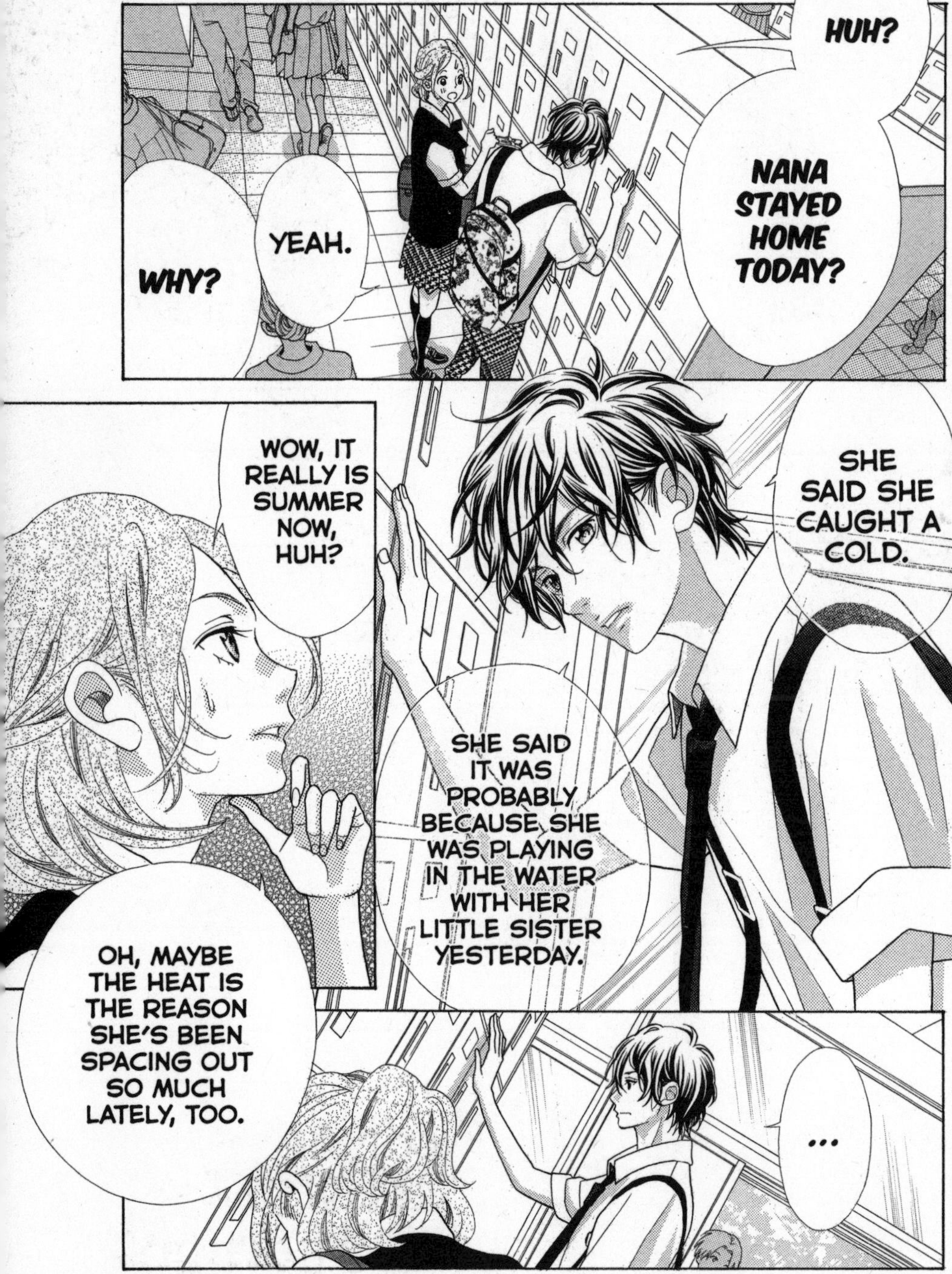
HUH?
NANA STAYED HOME TODAY?
YEAH.
WHY?
SHE SAID SHE CAUGHT A COLD.
SHE SAID IT WAS PROBABLY BECAUSE SHE WAS PLAYING IN THE WATER WITH HER LITTLE SISTER YESTERDAY.
WOW, IT REALLY IS SUMMER NOW, HUH?
...
OH, MAYBE THE HEAT IS THE REASON SHE'S BEEN SPACING OUT SO MUCH LATELY, TOO.

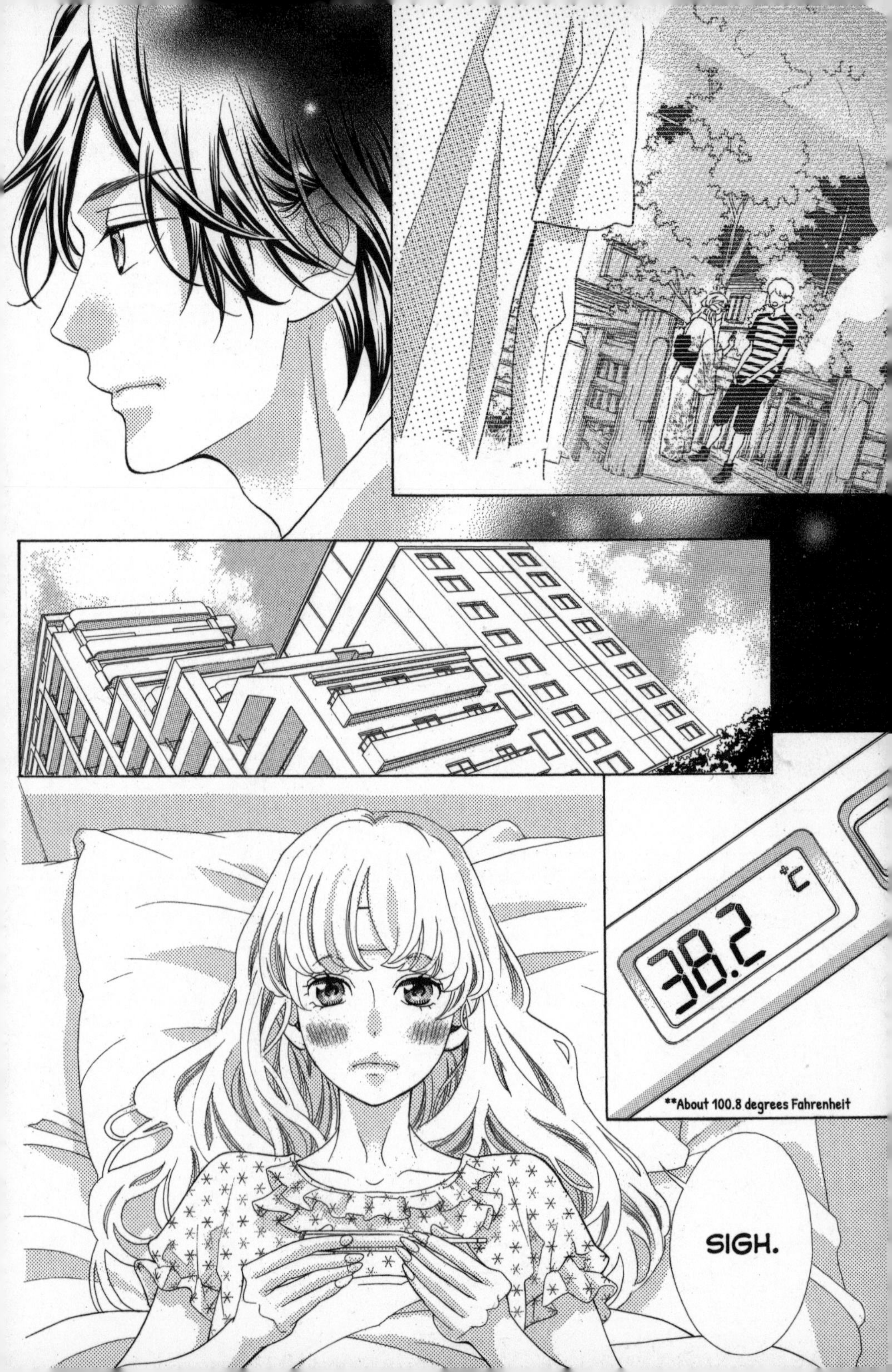
38.2 °C
**About 100.8 degrees Fahrenheit
SIGH.

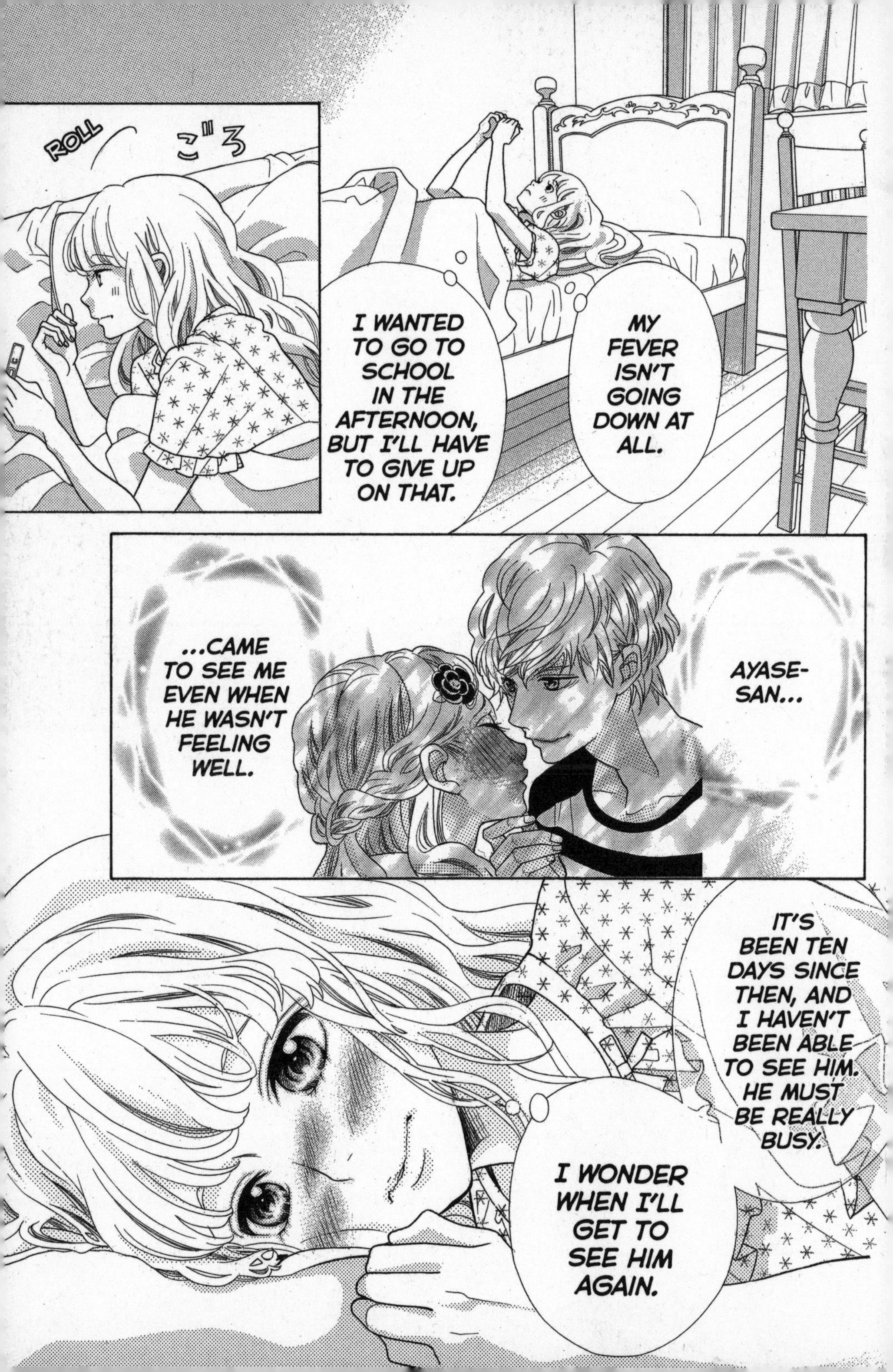
MY FEVER ISN'T GOING DOWN AT ALL.
I WANTED TO GO TO SCHOOL IN THE AFTERNOON, BUT I'LL HAVE TO GIVE UP ON THAT.
ROLL
ごろ
AYASE-SAN...
...CAME TO SEE ME EVEN WHEN HE WASN'T FEELING WELL.
IT'S BEEN TEN DAYS SINCE THEN, AND I HAVEN'T BEEN ABLE TO SEE HIM. HE MUST BE REALLY BUSY.
I WONDER WHEN I'LL GET TO SEE HIM AGAIN.

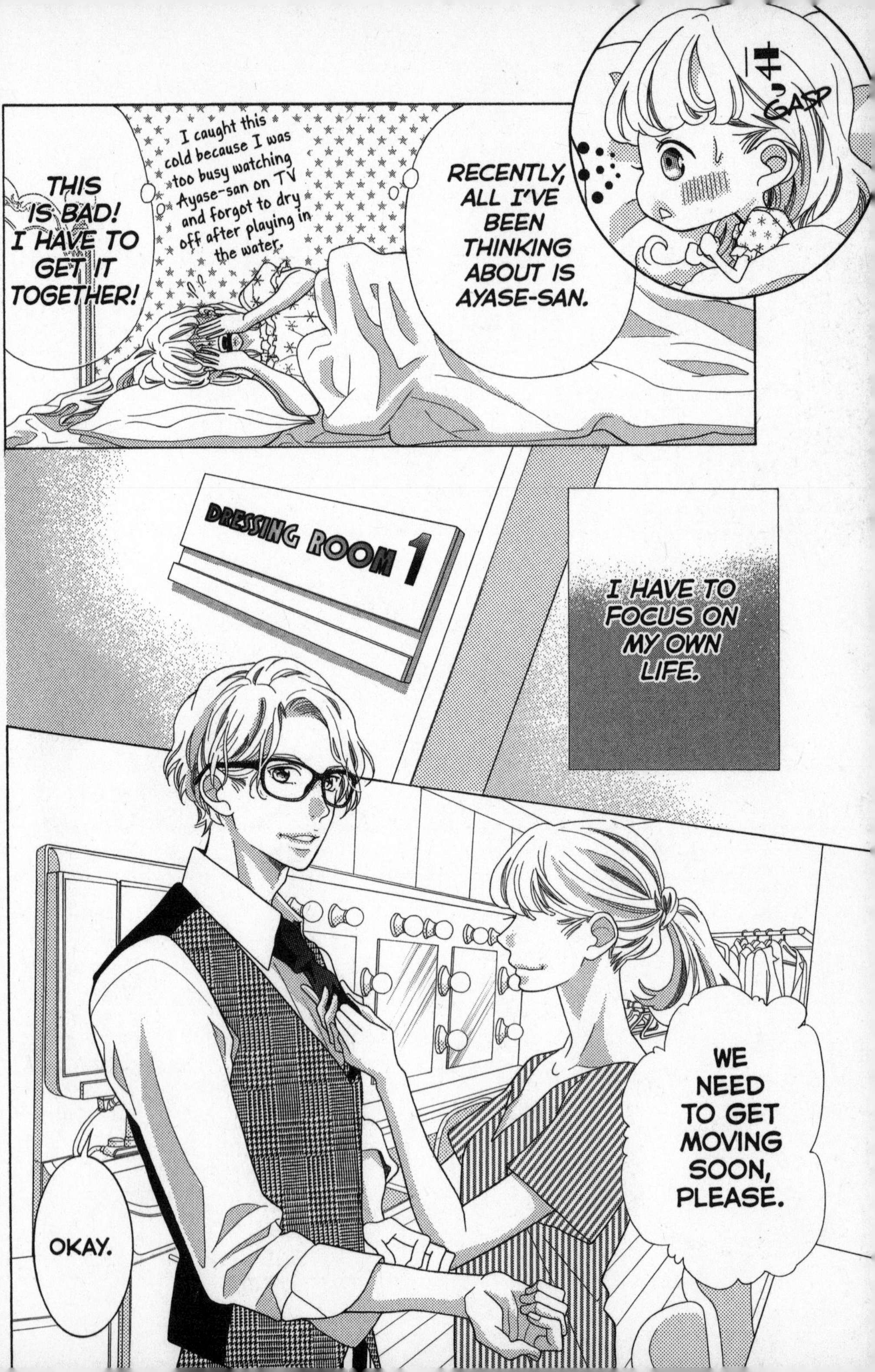
はっ
GASP
RECENTLY, ALL I'VE BEEN THINKING ABOUT IS AYASE-SAN.
I caught this cold because I was too busy watching Ayase-san on TV and forgot to dry off after playing in the water.
THIS IS BAD! I HAVE TO GET IT TOGETHER!
I HAVE TO FOCUS ON MY OWN LIFE.
DRESSING ROOM 1
WE NEED TO GET MOVING SOON, PLEASE.
OKAY.

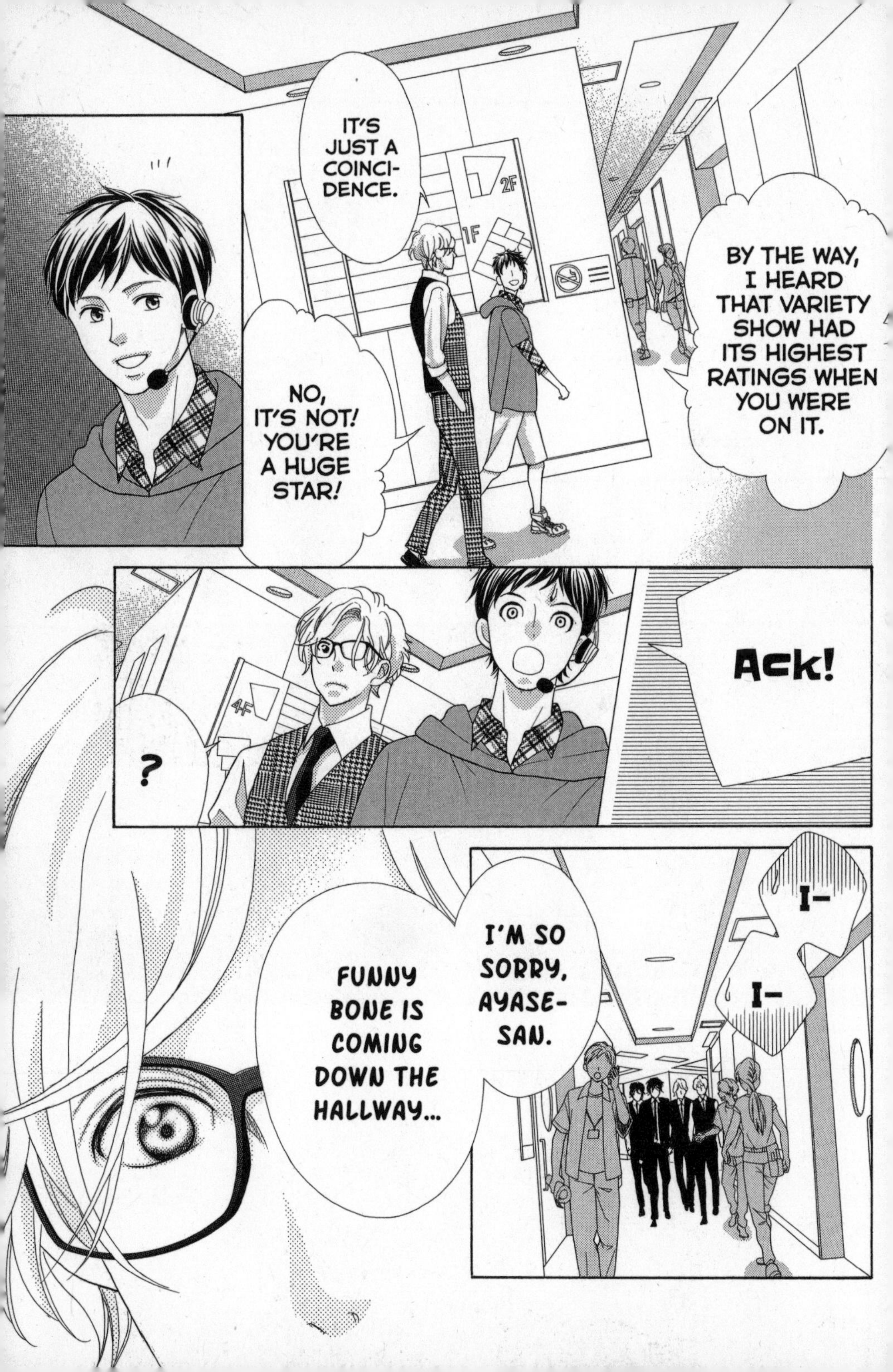
BY THE WAY, I HEARD THAT VARIETY SHOW HAD ITS HIGHEST RATINGS WHEN YOU WERE ON IT.
IT'S JUST A COINCIDENCE.
NO, IT'S NOT! YOU'RE A HUGE STAR!
ACK!
?
I-
I-
I'M SO SORRY, AYASE-SAN.
FUNNY BONE IS COMING DOWN THE HALLWAY...

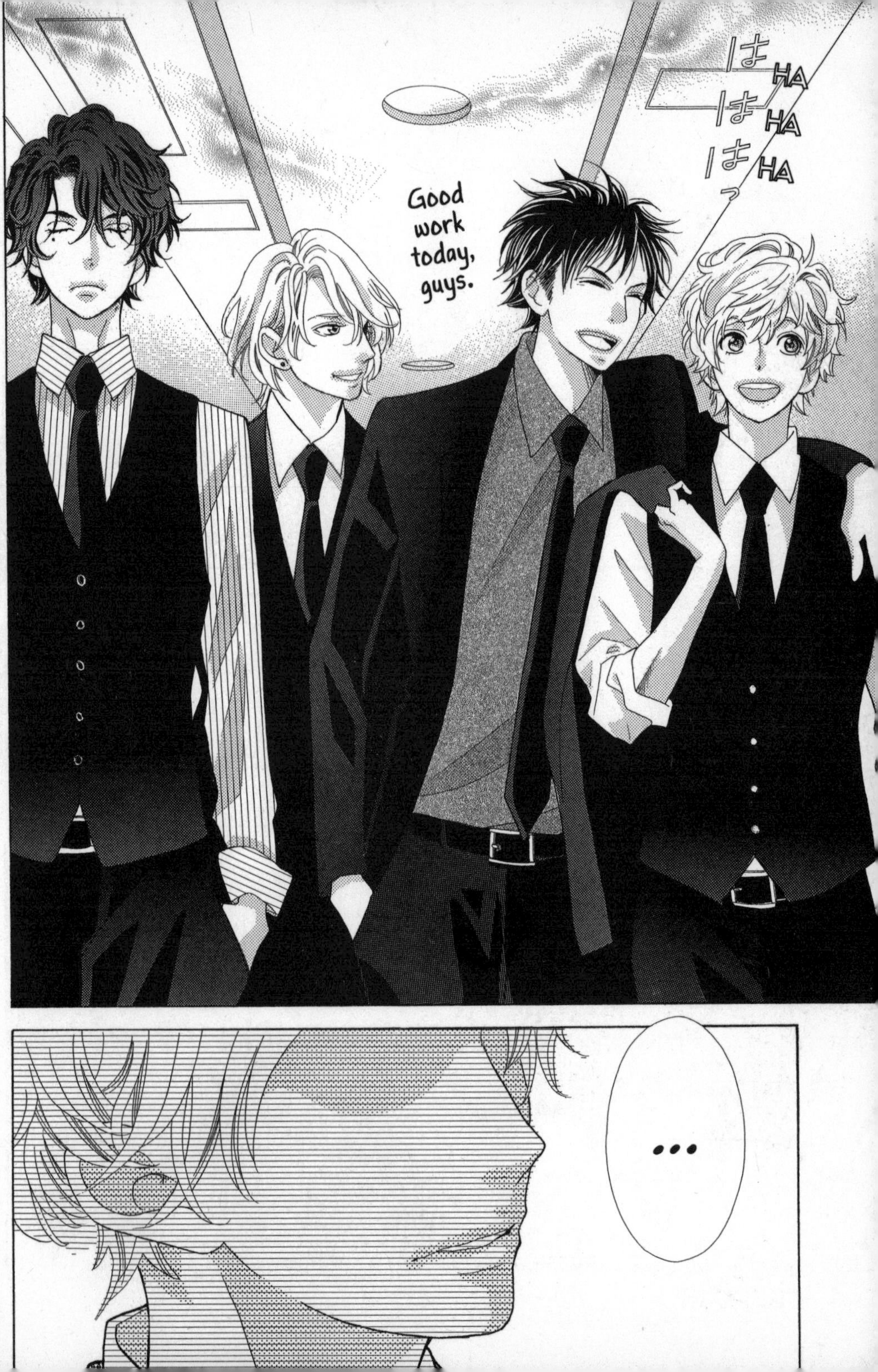
はははっ HA HA HA
Good work today, guys.
...

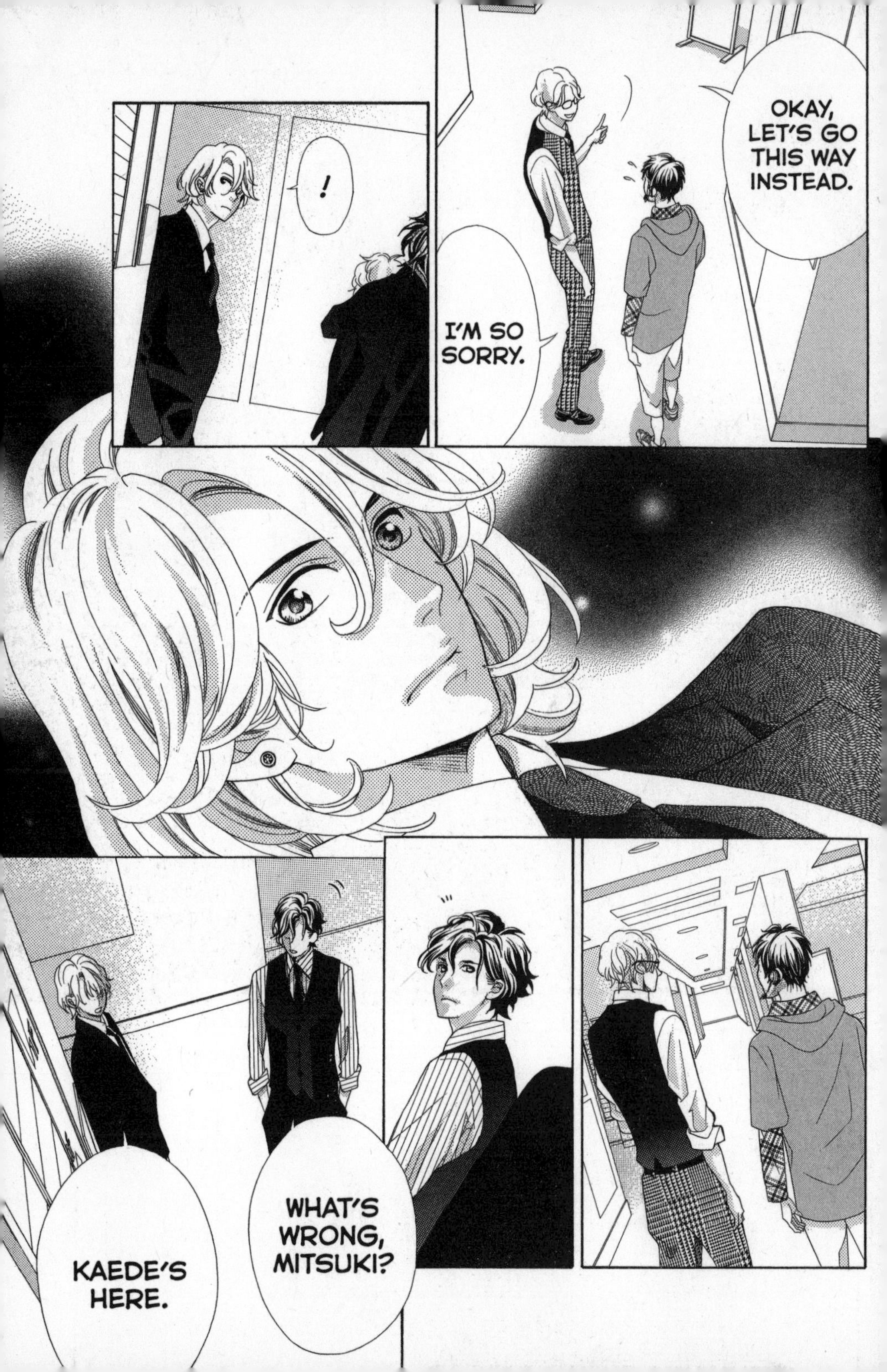
OKAY, LET'S GO THIS WAY INSTEAD.
I'M SO SORRY.
!
WHAT'S WRONG, MITSUKI?
KAEDE'S HERE.

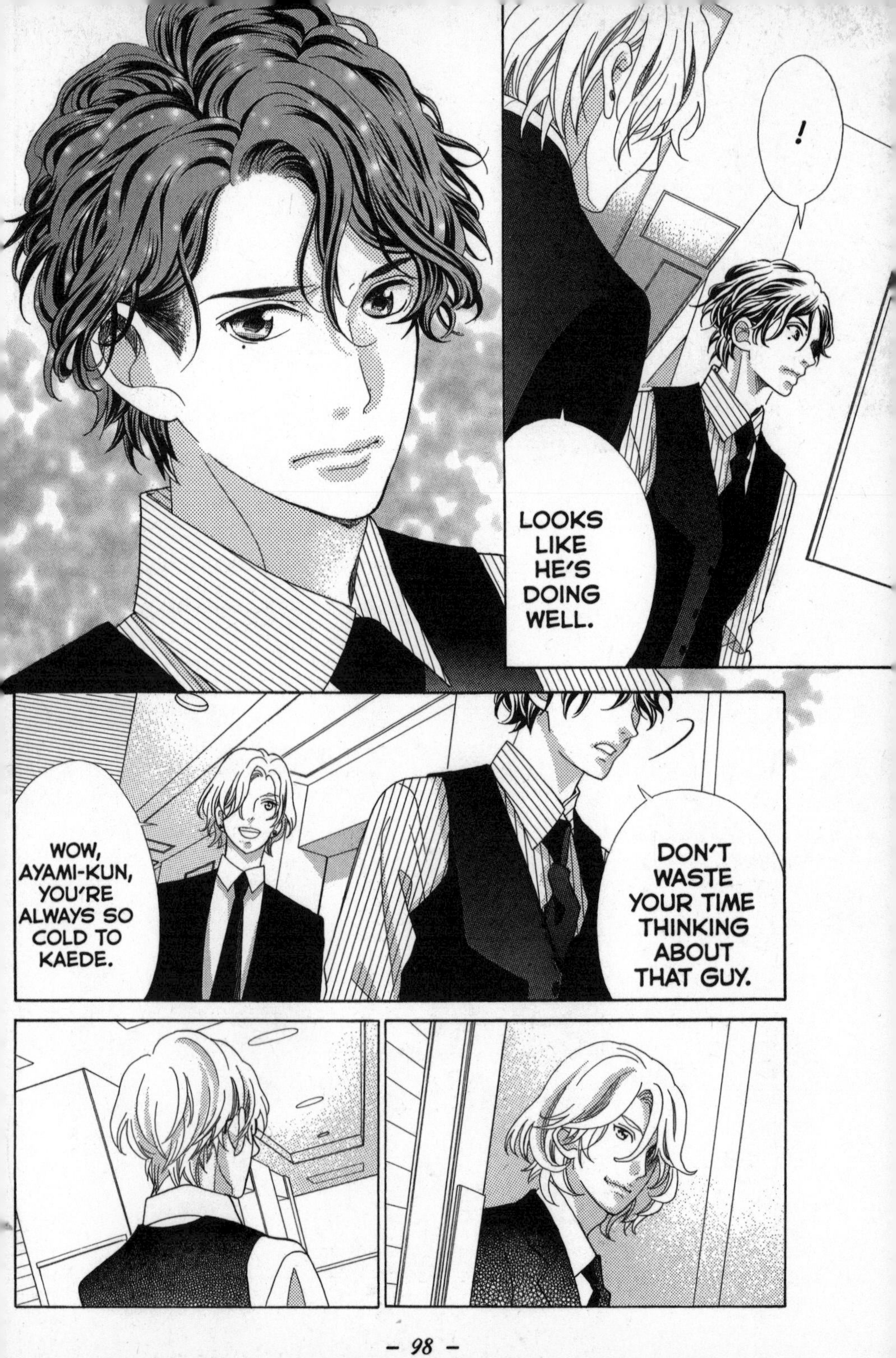
!
LOOKS LIKE HE'S DOING WELL.
DON'T WASTE YOUR TIME THINKING ABOUT THAT GUY.
WOW, AYAMI-KUN, YOU'RE ALWAYS SO COLD TO KAEDE.

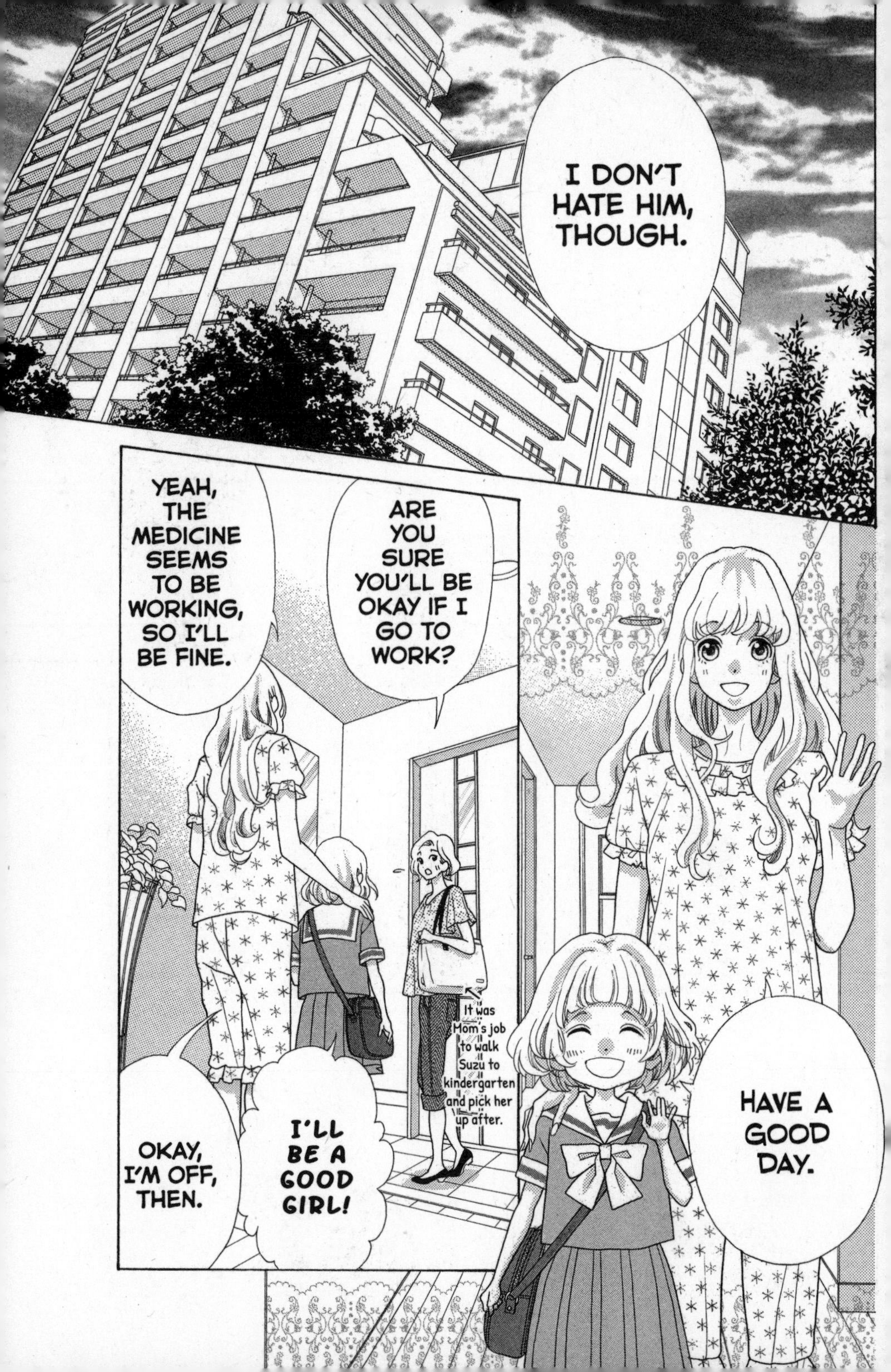
I DON'T HATE HIM, THOUGH.
ARE YOU SURE YOU'LL BE OKAY IF I GO TO WORK?
YEAH, THE MEDICINE SEEMS TO BE WORKING, SO I'LL BE FINE.
It was Mom's job to walk Suzu to kindergarten and pick her up after.
OKAY, I'M OFF, THEN.
I'LL BE A GOOD GIRL!
HAVE A GOOD DAY.

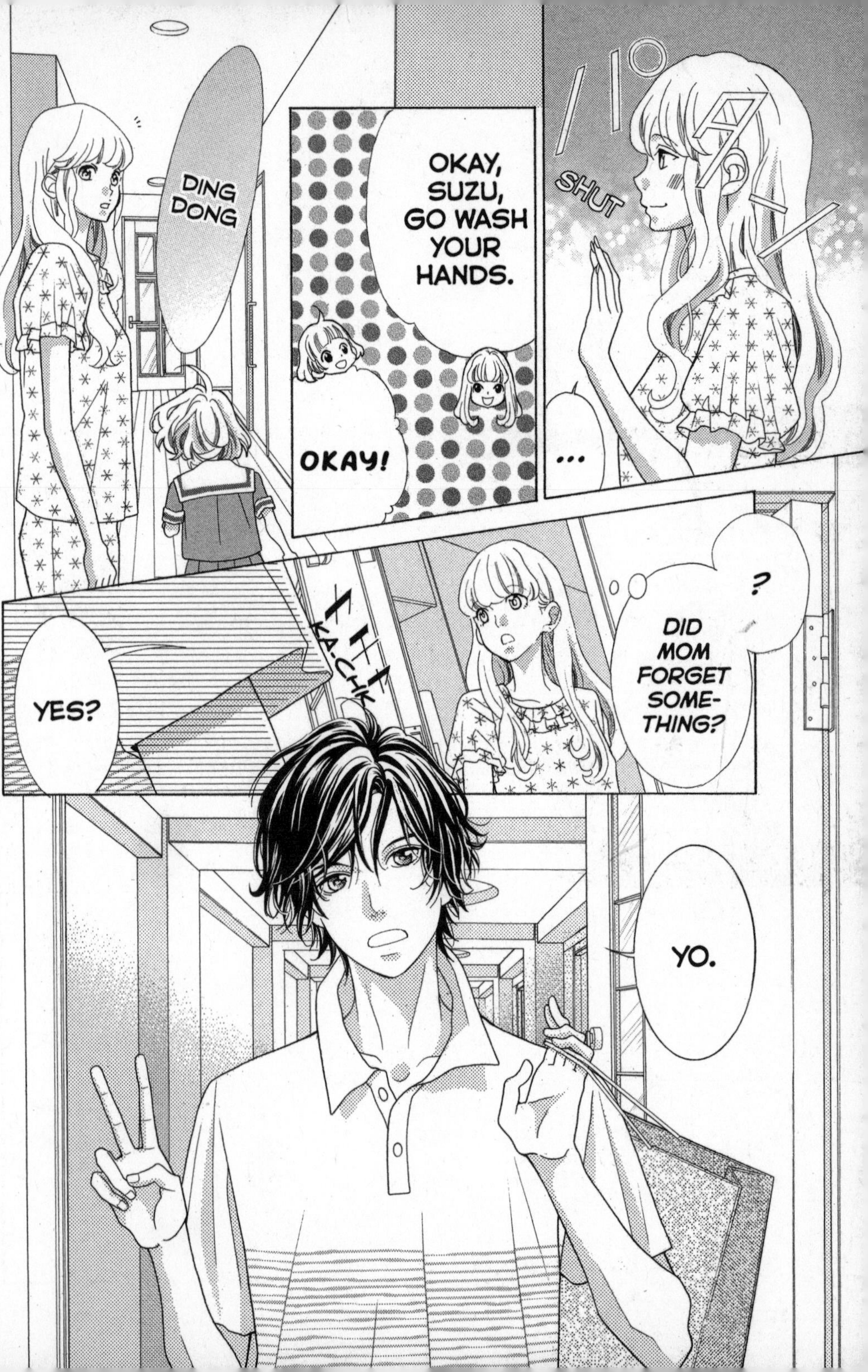
SHUT
...
OKAY, SUZU, GO WASH YOUR HANDS.
OKAY!
DING DONG
?
DID MOM FORGET SOME-THING?
KA-CHIK
YES?
YO.

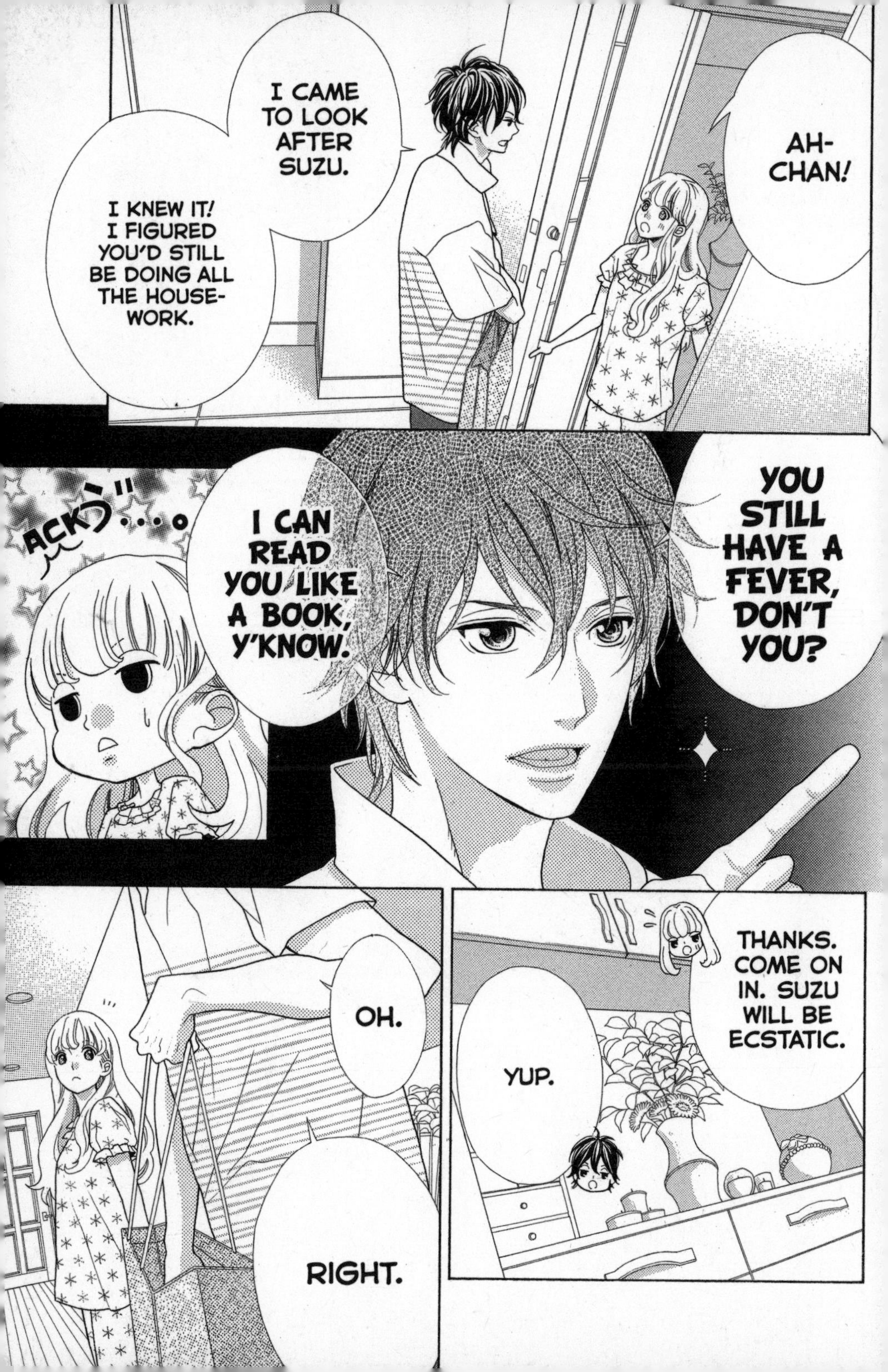
AH-CHAN!
I CAME TO LOOK AFTER SUZU.
I KNEW IT! I FIGURED YOU'D STILL BE DOING ALL THE HOUSE-WORK.
YOU STILL HAVE A FEVER, DON'T YOU?
I CAN READ YOU LIKE A BOOK, Y'KNOW.
ACK
THANKS. COME ON IN. SUZU WILL BE ECSTATIC.
YUP.
OH.
RIGHT.

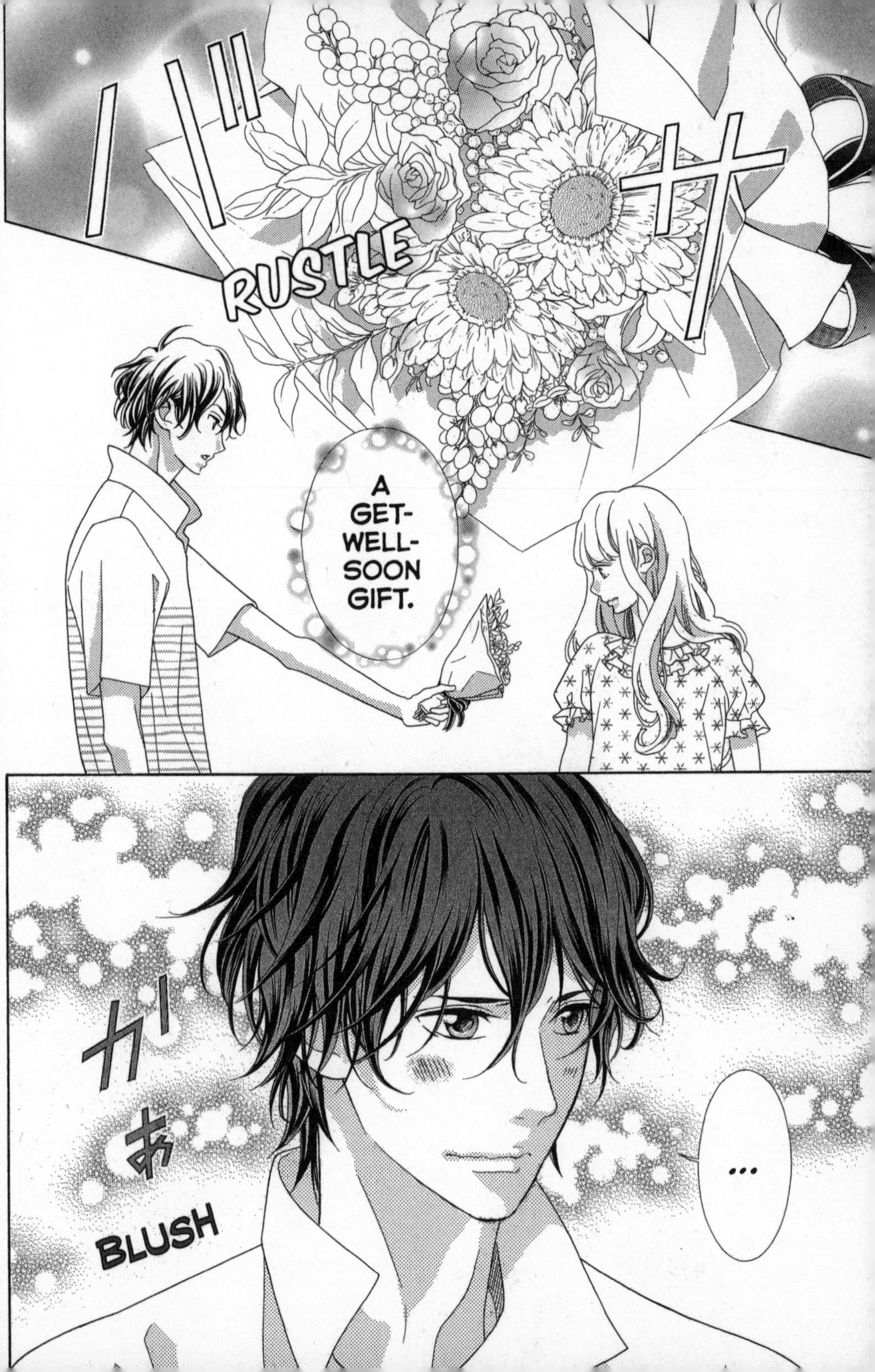
RUSTLE
A GET-WELL-SOON GIFT.
...
BLUSH

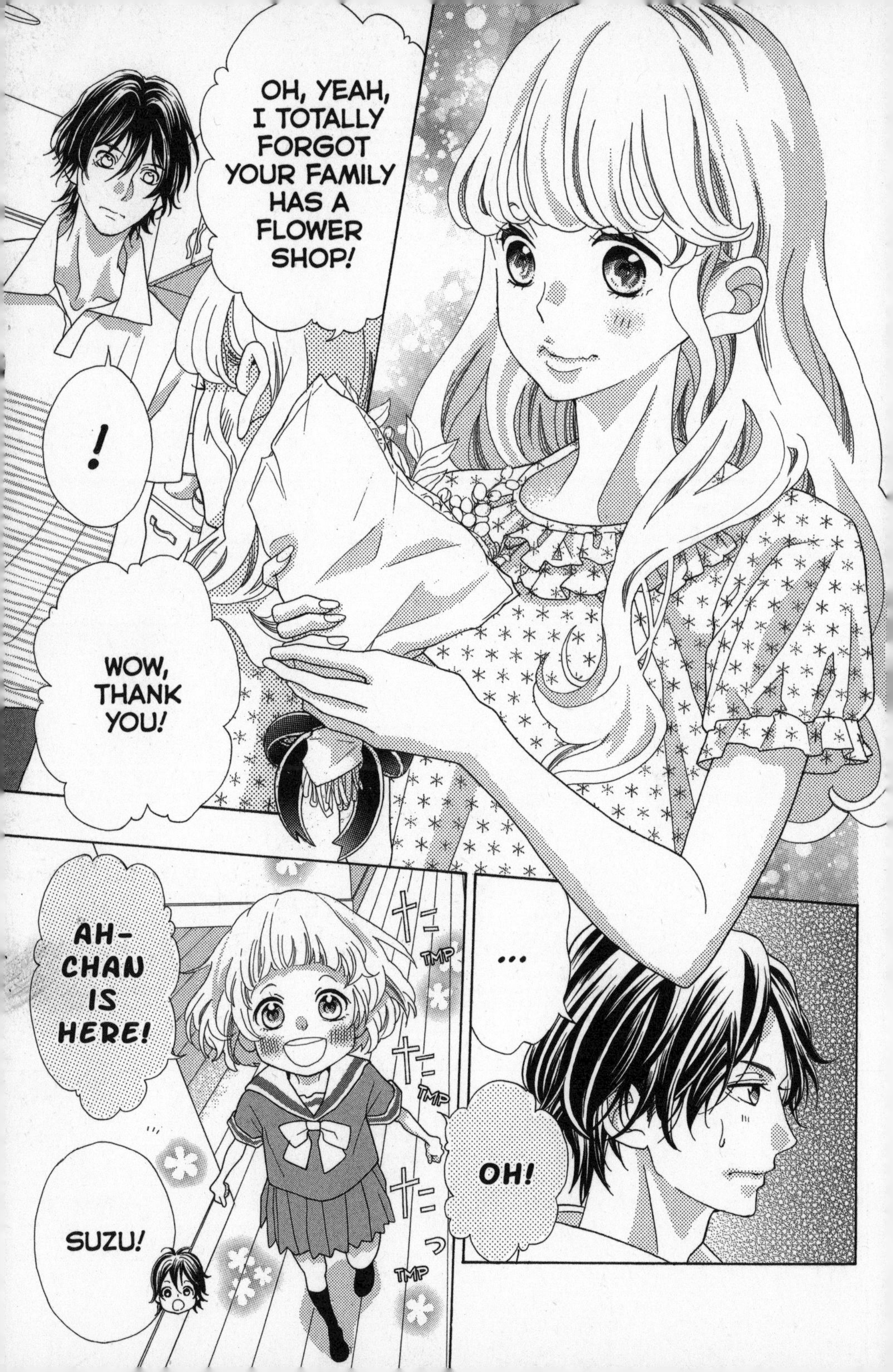
OH, YEAH, I TOTALLY FORGOT YOUR FAMILY HAS A FLOWER SHOP!
!
WOW, THANK YOU!
...
OH!
AH-CHAN IS HERE!
TMP
TMP
TMP
SUZU!

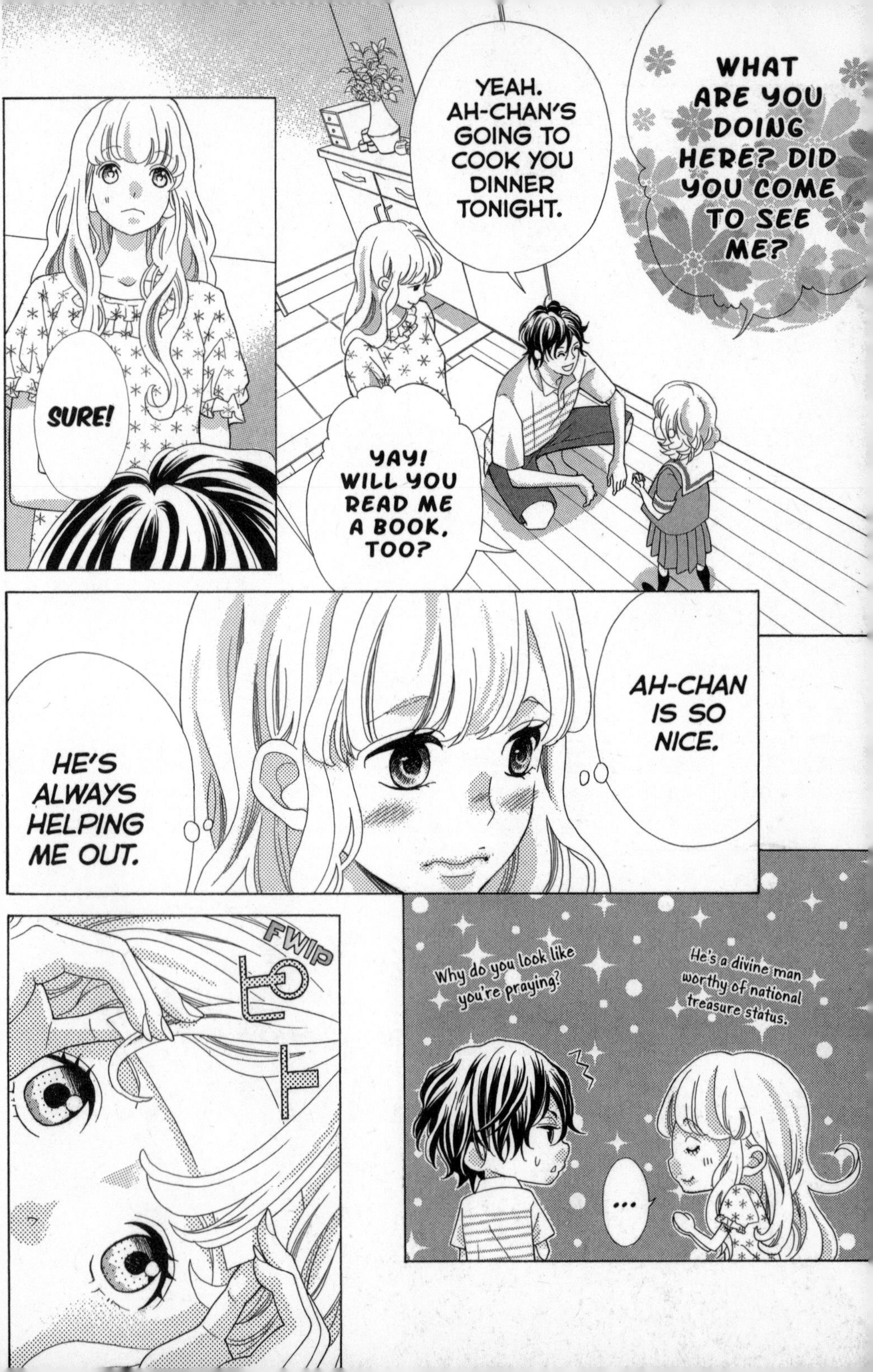
WHAT ARE YOU DOING HERE? DID YOU COME TO SEE ME?
YEAH. AH-CHAN'S GOING TO COOK YOU DINNER TONIGHT.
YAY! WILL YOU READ ME A BOOK, TOO?
SURE!
AH-CHAN IS SO NICE.
HE'S ALWAYS HELPING ME OUT.
He's a divine man worthy of national treasure status.
Why do you look like you're praying?
...
FWIP

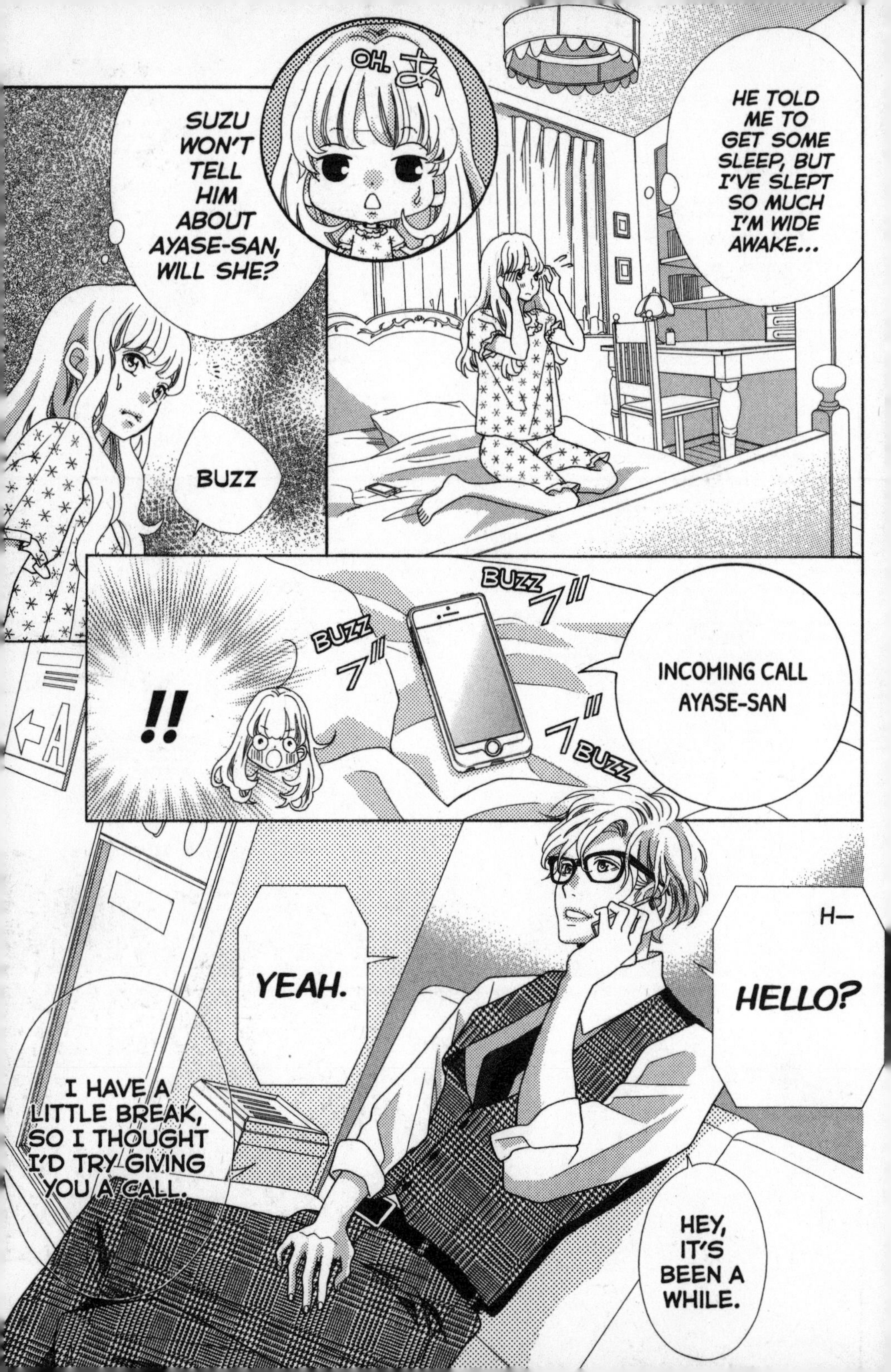
HE TOLD ME TO GET SOME SLEEP, BUT I'VE SLEPT SO MUCH I'M WIDE AWAKE...
OH. あ
SUZU WON'T TELL HIM ABOUT AYASE-SAN, WILL SHE?
BUZZ
BUZZ
INCOMING CALL AYASE-SAN
BUZZ
BUZZ
!!
H—
HELLO?
YEAH.
HEY, IT'S BEEN A WHILE.
I HAVE A LITTLE BREAK, SO I THOUGHT I'D TRY GIVING YOU A CALL.

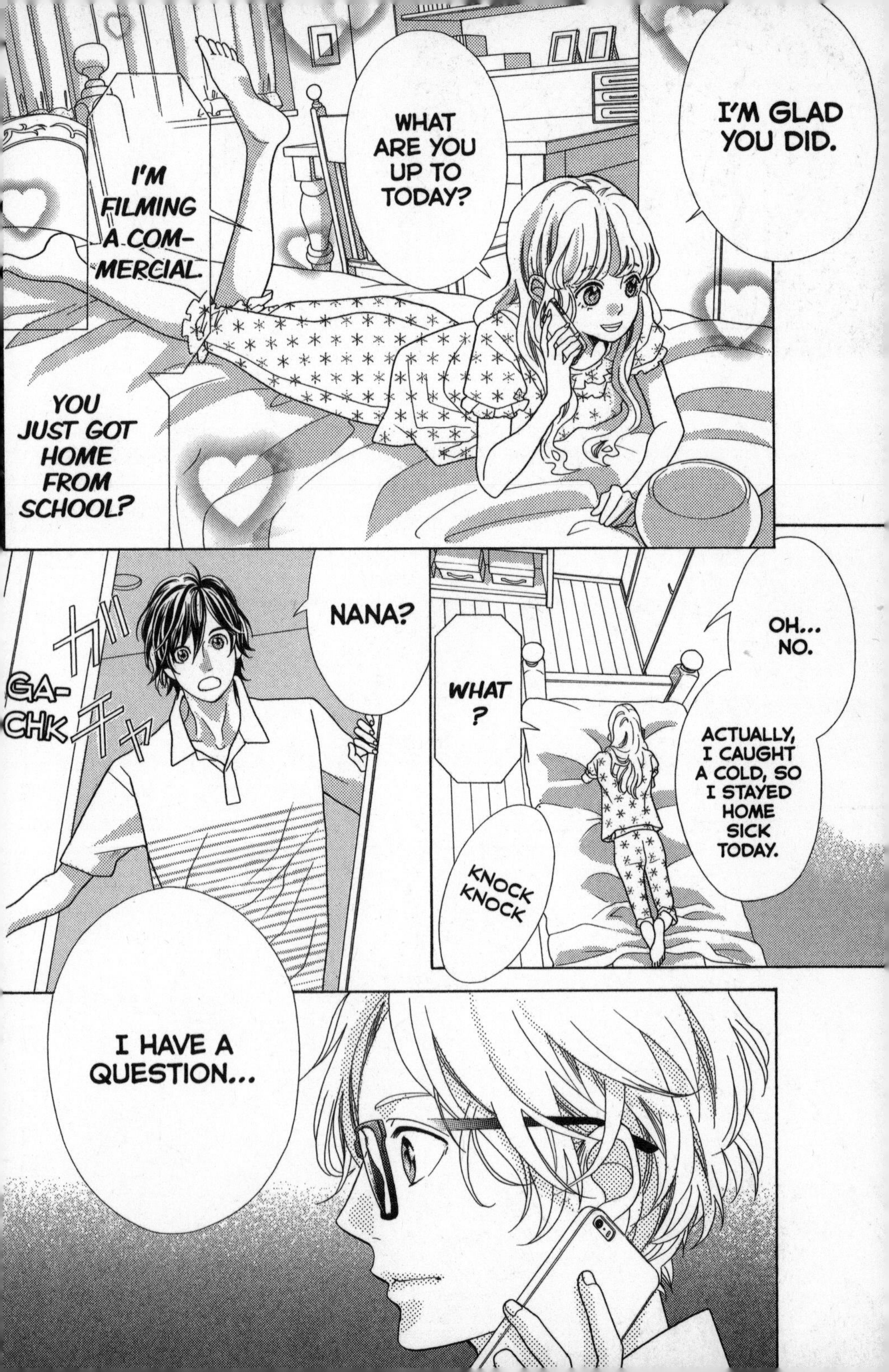
I'M GLAD YOU DID.
WHAT ARE YOU UP TO TODAY?
I'M FILMING A COM-MERCIAL
YOU JUST GOT HOME FROM SCHOOL?
OH... NO.
ACTUALLY, I CAUGHT A COLD, SO I STAYED HOME SICK TODAY.
WHAT?
KNOCK KNOCK
NANA?
GA-CHK
I HAVE A QUESTION...

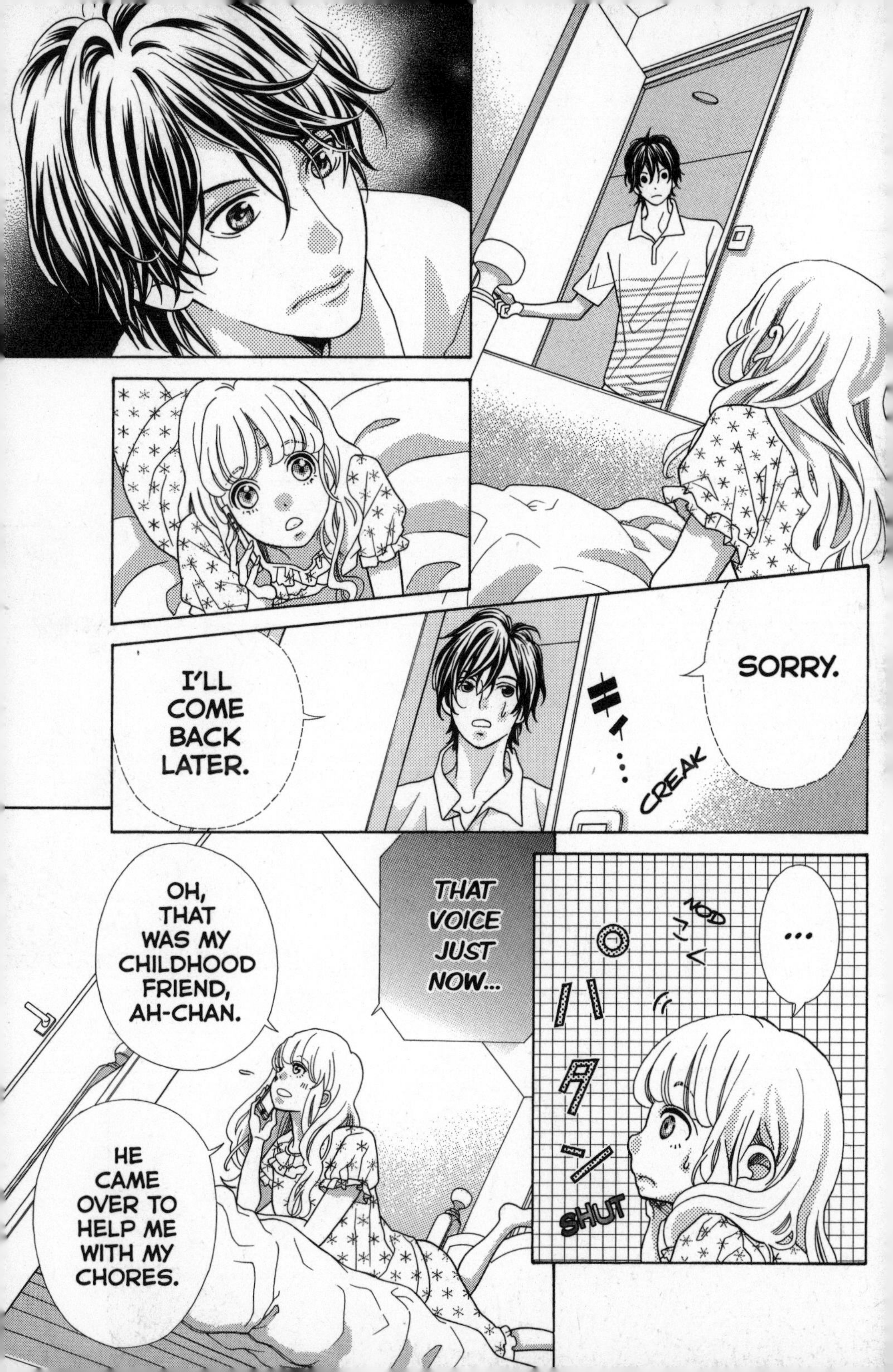
SORRY.
CREAK
I'LL COME BACK LATER.
...
NOD
SHUT
THAT VOICE JUST NOW...
OH, THAT WAS MY CHILDHOOD FRIEND, AH-CHAN.
HE CAME OVER TO HELP ME WITH MY CHORES.

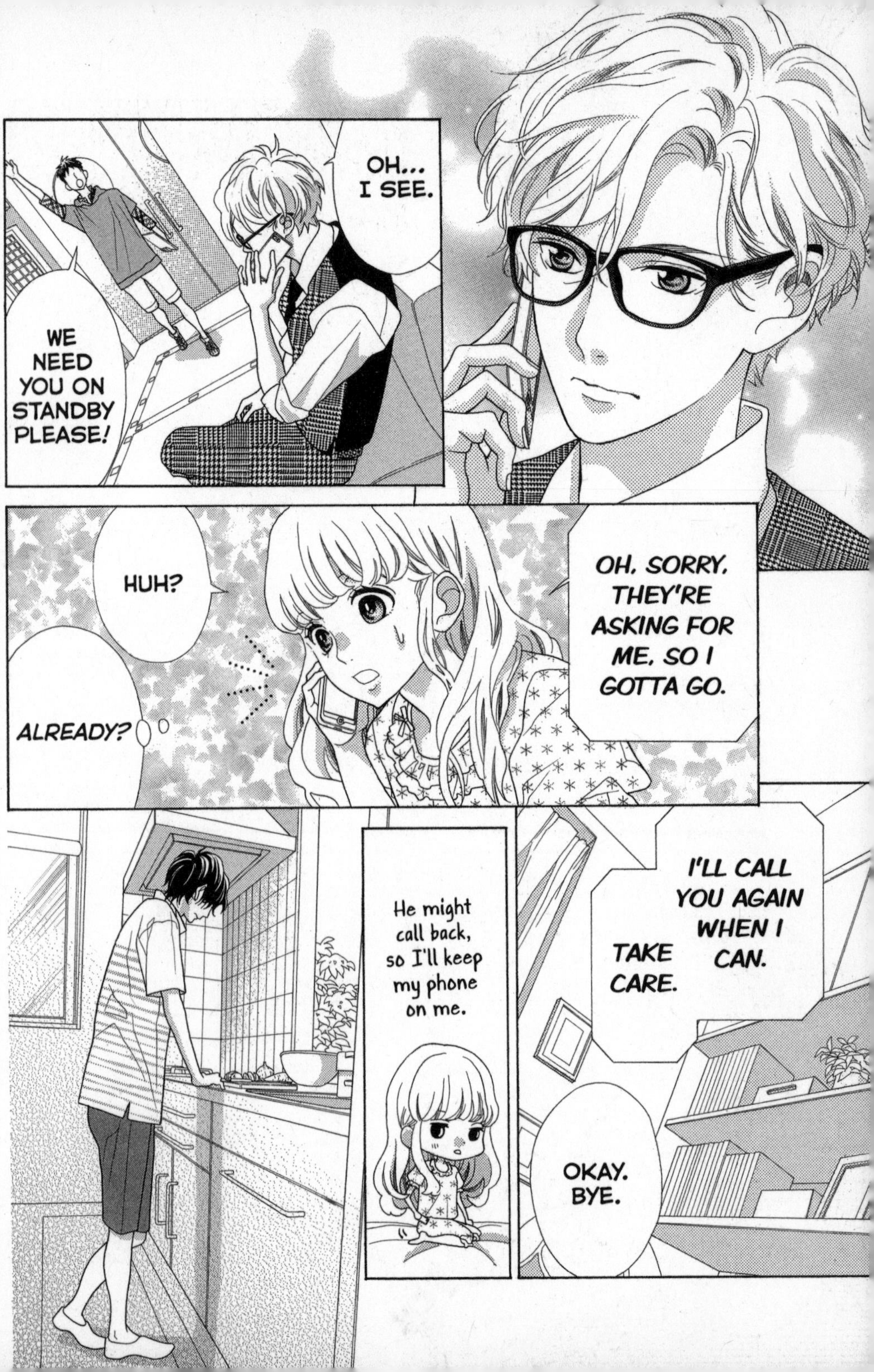
OH... I SEE.
WE NEED YOU ON STANDBY PLEASE!
OH. SORRY. THEY'RE ASKING FOR ME, SO I GOTTA GO.
HUH?
ALREADY?
I'LL CALL YOU AGAIN WHEN I CAN.
TAKE CARE.
OKAY. BYE.
He might call back, so I'll keep my phone on me.

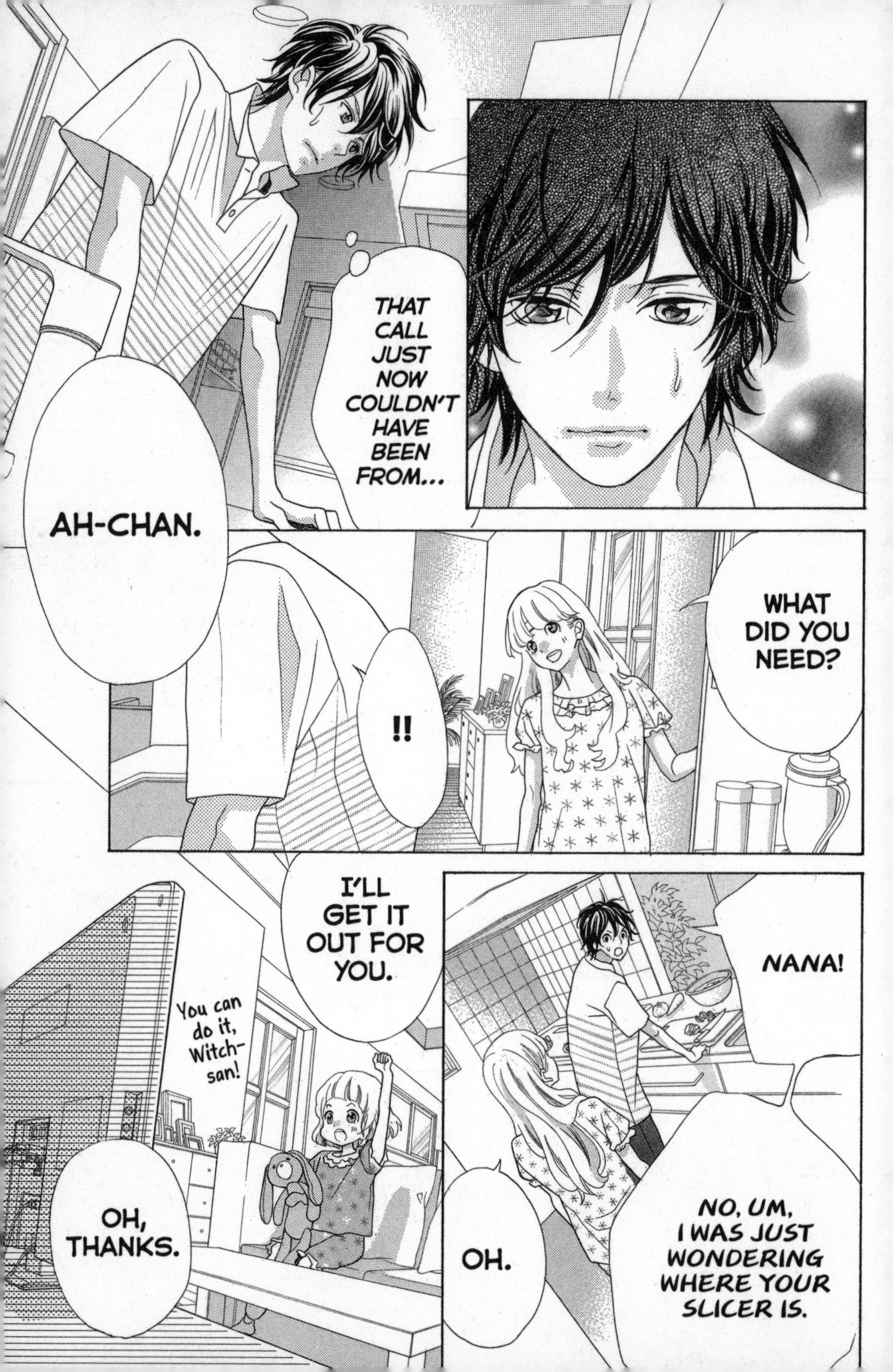
THAT CALL JUST NOW COULDN'T HAVE BEEN FROM...
AH-CHAN.
WHAT DID YOU NEED?
!!
NANA!
NO, UM, I WAS JUST WONDERING WHERE YOUR SLICER IS.
OH.
I'LL GET IT OUT FOR YOU.
You can do it, Witch-san!
OH, THANKS.

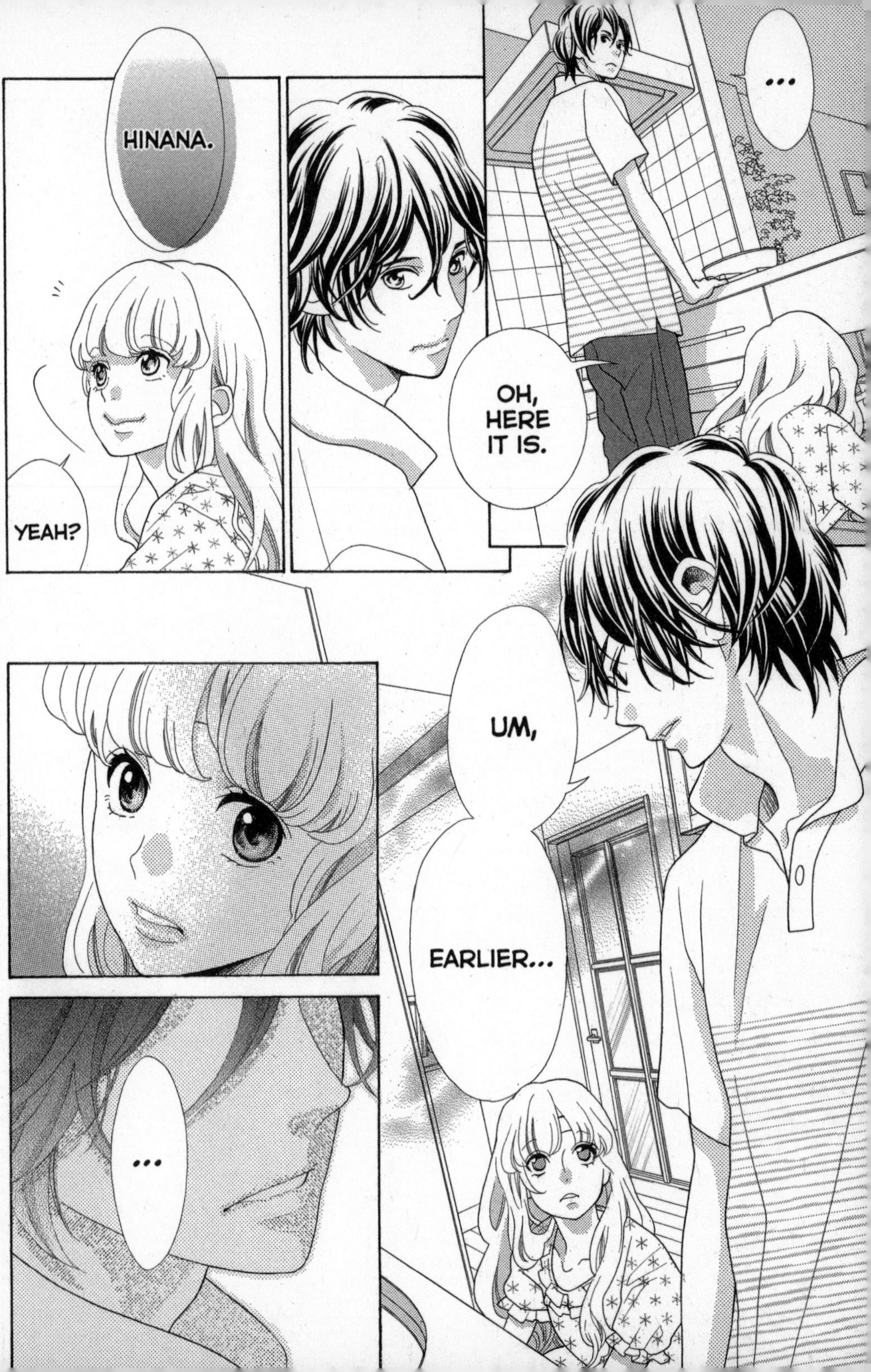
...
OH, HERE IT IS.
HINANA.
YEAH?
UM,
EARLIER...
...

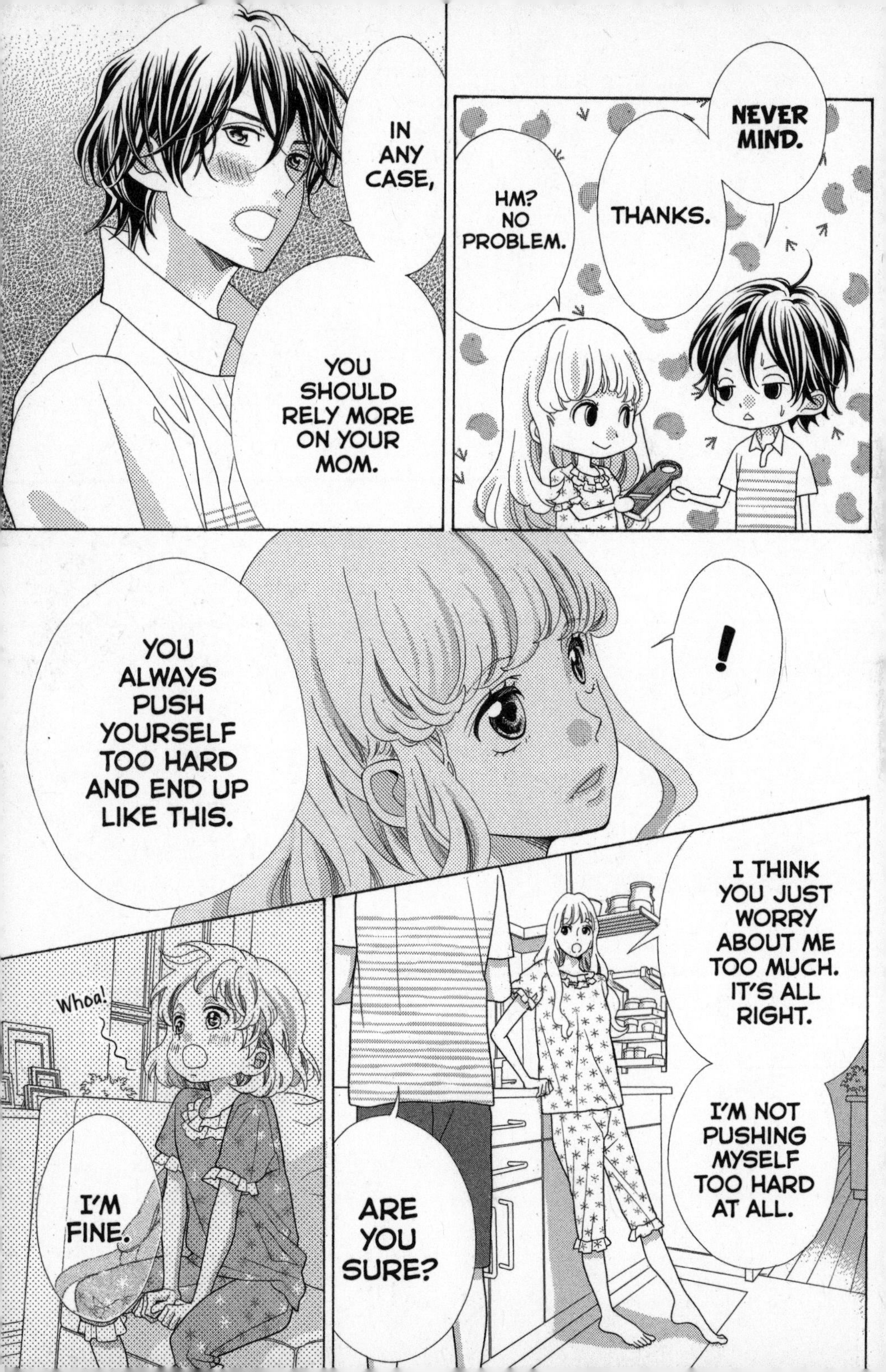
NEVER MIND.
THANKS.
HM? NO PROBLEM.
IN ANY CASE,
YOU SHOULD RELY MORE ON YOUR MOM.
!
YOU ALWAYS PUSH YOURSELF TOO HARD AND END UP LIKE THIS.
I THINK YOU JUST WORRY ABOUT ME TOO MUCH. IT'S ALL RIGHT.
I'M NOT PUSHING MYSELF TOO HARD AT ALL.
ARE YOU SURE?
Whoa!
I'M FINE.

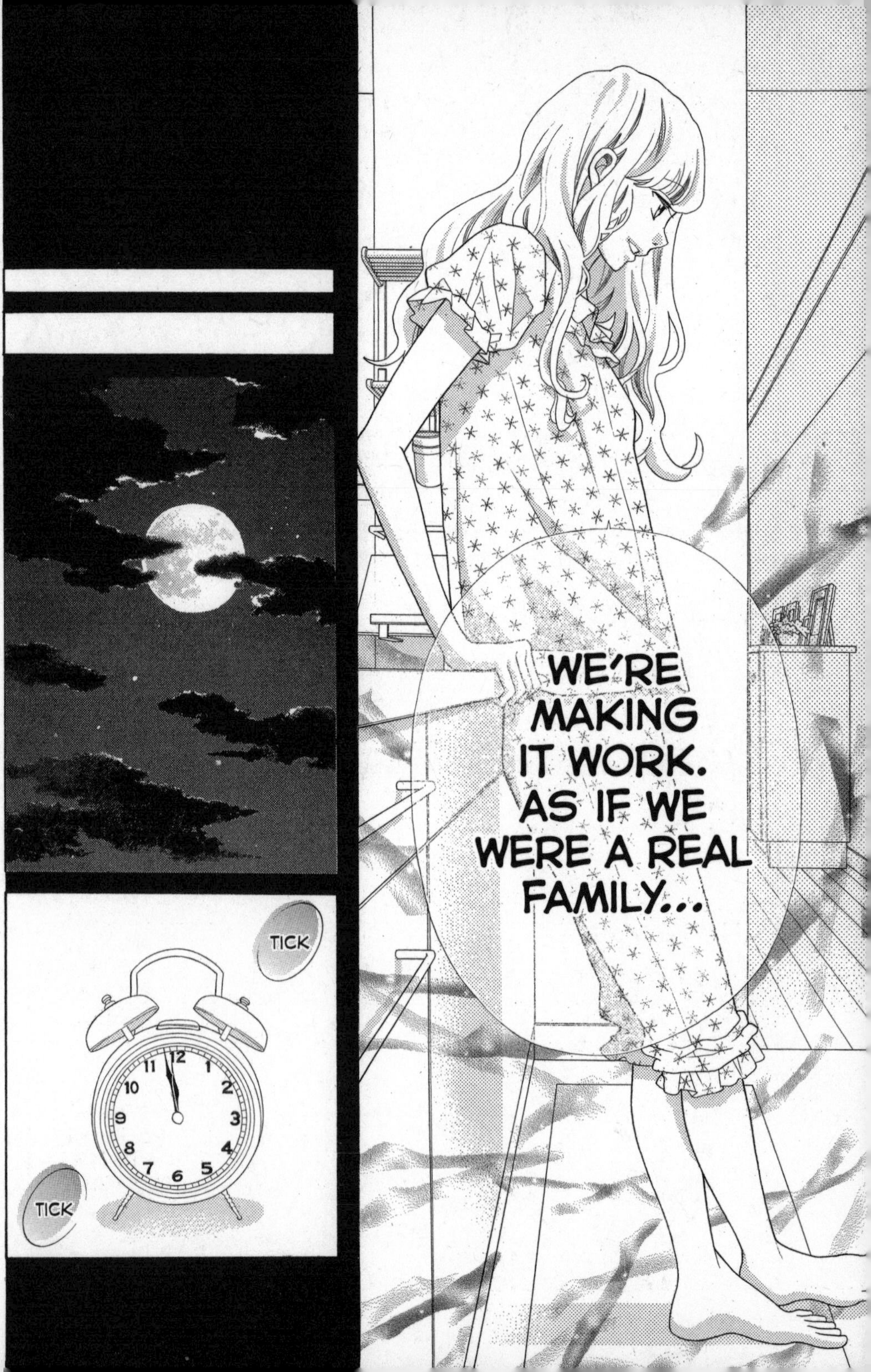
WE'RE MAKING IT WORK. AS IF WE WERE A REAL FAMILY...
TICK
TICK

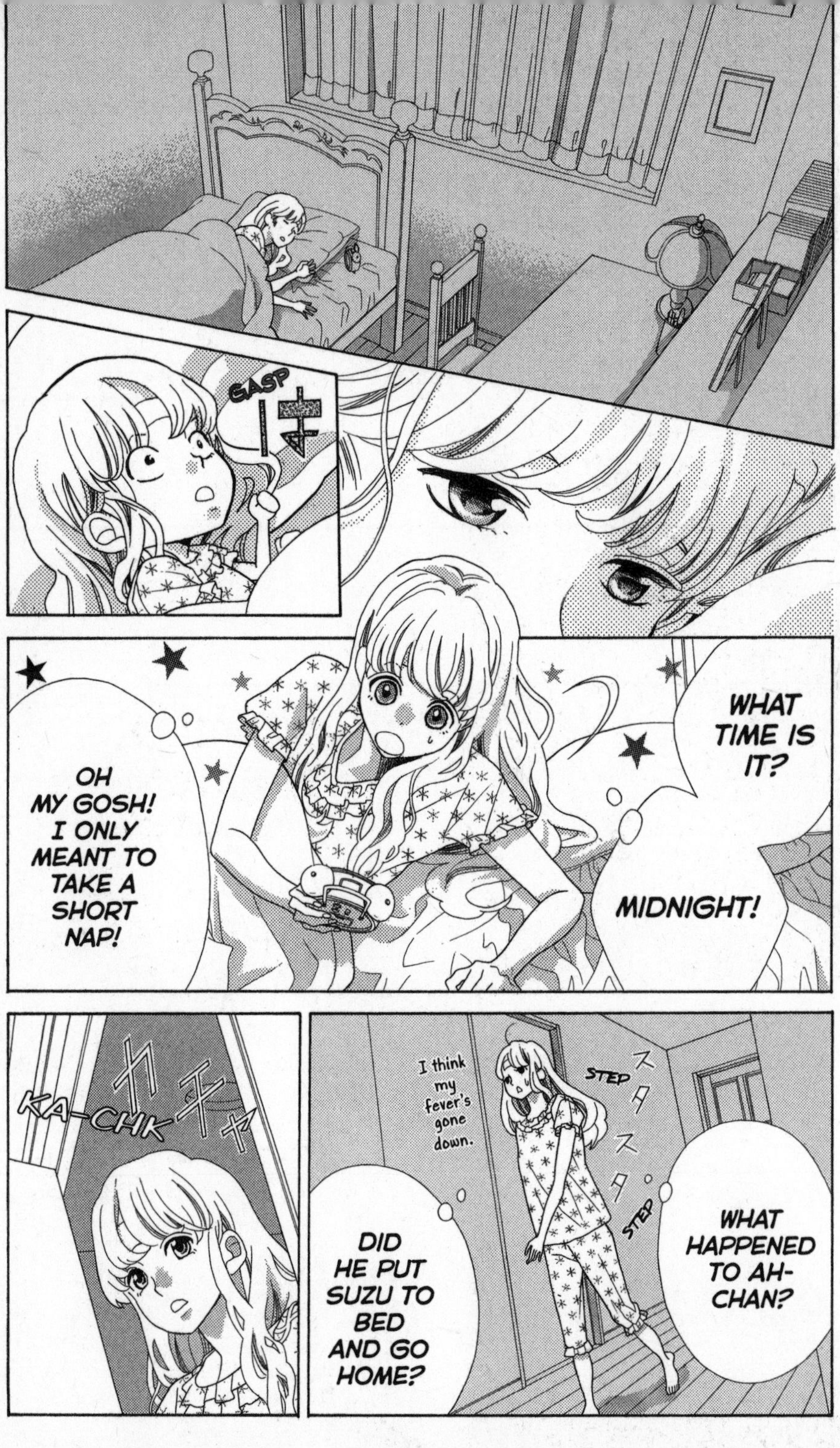

GASP
WHAT TIME IS IT?
MIDNIGHT!
OH MY GOSH! I ONLY MEANT TO TAKE A SHORT NAP!
I think my fever's gone down.
STEP
スタスタ
STEP
WHAT HAPPENED TO AH-CHAN?
DID HE PUT SUZU TO BED AND GO HOME?
KA-CHK
カチャ

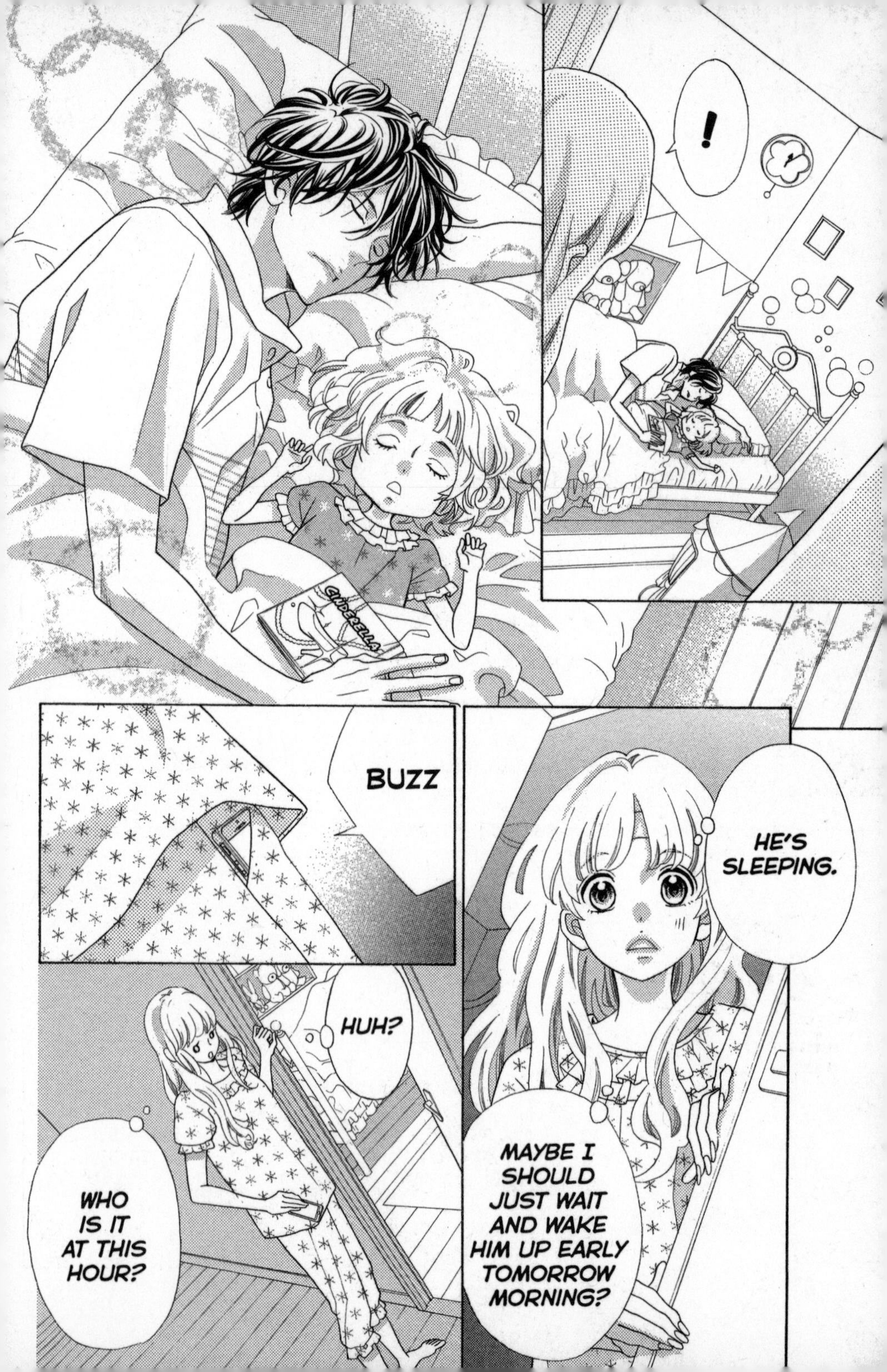
!
HE'S SLEEPING.
MAYBE I SHOULD JUST WAIT AND WAKE HIM UP EARLY TOMORROW MORNING?
BUZZ
HUH?
WHO IS IT AT THIS HOUR?
CINDERELLA

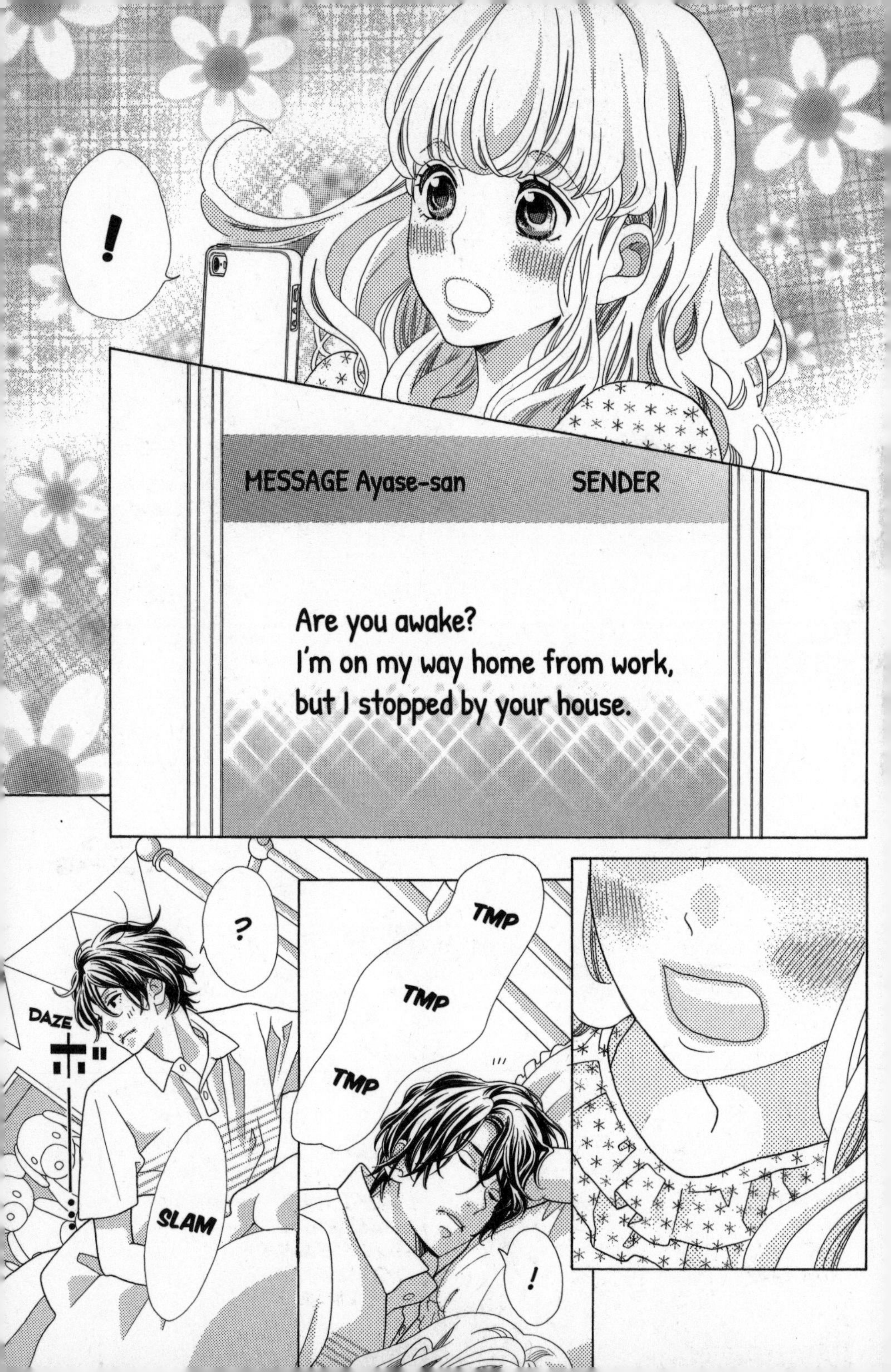
!
MESSAGE Ayase-san
SENDER
Are you awake?
I'm on my way home from work,
but I stopped by your house.
TMP
TMP
TMP
!
?
DAZE
SLAM

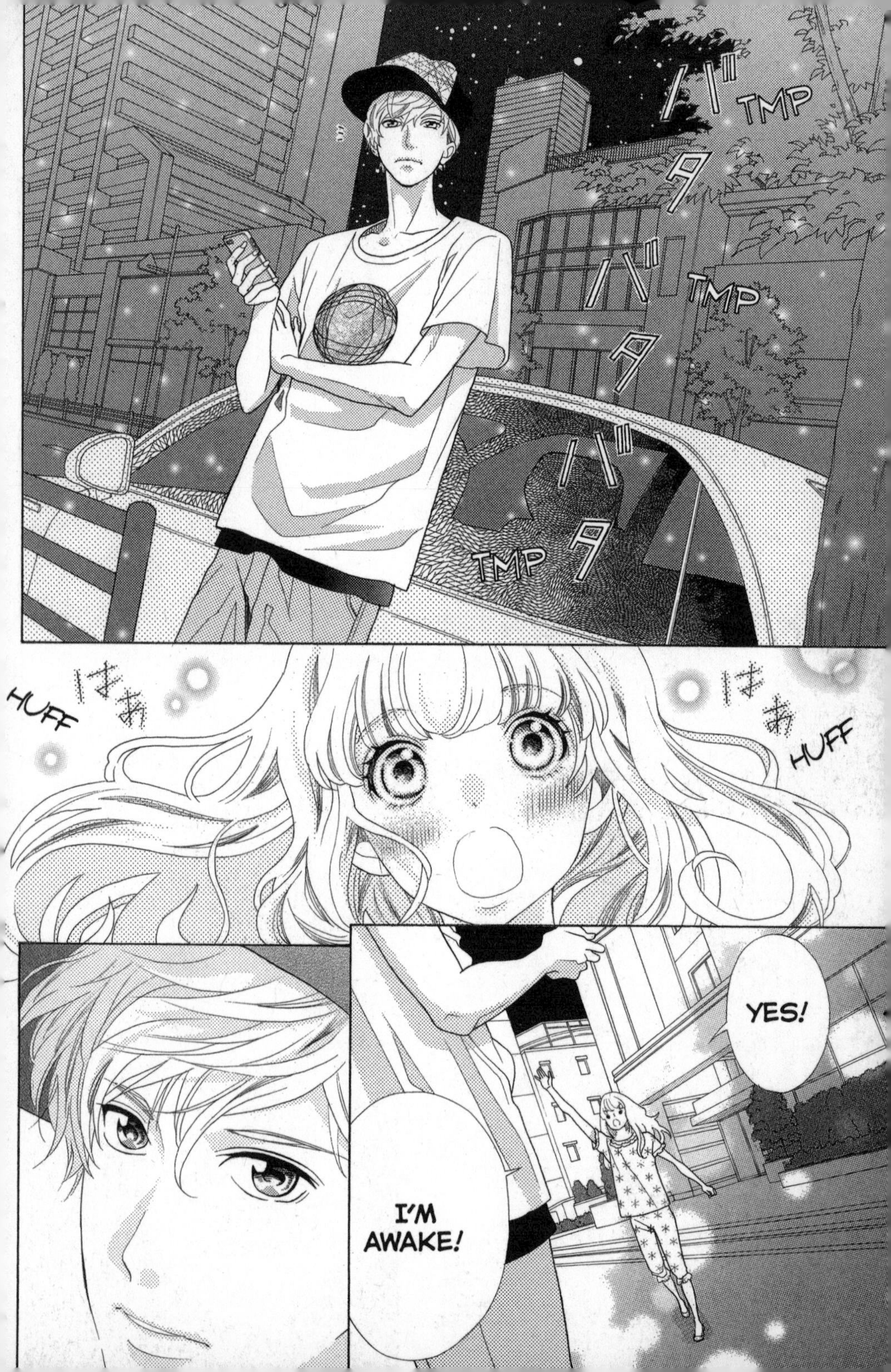
バ
TMP
タ
バ
TMP
タ
バ
タ
TMP
はあ
HUFF
はあ
HUFF
YES!
I'M AWAKE!

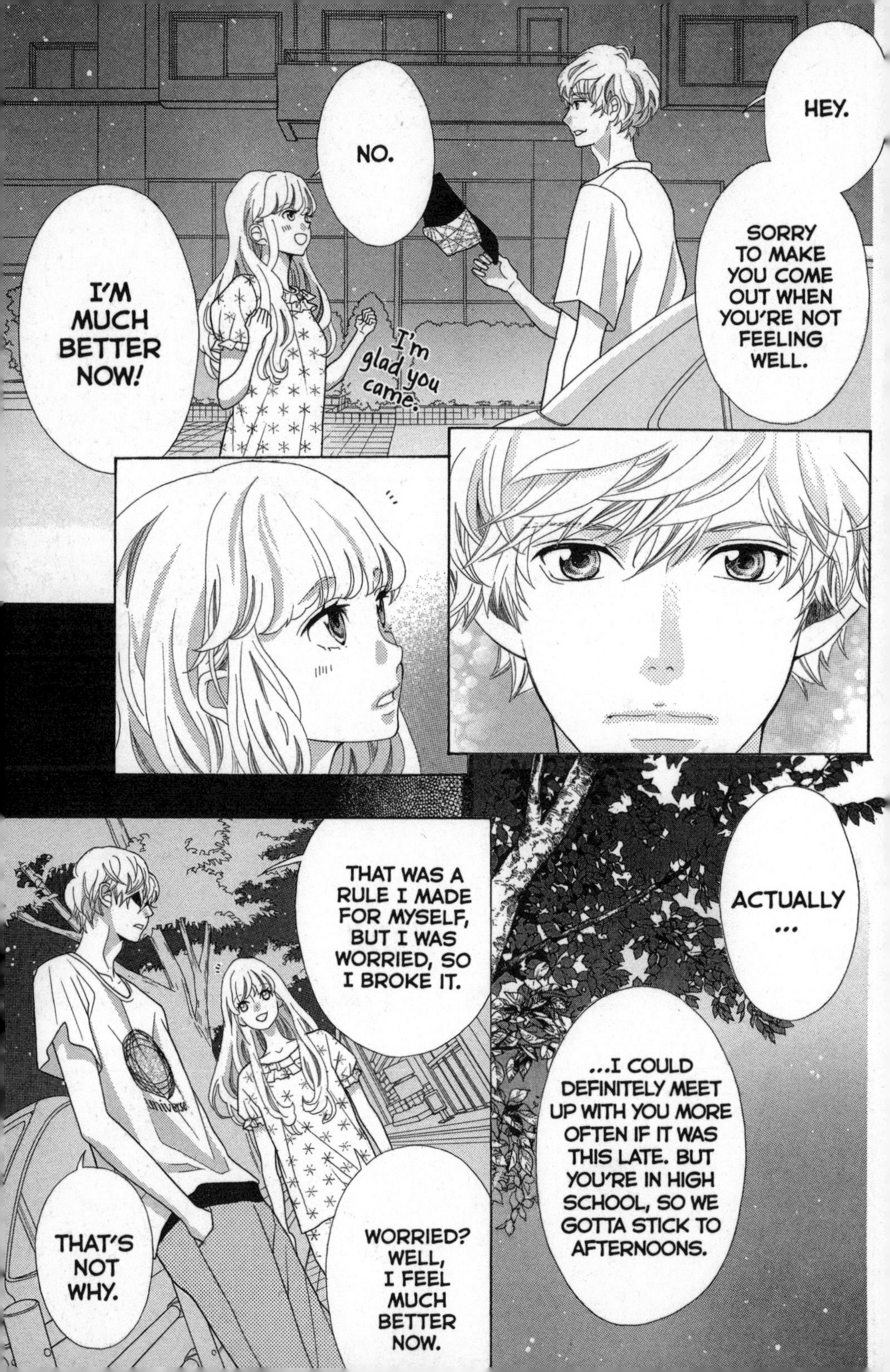
HEY.
SORRY TO MAKE YOU COME OUT WHEN YOU'RE NOT FEELING WELL.
NO.
I'm glad you came.
I'M MUCH BETTER NOW!
ACTUALLY...
...I COULD DEFINITELY MEET UP WITH YOU MORE OFTEN IF IT WAS THIS LATE. BUT YOU'RE IN HIGH SCHOOL, SO WE GOTTA STICK TO AFTERNOONS.
THAT WAS A RULE I MADE FOR MYSELF, BUT I WAS WORRIED, SO I BROKE IT.
WORRIED? WELL, I FEEL MUCH BETTER NOW.
THAT'S NOT WHY.

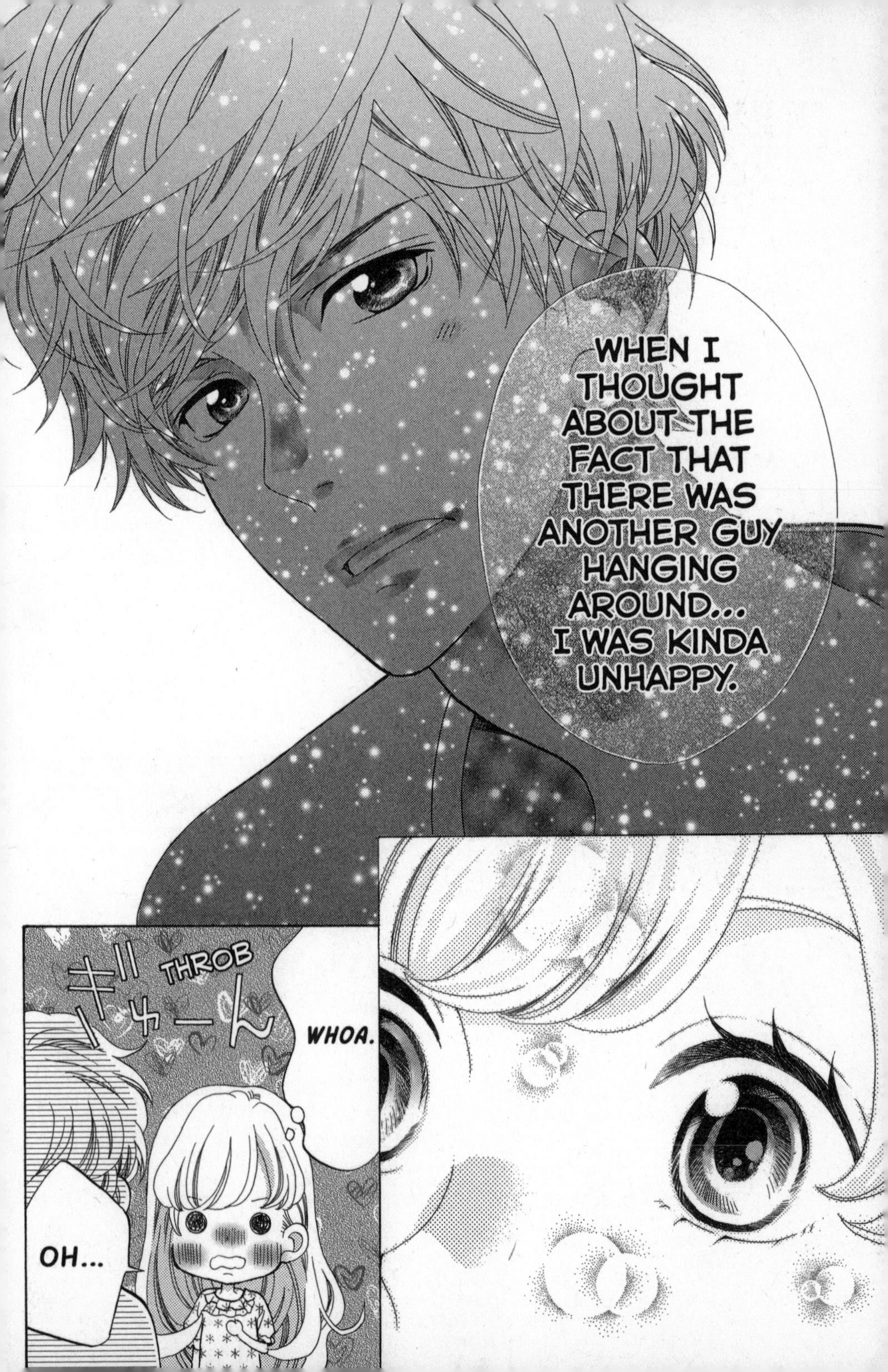
WHEN I THOUGHT ABOUT THE FACT THAT THERE WAS ANOTHER GUY HANGING AROUND... I WAS KINDA UNHAPPY.
きゅーん
THROB
WHOA.
OH...

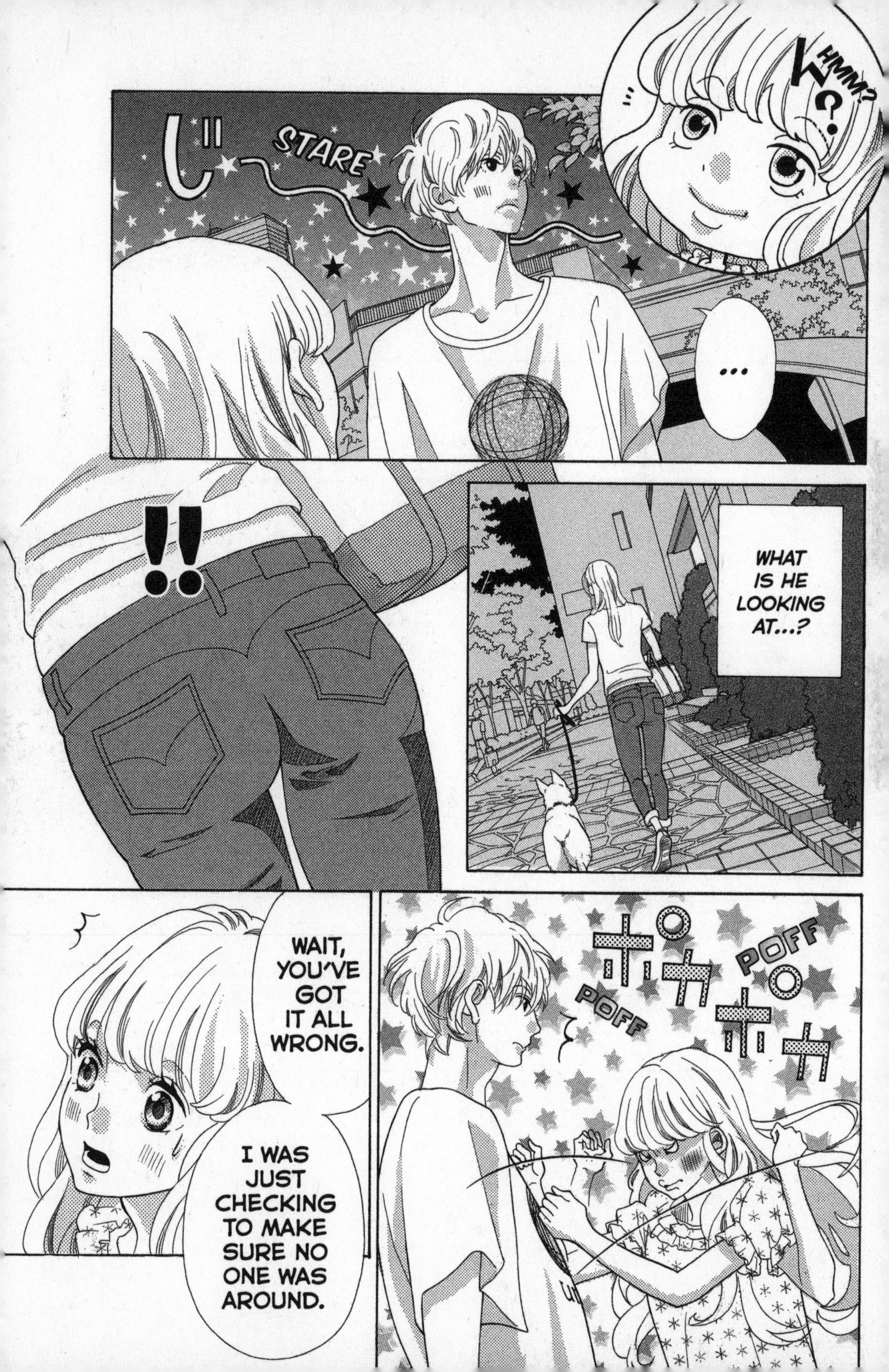
HMM?
...
STARE
WHAT IS HE LOOKING AT...?
!!
POFF
POFF
WAIT, YOU'VE GOT IT ALL WRONG.
I WAS JUST CHECKING TO MAKE SURE NO ONE WAS AROUND.

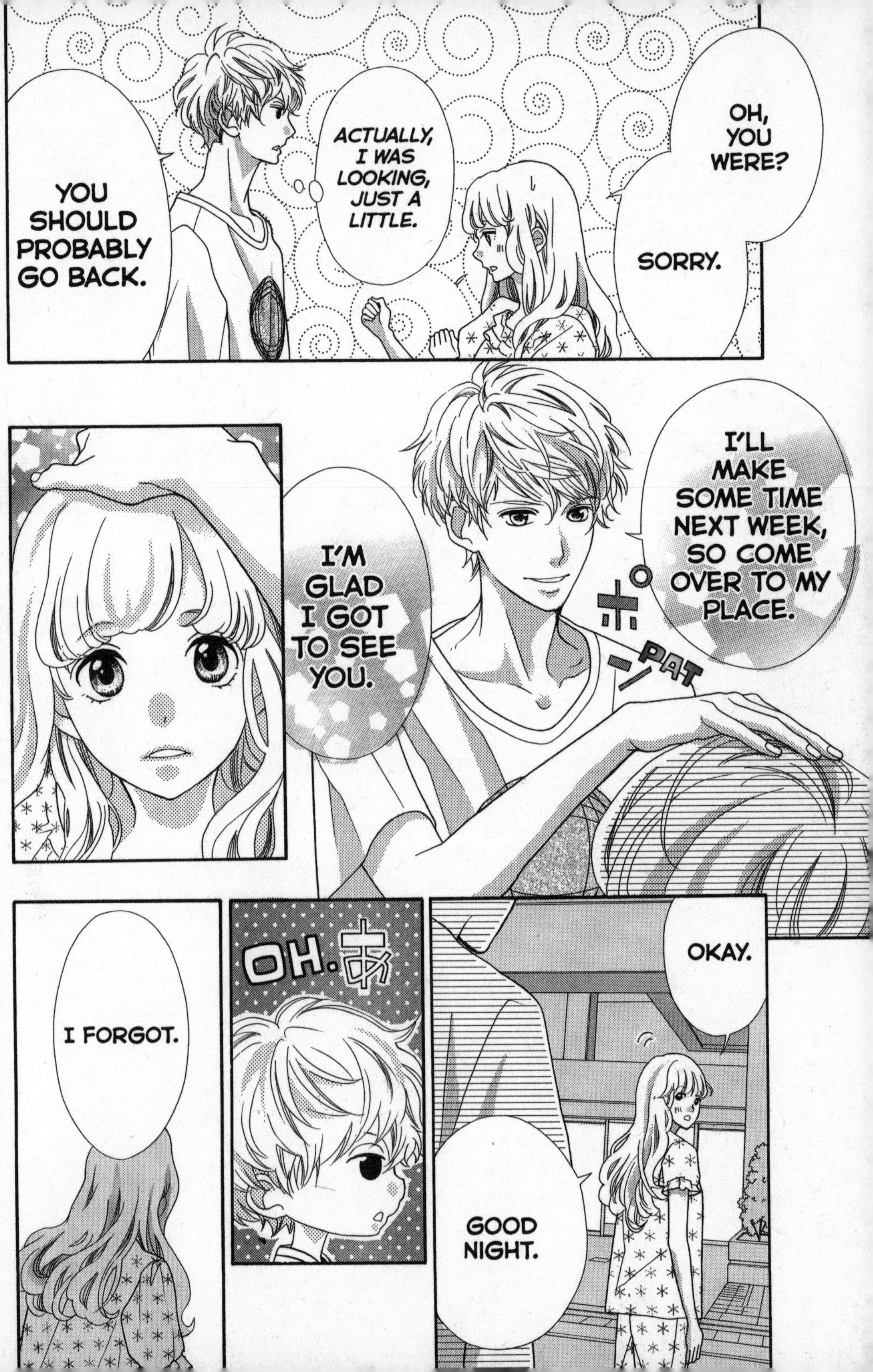
OH, YOU WERE?
SORRY.
ACTUALLY, I WAS LOOKING, JUST A LITTLE.
YOU SHOULD PROBABLY GO BACK.
I'LL MAKE SOME TIME NEXT WEEK, SO COME OVER TO MY PLACE.
PAT
I'M GLAD I GOT TO SEE YOU.
OKAY.
GOOD NIGHT.
OH.
I FORGOT.

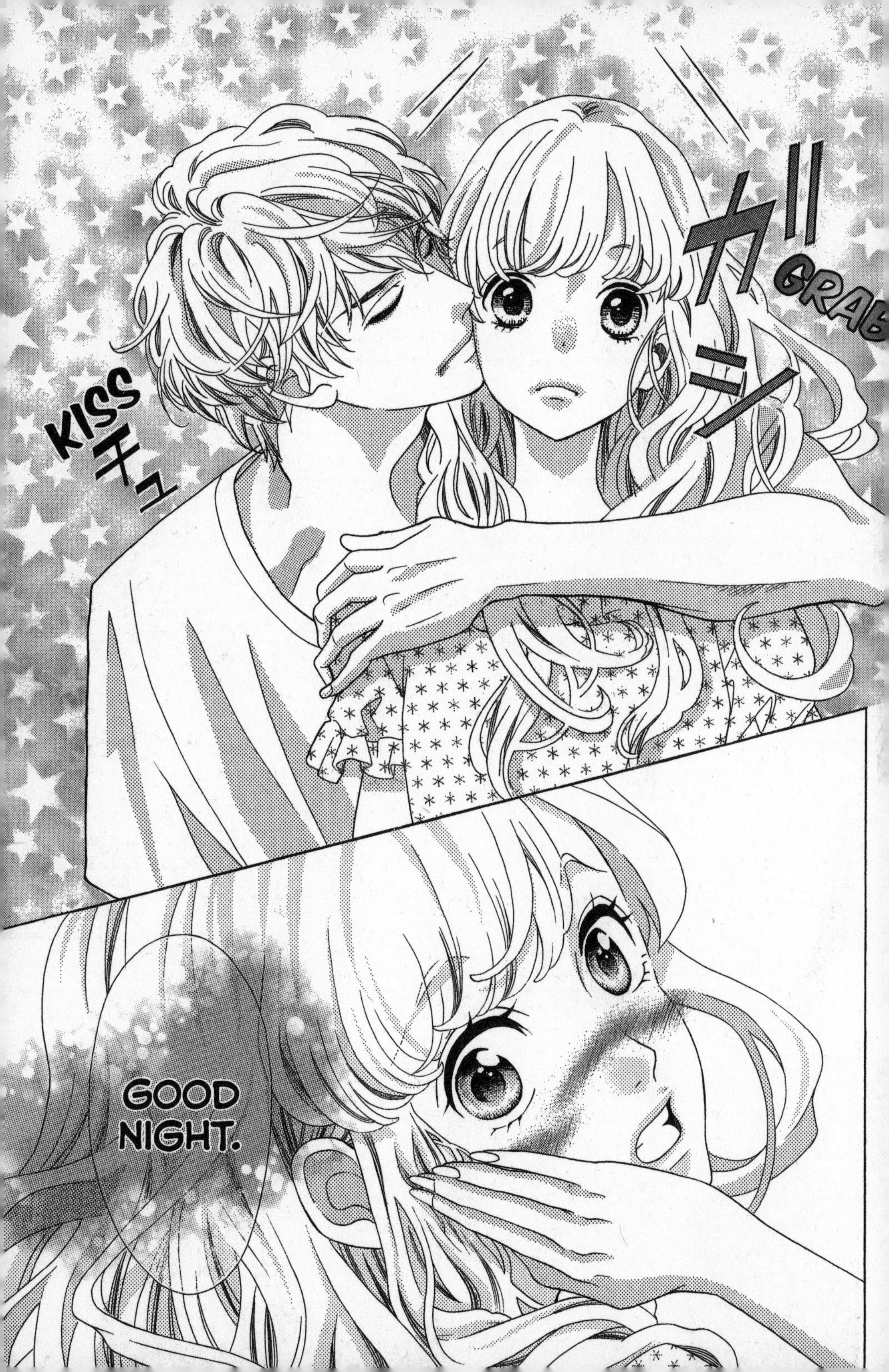
GRAB
KISS チュ
GOOD NIGHT.

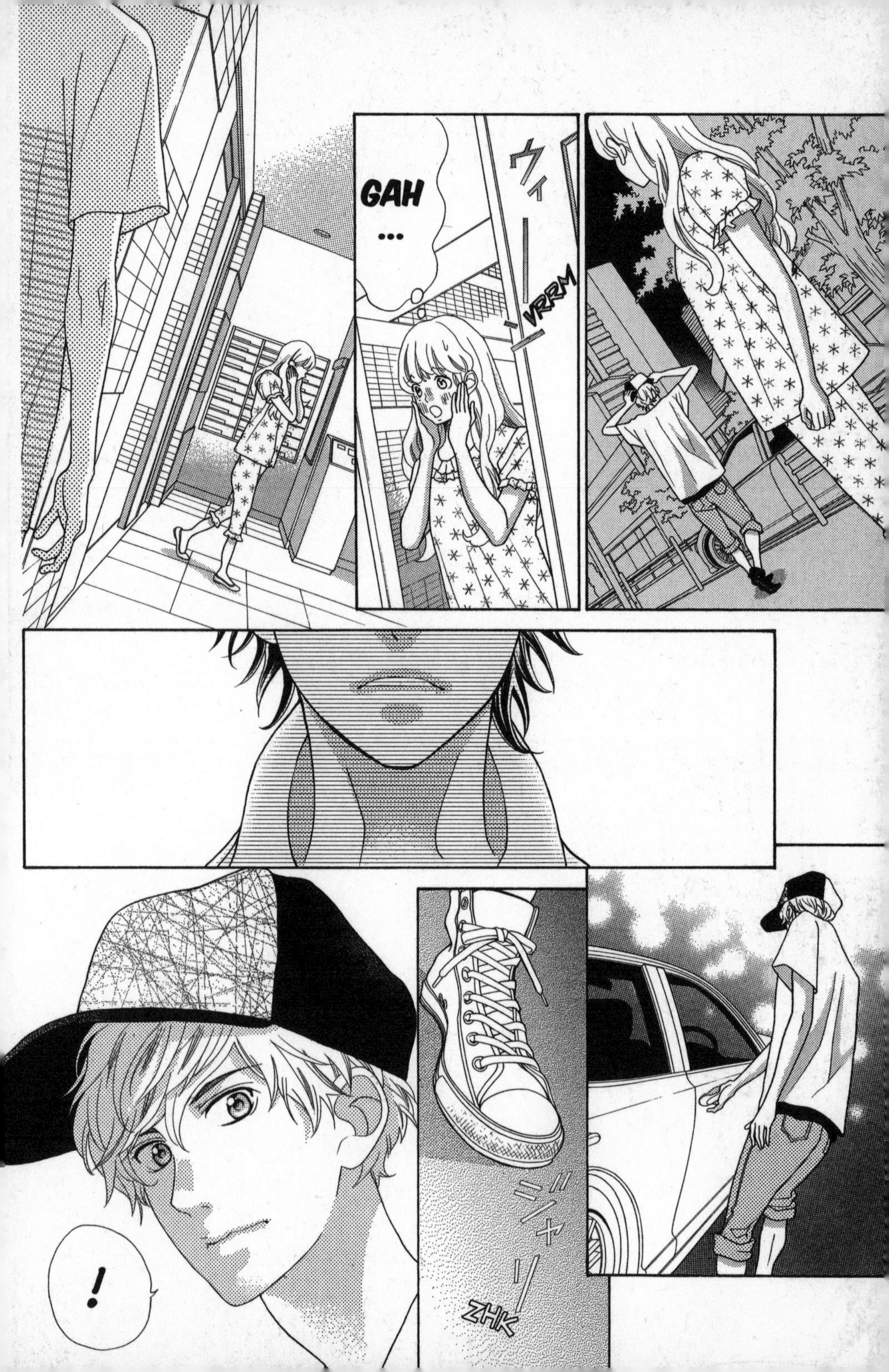
GAH
...
ヴィー
VRRM
ジャー
ZHK
!

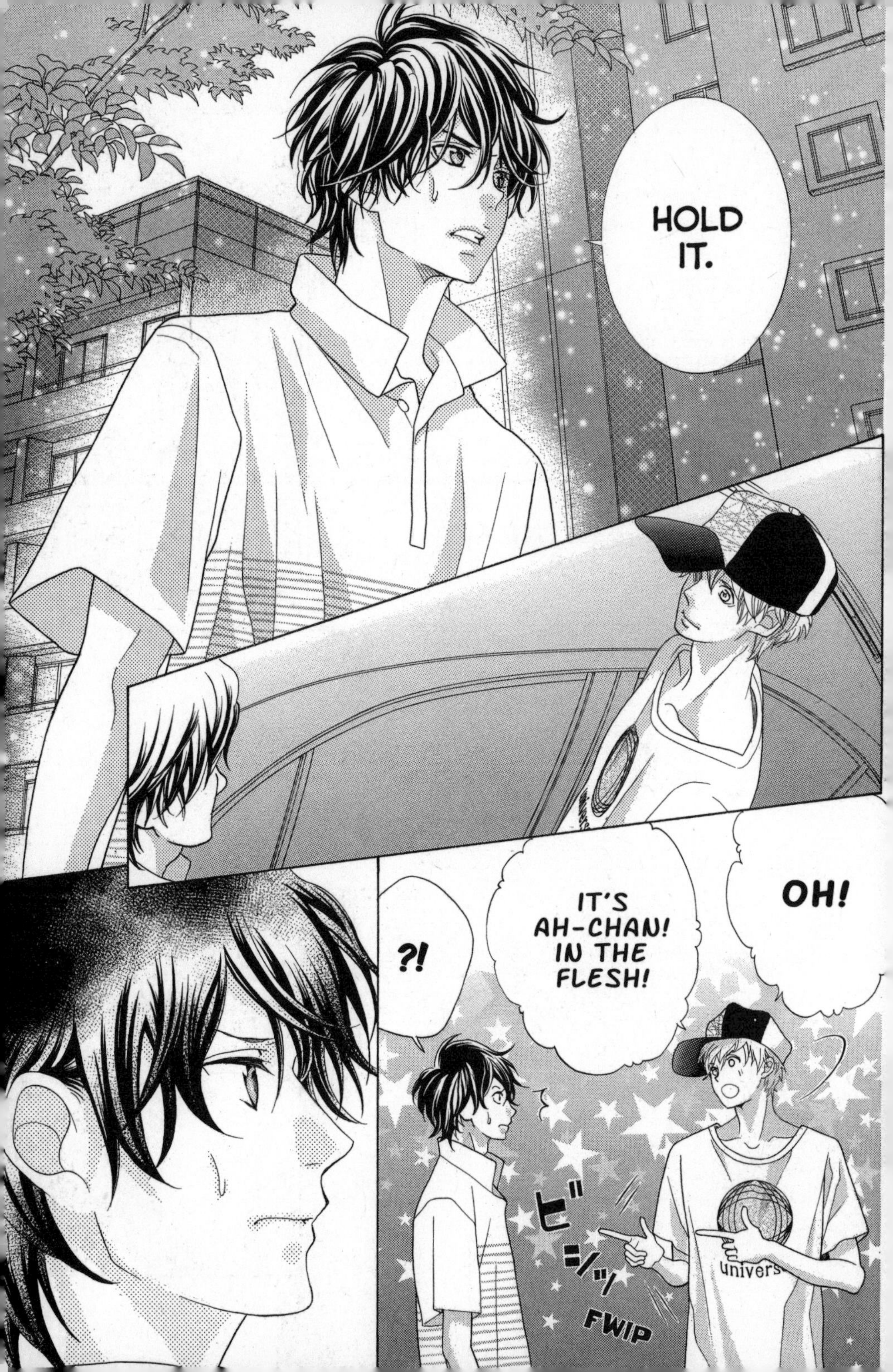
HOLD IT.
OH!
IT'S AH-CHAN! IN THE FLESH!
?!
ビシッ
FWIP

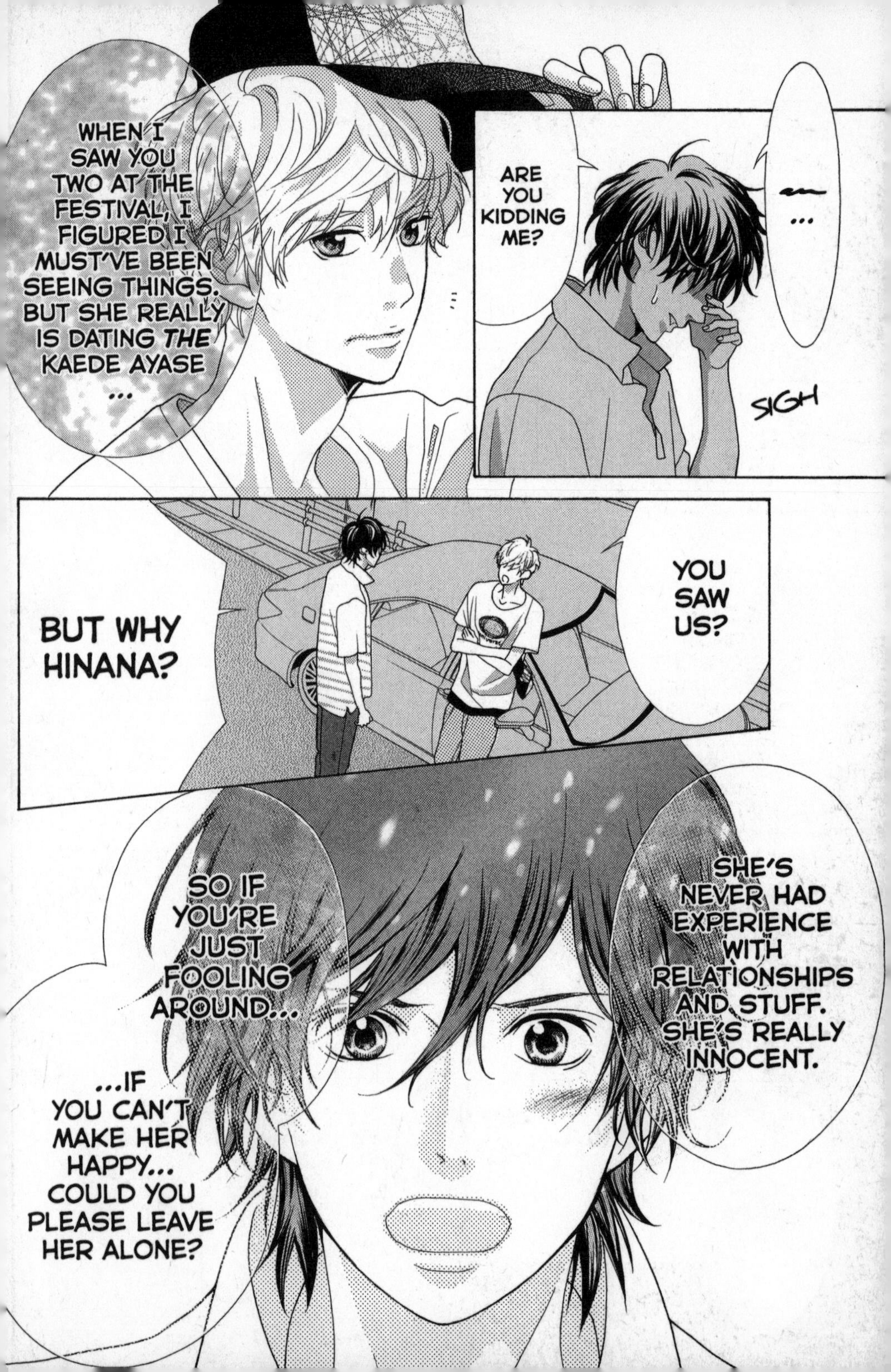
—...
ARE YOU KIDDING ME?
SIGH
WHEN I SAW YOU TWO AT THE FESTIVAL, I FIGURED I MUST'VE BEEN SEEING THINGS. BUT SHE REALLY IS DATING *THE* KAEDE AYASE...
YOU SAW US?
BUT WHY HINANA?
SHE'S NEVER HAD EXPERIENCE WITH RELATIONSHIPS AND STUFF. SHE'S REALLY INNOCENT.
SO IF YOU'RE JUST FOOLING AROUND...
...IF YOU CAN'T MAKE HER HAPPY... COULD YOU PLEASE LEAVE HER ALONE?

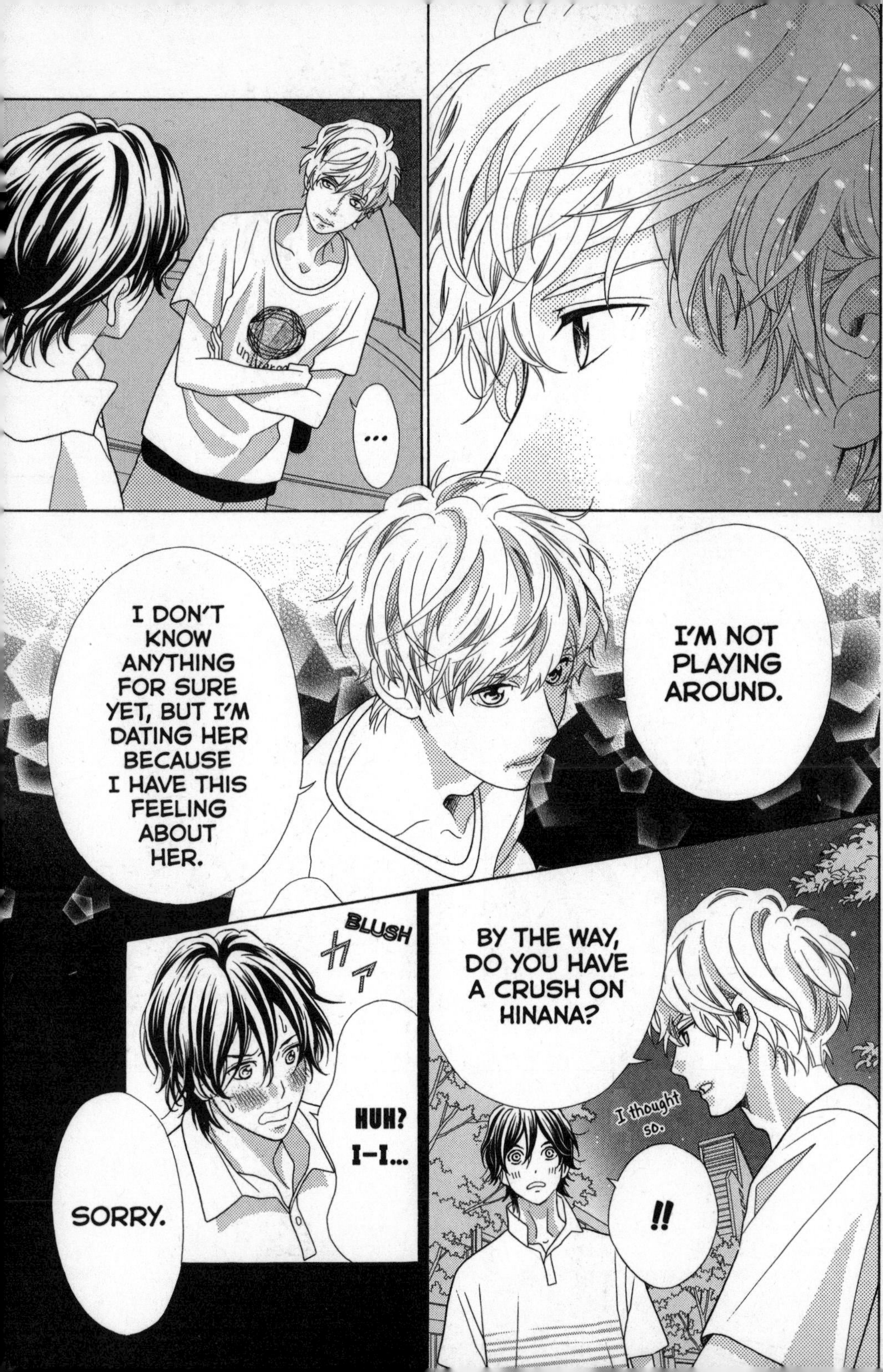
...
I'M NOT PLAYING AROUND.
I DON'T KNOW ANYTHING FOR SURE YET, BUT I'M DATING HER BECAUSE I HAVE THIS FEELING ABOUT HER.
BY THE WAY, DO YOU HAVE A CRUSH ON HINANA?
I thought so.
!!
BLUSH
カァ
HUH? I-I...
SORRY.

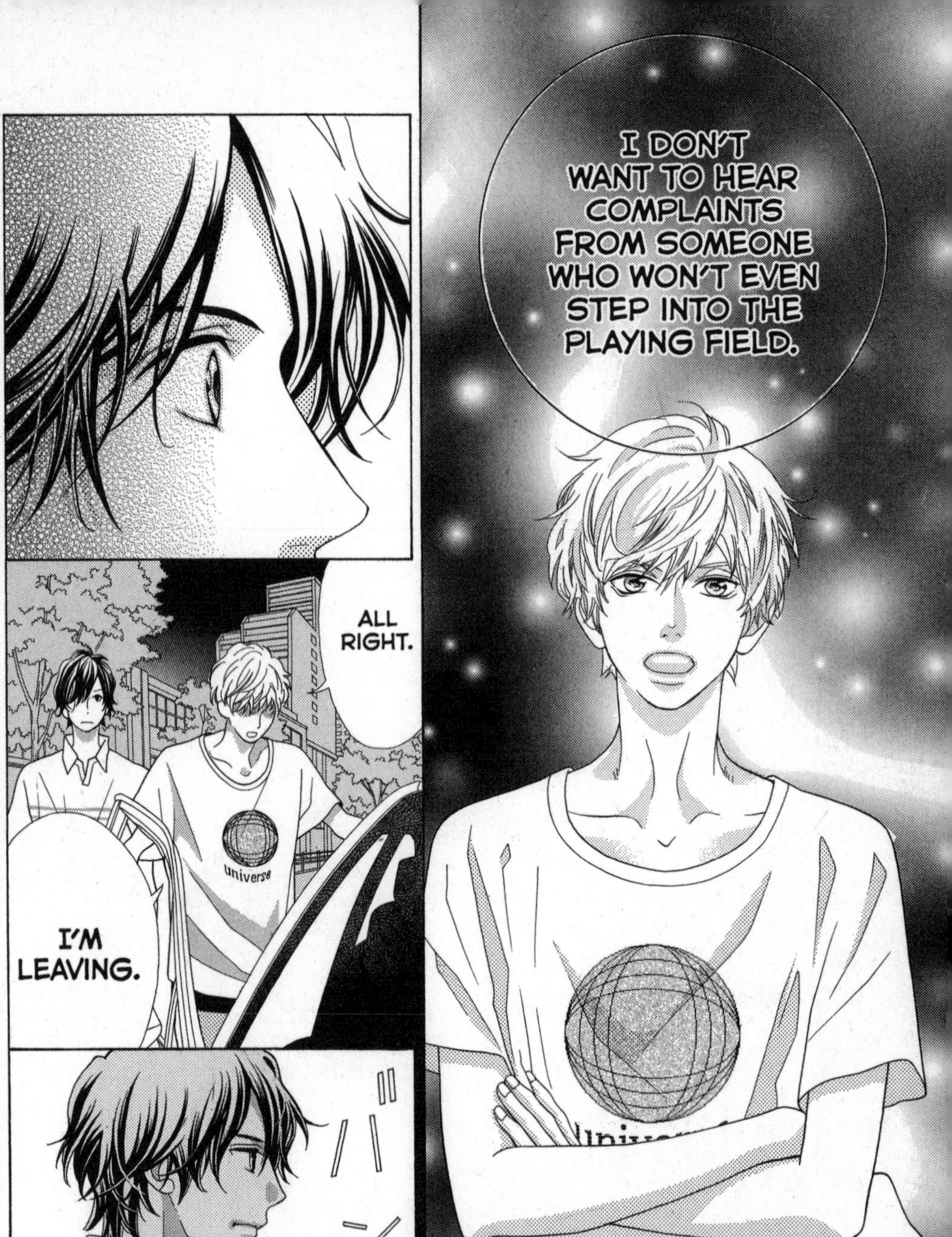
I DON'T WANT TO HEAR COMPLAINTS FROM SOMEONE WHO WON'T EVEN STEP INTO THE PLAYING FIELD.
universe
ALL RIGHT.
universe
I'M LEAVING.
SLAM

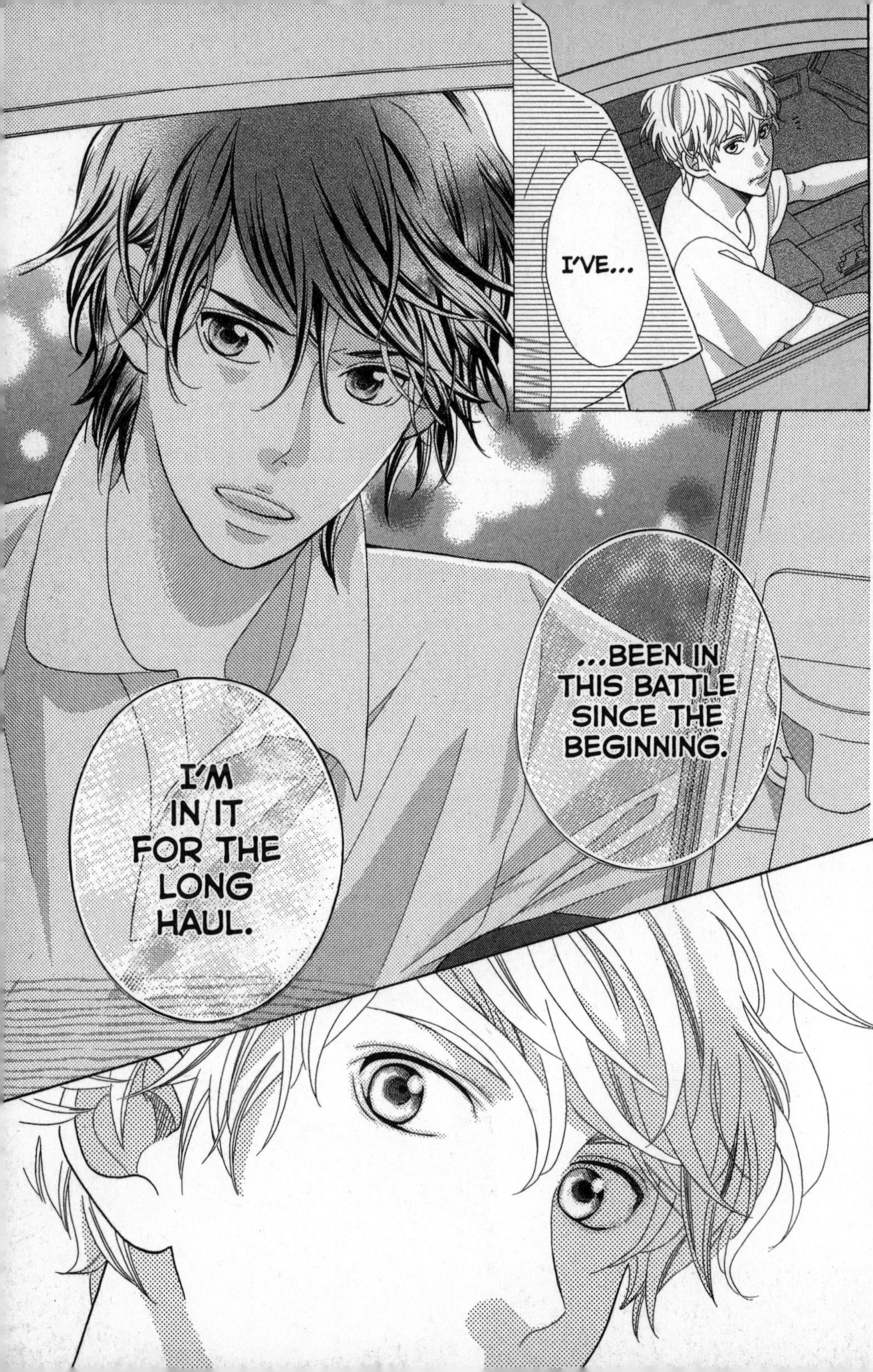
I'VE...
...BEEN IN THIS BATTLE SINCE THE BEGINNING.
I'M IN IT FOR THE LONG HAUL.

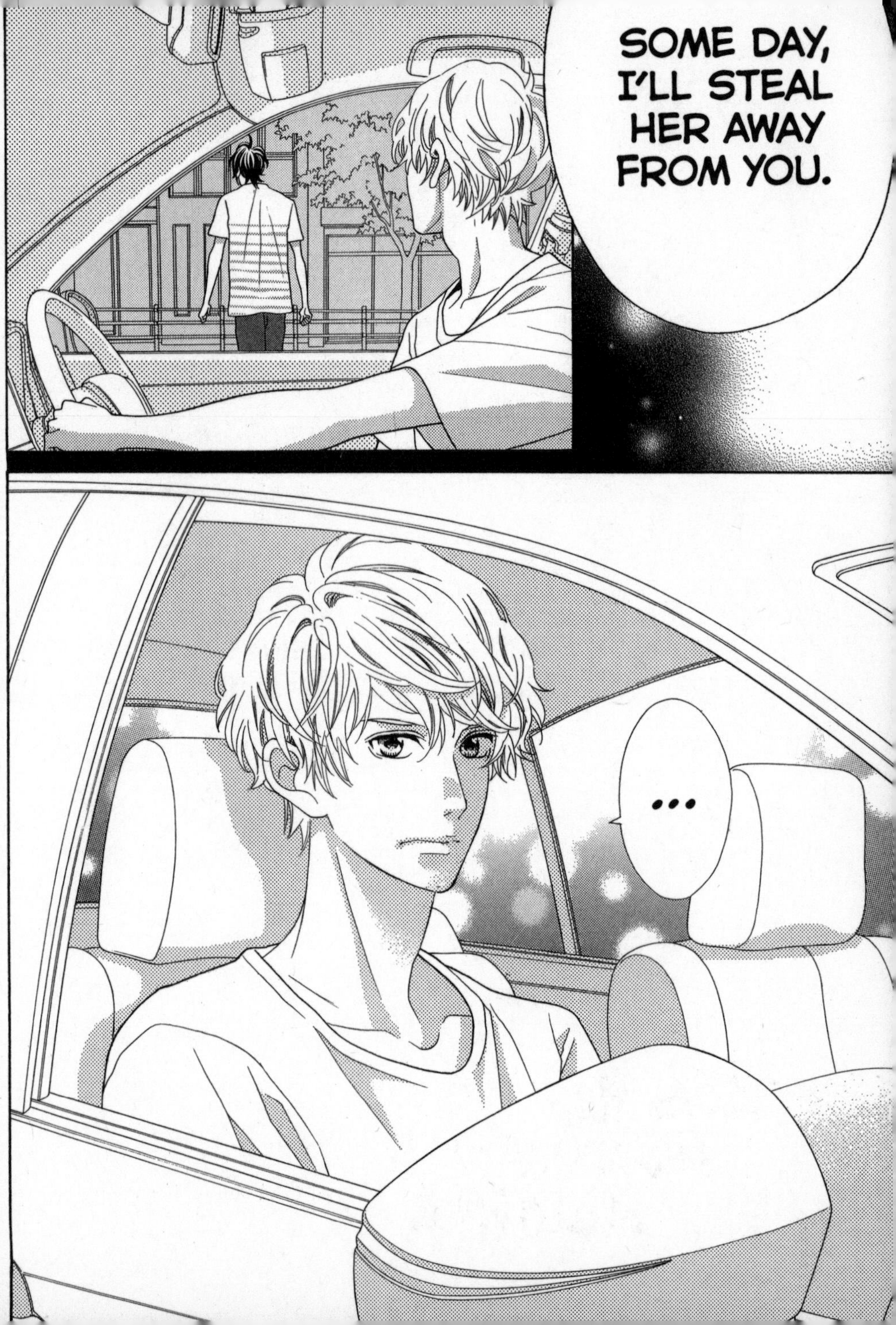
SOME DAY, I'LL STEAL HER AWAY FROM YOU.
...

Kiss Me at the Stroke of Midnight

AH-CHAN WAS KEEPING HIS FANBOY HEART AT BAY.

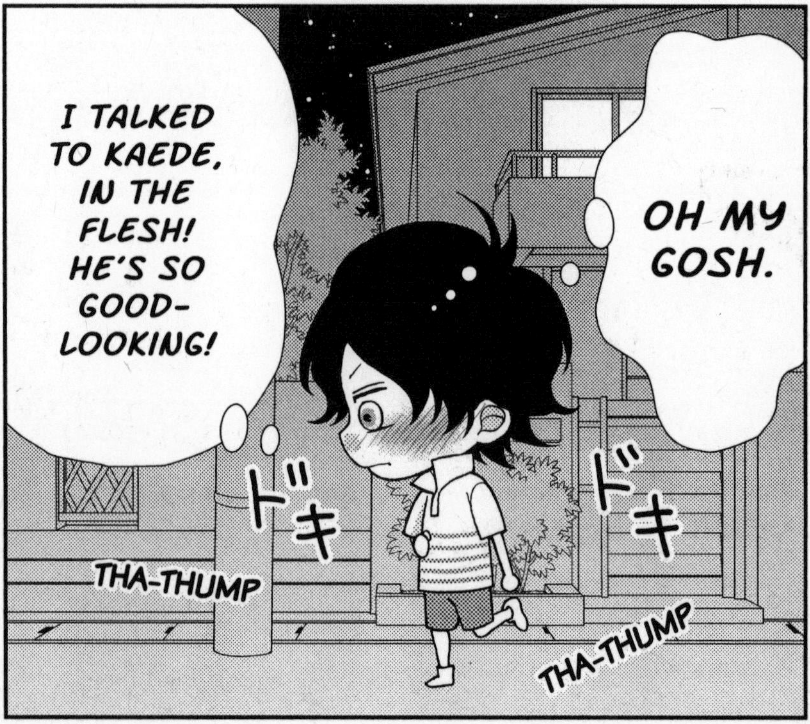
OH MY GOSH.
I TALKED TO KAEDE, IN THE FLESH! HE'S SO GOOD-LOOKING!
ドキ
THA-THUMP
ドキ
THA-THUMP

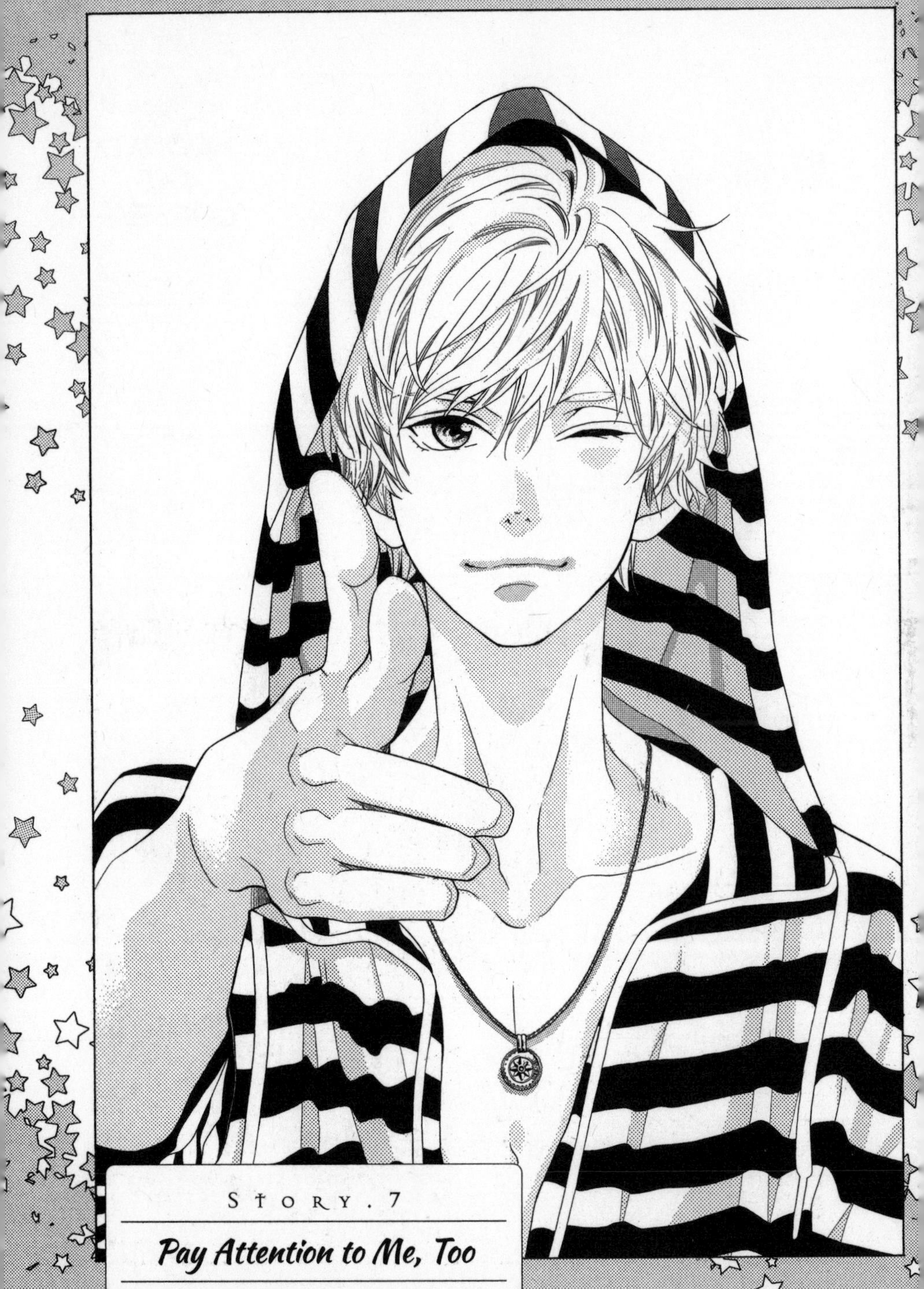
STORY . 7
Pay Attention to Me, Too

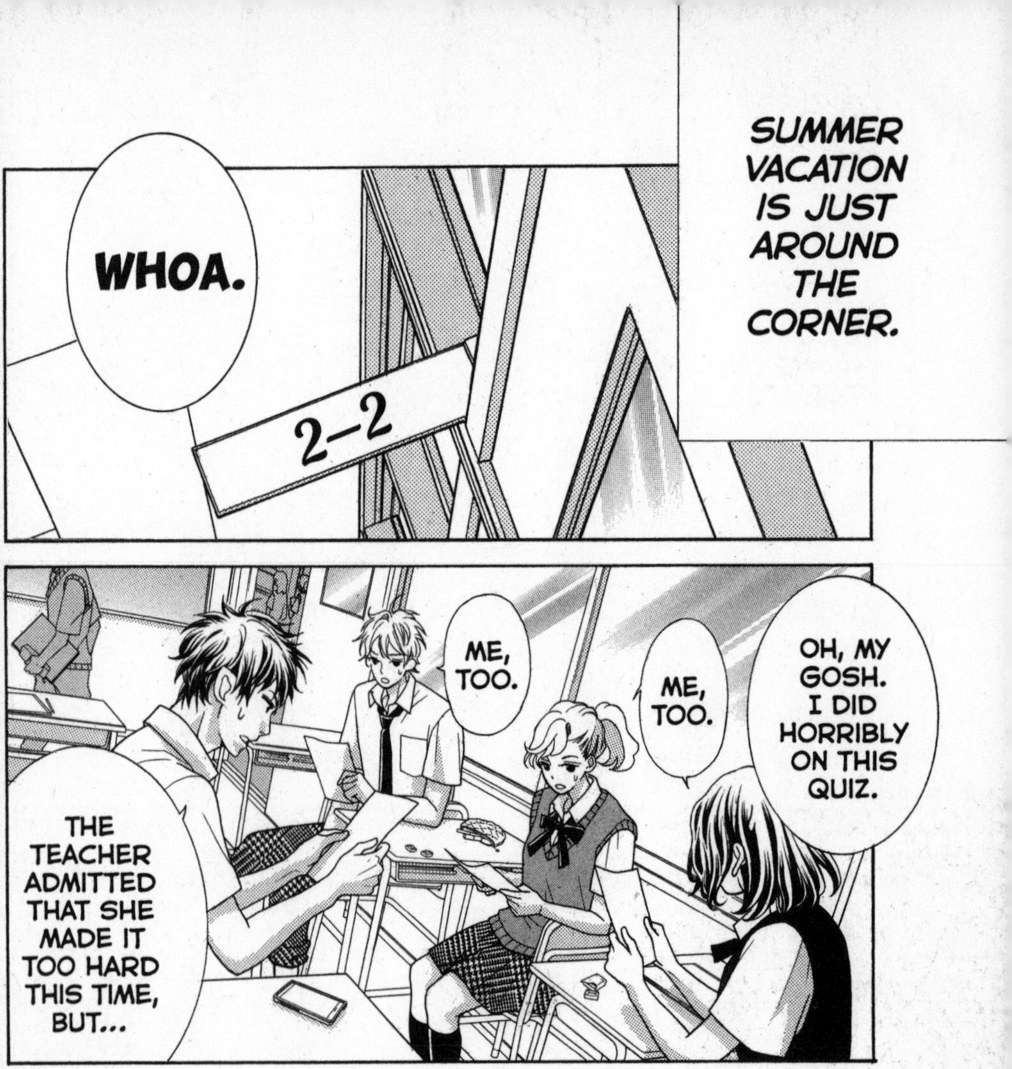
SUMMER VACATION IS JUST AROUND THE CORNER.
WHOA.
2–2
OH, MY GOSH. I DID HORRIBLY ON THIS QUIZ.
ME, TOO.
ME, TOO.
THE TEACHER ADMITTED THAT SHE MADE IT TOO HARD THIS TIME, BUT...

Kiss Me at the Stroke of Midnight

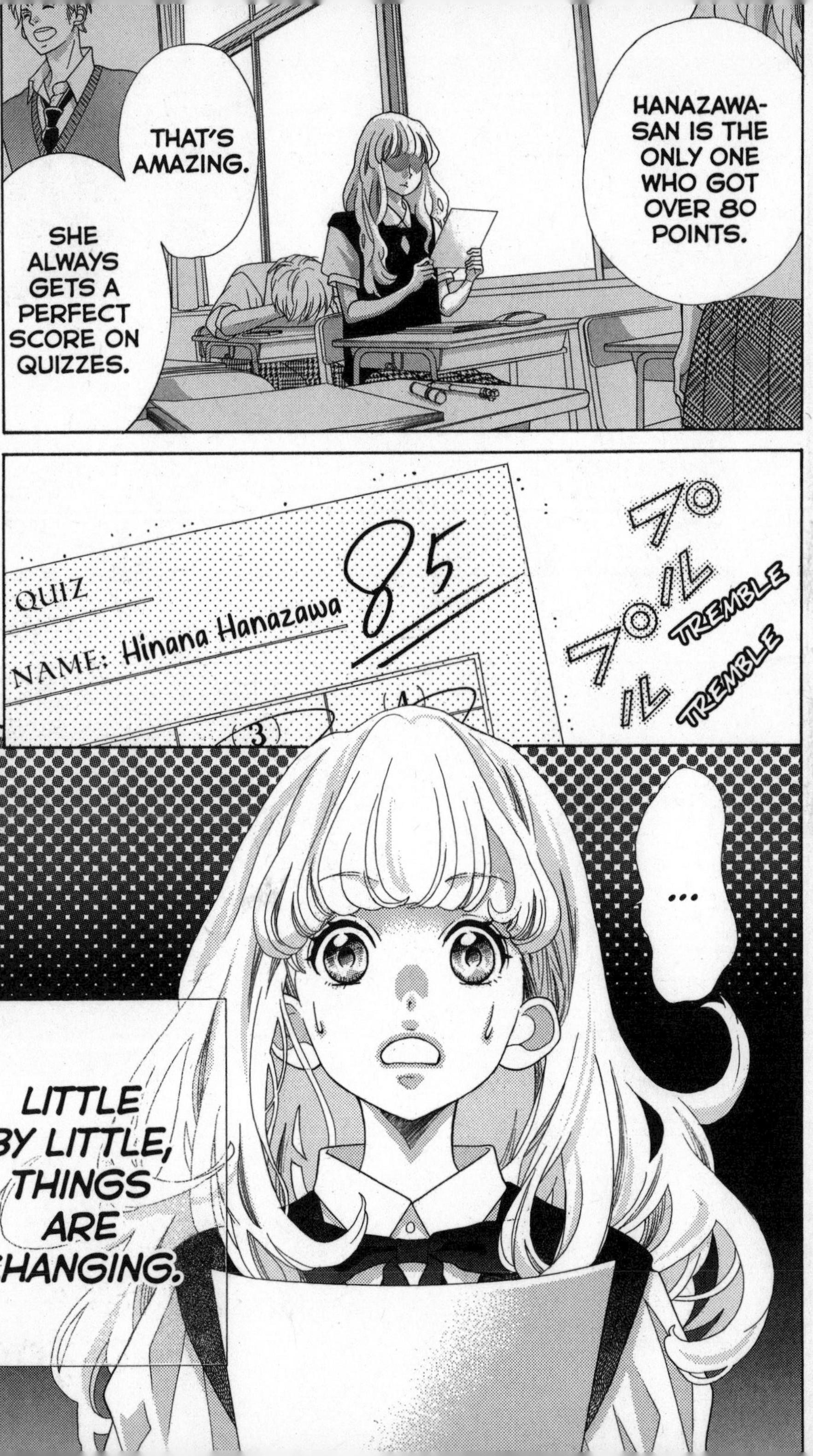
HANAZAWA-SAN IS THE ONLY ONE WHO GOT OVER 80 POINTS.
THAT'S AMAZING.
SHE ALWAYS GETS A PERFECT SCORE ON QUIZZES.
プルプル
TREMBLE TREMBLE
QUIZ
NAME: Hinana Hanazawa
85
...
LITTLE BY LITTLE, THINGS ARE CHANGING.

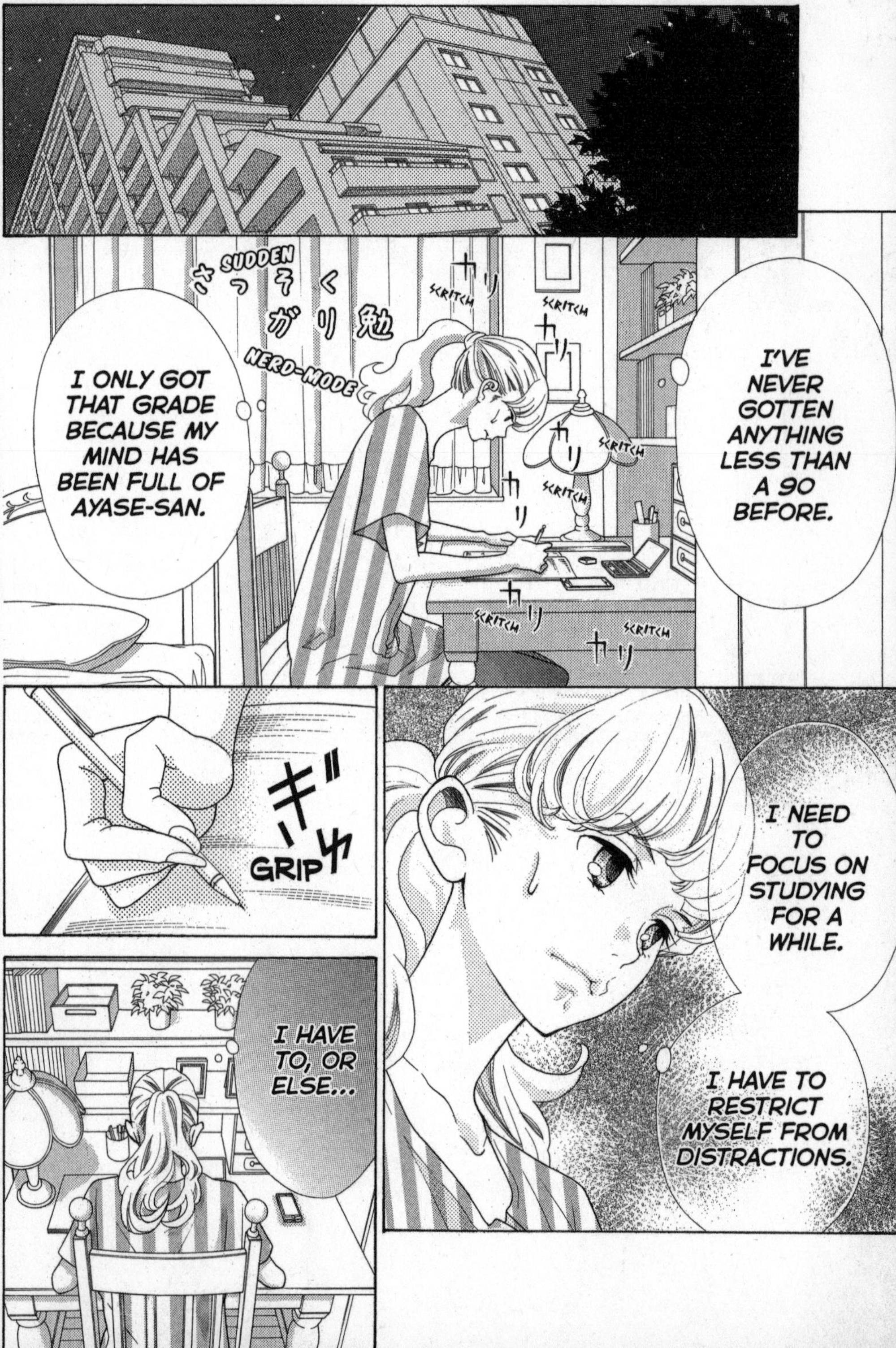
I'VE NEVER GOTTEN ANYTHING LESS THAN A 90 BEFORE.
SCRITCH
さっそくガリ勉
SUDDEN
NERD-MODE
カリ
SCRITCH
I ONLY GOT THAT GRADE BECAUSE MY MIND HAS BEEN FULL OF AYASE-SAN.
I NEED TO FOCUS ON STUDYING FOR A WHILE.
I HAVE TO RESTRICT MYSELF FROM DISTRACTIONS.
ぎゅ
GRIP
I HAVE TO, OR ELSE...

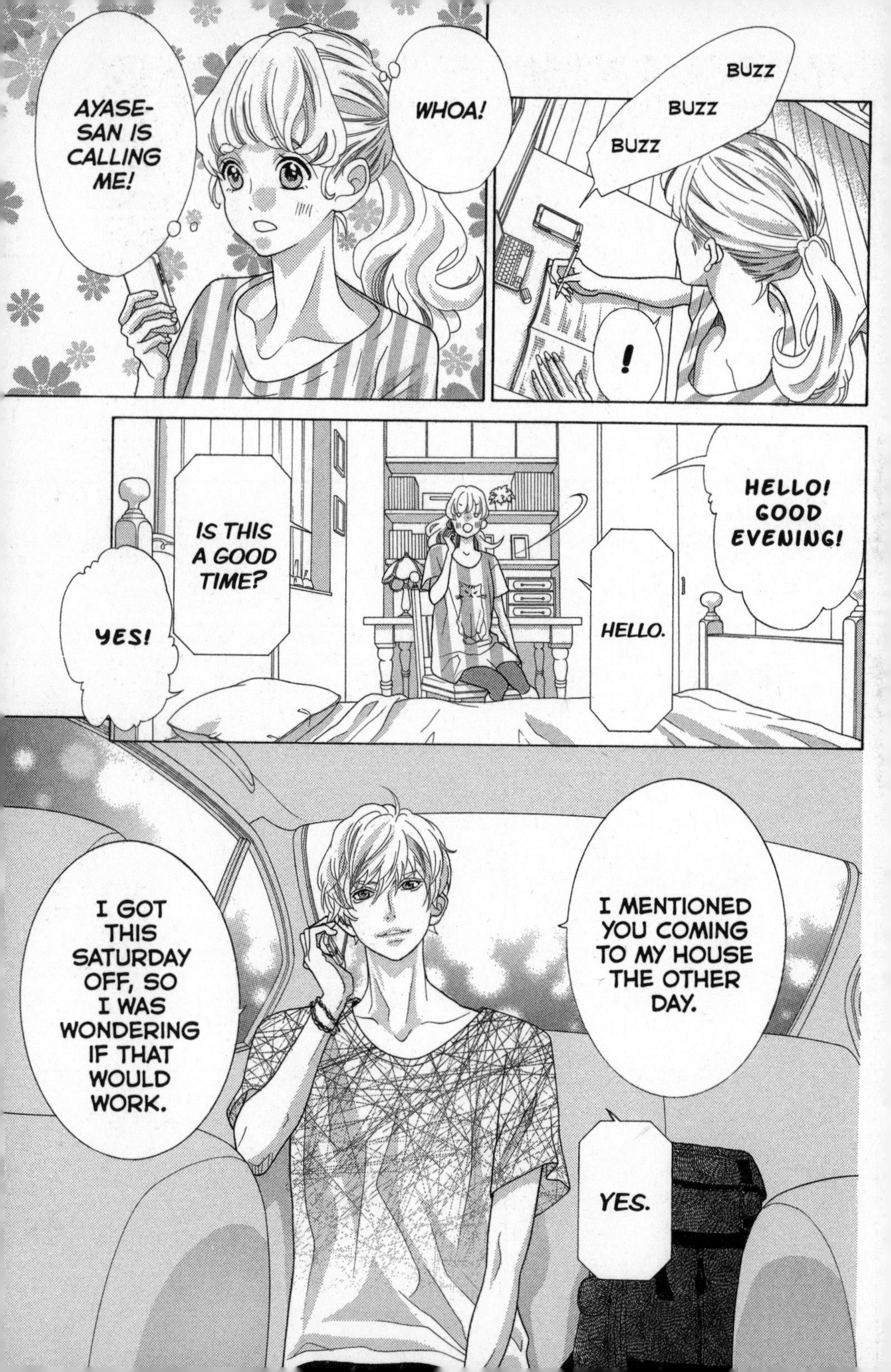
BUZZ
BUZZ
BUZZ
!
WHOA!
AYASE-SAN IS CALLING ME!
HELLO! GOOD EVENING!
HELLO.
IS THIS A GOOD TIME?
YES!
I MENTIONED YOU COMING TO MY HOUSE THE OTHER DAY.
YES.
I GOT THIS SATURDAY OFF, SO I WAS WONDERING IF THAT WOULD WORK.

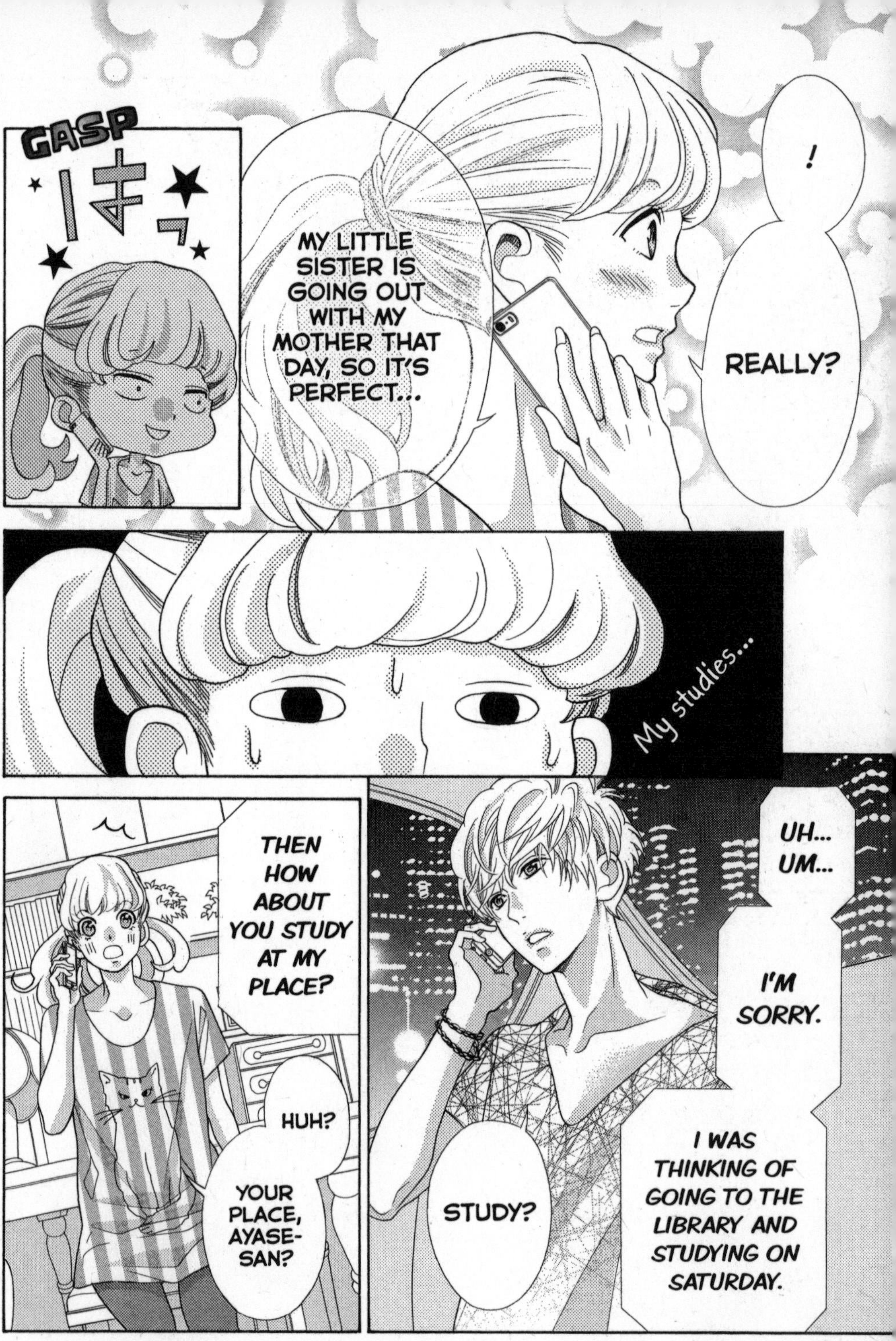
!
REALLY?
MY LITTLE SISTER IS GOING OUT WITH MY MOTHER THAT DAY, SO IT'S PERFECT...
GASP
はっ
My studies...
UH... UM...
I'M SORRY.
I WAS THINKING OF GOING TO THE LIBRARY AND STUDYING ON SATURDAY.
STUDY?
THEN HOW ABOUT YOU STUDY AT MY PLACE?
HUH?
YOUR PLACE, AYASE-SAN?

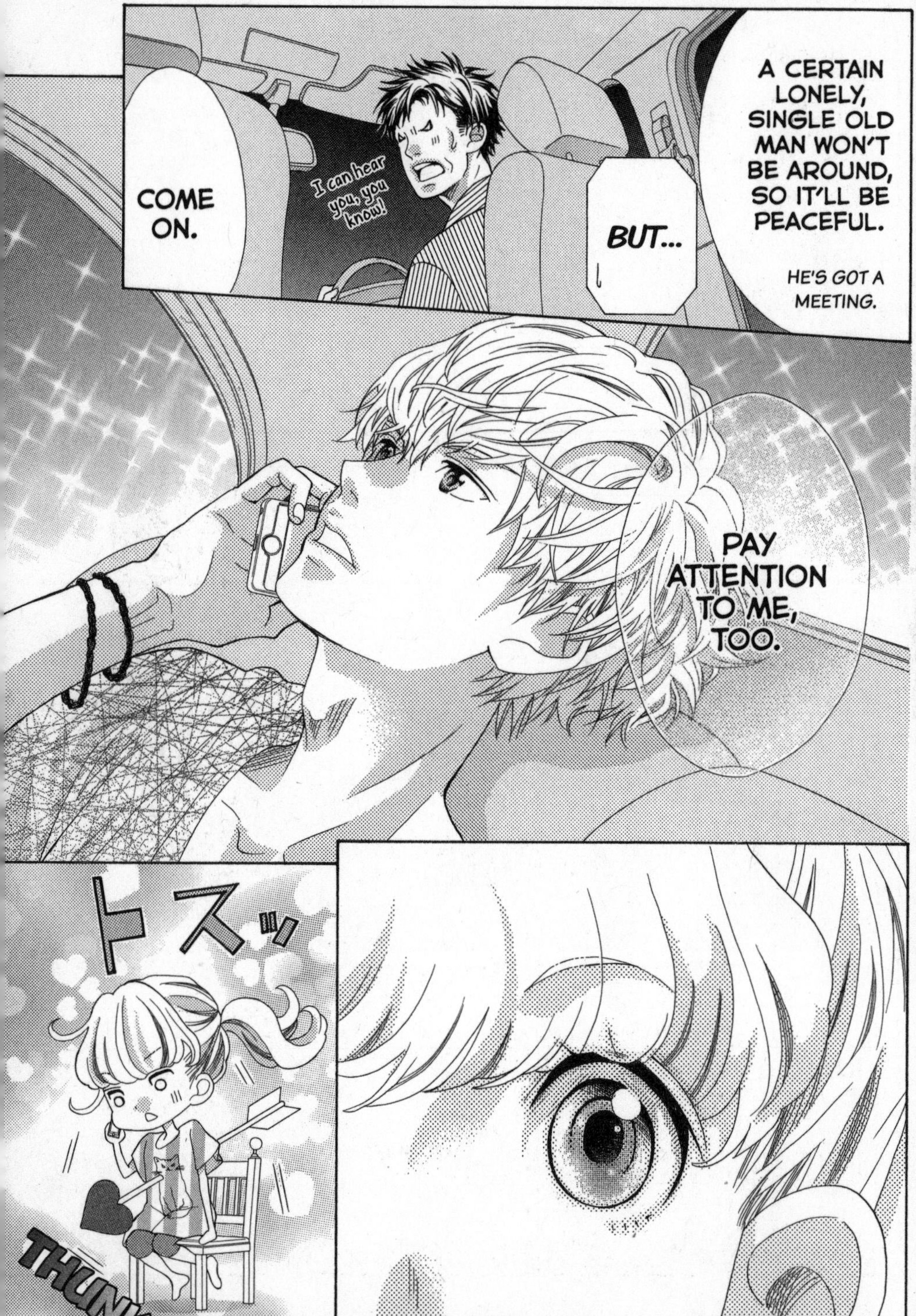
A CERTAIN LONELY, SINGLE OLD MAN WON'T BE AROUND, SO IT'LL BE PEACEFUL.
HE'S GOT A MEETING.
BUT...
I can hear you, you know!
COME ON.
PAY ATTENTION TO ME, TOO.
トスッ
THUNK

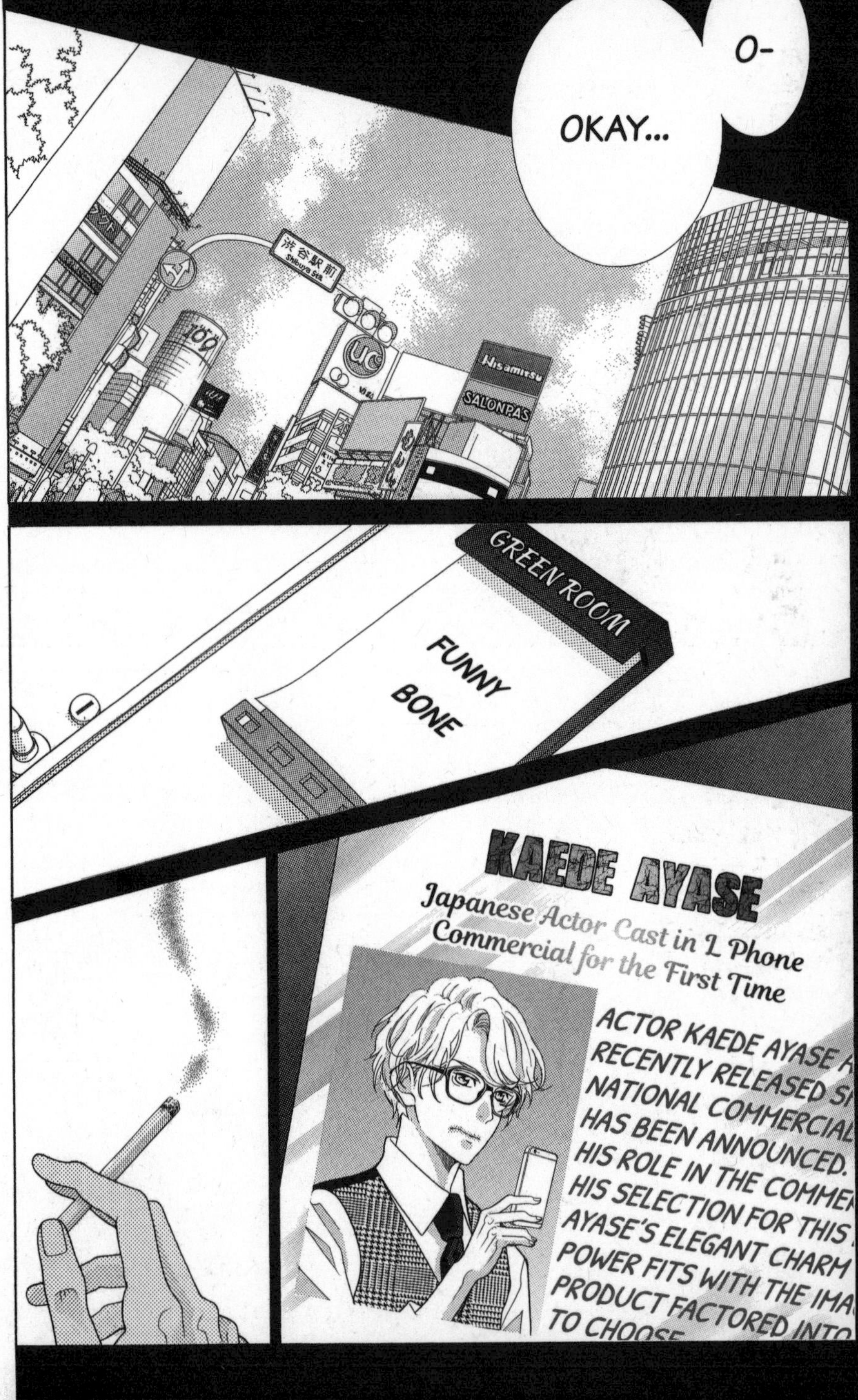
O-
OKAY...
渋谷駅前
Shibuya Sta.
109
Hisamitsu
SALONPAS
GREEN ROOM
FUNNY BONE
KAEDE AYASE
Japanese Actor Cast in L Phone Commercial for the First Time
ACTOR KAEDE AYASE
RECENTLY RELEASED
NATIONAL COMMERCIAL
HAS BEEN ANNOUNCED.
HIS ROLE IN THE COMME
HIS SELECTION FOR THIS
AYASE'S ELEGANT CHARM
POWER FITS WITH THE IMA
PRODUCT FACTORED INTO
TO CHOOSE

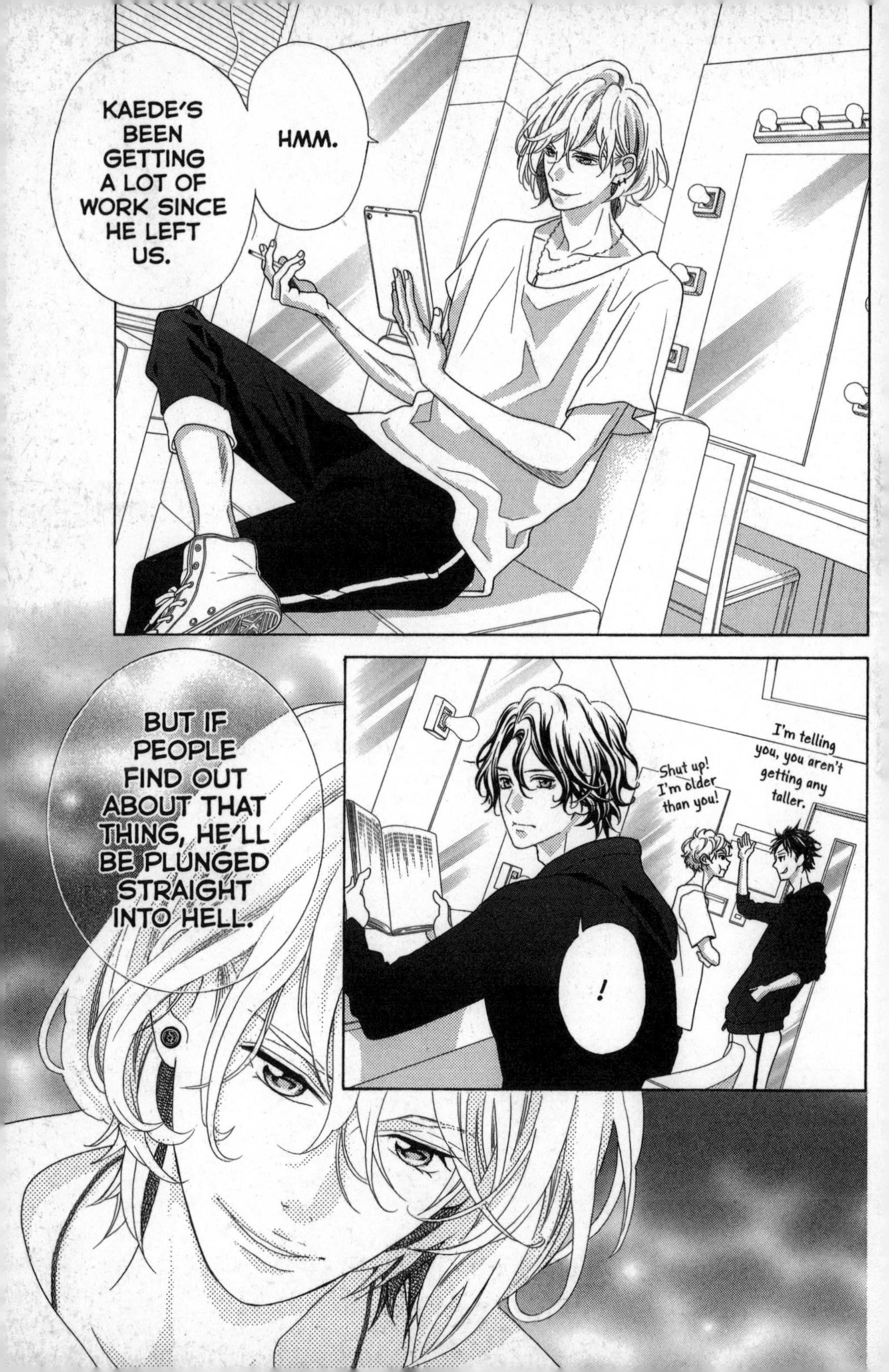
HMM.
KAEDE'S BEEN GETTING A LOT OF WORK SINCE HE LEFT US.
I'm telling you, you aren't getting any taller.
Shut up! I'm older than you!
!
BUT IF PEOPLE FIND OUT ABOUT THAT THING, HE'LL BE PLUNGED STRAIGHT INTO HELL.

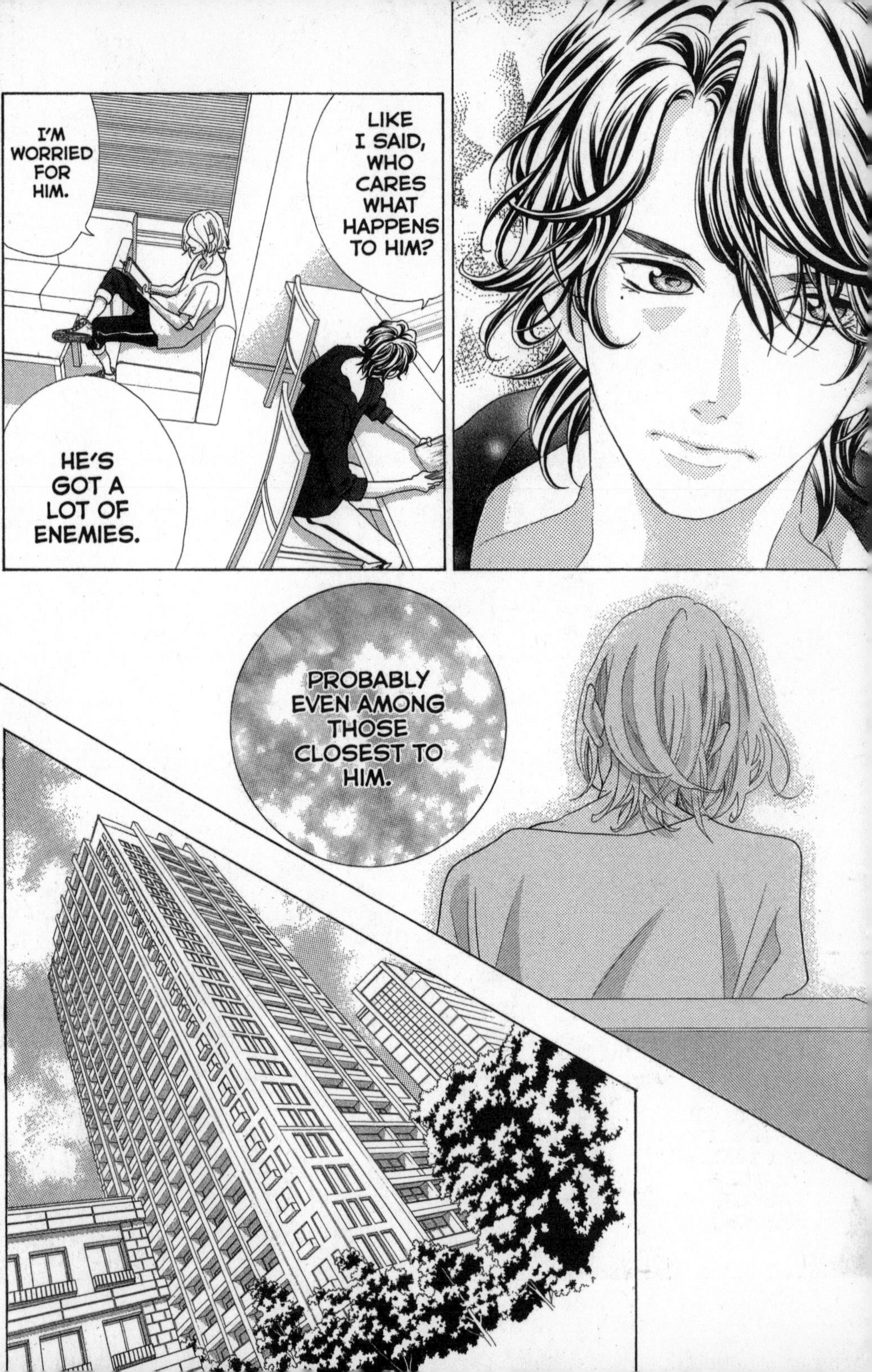
LIKE I SAID, WHO CARES WHAT HAPPENS TO HIM?
I'M WORRIED FOR HIM.
HE'S GOT A LOT OF ENEMIES.
PROBABLY EVEN AMONG THOSE CLOSEST TO HIM.

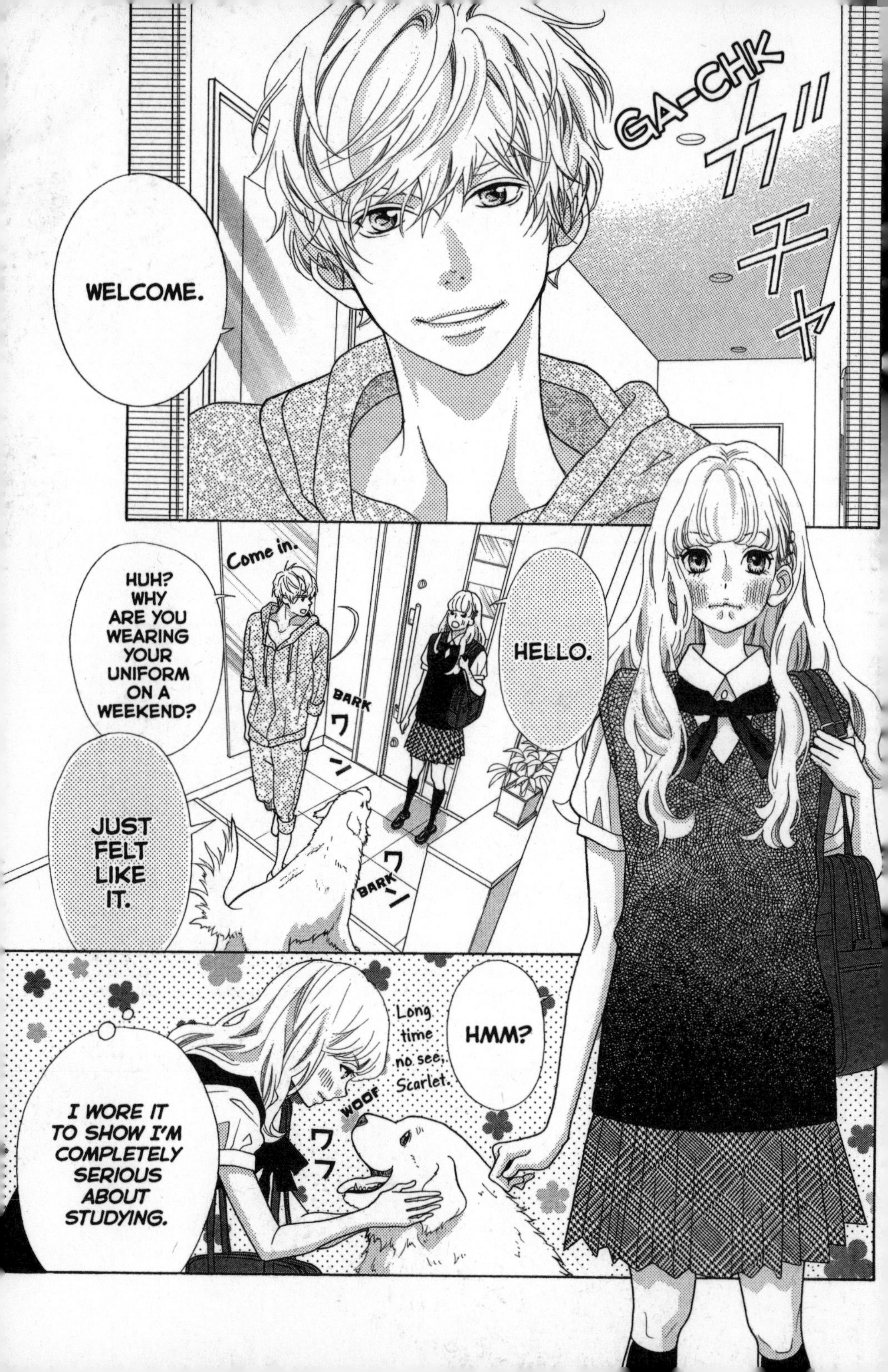
GA-CHK
カチャ
WELCOME.
HELLO.
Come in.
HUH? WHY ARE YOU WEARING YOUR UNIFORM ON A WEEKEND?
BARK
ワン
BARK
ワン
JUST FELT LIKE IT.
HMM?
Long time no see, Scarlet.
WOOF
ワフ
I WORE IT TO SHOW I'M COMPLETELY SERIOUS ABOUT STUDYING.

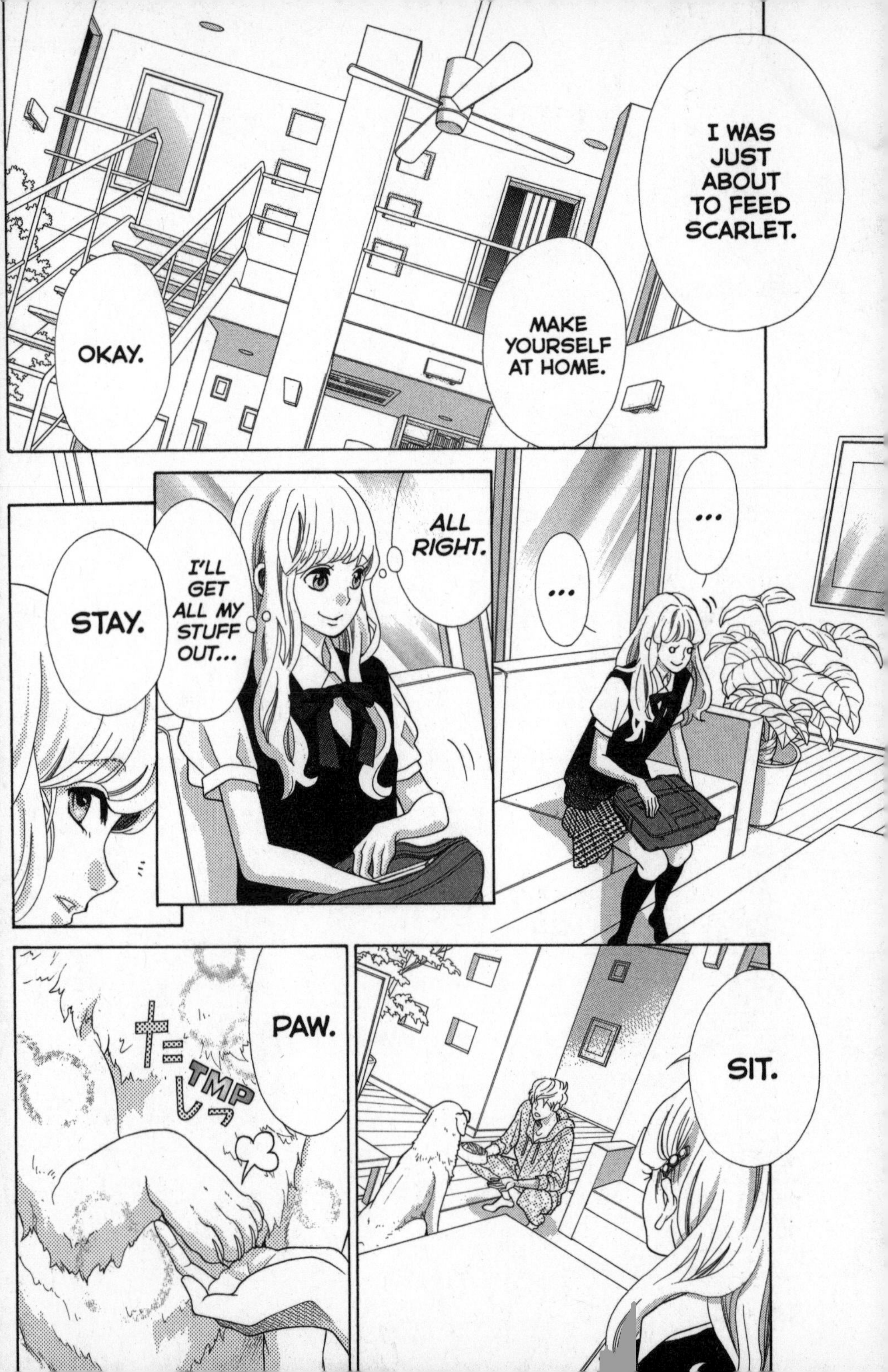
I WAS JUST ABOUT TO FEED SCARLET.
MAKE YOURSELF AT HOME.
OKAY.
...
...
ALL RIGHT.
I'LL GET ALL MY STUFF OUT...
STAY.
SIT.
PAW.
TMP

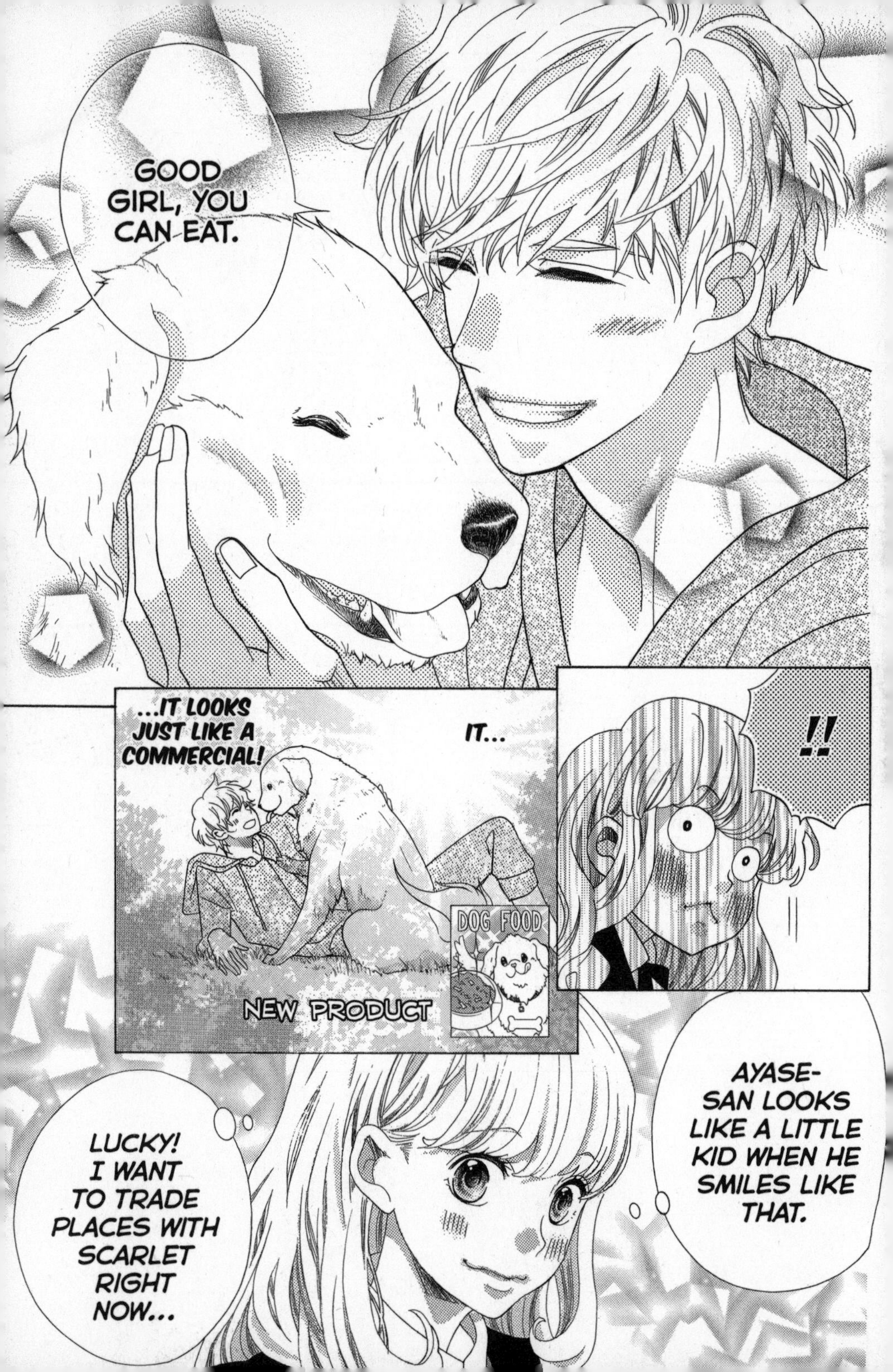
GOOD GIRL, YOU CAN EAT.
!!
IT...
...IT LOOKS JUST LIKE A COMMERCIAL!
DOG FOOD
NEW PRODUCT
AYASE-SAN LOOKS LIKE A LITTLE KID WHEN HE SMILES LIKE THAT.
LUCKY! I WANT TO TRADE PLACES WITH SCARLET RIGHT NOW...

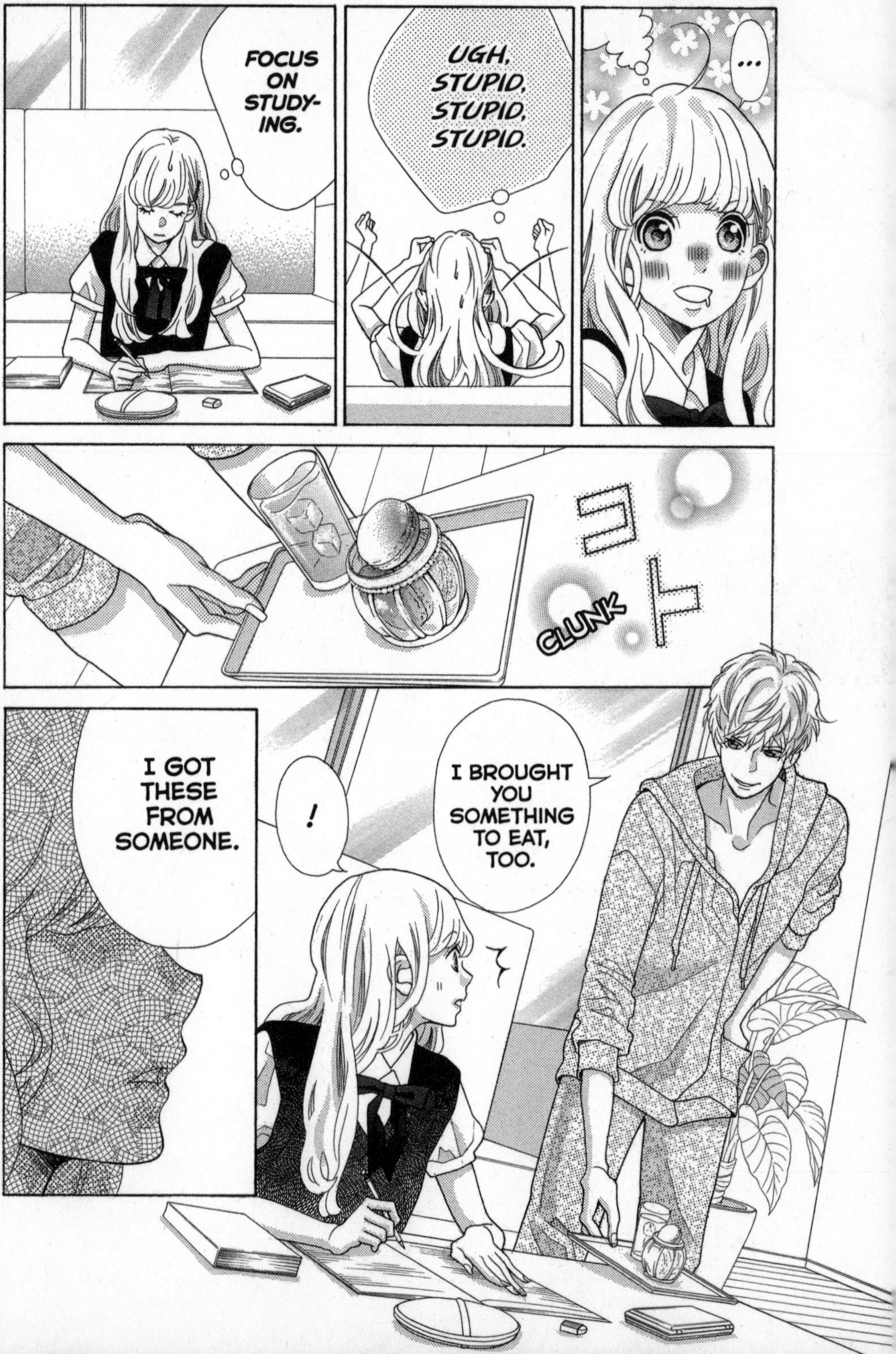
...
UGH, STUPID, STUPID, STUPID.
FOCUS ON STUDY-ING.
コト
CLUNK
I BROUGHT YOU SOMETHING TO EAT, TOO.
!
I GOT THESE FROM SOMEONE.

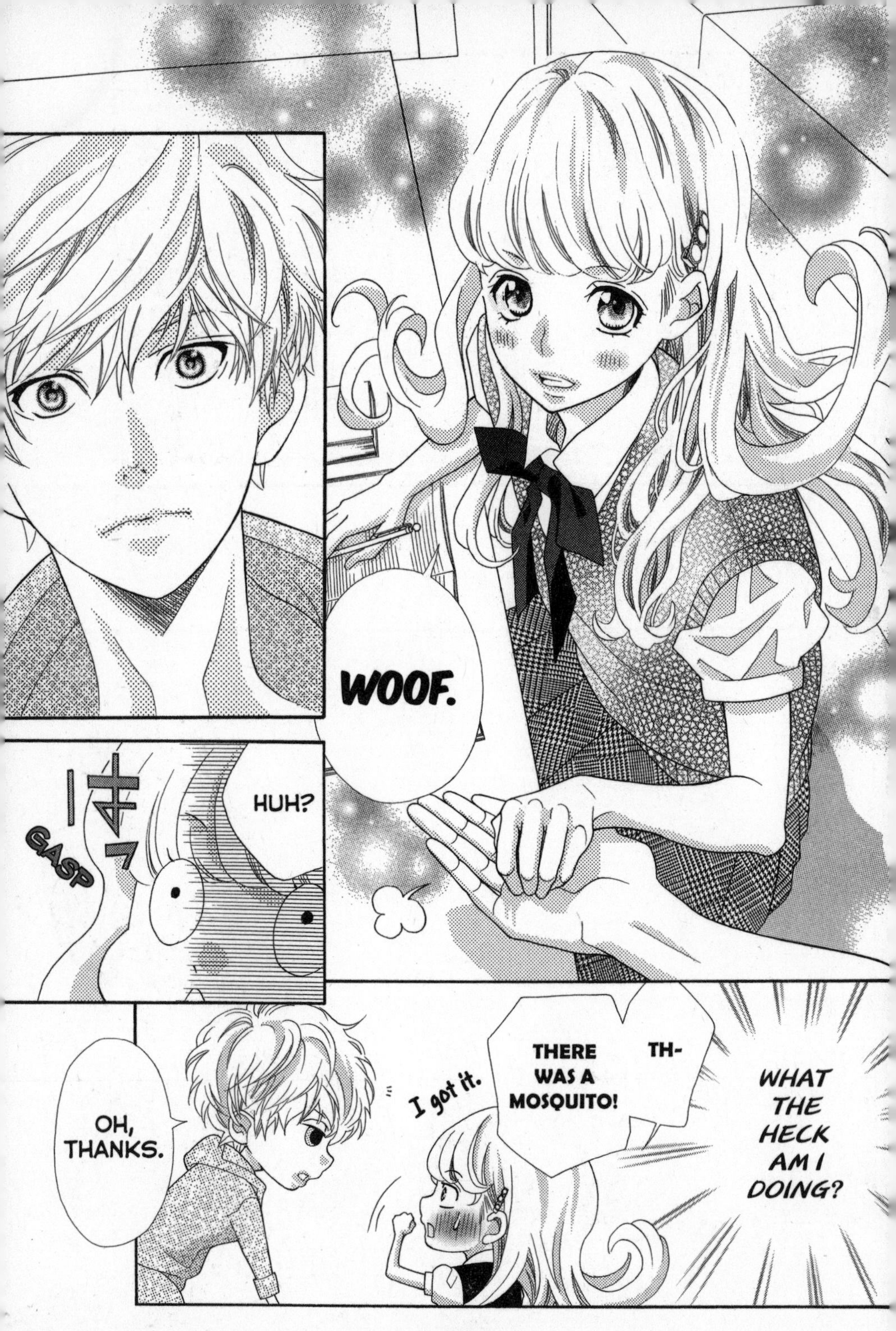
WOOF.
HUH?
GASP
WHAT THE HECK AM I DOING?
TH- THERE WAS A MOSQUITO!
I got it.
OH, THANKS.

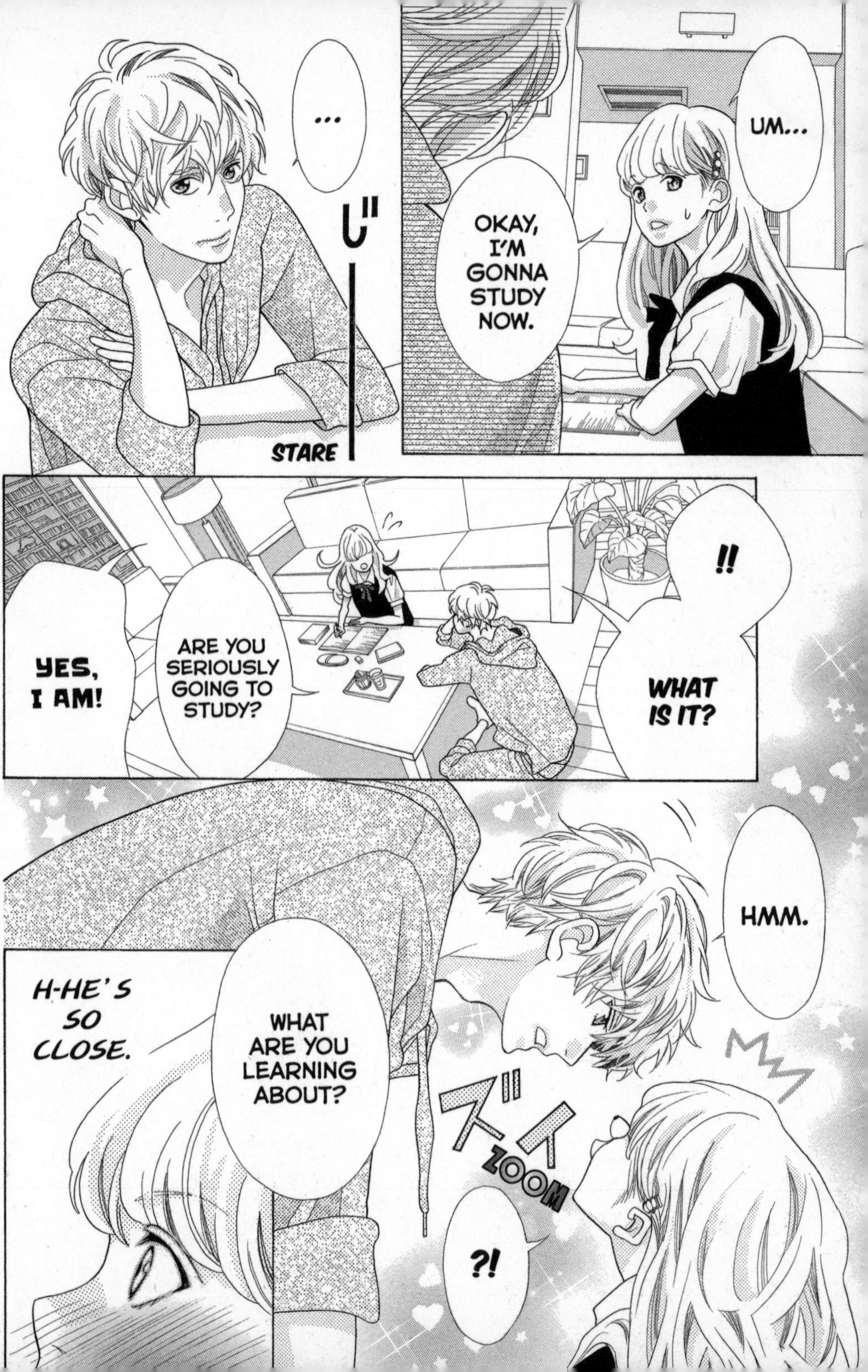
UM...
OKAY, I'M GONNA STUDY NOW.
...
じー
STARE
!!
WHAT IS IT?
ARE YOU SERIOUSLY GOING TO STUDY?
YES, I AM!
HMM.
WHAT ARE YOU LEARNING ABOUT?
H-HE'S SO CLOSE.
ズイ
ZOOM
?!

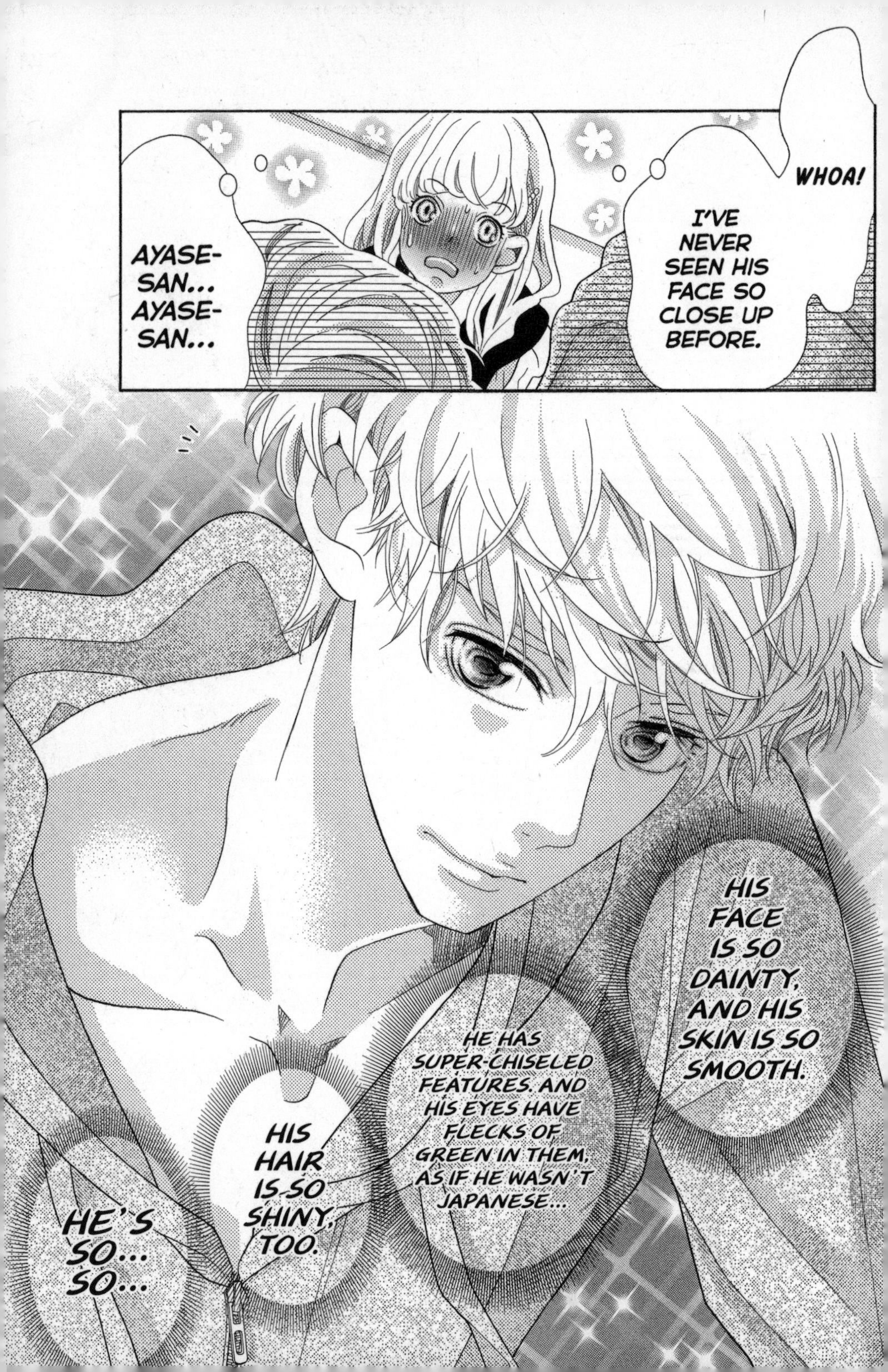
WHOA!
I'VE NEVER SEEN HIS FACE SO CLOSE UP BEFORE.
AYASE-SAN... AYASE-SAN...
HIS FACE IS SO DAINTY, AND HIS SKIN IS SO SMOOTH.
HE HAS SUPER-CHISELED FEATURES. AND HIS EYES HAVE FLECKS OF GREEN IN THEM, AS IF HE WASN'T JAPANESE...
HIS HAIR IS SO SHINY, TOO.
HE'S SO... SO...

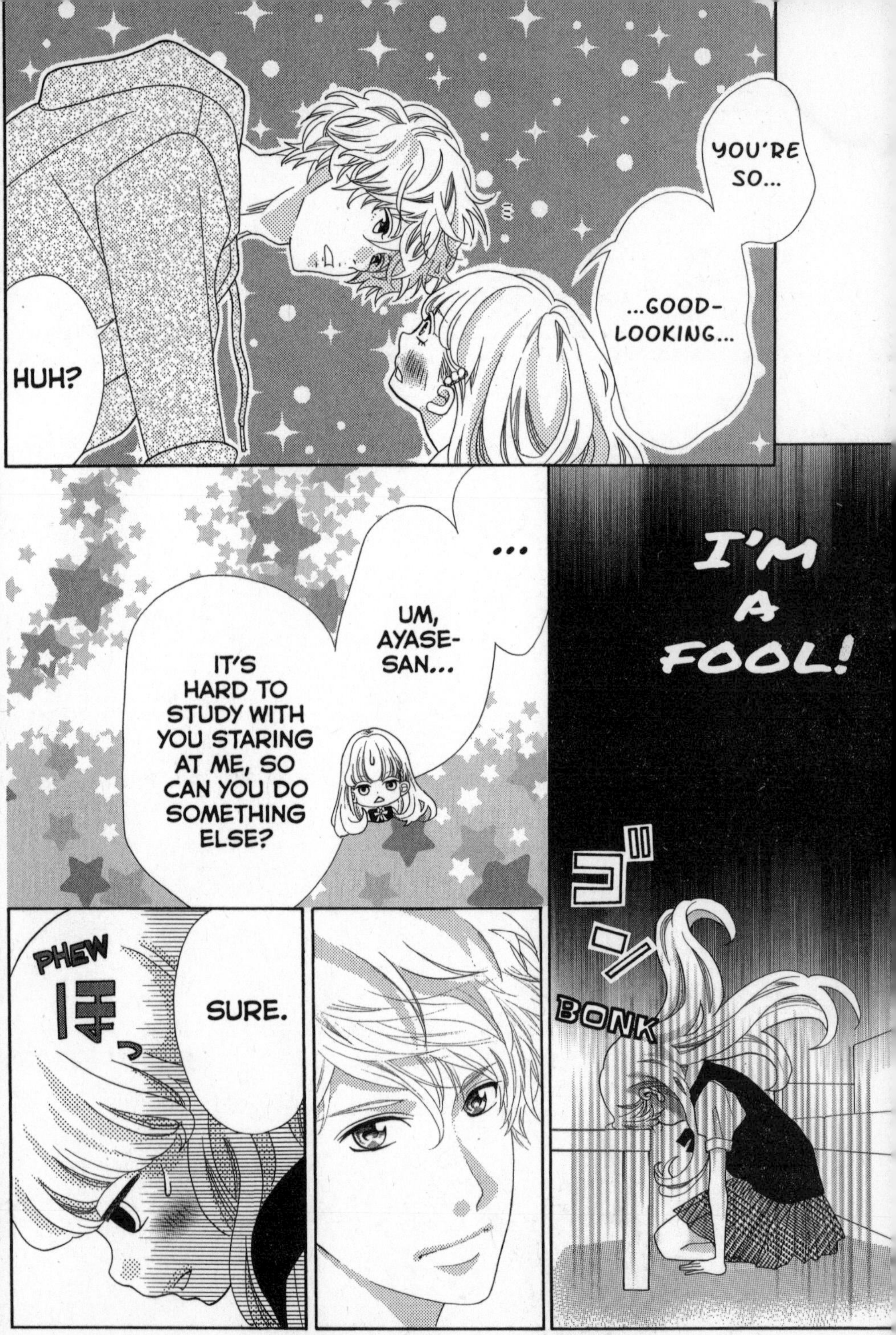
YOU'RE SO...
...GOOD-LOOKING...
HUH?
I'M A FOOL!
ゴン
BONK
...
UM, AYASE-SAN...
IT'S HARD TO STUDY WITH YOU STARING AT ME, SO CAN YOU DO SOMETHING ELSE?
SURE.
ほっ
PHEW

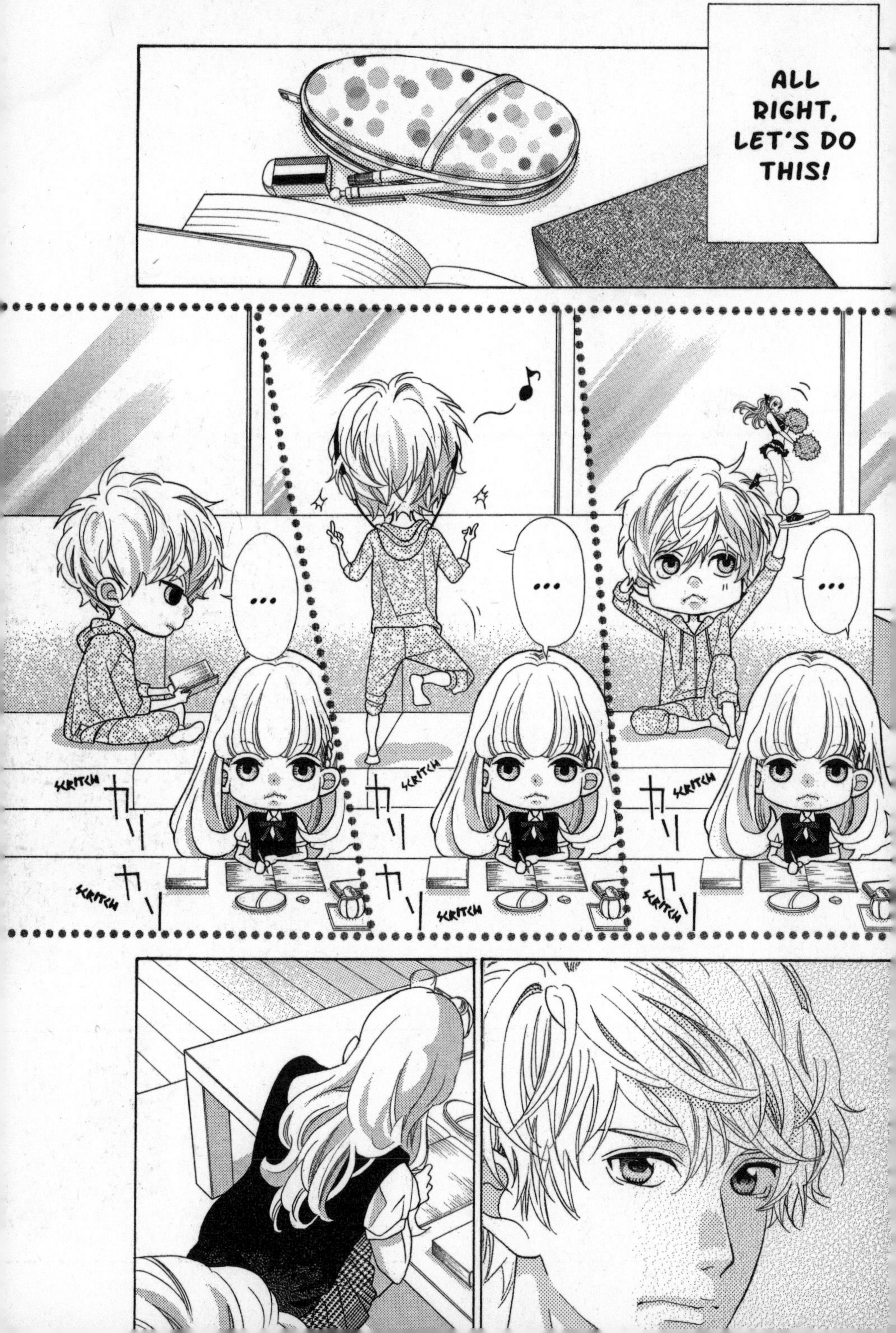
ALL RIGHT, LET'S DO THIS!
...
SCRITCH
SCRITCH
...
SCRITCH
SCRITCH
...
SCRITCH
SCRITCH

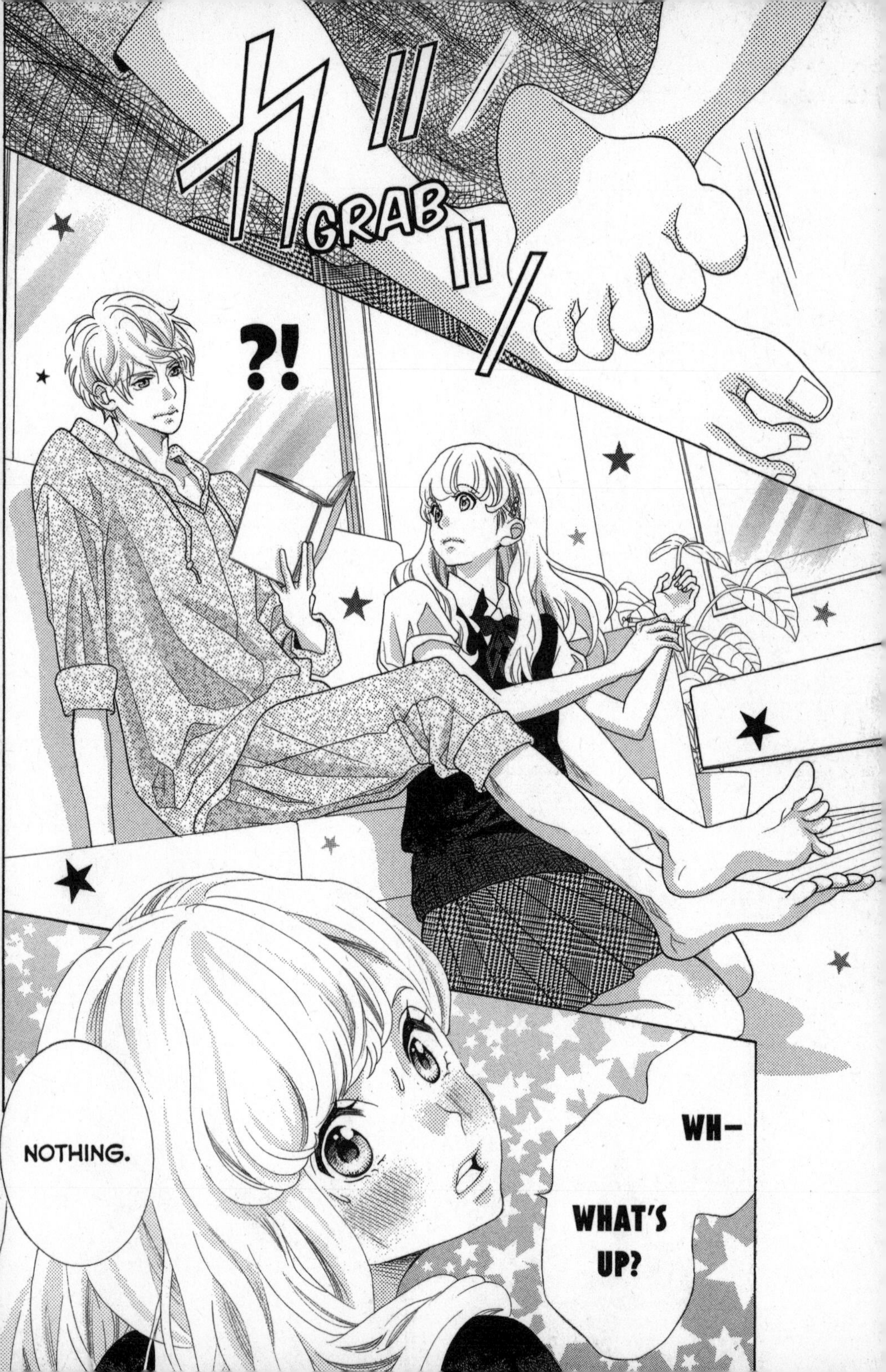
GRAB
?!
WH— WHAT'S UP?
NOTHING.

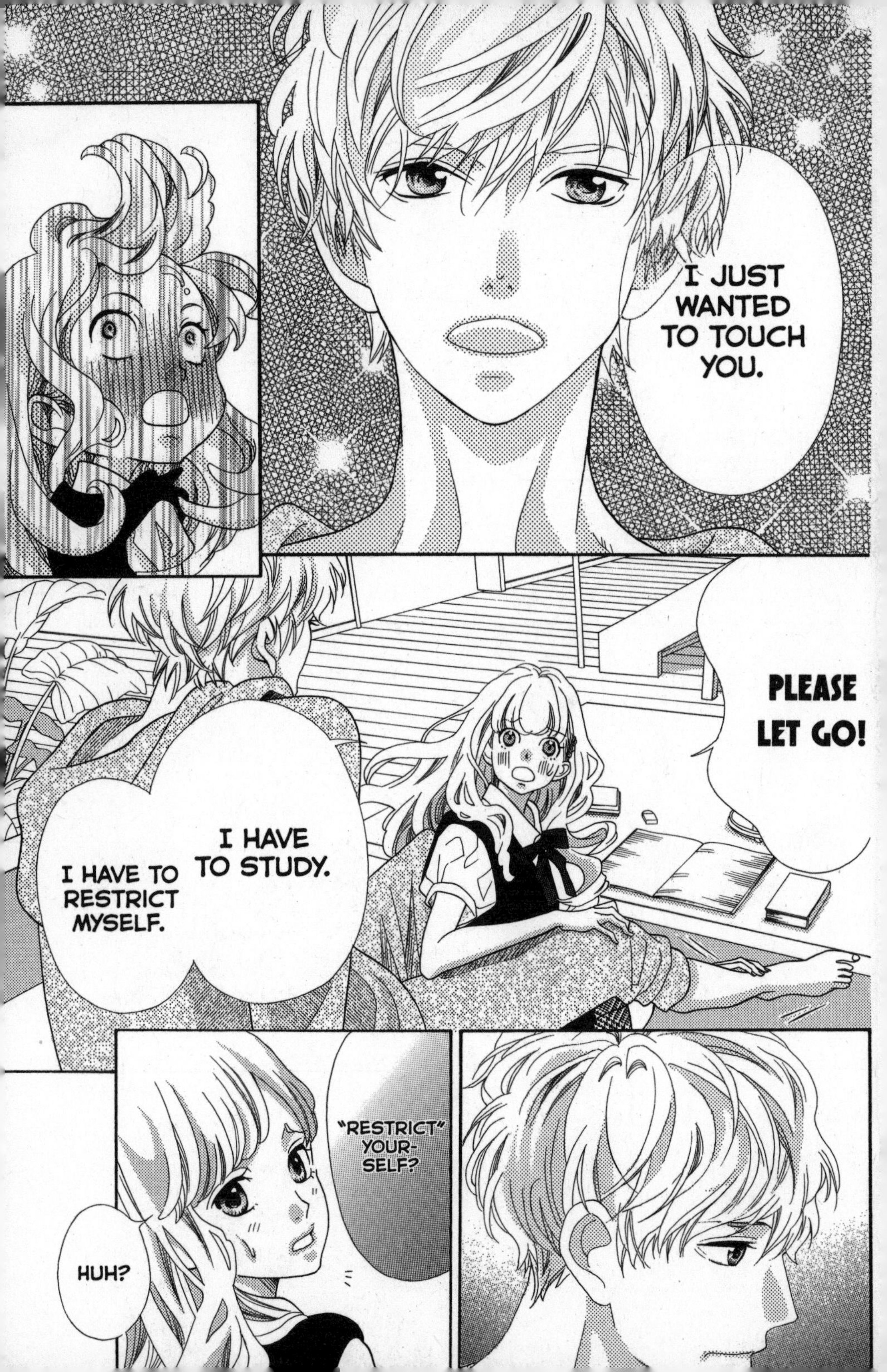
I JUST WANTED TO TOUCH YOU.
PLEASE LET GO!
I HAVE TO STUDY.
I HAVE TO RESTRICT MYSELF.
"RESTRICT" YOUR-SELF?
HUH?

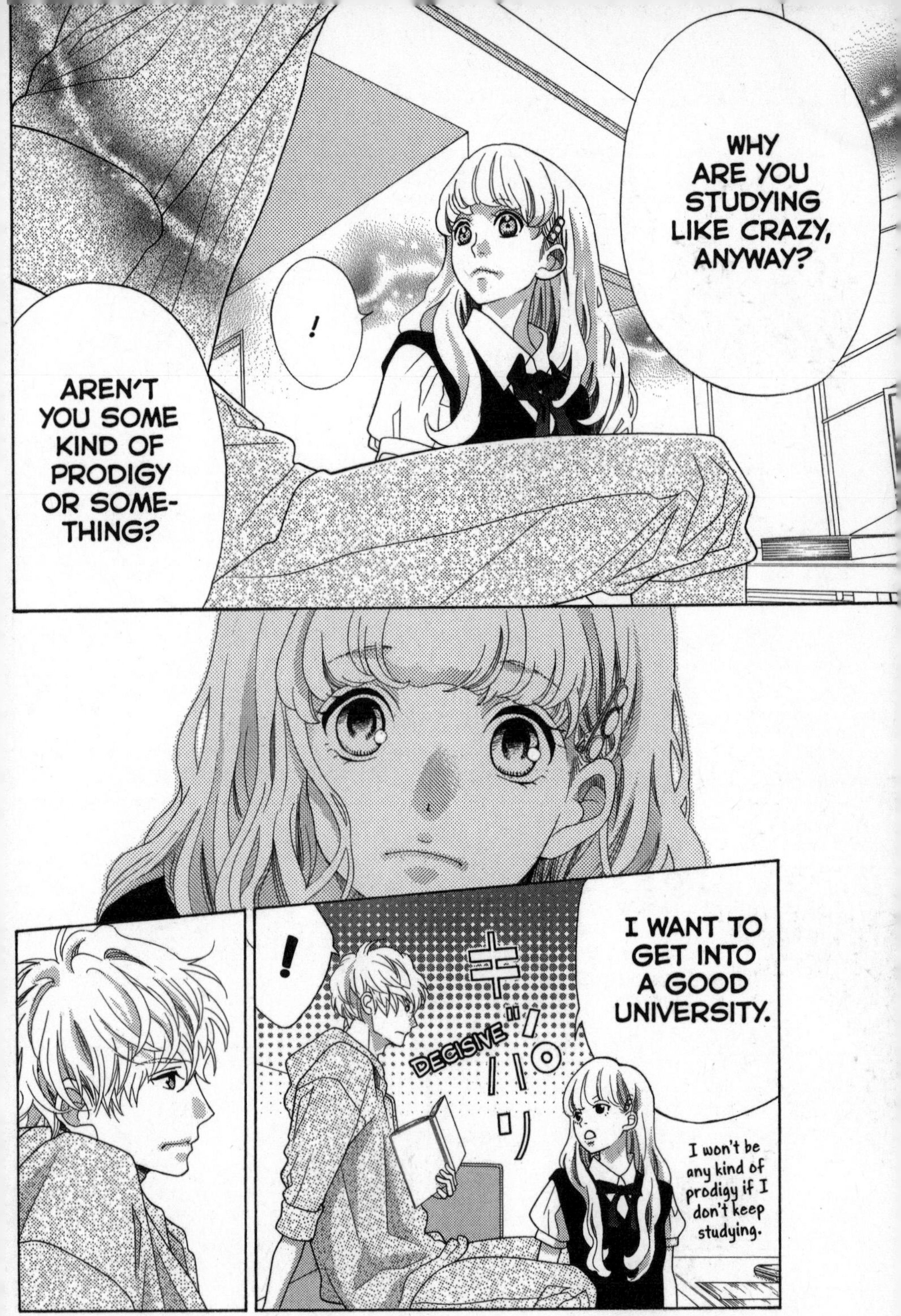
WHY ARE YOU STUDYING LIKE CRAZY, ANYWAY?
!
AREN'T YOU SOME KIND OF PRODIGY OR SOME-THING?
I WANT TO GET INTO A GOOD UNIVERSITY.
!
DECISIVE
I won't be any kind of prodigy if I don't keep studying.

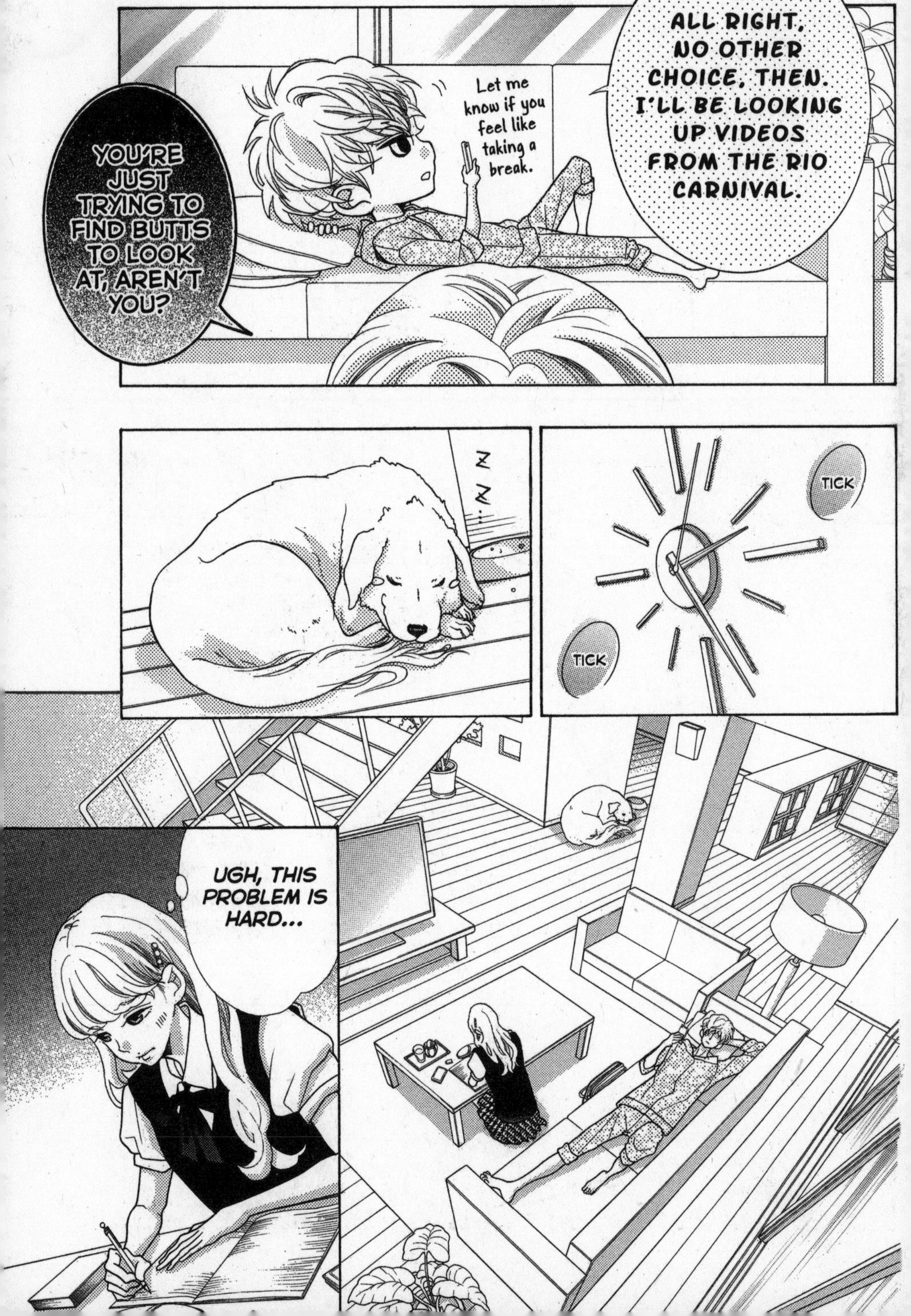
ALL RIGHT, NO OTHER CHOICE, THEN. I'LL BE LOOKING UP VIDEOS FROM THE RIO CARNIVAL.
Let me know if you feel like taking a break.
YOU'RE JUST TRYING TO FIND BUTTS TO LOOK AT, AREN'T YOU?
TICK
TICK
Z Z...
UGH, THIS PROBLEM IS HARD...

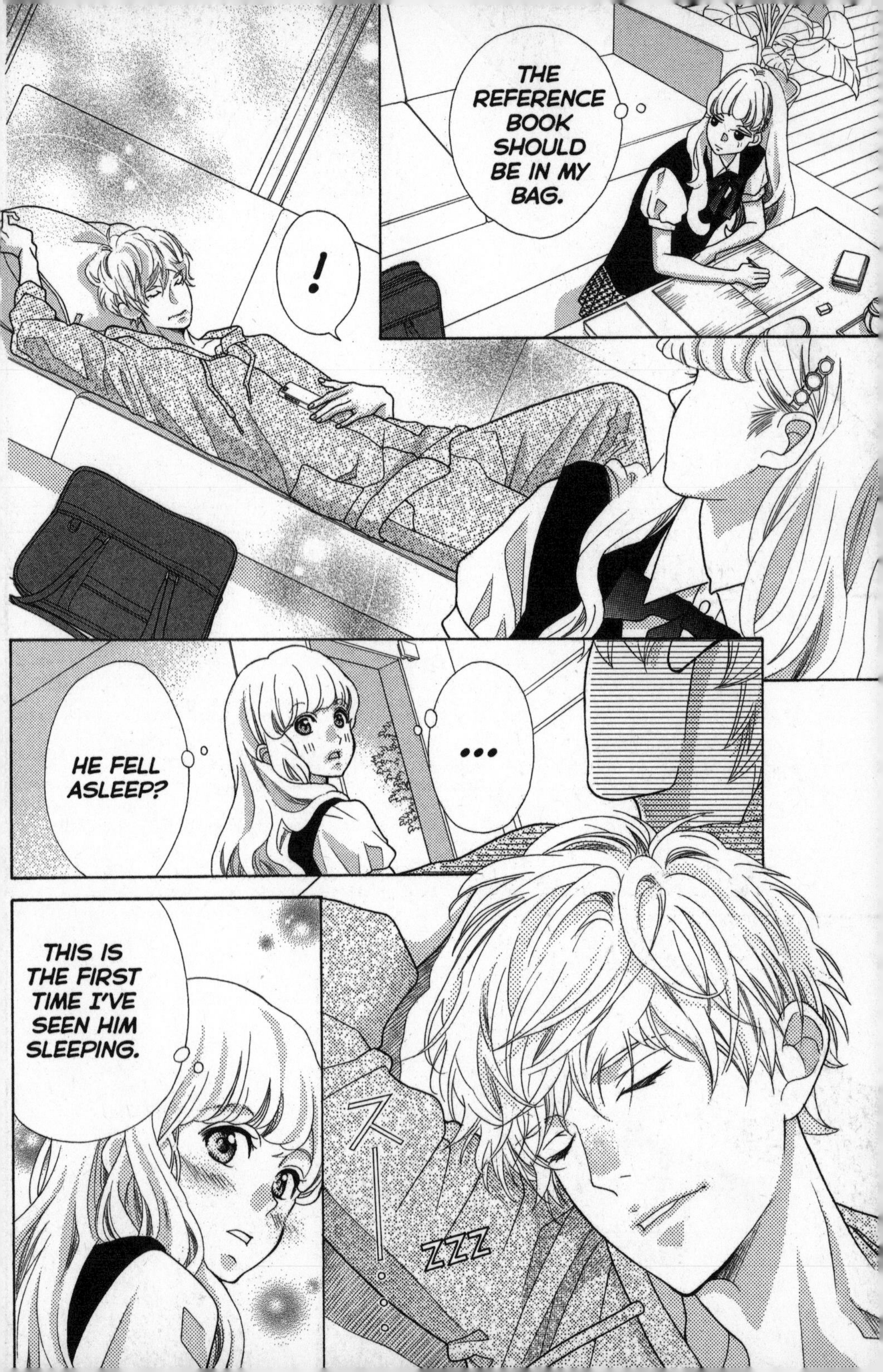
THE REFERENCE BOOK SHOULD BE IN MY BAG.
!
...
HE FELL ASLEEP?
THIS IS THE FIRST TIME I'VE SEEN HIM SLEEPING.
ZZZ

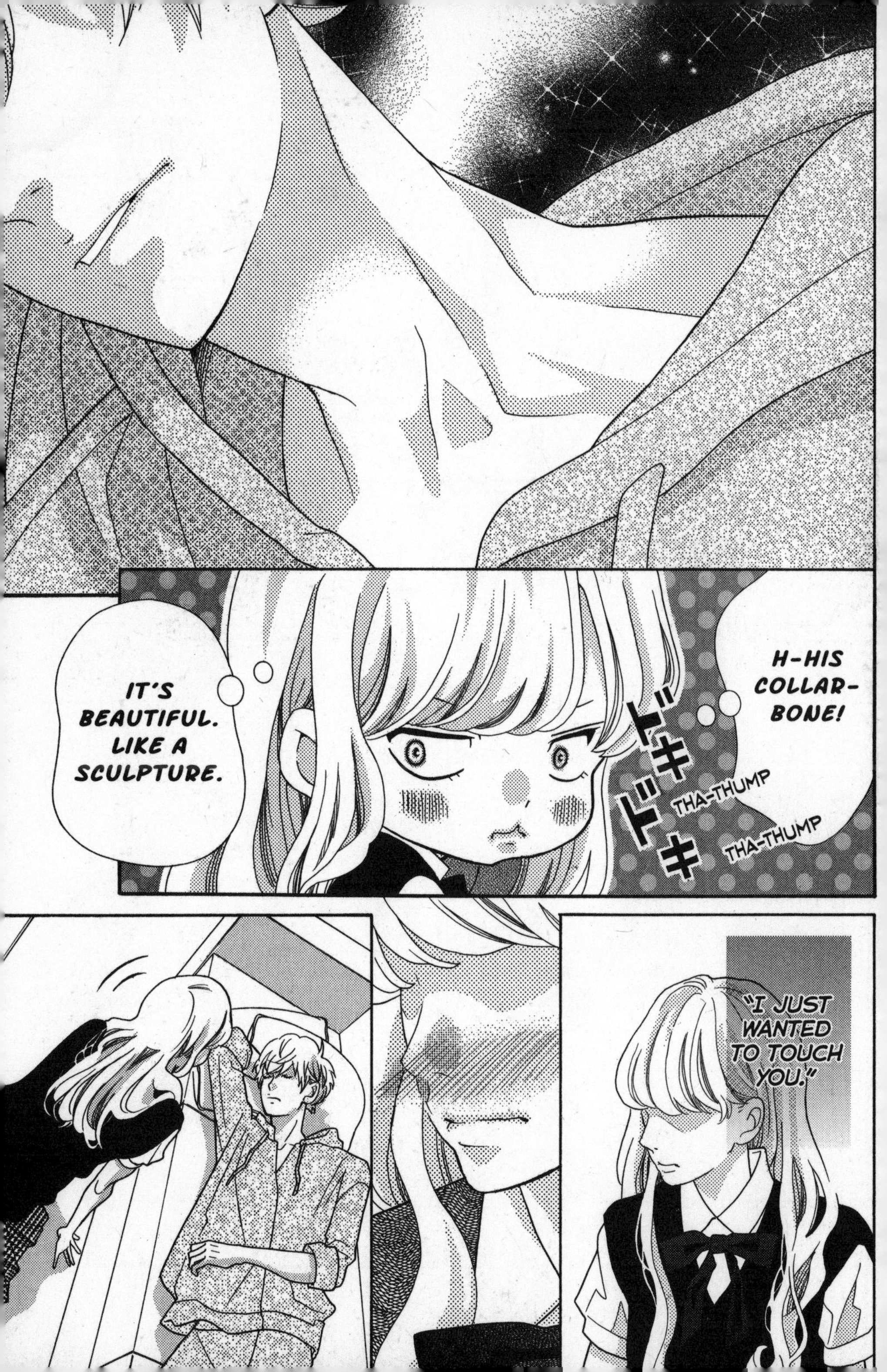
H-HIS COLLAR-BONE!
ドキ ドキ
THA-THUMP THA-THUMP
IT'S BEAUTIFUL. LIKE A SCULPTURE.
"I JUST WANTED TO TOUCH YOU."

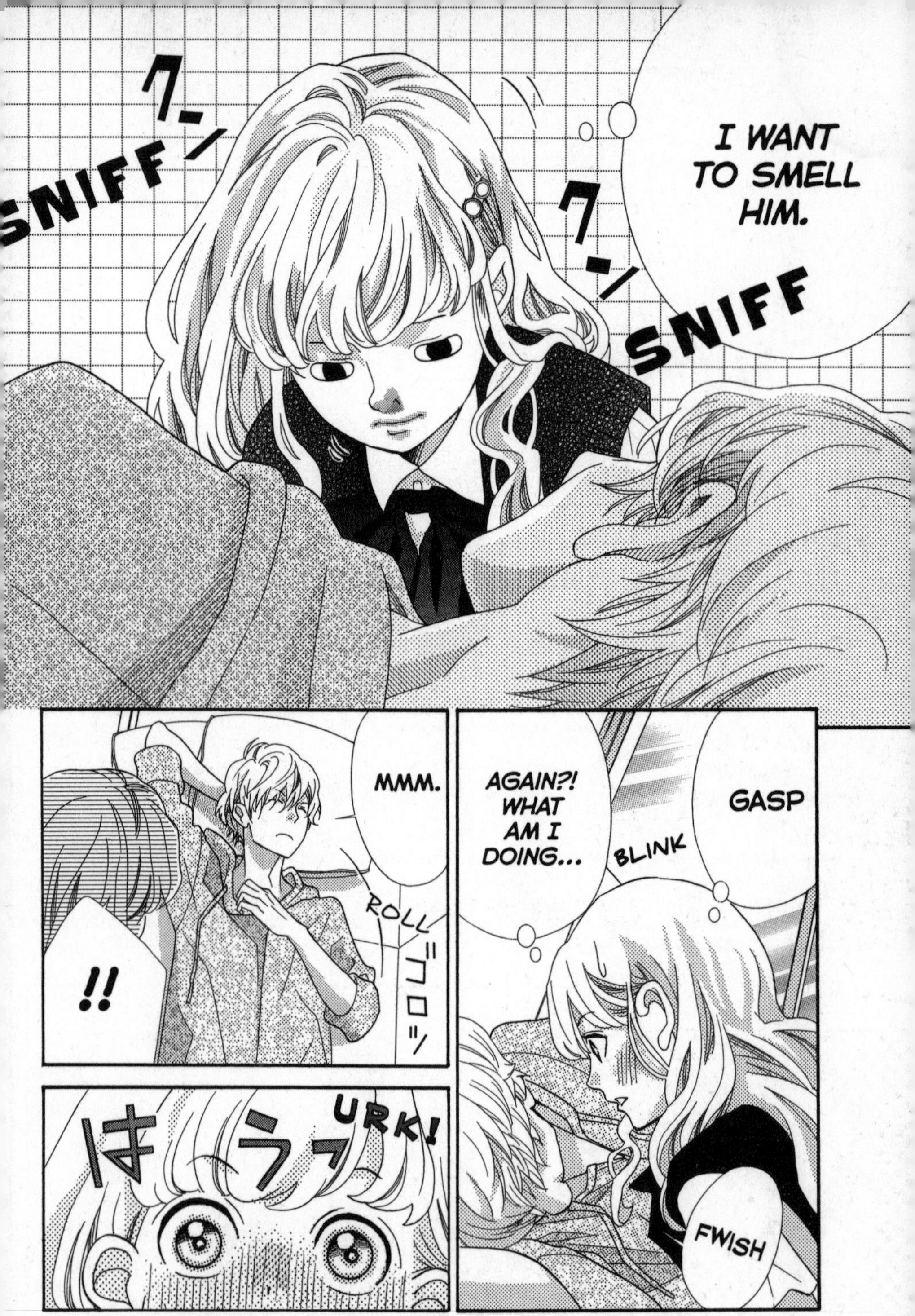
I WANT TO SMELL HIM.
クン
SNIFF
クン
SNIFF
GASP
BLINK
AGAIN?! WHAT AM I DOING...
FWISH
MMM.
ROLL
ゴロッ
!!
URK!
はっ

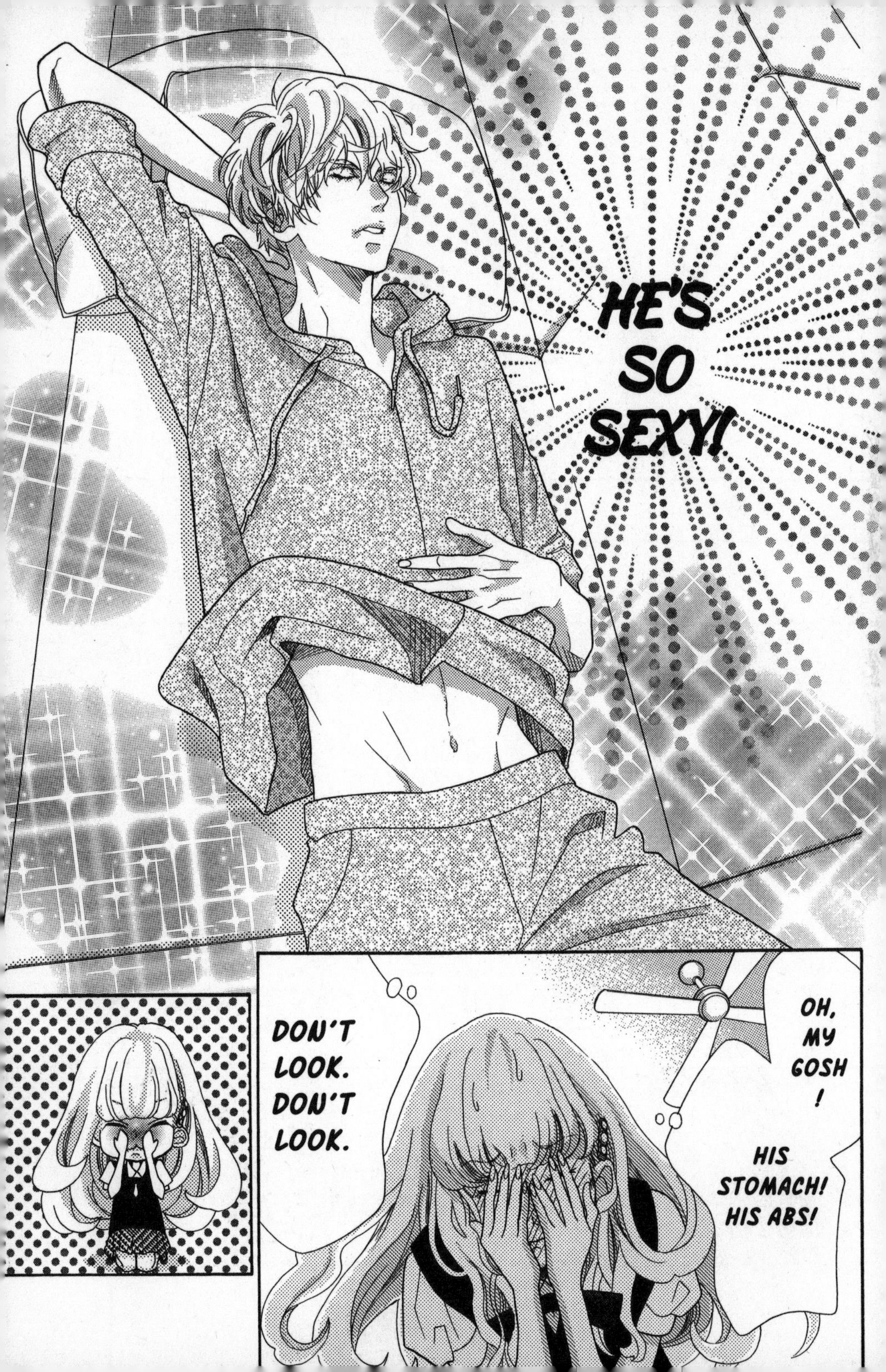
HE'S SO SEXY!
OH, MY GOSH!
HIS STOMACH! HIS ABS!
DON'T LOOK. DON'T LOOK.

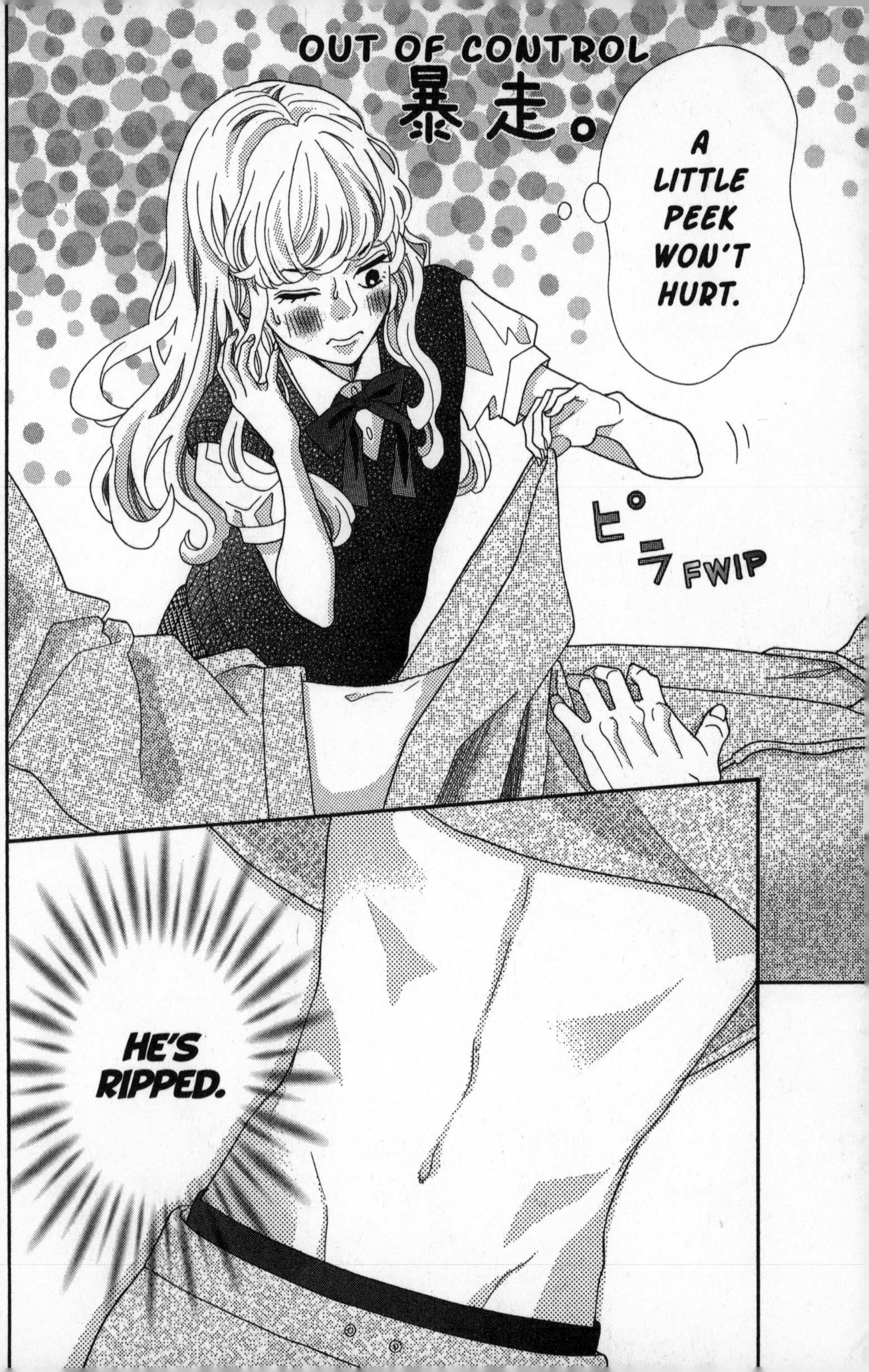
OUT OF CONTROL
暴走。
A LITTLE PEEK WON'T HURT.
ピラ FWIP
HE'S RIPPED.

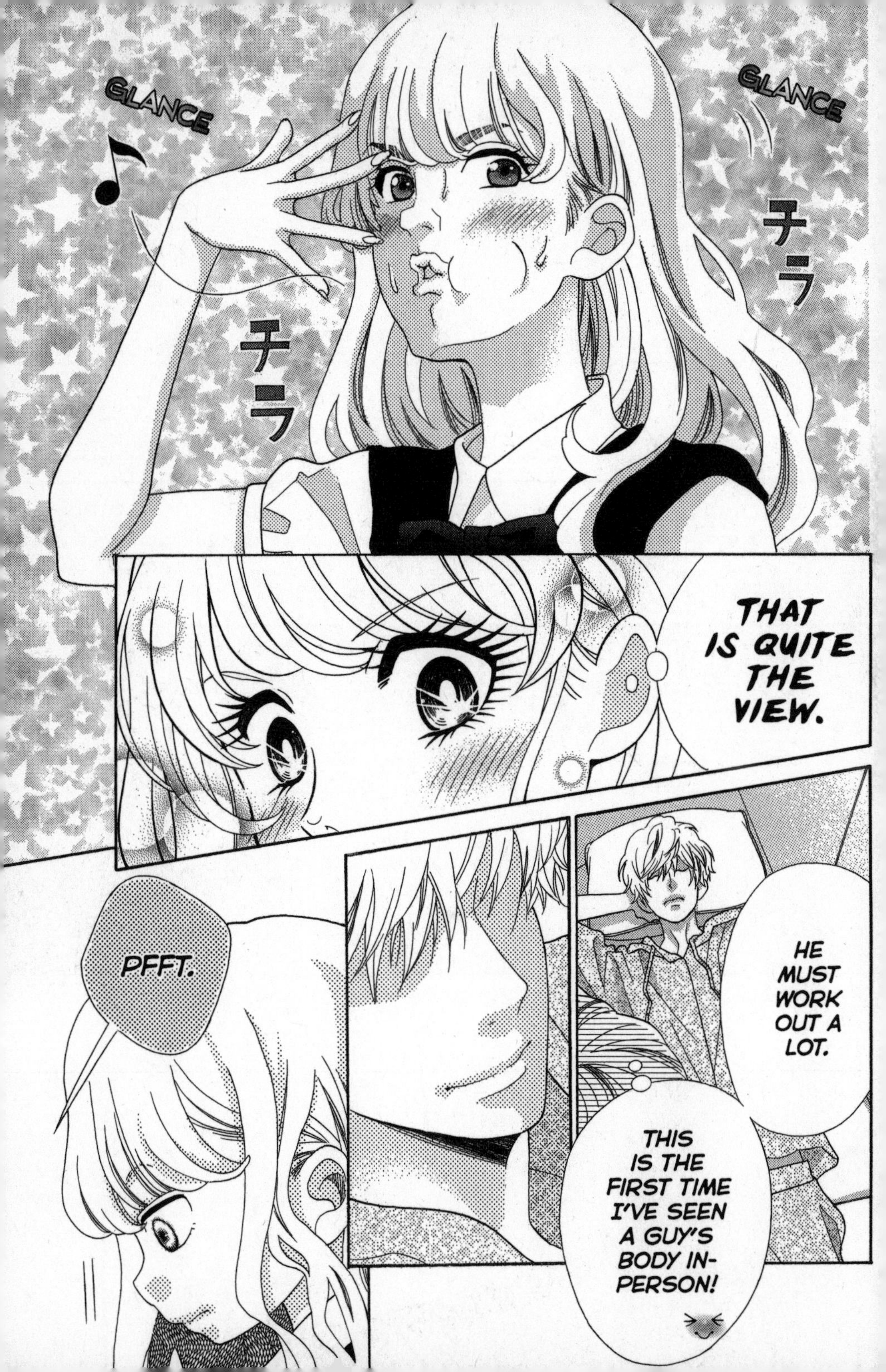
GLANCE
チラ
GLANCE
チラ
THAT IS QUITE THE VIEW.
HE MUST WORK OUT A LOT.
THIS IS THE FIRST TIME I'VE SEEN A GUY'S BODY IN-PERSON!
PFFT.

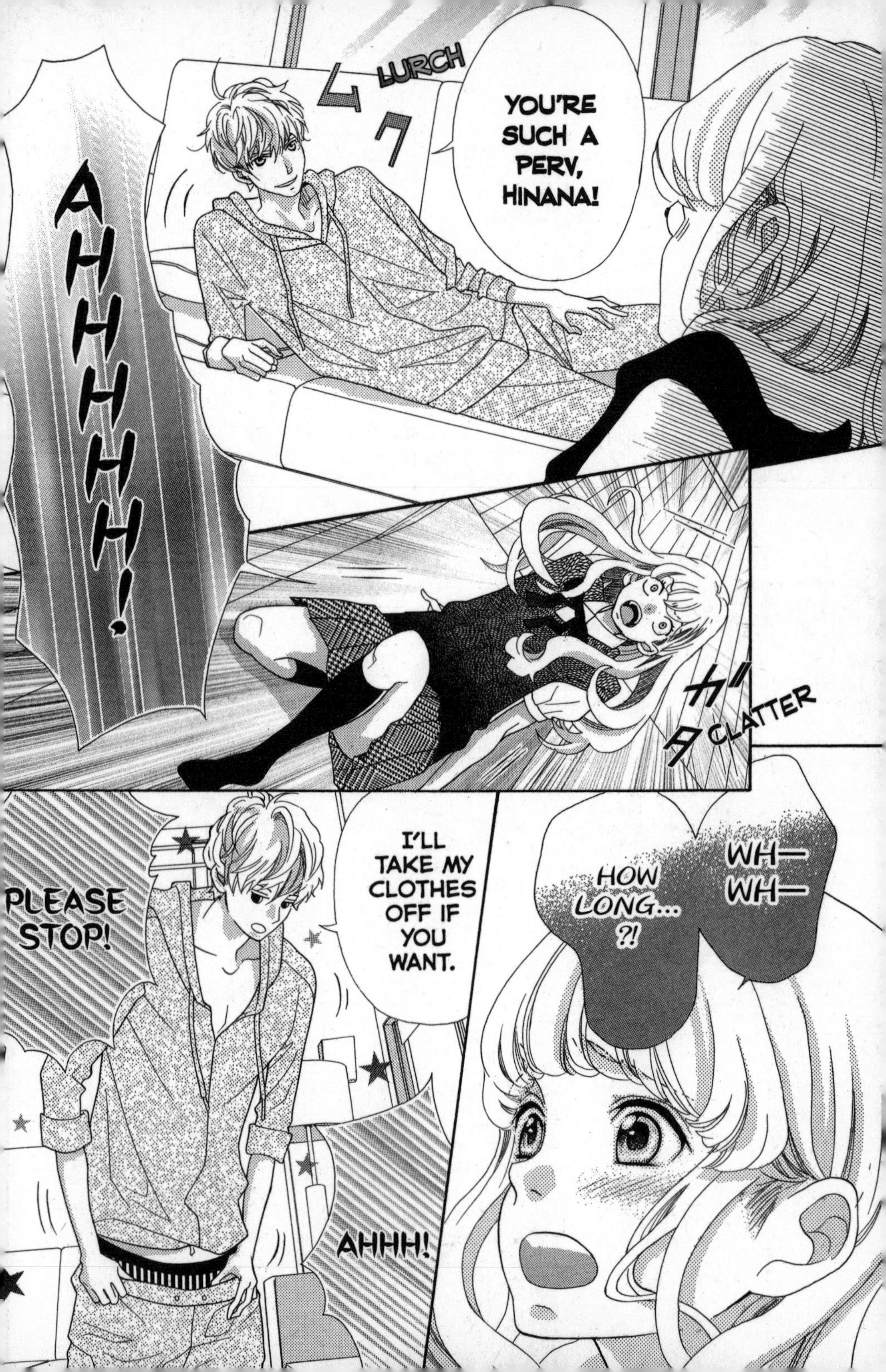
YOU'RE SUCH A PERV, HINANA!
ムク LURCH
ガタ CLATTER
AHHHHHH!
WH— WH—
HOW LONG...?!
I'LL TAKE MY CLOTHES OFF IF YOU WANT.
AHHH!
PLEASE STOP!

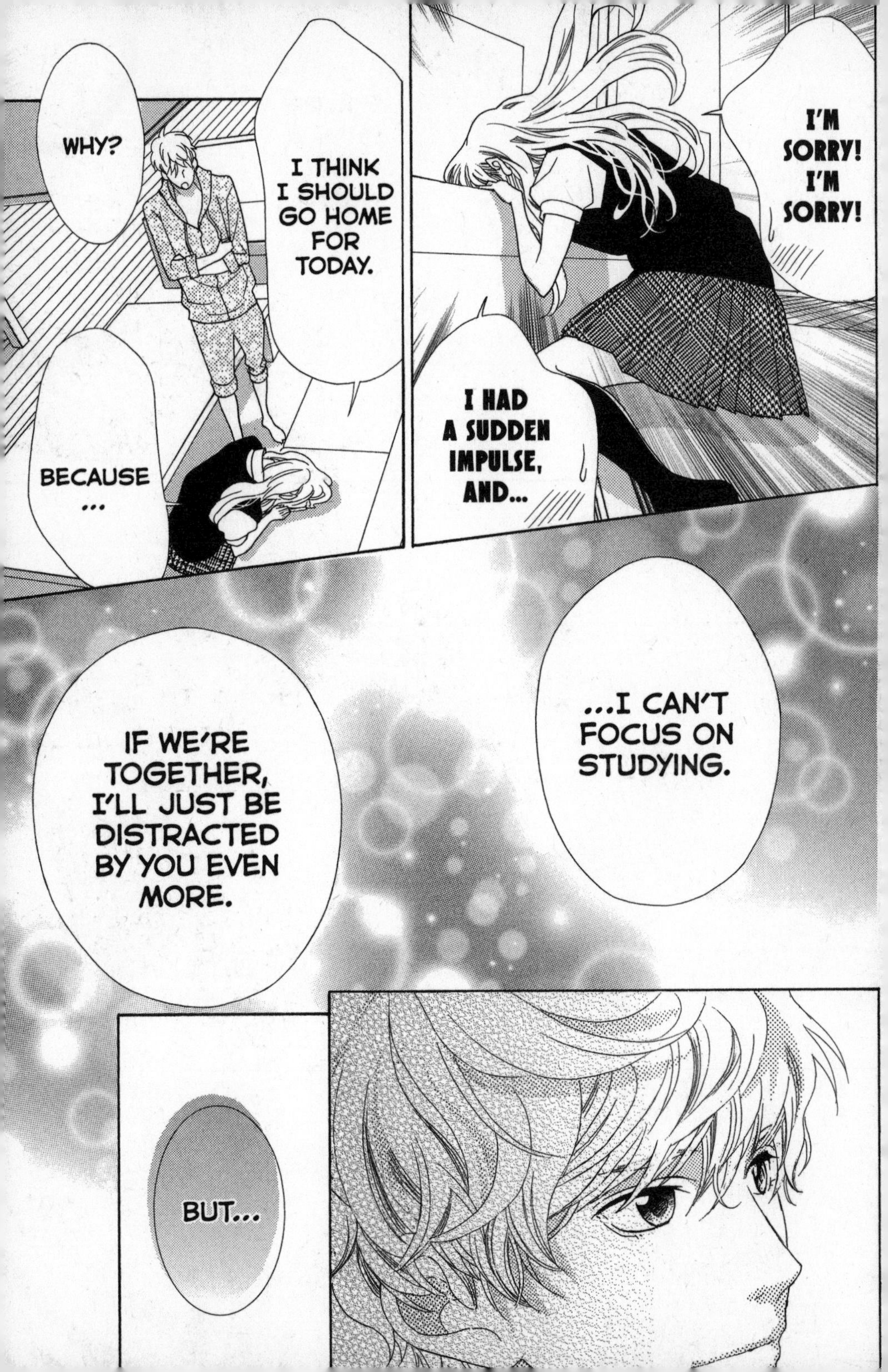
I'M SORRY! I'M SORRY!
I HAD A SUDDEN IMPULSE, AND...
I THINK I SHOULD GO HOME FOR TODAY.
WHY?
BECAUSE ...
...I CAN'T FOCUS ON STUDYING.
IF WE'RE TOGETHER, I'LL JUST BE DISTRACTED BY YOU EVEN MORE.
BUT...

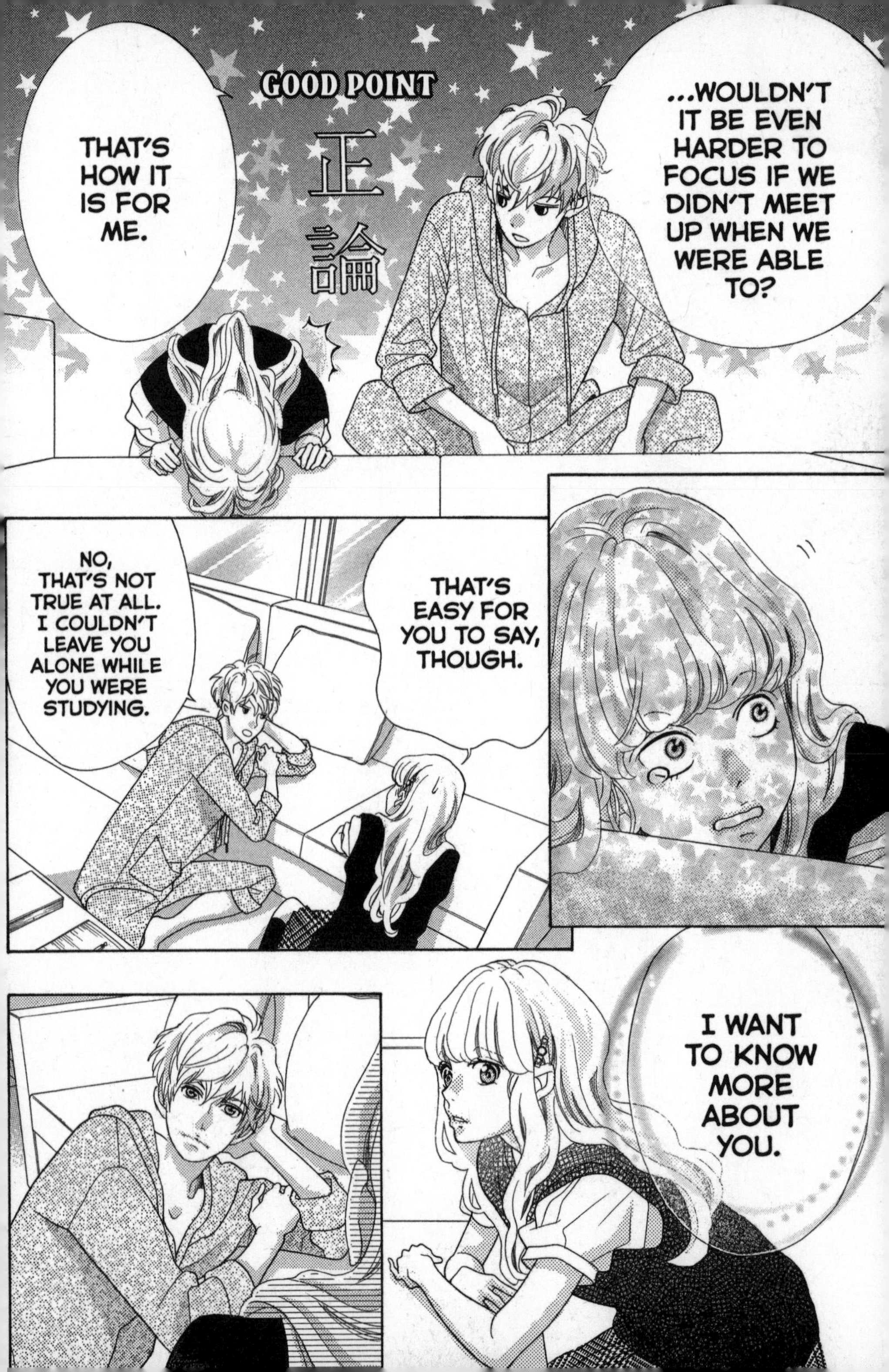
...WOULDN'T IT BE EVEN HARDER TO FOCUS IF WE DIDN'T MEET UP WHEN WE WERE ABLE TO?
GOOD POINT
正論
THAT'S HOW IT IS FOR ME.
THAT'S EASY FOR YOU TO SAY, THOUGH.
NO, THAT'S NOT TRUE AT ALL. I COULDN'T LEAVE YOU ALONE WHILE YOU WERE STUDYING.
I WANT TO KNOW MORE ABOUT YOU.

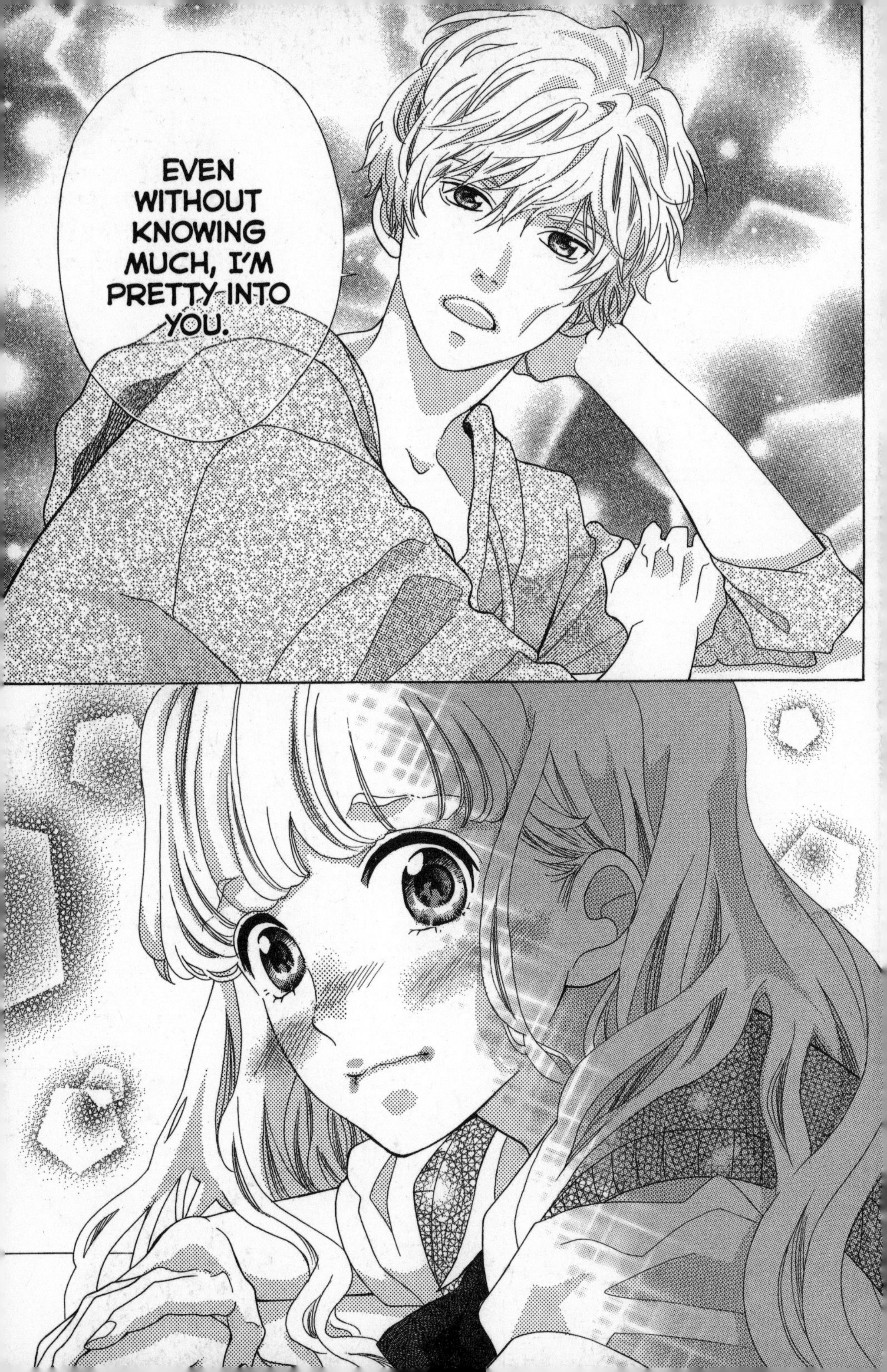
EVEN WITHOUT KNOWING MUCH, I'M PRETTY INTO YOU.

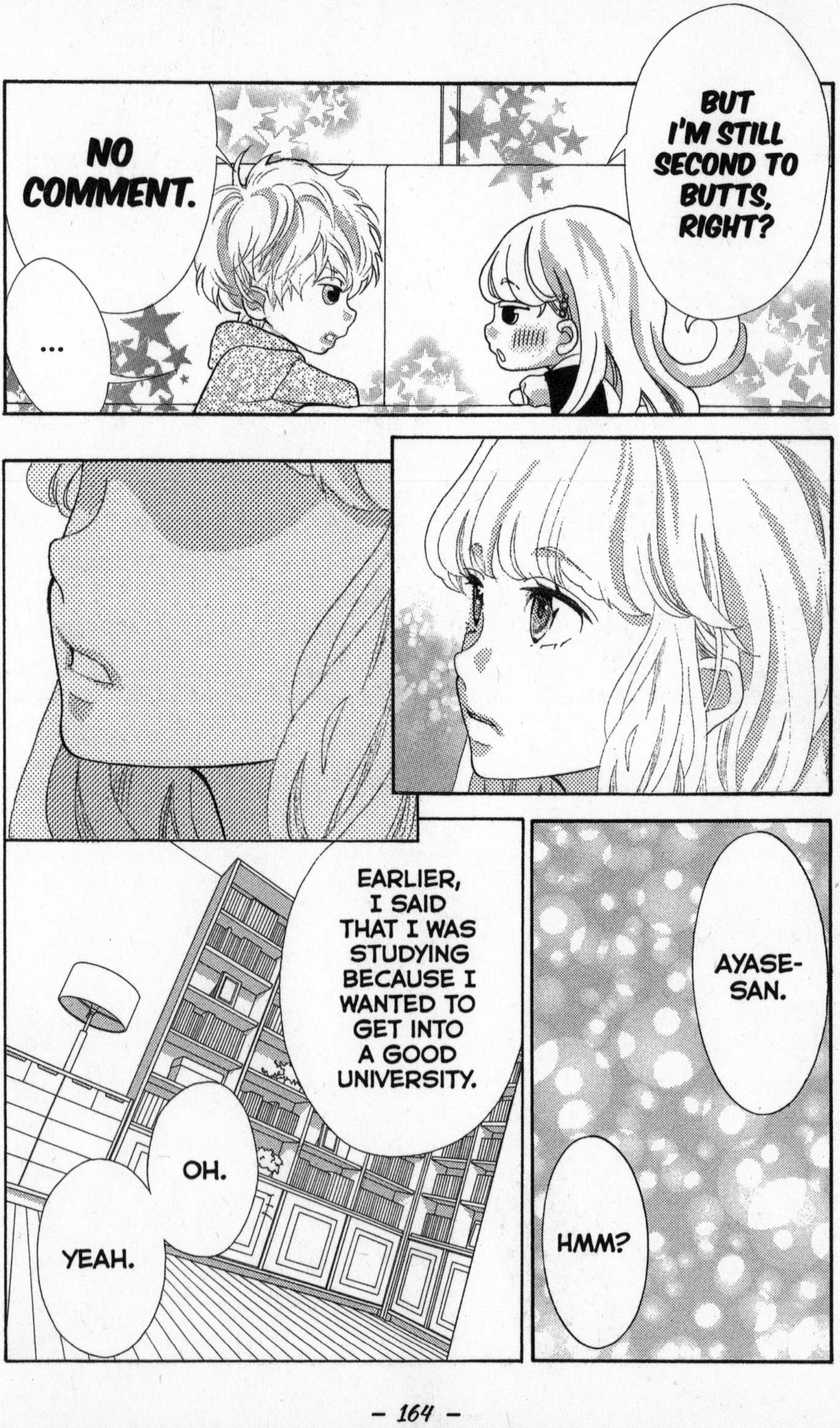
BUT I'M STILL SECOND TO BUTTS, RIGHT?
NO COMMENT.
...
AYASE-SAN.
HMM?
EARLIER, I SAID THAT I WAS STUDYING BECAUSE I WANTED TO GET INTO A GOOD UNIVERSITY.
OH.
YEAH.

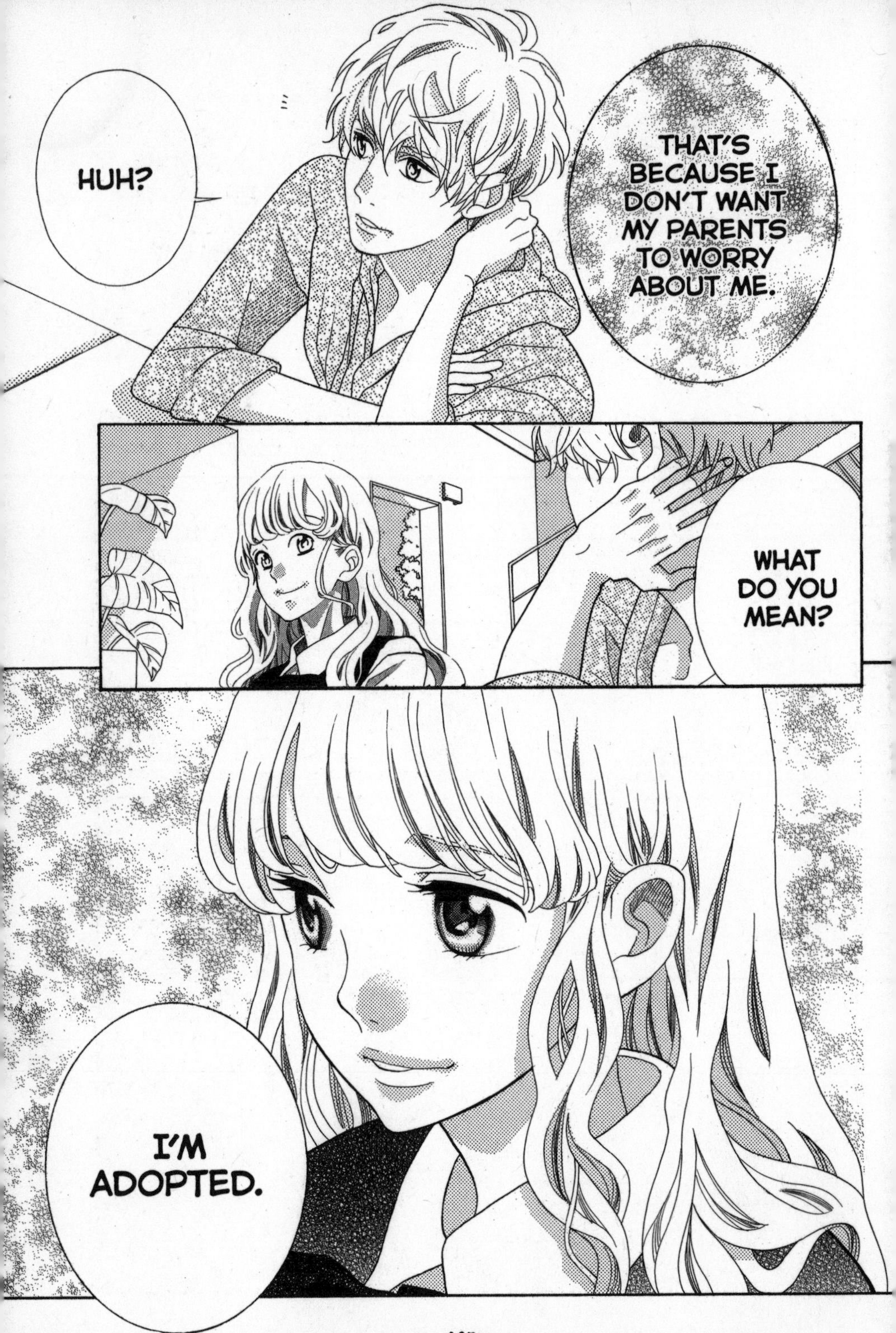
THAT'S BECAUSE I DON'T WANT MY PARENTS TO WORRY ABOUT ME.
HUH?
WHAT DO YOU MEAN?
I'M ADOPTED.

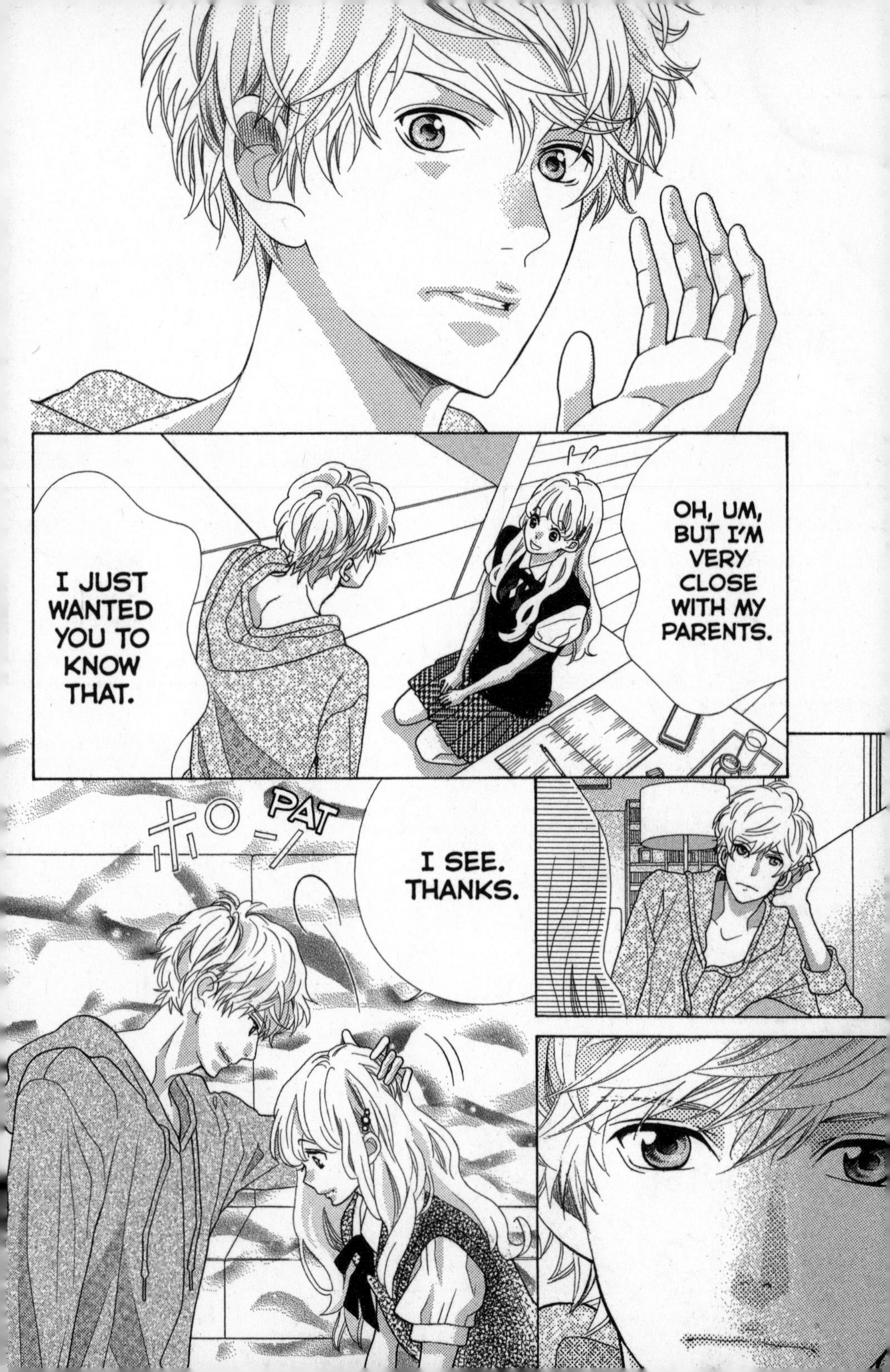
OH, UM, BUT I'M VERY CLOSE WITH MY PARENTS.
I JUST WANTED YOU TO KNOW THAT.
I SEE. THANKS.
PAT

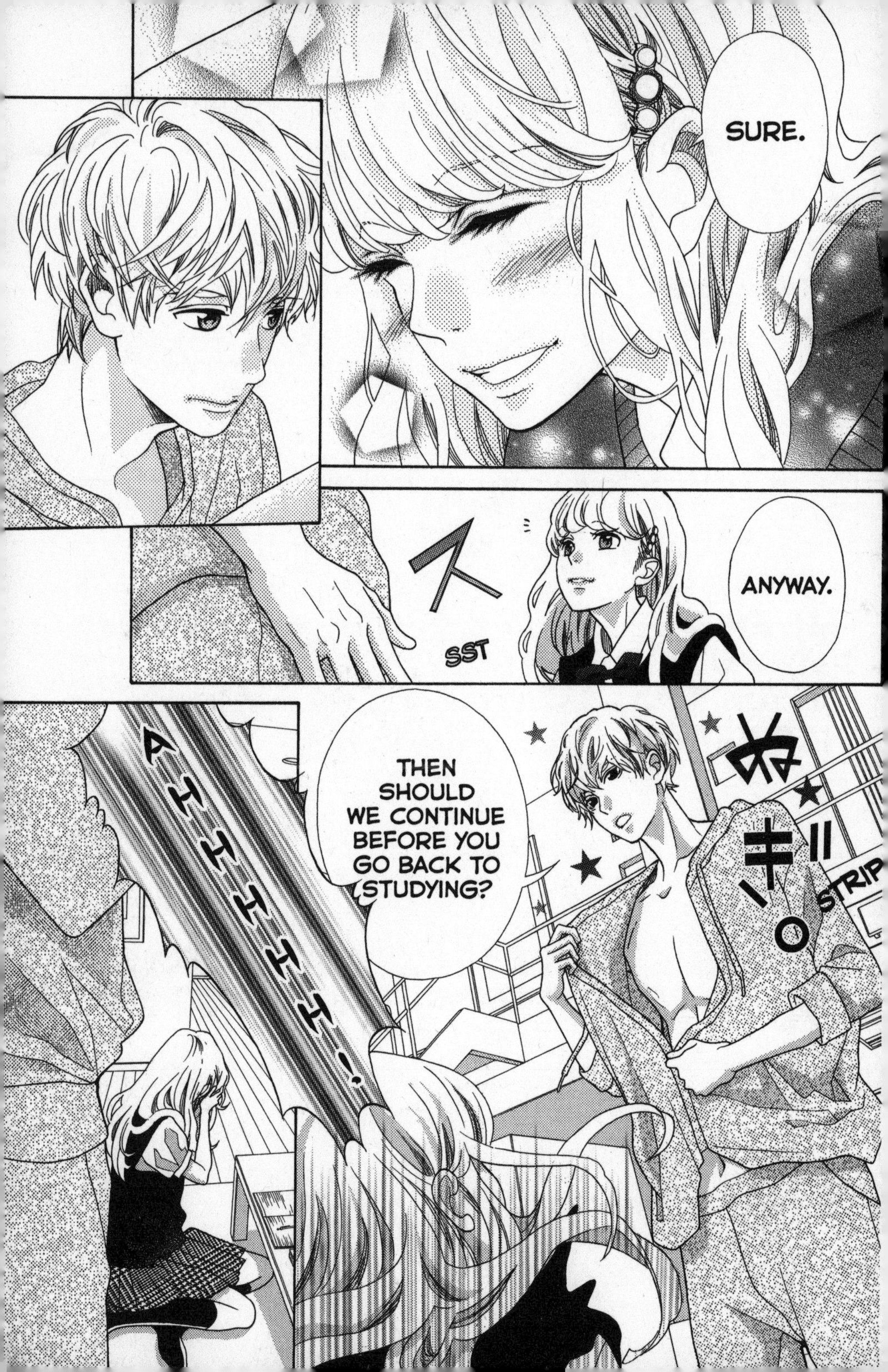
SURE.
ANYWAY.
SST
STRIP
THEN SHOULD WE CONTINUE BEFORE YOU GO BACK TO STUDYING?
AHHHHHH!!

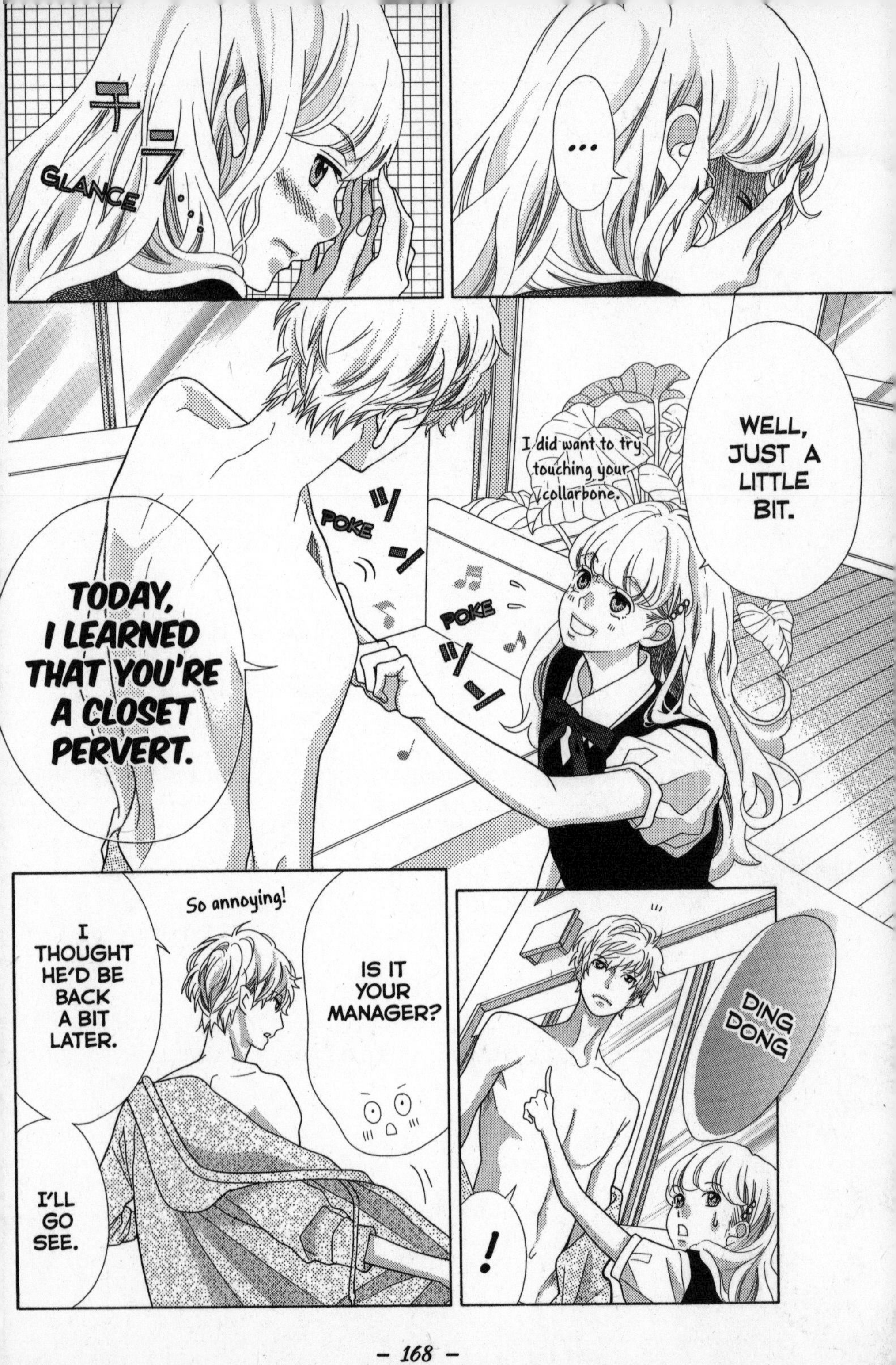

...
GLANCE
WELL, JUST A LITTLE BIT.
I did want to try touching your collarbone.
POKE
POKE
TODAY, I LEARNED THAT YOU'RE A CLOSET PERVERT.
DING DONG
!
IS IT YOUR MANAGER?
So annoying!
I THOUGHT HE'D BE BACK A BIT LATER.
I'LL GO SEE.

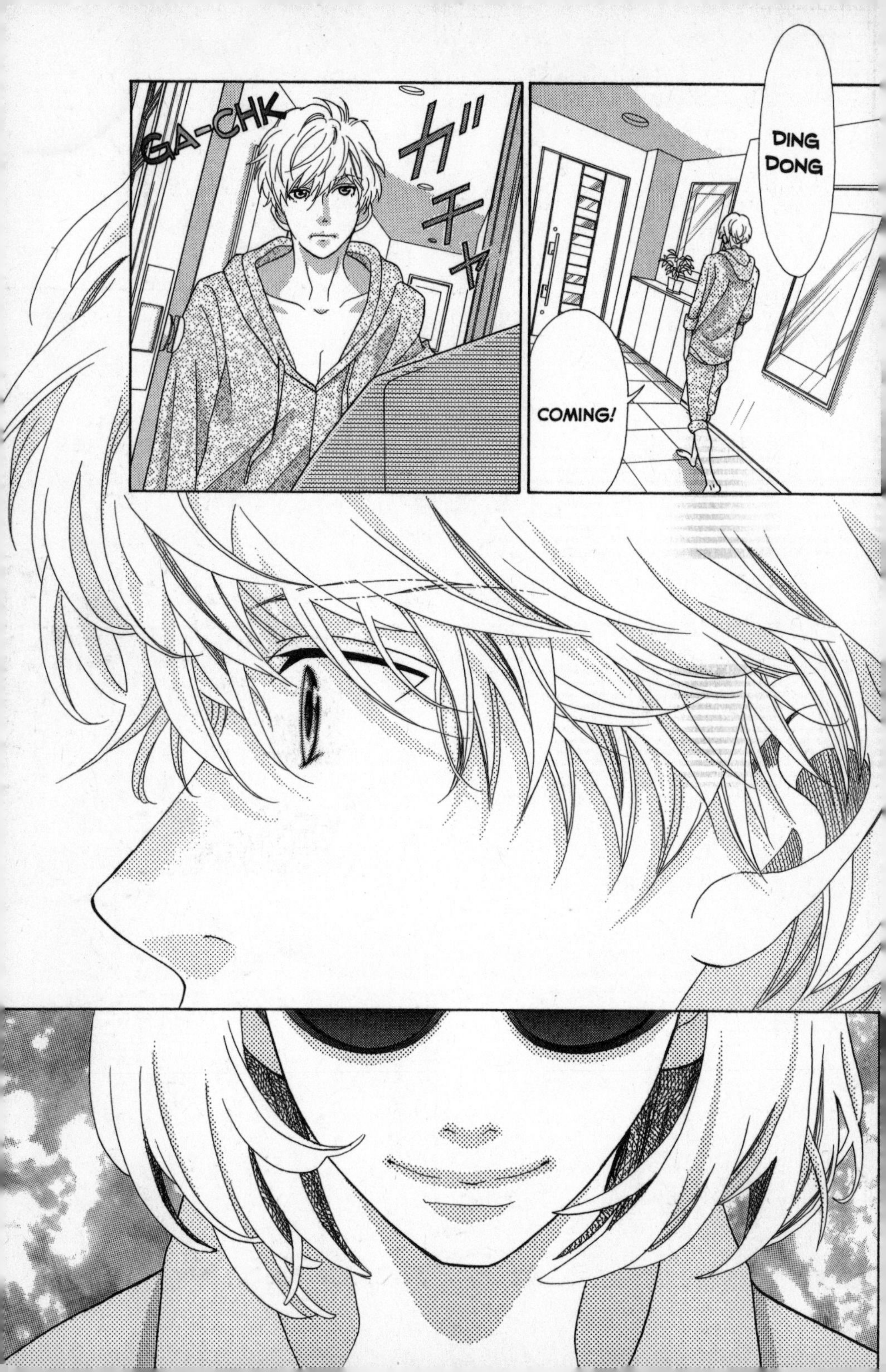
DING DONG
COMING!
GA-CHK
ガチャ

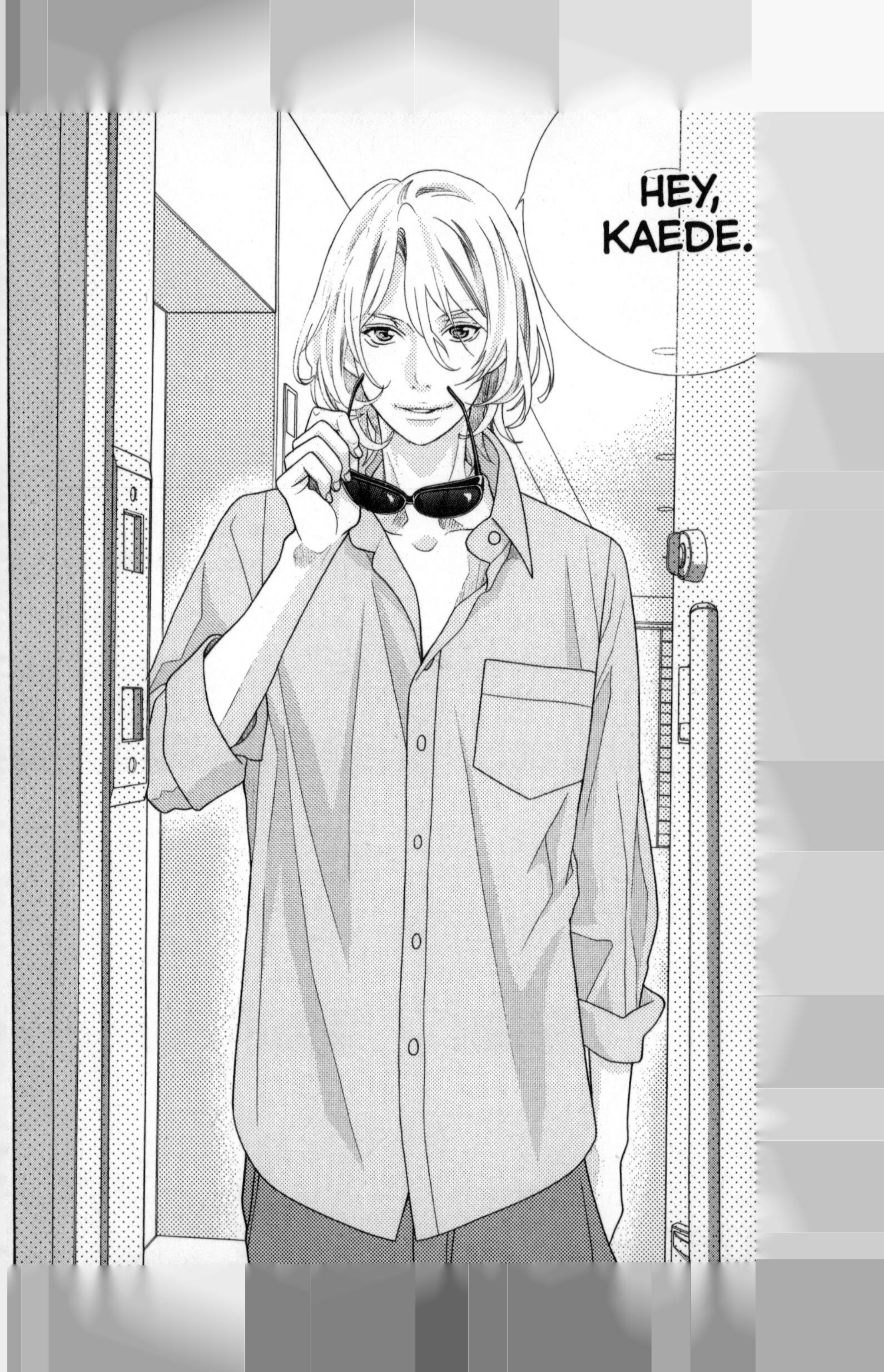
HEY, KAEDE.

TO BE CONTINUED IN
KISS ME AT THE STROKE OF MIDNIGHT
VOLUME 3

AFTERWORD

HELLO, EVERYONE!

THANK YOU FOR READING VOLUME 2!

DID YOU HAVE FUN?

WHEN THE FIRST VOLUME WAS PUBLISHED, I RECEIVED SEVERAL QUESTIONS ASKING ABOUT WHO KAEDE WAS BASED ON, BUT HE ISN'T BASED ON ANYONE IN PARTICULAR. PERSONALLY, HE WAS SORT OF A MISH-MASH OF TWO PEOPLE I HAD IN MIND. BUT I'M KEEPING IT A SECRET BECAUSE I'M IN AWE OF THEM BASED ON MY OWN INTERPRETATIONS. FUNNY BONE ALSO SHOWS UP IN THIS VOLUME, BUT THESE GUYS ALSO AREN'T BASED ON ANYONE FROM REAL LIFE.

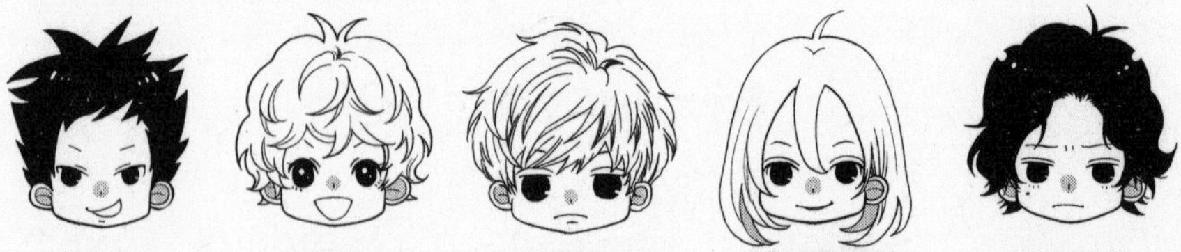

NAOTO **YUTA** **KAEDE** **MITSUKI** **AYAMI**

(NAOTO'S THE ONLY ONE WHO HASN'T BEEN REVEALED BY NAME YET, SO HERE HE IS!)

I'M NOT SURE WHAT KIND OF TROUBLE THESE GUYS WILL BE STIRRING UP UNTIL I'M FINISHED WRITING. BUT I'M GOING TO BE HAVING A LOT OF FUN WHILE DRAWING IT!

I HOPE YOU ENJOY VOLUME 3, TOO!

11.2015 -RIN MIKIMOTO

TWITTER: @RINMIKIRIN

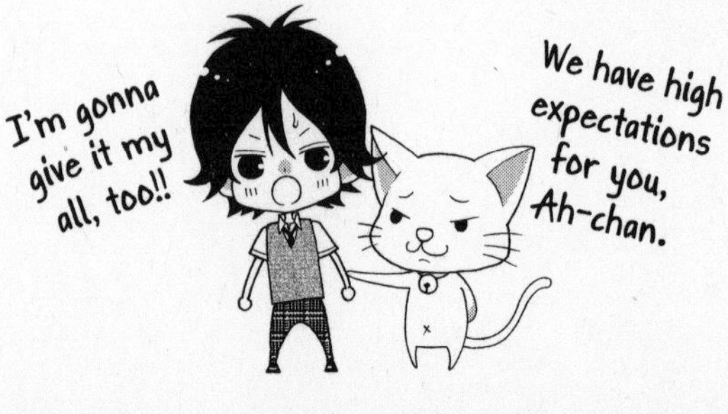
We have high expectations for you, Ah-chan.
I'm gonna give it my all, too!!

Special thanx

S.sato

H.saijyo

M.kawai

M.takayashiki

K.kaneko

Every one of the staff

Everyone in the editorial department

Horiuchi-sama

Morita-san

Saiki-san

arcoinc Kusume-sama

&U

I LOVE YOU

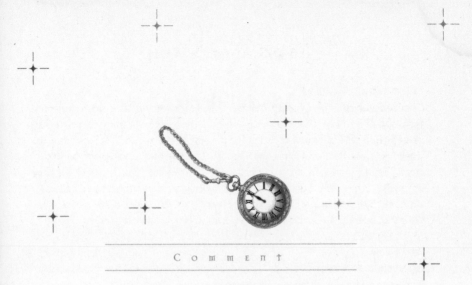

Comment

Ever since I started writing this series, I've had lots of opportunities to study up on celebrity topics. I love doing research! Unrelated to this manga, I'm currently looking into insects. It sounds dull, but I look forward to it every night before bed! Hope you enjoy Volume 2!

Rin Mikimoto

TRANSLATION NOTES

TANABATA FESTIVAL, P.57

"Tanabata," which literally translates to "the seventh evening," is a Japanese summer festival that comes from the Chinese Qixi Festival. It is most commonly held on July seventh, with several events occuring for the rest of the month. This is because, as legend goes, the deities Orihime and Hikoboshi can only meet once a year, on this night. The story revolves around Princess Orihime, the daughter of Tentei, the King of the Sky. She is skilled at weaving, and spends all her days hard at work. Because she is sad that she does not have time to meet a partner, Tentei introduces her to Hikoboshi, a boy who is talented at cowherding. When the two meet and fall in love, they forgo their weaving and cowherding, which upsets Tentei. The King forbids them from seeing each other ever again, but is later moved by his daughter's pleas, and so, he allows the couple to meet on the seventh day of the seventh month. Orihime is represented by the star Vega, and Hikoboshi is represented by the star Altair. In addition to the festival, it is custom for people to write their wishes on strips of paper and hang them on bamboo.

YUKATA, P.60

A casual summer kimono often worn to summer festivals. It is made from a much lighter cloth than regular kimono, and is easier to wear and prepare.

Based on the critically acclaimed classic horror manga

The first new *Parasyte* manga in over 20 years!

NEO PARASYTE f

BY ASUMIKO NAKAMURA, EMA TOYAMA, MIKI RINNO, LALAKO KOJIMA, KAORI YUKI, BANKO KUZE, YUUKI OBATA, KASHIO, YUI KUROE, ASIA WATANABE, MIKIMAKI, HIKARU SURUGA, HAJIME SHINJO, RENJURO KINDAICHI, AND YURI NARUSHIMA

A collection of chilling new *Parasyte* stories from Japan's top shojo artists!

Parasites: shape-shifting aliens whose only purpose is to assimilate with and consume the human race... but do these monsters have a different side? A parasite becomes a prince to save his romance-obsessed female host from a dangerous stalker. Another hosts a cooking show, in which the real monsters are revealed. These and 13 more stories, from some of the greatest shojo manga artists alive today, together make up a chilling, funny, and entertaining tribute to one of manga's horror classics!

KC
KODANSHA COMICS

WELCOME TO THE BALLROOM

By Tomo Takeuchi

Feckless high school student Tatara Fujita wants to be good at something—anything. Unfortunately, he's about as average as a slouchy teen can be. The local bullies know this, and make it a habit to hit him up for cash, but all that changes when the debonair Kaname Sengoku sends them packing. Sengoku's not the neighborhood watch, though. He's a professional ballroom dancer. And once Tatara Fujita gets pulled into the world of ballroom, his life will never be the same.

KC
KODANSHA
COMICS

The Black Museum The Ghost and the Lady

By Kazuhiro Fujita

Deep in Scotland Yard in London sits an evidence room dedicated to the greatest mysteries of British history. In this "Black Museum" sits a misshapen hunk of lead—two bullets fused together—the key to a wartime encounter between Florence Nightingale, the mother of modern nursing, and a supernatural Man in Grey. This story is unknown to most scholars of history, but a special guest of the museum will tell the tale of The Ghost and the Lady...

Praise for Kazuhiro Fujita's *Ushio and Tora*

"A charming revival that combines a classic look with modern depth and pacing... **Essential viewing both for curmudgeons and new fans alike.**" — Anime News Network

"**GREAT!** The first episode of Ushio and Tora captures the essence of '90s anime." — IGN

H A P P I N E S S
——ハピネス——
By **Shuzo Oshimi**

From the creator of *The Flowers of Evil*

Nothing interesting is happening in Makoto Ozaki's first year of high school. His life is a series of quiet humiliations: low-grade bullies, unreliable friends, and the constant frustration of his adolescent lust. But one night, a pale, thin girl knocks him to the ground in an alley and offers him a choice. Now everything is different. Daylight is searingly bright. Food tastes awful. And worse than anything is the terrible, consuming thirst...

Praise for Shuzo Oshimi's *The Flowers of Evil*

"A shockingly readable story that vividly—one might even say queasily—evokes the fear and confusion of discovering one's own sexuality. Recommended." —The Manga Critic

"A page-turning tale of sordid middle school blackmail." —Otaku USA Magazine

"A stunning new horror manga." —Third Eye Comics

KC/
KODANSHA COMICS

The award-winning manga about what happens inside you!

"Far more entertaining than it ought to be... what kid doesn't want to think that every time they sneeze a torpedo shoots out their nose?"
–Anime News Network

Strep throat! Hay fever! Influenza! The world is a dangerous place for a red blood cell just trying to get her deliveries finished. Fortunately, she's not alone...she's got a whole human body's worth of cells ready to help out! The mysterious white blood cells, the buff and brash killer T cells, even the cute little platelets— everyone's got to come together if they want to keep you healthy!

Cells at Work!

はたらく細胞

By Akane Shimizu

A new series from the creator of *Soul Eater*, the megahit manga and anime seen on Toonami!

"Fun and lively... a great start!"
  -Adventures in Poor Taste

FIRE FORCE

By Atsushi Ohkubo

The city of Tokyo is plagued by a deadly phenomenon: spontaneous human combustion! Luckily, a special team is there to quench the inferno: The Fire Force! The fire soldiers at Special Fire Cathedral 8 are about to get a unique addition. Enter Shinra, a boy who possesses the power to run at the speed of a rocket, leaving behind the famous "devil's footprints" (and destroying his shoes in the process). Can Shinra and his colleagues discover the source of this strange epidemic before the city burns to ashes?

Kiss Me at the Stroke of Midnight volume 2 is a work of fiction. Names, characters, places, and incidents are the products of the author's imagination or are used fictitiously. Any resemblance to actual events, locales, or persons, living or dead, is entirely coincidental.

A Kodansha Comics Trade Paperback Original.

Published in the United States by Kodansha Comics, an imprint of Kodansha USA Publishing, LLC, New York.

Publication rights for this English edition arranged through Kodansha Ltd., Tokyo.

First published in Japan in 2015 by Kodansha Ltd., Tokyo, as *Gozen Reiji, Kiss Shi ni Kiteyo* volume 2.

Cover Design: Tomohiro Kusume (arcoinc)

ISBN 978-1-63236-495-1

Printed in the United States of America.

www.kodanshacomics.com

9 8 7 6 5 4 3 2 1

Translation: Melissa Goldberg
Lettering: Bunny To, Scott O. Brown
Editing: Haruko Hashimoto, Dawne Law
Editorial Assistance: YKS Services LLC/SKY Japan, INC.
Kodansha Comics Edition Cover Design: Phil Balsman